ECONOGUIDE™ SERIES

ECONOGUIDE® DISNEYLAND® RESORT, UNIVERSAL STUDIOS HOLLYWOOD® 2003

And Other Major Southern California Attractions Including Disney's California Adventure

COREY SANDLER

The
Globe
Pequot
Press

GUILFORD, CONNECTICUT

> The prices and rates listed in this guidebook were confirmed at press time. We recommend, however, that you call establishments to obtain current information before traveling.

Text design by Lesley Weissman-Cook

Maps created by Stefanie Ward © The Globe Pequot Press

ISSN 1541-7158

ISBN 0-7627-2496-X

Manufactured in the United States of America

First Globe Pequot Press Edition/First Printing

To Willie and Tessa,
May their lives always be a magic theme park

CONTENTS

PART V: SIX FLAGS CALIFORNIA

PART VI: SLEEPING AND EATING FOR LESS

PART VII: BEYOND THE THEME PARKS

Acknowledgments

As always, dozens of hard-working and creative people helped move my words from the keyboard to the book you hold in your hands.

Among the many to thank are Mary Luders Norris of Globe Pequot Press; we look forward to many years of partnership. Thanks, too, to editorial and production staff at Globe Pequot, including Elizabeth Taylor, Melissa Evarts, Josh Rosenberg, Joanna Beyer, Casey Shain, Lesley Weissman-Cook, and Donna Dowler.

Gene Brissie has been a believer for a decade, and the feeling is mutual.

My appreciation extends to the public relations staffs who helped me with my research.

As always, thanks to Janice Keefe for running the office and putting up with me, a pair of major assignments. Thanks also to *Econoguide* staffers Michael Lawrence and Maureen Moriarty.

And thanks to you for buying this book. We all hope you find it of value; please let us know how we can improve the book in future editions. (Please enclose a stamped envelope if you'd like a reply; no phone calls, please.)

Corey Sandler
Econoguide Travel Books
P.O. Box 2779
Nantucket, MA 02584

To send electronic mail, use the following address:
info@econoguide.com.
You can also consult our Web page at:
www.econoguide.com.

I hope you'll also consider the other books in the Econoguide series. You can find them at bookstores, or ask your bookseller to order them. All are written by Corey Sandler.

Econoguide Walt Disney World, Universal Orlando
Econoguide Las Vegas
Econoguide to Buying or Leasing a Car
Econoguide to Buying and Selling a Home
Econoguide Cruises

Also by Corey Sandler:
Fix Your Own PC, Seventh Edition

INTRODUCTION TO THE
2003 EDITION

Disneyland occupies a critical piece of our cultural DNA. There's not a place on the planet where Mickey Mouse, and the fantasy world built to celebrate his creator's vision, is not known.

If you've never been to Disneyland, you need to make a pilgrimage. If you haven't been there in years, you'll hardly recognize the place: there are now two parks in Anaheim—the original happiest place on earth and a new salute to the Golden State. And while you're in the neighborhood, take the time to explore Los Angeles and Orange County.

We love L.A. . . . from the historic city itself to the make-believe world of Hollywood to the very real world of the mountains and canyons of Southern California; from the spectacular museums of Los Angeles to the pounding surf. I don't know of many other places with so much to do, so many interesting places to visit . . . and so many ways to spend your hard-earned dollars.

This book is not a guide to California on $5.00 a day; that's not a realistic goal, and it's not the way we look at the world. Rather, our goal is to help readers get the most for their time and money at whatever level they travel, ultra-luxury to super-budget. If there's a way to get more and pay less, we'll help you find it; if an attraction is not worth a visit, you won't find it here.

We cover familiar—and rapidly changing—places, including Disneyland, Disney's California Adventure, Universal Studios Hollywood, Universal Studios CityWalk, Knott's Berry Farm, Six Flags Magic Mountain, the big-city appeals of Los Angeles, and the tinsel dreams of Hollywood. We also journey farther afield in Southern California, from Palm Springs, Santa Barbara, and Malibu down to San Juan Capistrano and SeaWorld in San Diego.

You'll find our selection shows the best places to visit and the best ways to do so. We've included Web addresses, telephone numbers, and price ranges for hundreds of attractions, museums, and hotels.

The Econoguide Best of Los Angeles and Southern California

▶ Disneyland

▶ Disney's California Adventure

▶ Downtown Disney

▶ Universal Studios Hollywood

▶ Universal CityWalk

▶ Knott's Berry Farm

▶ Six Flags Magic Mountain

▶ SeaWorld California

▶ Paramount Studios Tour

▶ Warner Bros. Studio VIP Tours

▶ The *Queen Mary*

▶ Downtown Los Angeles Museums

That other book about Disneyland, the one with "The Official Guide" on its cover, is an interesting collection of material. But in our humble opinion it suffers from a fatal closeness to its subject: It is prepared by the Walt Disney Company. We suspect that explains why it finds very little that is anything less than wonderful within the boundaries of the Disneyland Resort, and why it almost ignores the world outside.

Another feature of this book is the exclusive section of special offers to travelers. A savvy consumer can easily save hundreds of dollars on a trip by using some of the discount coupons we publish. An important note: The author and publisher of this book have no connection or financial interest in any of the coupons or companies presented.

PART I

SOUTHERN CALIFORNIA–BOUND

CHAPTER ONE

PLANES, TRAINS, AND AUTOMOBILES

I LOVE TO TRAVEL but I hate to waste time and money. It all but kills me to know that I spent $200 more than I should have for an airline ticket, or that the next guy over has a nicer hotel room at a better price. Put another way, my goal is to take more vacations and spend more time in wondrous places than most people, and to have a better time while I'm at it.

Let's get something straight here, though: This book is not a guide for the cheapskate who wants a $10-a-night tour of dreadful dives and uninspiring-but-free sights. I'm perfectly willing to spend a reasonable amount of money for good value. In this book, I'll help you make the same sort of good use of your own money and time.

AIR TRAVEL

The way I figure it, one major airline is pretty much like another. Sure, one company may offer a larger bag of peanuts while the other promises its flight attendants have more accommodating smiles. Me, I'm much more interested in other things:

1. Safety
2. The most convenient schedule
3. The lowest price

Though I'm sometimes willing to trade price for convenience, I'll never risk my neck for a few dollars. But that doesn't mean I don't try my hardest to get the very best price on airline tickets. I watch the newspapers for seasonal sales and price wars, clip coupons from the usual and not-so-usual sources, consult the burgeoning world of Internet travel agencies, and happily play one airline against the other.

LOS ANGELES AREA

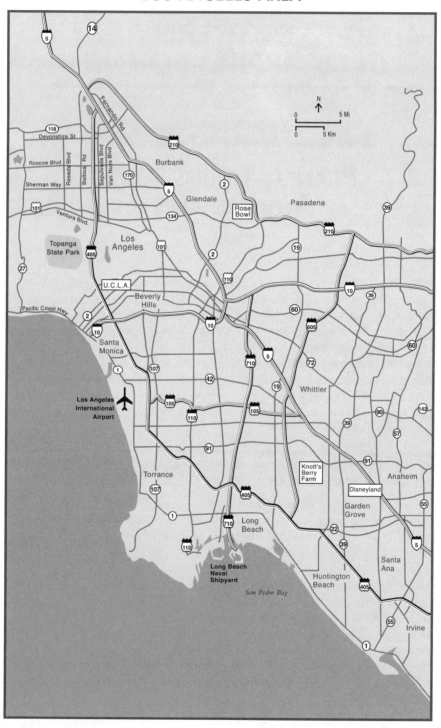

Let's start with a very real-life scenario: It's June 2002, and I'm flying west from Boston to Los Angeles. My ticket, which I bought in advance as a bargain special on a Web site and includes a Saturday night stayover, cost a mere $234 for a round-trip. If I had called the airline directly, the best standard fare for the same flights would have been $390. The businessman across the aisle, who is flying out on a Monday and back on a Friday, will suffer through the same plastic baggie of fried something-or-other, watch the same crummy movie, and arrive in Los Angeles at the same millisecond I do. The only difference will be that he paid $425 for his ticket. Someone in first class who (in my humble opinion) has more money than sense has paid an astounding $3,843 for a slightly wider, slightly plusher seat and a relatively better meal. (I'd rather spend just some of that money on a better place to sleep and a meal at a restaurant where half the meal doesn't end up in your lap.)

All of those prices are real, as I write these words. Now, consider a few more positive examples.

Somewhere else on this same plane is a couple who were bumped off a previous flight because of overbooking. They are happily discussing where to use the two free round-trip tickets they received in compensation. Up front in first class where you arrive a millisecond earlier, a family of four is traveling on free tickets earned through Mom's frequent flier plan.

Me, I'm perfectly happy with that cut-rate ticket. I use some of the money I saved to buy a bag lunch to eat on the plane, and I'm daydreaming about where to use the frequent flyer miles I'm earning on the airfare, hotel, and car rental. And on my trip back home, I will try to get on the flight I really wanted to take instead of the less convenient reservation I was forced to sign up for when I bought that cut-rate ticket. How will I do this? Read on.

■ ALICE IN AIRLINELAND

In today's strange world of air travel, there is a lot of room for the dollarwise and clever traveler to wiggle. You can pay an inflated full price, you can take advantage of the lowest fares, or you can play the ultimate game and parlay tickets into free travel.

There are three golden rules when it comes to saving hundreds of dollars on travel—be flexible, be flexible, and be flexible. Here's how to translate that flexibility into extra dollars in your pocket:

■ Be flexible about when you choose to travel. Go during the off-season or low-season when airfares, hotel rooms, cruises, and attractions are offered at substantial discounts. Try to avoid school vacations, spring break, and the prime summer travel months of July and August, unless you enjoy a lot of company.

■ Be flexible about the day of the week you travel. In many cases you can save hundreds of dollars by bumping your departure date one or two days in either direction. Ask your travel agent or airline ticket

Double Indemnity

Your homeowner's or renter's insurance policy may include coverage for theft of your possessions while you travel, making it unnecessary to purchase a special policy. Check with your insurance agent.

agent for current fare rules and restrictions. If this puts you into your destination a day or two ahead of your intended arrival, use the time to become acclimated to a new time zone and to explore.

The days of lightest air travel are generally midweek, Saturday afternoon, and Sunday morning. The busiest days are Sunday evening, Monday morning, and Friday afternoon and evening.

In general you will receive the lowest possible fare if your stay includes all day Saturday; this class of ticket is sold as an excursion fare. Airlines use this as a way to exclude business travelers from the cheapest fares, assuming that business-people will want to be home by Friday night. (There has been *some* movement to dispense with this class of fares, but you're still likely to run into excursion fare requirements on many airlines.)

▪ Be flexible about the hour of your departure. There is generally lower demand—and therefore lower prices—for flights that leave in the middle of the day or very late at night. The highest rates are usually assigned to breakfast-time (7:00–11:00 A.M.) and cocktail-hour (4:00–7:00 P.M.) departures.

▪ Be flexible on the route you will take and be willing to put up with a change of plane or stopover. Once again, you are putting the law of supply and demand in your favor. For example, a nonstop flight from Boston to Los Angeles for a family of four may cost hundreds more than a flight from Boston that includes a change of planes in Chicago before proceeding on to California.

(You should also understand that in airline terminology, a "direct" flight does not mean a "nonstop" flight. Nonstop means the plane goes from Point A to Point B without stopping anywhere else. A direct flight may go from Point A to Point B, but may include a stopover at Point C or at more than one airport along the way. A connecting flight means you must get off the plane at an airport en route and change to another plane. And just to add one more level of confusion, some airlines have "direct" flights that involve a change of plane along the way—the flight number stays the same but passengers have to get off at an intermediate stop, dragging all their carry-on luggage to another gate and aircraft. Go figure.)

Consider flying on one of the newer, deep-discount airlines, but don't let economy cloud your judgment. Some carriers are simply better run than others. Read the newspapers, check with a trusted travel agent, and use common sense. As far as I'm concerned, the best thing about the cheapo airlines is the pressure they put on the established carriers to lower prices or even to match fares on certain flights. Look for the cheapest fare you can find and then call your favorite big airline and see if it will sell you a ticket at the same price—it just might work.

▪ Don't overlook the possibility of flying out of a different airport either. For example, metropolitan New Yorkers can find domestic flights from LaGuardia, Newark, White Plains, and a developing discount mecca at Islip. Suburbanites of Boston might want to consider flights from Providence as possibly cheaper alternatives to Logan Airport. Chicago has O'Hare and Midway. From Southern California there are major airports at Los Angeles, Orange County, Burbank, and San Diego.

■ Plan way ahead of time and purchase the most deeply discounted advance tickets, which usually are noncancelable. Most carriers limit the number of discount tickets on any particular flight. Although there may be plenty of seats left on the day you want to travel, they may be offered at higher rates.

■ Understand the difference between nonrefundable and noncancelable. Most airlines interpret *nonrefundable* to mean that they can keep all your money if you cancel a reservation or fail to show up for a flight. A *noncancelable* fare means that if your plans change or you are forced to cancel your trip, your tickets retain their value and can be applied against another trip. In mid-2002, most airlines charged a fee of about $75 to $100 to reissue a noncancelable ticket. Many deep-discount tickets sold on airline Web sites are nonrefundable. Of course, if the airline cancels your flight or makes a schedule or routing change you find does not meet your needs, you are entitled to a refund of your fare.

■ If you're feeling adventurous, you can take a big chance and wait for the last possible moment, keeping in contact with charter tour operators and accepting a bargain price on a leftover seat and hotel reservation. You may also find that some airlines will reduce the prices on leftover seats within a few weeks of your departure date; don't be afraid to check with the airline regularly or ask your travel agent to do it for you. In fact, some travel agencies have automated computer programs that keep a constant electronic eagle eye on available seats and fares.

■ Take advantage of special discount programs such as senior citizens' clubs, military discounts, or offerings from other organizations to which you may belong. If you are in the broadly defined "senior" category, you may not even have to belong to a group such as AARP; simply ask the airline ticket agent if there is a discount available. You may have to prove your age or show a membership card when you pick up your ticket or boarding pass.

■ Consider doing business with discounters, known in the industry as consolidators or, less flatteringly, as bucket shops. These companies buy the airlines' slow-to-sell tickets in volume and resell them to consumers at rock-bottom prices. Look for their ads in the classified listings of many Sunday newspaper travel sections. Be sure to study and understand the restrictions; if they fit your needs and wants, this is a good way to fly.

You can also find ticket broker and bucket shop ads on-line and in classified ads in the *USA Today,* the "Mart" section of the *Wall Street Journal,* the back pages of *The Village Voice,* or in specialty magazines aimed at frequent flyers.

Some travel agencies can also offer you consolidator tickets. Just be sure to weigh the savings on the ticket price against any restrictions attached to the tickets; for example, they may not be changeable, and they usually don't accrue frequent flyer mileage.

■ Shop on-line through one of the Internet travel sites or the Web sites of individual airlines. You can expect to receive the lowest possible airfares—usually a few percent below the best prices offered if you call the airline directly—but little assistance in choosing among the offerings. Be sure to pay close attention to details such as the number of connections required between origin and destina-

Mileage to/from Disneyland and Los Angeles

MILEAGE TO/FROM DISNEYLAND	Miles	Time
San Juan Capistrano	27	0:31
Los Angeles	28	0:42
Hollywood	34	0:53
San Diego	93	1:49
Palm Springs	96	1:47
Santa Barbara	129	2:39
Las Vegas, NV	271	4:56
San Francisco	407	7:54
South Lake Tahoe	498	9:48
Disney World, FL	2,512	46:14

MILEAGE TO/FROM LOS ANGELES	Miles	Time
Hollywood	6	0:11
Disneyland	28	0:42
San Juan Capistrano	54	1:13
Santa Barbara	102	1:57
Palm Springs	105	2:06
San Diego	121	2:31
Las Vegas, NV	271	5:04
San Francisco	380	7:14
South Lake Tahoe	471	9:08
Disney World, FL	2,521	46:33

tion. Note, too, that tickets sold in this way may have severe restrictions on changes and cancellations.

Some of the best Internet agencies include:

- **Atevo,** www.atevo.com
- **Cheap Tickets,** www.cheaptickets.com
- **Microsoft Expedia,** www.expedia.com
- **Travelocity,** www.travelocity.com
- **Trip.com,** www.trip.com

Among the airlines that offer on-line booking are:

- **American Airlines,** www.aa.com
- **Continental Airlines,** www.continental.com
- **Delta Airlines,** www.deltaairlines.com
- **Northwest Airlines,** www.nwa.com
- **Southwest Airlines,** www.iflyswa.com
- **United Airlines,** www.ual.com
- **USAirways,** www.usairways.com

- Consider, very carefully, buying tickets from an on-line travel auction site such as www.priceline.com or www.hotwire.com. These sites promise to match your travel plans with available seats on major airlines at deep-discount prices; you will not be able to choose departure or arrival times or a particular airline. The way to use these sites is to do your research beforehand on one of the regular Web sites to find the best price you can; compare that to the "blind" offerings from the auction sites. Although the auction sites can often deliver the best prices, the tickets come with some detractions: You cannot time your arrival to meet a particular schedule and may have to build in an extra hotel stay at each end of the trip; it may be impossible to make changes or obtain a refund if your plans change; and you may not be permitted to stand by for another flight with your limited ticket. And read the fine print carefully: prices may not include taxes and fees, and the sites may tack on a service charge. Be sure to compare the true bottom line to the price quoted on other Web sites or from a travel agent.
- The day of the week on which you buy your tickets may also make a price difference. Airlines often test out higher fares over the relatively quiet weekends. They're looking to see if their competitors will match their higher rates; if the other carriers don't bite, the fares often float back down by Monday morning. Shop during the week.

OTHER MONEY-SAVING STRATEGIES

Airlines are forever weeping and gnashing their teeth about huge losses due to cutthroat competition. And then they regularly turn around and drop their prices radically with major sales. I don't waste time worrying about the bottom line of the airlines; it's my own wallet I want to keep full. Therefore, the savvy traveler keeps an eye out for airline fare wars all the time. Read the ads in newspapers and keep an ear open for news broadcasts that often cover the outbreak of price drops. If you have a good relationship with a travel agent, you can ask to be notified of any fare sales.

The most common times for airfare wars are in the weeks leading up to the quietest seasons for carriers, including the period from mid-May to mid-June (except the Memorial Day weekend), between Labor Day and Thanksgiving, and again in the winter with the exception of Christmas, New Year's, and President's Day holiday periods.

Don't be afraid to ask for a refund on previously purchased tickets if fares go down for the period of your travel. The airline may refund the difference, or you may be able to reticket your itinerary at the new fare, paying a $75 penalty for cashing in the old tickets. Be persistent: if the difference in fare is significant, it may be worth making a visit to the airport to meet with a supervisor at the ticket counter.

Study the fine print on discount coupons distributed by the airlines or third parties such as supermarkets, catalog companies, and direct marketers. In my experience, these coupons are often less valuable than they seem. Read the fine print carefully and be sure to ask the reservationist if the price quoted with the coupon is higher than another fare for which you qualify.

■ YOUR RIGHTS AS A CONSUMER

The era of airline deregulation has been a mixed blessing for the industry and the consumer. After an era of wild competition based mostly on price, we now are left with fewer but larger airlines and a dizzying array of confusing rules. The U.S. Department of Transportation and its Federal Aviation Administration (FAA) still regulate safety issues. Almost everything else is between you and the airline.

Policies on fares, cancellations, reconfirmation, check-in requirements, and compensation for lost or damaged baggage or for delays all vary by airline. Your rights are limited and defined by the terms of the contract you make with an airline when you buy your ticket. You may find the contract included with the ticket you purchase, or the airlines may "incorporate terms by reference" to a separate document that you will have to request to see.

Whether you are buying your ticket through a travel agent or dealing directly with the airline, here are some important questions to ask:

- Is the price guaranteed, or can it change from the time of the reservation until you actually purchase the ticket?
- Can the price change between the time you buy the ticket and the date of departure?
- Is there a penalty for cancellation of the ticket?
- Can the reservation be changed without penalty or for a reasonable fee? Be sure you understand the sort of service you are buying.
- Is this a nonstop flight, a direct flight, or a flight that requires you to change planes one or more times?
- What seat has been issued? Do you really want the center seat in a three-seat row, between two strangers?

You might also want to ask your travel agent:

- Is there anything I should know about the financial health of this airline?
- Are you aware of any threats of work stoppages or legal actions that could ruin my trip?

■ BEATING THE AIRLINES AT THEIR OWN GAME

In my opinion, the airlines deserve all the headaches we travelers can give them because of the costly pricing schemes they throw at us—deals such as take-it-or-leave-it fares of $350 to fly 90 miles between two cities where they hold a monopoly, and $198 bargain fares to travel 3,000 miles across the nation. Or round-trip fares of $300 if you leave on a Thursday and return on a Monday, but $1,200 if you leave on Monday and return the next Thursday.

But a creative traveler can find ways to work around most of these roadblocks. Nothing I'm going to suggest here is against the law; some of the tips, though, are against the rules of some airlines. Here are a couple of strategies.

Nested Tickets. This scheme generally works in either of two situations: where regular fares are more than twice as high as excursion fares that include a Saturday night stay over, or in situations where you plan to fly between two locations twice in less than a year.

Let's say you want to fly from Boston to Los Angeles. Buy two sets of tickets in your name. The first is from Boston to Los Angeles and back. This set has the return date for when you want to come back from your second trip. The other set of tickets is from Los Angeles to Boston and back to Los Angeles, this time making the first leg of the ticket for the date you want to come back from the first trip, and the second leg of the trip the date you want to depart for the second trip.

If this sounds complicated, that's because it is. It will be up to you to keep your tickets straight when you travel. Some airlines have threatened to crack down on such practices by searching their computer databases for multiple reservations. That doesn't mean you can't buy such tickets. Check with a travel agent for advice. One solution: buy one set of tickets on one airline and the other set on another carrier.

Split Tickets. Fare wars sometimes result in super-cheap fares through a connecting city. For example, an airline seeking to boost traffic through a hub in Cincinnati creates a situation in which it is less expensive to get from New York to Los Angeles by buying a round-trip ticket from New York to Cincinnati, and then a separate round-trip ticket from Cincinnati to Los Angeles.

Be sure to book a schedule that allows enough time between flights; if you miss your connection you could end up losing time and money.

■ STANDING UP FOR STANDING BY

One of the little-known secrets of air travel on most airlines and most types of tickets is the fact that travelers with valid tickets are allowed to stand by for flights other than the ones for which they have reservations; if there are empty seats on the flight, standby ticket holders are permitted to board.

Some airlines are very liberal in their acceptance of standbys within a few days of the reserved flight, while others will charge a fee for changes in itinerary. And some airline personnel are stricter about regulations than others.

Here's what I do know: If I can't get the exact flight I want for a trip, I make the closest acceptable reservations available after that flight and then show

The Best Policy

Consider buying trip cancellation insurance from a travel agency, tour operator, or directly from an insurance company (ask your insurance agent for advice). The policies are intended to reimburse you for any lost deposits or prepayments if you must cancel a trip because you or certain members of your family become ill. Read the policy carefully to understand the circumstances under which the company will pay.

Take care not to purchase more coverage than you need; if your tour package costs $5,000 but you would lose only $1,000 in the event of a cancellation, then the amount of insurance required is just $1,000. Some policies will cover you for health and accident benefits while on vacation, excluding any preexisting conditions.

Be sure you understand your contract with your airline; you may be able to reschedule a flight or even receive a refund after payment of a service charge. Some airlines give full refunds or free rescheduling if you can prove a medical reason for the change.

up early at the airport and head for the check-in counter for the flight I really want to take. Unless you are seeking to travel during an impossibly overbooked holiday period or arrive on a bad weather day when flights have been canceled, your chances of successfully standing by for a flight are usually pretty good.

One trick is to call the airline the day before the flight and check on the availability of seats for the flight you want to try for. Some reservation clerks are very forthcoming with information; many times I have been told something like, "There are seventy seats open on that flight." Be careful with standby maneuvers if your itinerary requires a change of plane en route; you'll need to check the availability of seats on all of the legs of your journey. Some deep-discount fares may include prohibitions against standing by for other flights; read the fine print, especially if you are booking your own flight over the Internet.

The fly in the ointment in today's strict security environment is this: airlines are required to match bags to passengers before a flight takes off. It is difficult, if not impossible, to stand by for a flight other than the one you hold a ticket for if you have checked a bag. Your chances are much better if you limit yourself to carry-on bags. And, security screeners may not let you into the concourse for flights more than two hours before scheduled departure. Consult with the ticket agents at check-in counters outside of the security barriers for advice.

And a final note: Be especially careful about standing by for the very last flight of the night. If you somehow are unable to get on that flight, you're stuck for the night.

◼ OVERBOOKING

Overbooking is a polite industry term for the legal business practice of selling more than an airline can deliver. It all stems, alas, from the rudeness of many travelers who neglect to cancel flight reservations that will not be used. Airlines study the patterns on various flights and city pairs and apply a formula that allows them to sell more tickets than there are seats on the plane in the expectation that a certain percentage of ticket holders will not show up.

But what happens if all passengers holding a reservation do show up? Obviously, the result will be more passengers than seats, and some will have to be left behind. The involuntary bump list will begin with passengers who check in late. Airlines must ask for volunteers before bumping any passengers who have followed the rules on check-in. Assuming that no one is willing to give up his or her seat just for the fun of it, the airline will offer some sort of compensation—either a free ticket or cash, or both. It is up to the passenger and the airline to negotiate a deal.

Some air travelers, including this author, look forward to an overbooked flight when their schedules are flexible. My most profitable score: $4,000 in vouchers on a set of four $450 international tickets. The airline was desperate to clear a large block of seats, and it didn't matter to us if we arrived home a few hours late. We received the equivalent of three tickets for the price of one, and you can bet that we'll hope to earn some more free travel on future tickets purchased with those vouchers.

The U.S. Department of Transportation's consumer protection regulations set some minimum levels of compensation for passengers who are bumped from a flight due to overbooking. If you are bumped involuntarily, the airline must provide a ticket on its next available flight. Unfortunately, there is no guarantee there will be a seat on that plane or that it will arrive at your destination at a convenient time.

If the airline can get you on another flight that will get you to your destination within one hour of the original arrival time, no compensation need be paid. If you are scheduled to get to your destination more than one hour but less than two hours late, you're entitled to receive an amount equal to the one-way fare of the oversold flight, up to $200. If the delay is more than two hours, the bumpee will receive an amount equal to twice the one-way fare of the original flight, up to $400.

It is not considered bumping if a flight is canceled because of weather, equipment problems, or the lack of a flight crew. You are also not eligible for compensation if the airline substitutes a smaller aircraft for operational or safety reasons, or if the flight involves an aircraft with sixty seats or less.

■ HOW TO GET BUMPED

Why in the world would you want to be bumped? Well, perhaps you'd like to look at missing your plane as an opportunity to earn a little money for your time instead of an annoyance. Is a two-hour delay worth $100 an hour to you? For the inconvenience of waiting a few hours on the way home, a family of four might receive a voucher for $800—that could pay for a week's hotel plus a heck of a meal at the airport.

If you're not in a rush to get to your destination—or to get back home—you might want to volunteer to be bumped. We wouldn't recommend doing this on the busiest travel days of the year or if you are booked on the last flight of the day, unless you are also looking forward to a free night in an airport motel.

■ BAD WEATHER, BAD PLANES, STRIKES, AND OTHER HEADACHES

You don't want pilots to fly into weather they consider unsafe, of course. You also don't want them to take up a plane with a mechanical problem. No matter how you feel about unions, you probably don't want to cross a picket line to board a plane piloted by strikebreakers. And so, you should accept an airline's cancellation of a flight for any of these legitimate reasons.

Here's the bad news, though: if a flight is canceled for an "act of God" such as bad weather, an earthquake, or a plague of locusts, or because of a strike or labor dispute, the airline isn't required to do anything for you except refund your money. In practice, carriers will usually make a good effort to find another way to get you to your destination more or less on time, which could mean rebooking on another flight on the same airline or on a different carrier. But you could be facing a delay of a day or more in the worst situations, such as a major snowstorm.

Here is a summary of your rather limited rights as an air passenger:

■ An airline is required to compensate you above the cost of your ticket only if you're bumped from an oversold flight against your will.

■ If you volunteer to be bumped, you can negotiate for the best deal with the ticket agent or a supervisor; for your inconvenience, you can generally expect to be offered a free round-trip ticket on the airline.

■ If your scheduled flight is unable to deliver you directly to the destination on your ticket, and alternate transportation such as a bus or limousine is provided, the airline is required to pay you twice the amount of your one-way fare if your arrival on the alternate transportation will be more than two hours later than the original airline ticket promised.

■ If you purchased your ticket with a credit card, the airline must credit your account within seven days of receiving an application for a refund.

All that said, in many cases you will be able to convince an agent or a supervisor to go beyond the letter of the law. I've found that the best strategy is to politely but firmly stand your ground. Ask the ticket clerk for another flight, for a free night in a hotel and a flight in the morning, or for any other reasonable accommodation. Don't take no for an answer, but remain polite and ask for a supervisor, if necessary. Sooner or later, they'll do something to get you out of the way.

And then there are labor problems such as those that faced American Airlines and US Airways in recent years. Your best defense against a strike is to anticipate it before it happens; keep your ears open for labor problems when you make a reservation. Then keep in touch with your travel agent or the airline itself in the days leading up to any strike deadline. It is often easier to make alternate plans or seek a refund in the days immediately before a strike; wait until the last minute and you're going to be joining a very long line of upset people.

In the face of a strike, a major airline will attempt to reroute you on another airline if possible; if you buy your own ticket on another carrier, you're unlikely to be reimbursed. If your flight is canceled, you'll certainly be able to claim a full refund of your fare or obtain a voucher in its value without paying any penalties.

■ AIRLINE SAFETY

There are no guarantees in life, but in general, flying on an airplane is considerably safer than the drive to the airport. All the major air carriers have very good safety records; some are better than others. I pay attention to news reports about FAA inspections and rulings, and then make adjustments. And although I love to squeeze George Washington until he yelps, I avoid start-up and super-cut-rate airlines because I have my doubts about how much money they can afford to devote to maintenance.

Among major airlines, the fatal accident rate during the last twenty-five years stands somewhere between .3 and .74 incidents per million flights. Not included in these listings are small commuter airlines (except those that are affiliated with major carriers). Put another way, if you were to take one flight per day—randomly selected—chances are it would be about 22,000 years before you would end up as a statistic on a fatal crash.

The very low numbers over such a long period of time, experts say, make them poor predictors of future incidents. Instead, you should pay more attention to reports of FAA or National Transportation Safety Board (NTSB) rulings on maintenance and training problems.

■ THE NEW WORLD OF AIRPORT SECURITY

Travel has become all the more complicated and less convenient in the wake of the terrorist attacks of 2001. The bottom line for well-meaning, nonviolent business and pleasure travelers is this: you'll need to add an hour or more to the check-in process, and your options to stand by for a different flight or make other changes to your itinerary are severely limited.

Here are some things you can do to lessen the pain:

■ Consult with the airline or your travel agent about current policies regarding check-in times.

■ Consider your departure time; lines for check-in and security clearance are longest during peak travel times—early morning and late afternoon.

■ An alternate airport may have shorter lines. Some major hubs may, by necessity, be more efficient at processing huge crowds; at the same time, smaller airports with fewer crowds may be easier to navigate.

■ Try to avoid carrying unnecessary metallic items on your person. Choose a belt with a small buckle rather than the one with the three-pound world-championship steer wrestling medallion. Put your cell phone, keys, coins, and wristwatch in a plastic bag and place it in your carry-on bag as you approach the magnetometer; this will speed your passage and reduce the chances of losing items.

■ Be cooperative and remember that the screening is intended to keep you safe, and hope that the guards do their job well.

ABOUT TRAVEL AGENCIES

Here's my advice about travel agents in a nutshell: Get a good one, or go it alone. Good travel agents are those who remember who they work for: you. Of course there is a built-in major conflict of interest here, because the agent is in most cases paid by someone else. Agents receive a commission on airline tickets, hotel reservations, car rentals, and many other services they sell you. The more they sell (or the higher the price), the more they earn.

I would recommend you start the planning for any trip by calling airlines and a few hotels to determine the best package you can put together for yourself. Then call your travel agent and ask him or her to do better. If your agent contributes knowledge or experience, comes up with dollar-saving alternatives to your own package, or offers some other kind of convenience, then go ahead and book your trip through the agency. If, as I often find, you know a lot more about your destination and are willing to spend a lot more time to save money than is the agent, do it yourself.

A number of large agencies offer rebates on part of their commissions to trav-

Don't Wait to Drop a Card

If you have booked a trip through a travel agent or tour operator, keep in touch. In many cases they can anticipate major changes before departure time and will let you know. And many operators will try hard to keep you from demanding a refund if you find a major change unacceptable. They may offer a discount or upgrade on a substitute trip or adjust the price of the changed tour.

If you have booked a flight directly through an airline, make sure they have your phone number in case of a change in the schedule. Call the airline a few days before your first flight to confirm your reservation and check for any changes.

elers. Some of these companies cater only to frequent flyers who will bring in a lot of business; other rebate agencies offer only limited services to clients.

You can find discount travel agencies through many major credit card companies (Citibank and American Express among them) or through associations and clubs. Some warehouse shopping clubs have rebate travel agencies. If you establish a regular relationship with your travel agency and bring them enough business to make them glad to hear from you, don't be afraid to ask them for a discount equal to a few percentage points.

Internet travel agencies offer airline, hotel, car, cruise, and package reservations. You won't receive personalized assistance, but you will be able to make as many price checks and itinerary routings as you'd like without apology. Several of the services feature special deals, including companion fares and rebates you won't find offered elsewhere.

■ TOUR PACKAGES AND CHARTER FLIGHTS

Tour packages and flights sold by tour operators or travel agents may look similar, but the consumer may end up with significantly different rights. What you end up with is greatly dependent on whether the flight is a scheduled or nonscheduled flight. A scheduled flight is one that is published in the *Official Airline Guide* and available to the general public through a travel agent or from the airline. This doesn't mean that a scheduled flight will necessarily be on a major carrier or that you'll be flying on a 747 jumbo jet; it could just as easily be the propeller-driven pride of Hayseed Airlines. In any case, though, a scheduled flight does have to meet stringent federal government certification requirements.

A nonscheduled flight is also known as a "charter flight." The term is sometimes also applied to a complete package that includes a nonscheduled flight, hotel accommodations, ground transportation, and other elements. Charter flights are generally a creation of a tour operator who will purchase all the seats on a specific flight to a specific destination or who will rent an airplane and crew from an air carrier.

Charter flights and charter tours are regulated by the federal government, but your rights as a consumer are much more limited than those afforded to scheduled flight customers. You wouldn't buy a hamburger without knowing the price and specifications (two all-beef patties on a sesame seed bun, etc.). Why, then, would you spend hundreds or even thousands of dollars on a tour and not understand the contract that underlies the transaction?

When you purchase a charter flight or a tour package, you should review and sign a contract that spells out your rights. This contract is sometimes referred to as the "Operator Participant Contract" or the "Terms and Conditions." Look for this contract in the booklet or brochure that describes the packages; ask for it if one is not offered.

Remember that the contract is designed mostly to benefit the tour operator, and each contract may be different from others you have agreed to in the past. The basic rule here is this: If you don't understand it, don't sign it.

Second Chance

Most tour operators, if forced to cancel, will offer another package or other incentives as a goodwill gesture. If a charter flight or charter tour is canceled, the tour operator must refund your money within fourteen days.

■ HOW TO BOOK A PACKAGE OR CHARTER FLIGHT

For charter flights and packages, consider using a travel agent, preferably one you know and trust. The tour operator usually pays the agent's commission. Some tour packages, however, are available only from the operator who organized the tour; in certain cases, you may be able to negotiate a better price by dealing directly with the operator, although you are giving up one layer of protection for your rights.

Pay for your ticket with a credit card; I consider this a cardinal rule for almost any situation in which you're paying in advance for a service or product. If you end up in a dispute with the travel provider or a travel agency, you should be able to enlist the assistance of the credit card issuer on your behalf.

Keep in mind that charter airlines don't have fleets of planes available as substitutes in the event of a mechanical problem or an extensive weather delay. They may not be able to arrange for a substitute plane from another carrier.

If you're still willing to try a charter after all of these warnings, make one more check of the bottom line before you sign the contract.

■ First of all, is the air travel significantly less expensive than the lowest nonrefundable fare available from a scheduled carrier? (Remember that you are, in effect, buying a nonrefundable fare with most charter flight contracts.)

■ Have you included taxes, service charges, baggage transfer fees, or other charges the tour operator may put into the contract?

■ Are the savings significantly more than the 10 percent the charter operator may (typically) boost the price without your permission? Do any savings come at a cost of time? Put a value on your time.

■ Finally, don't buy a complete package until you have compared it to the a la carte cost of such a trip. Call the hotels offered by the tour operator, or similar ones in the same area, and ask them a simple question: "What is your best price for a room?" Be sure to mention any discount programs that are applicable, including the American Automobile Association (AAA) or other organizations.

Lug It Yourself

If you are using a scheduled airline to connect with a charter flight, or the other way around, your baggage will not be automatically transferred. You must make the transfer yourself.

Charter and tour flights operate independently of other flights. If you are on a trip that combines scheduled and nonscheduled flights, or two unrelated charter flights, you may end up losing your money and flight because of delays. It may make sense to avoid such combinations for that reason, or to leave extra hours or even days between connections. Some tour operators offer travel-delay insurance that pays for accommodations or alternative travel arrangements necessitated by certain types of delays.

Do the same for car rental agencies, and place a call to any attractions you plan to visit to get current prices.

LOS ANGELES INTERNATIONAL AIRPORT (LAX)

Information: (310) 646–5252. www.lawa.org.

LAX is located in Westchester, at the intersections of Century and Sepulveda Boulevards. The airport is near the Inglewood/Century Boulevard exit of Interstate 405.

An MTA bus stop is located between the passenger terminals. Call (213) 626–4455 for schedules.

Terminal 1: America West, Southwest, US Airways

Terminal 2: Air Canada, Air China, Air New Zealand, American Trans Air, Avianca, Hawaiian Airlines, KLM, Northwest, Omni, Virgin Atlantic, World

Terminal 3: Alaska, American Express (Western destinations and Orlando) Frontier, Horizon, Midwest Express

Bradley International Terminal: Aero California, Aeroflot, Aer Lingus, Air France, Air Liberté, Air Pacific, Alitalia, ANA (All Nippon), Asiana, British Airways, Canada 3000, Cathay Pacific, China Airlines, China Eastern, Copa Airlines, Egyptair, El Al, Eva Air, Japan Airlines, Korean Airlines, LACSA, Lan Chile, LTU, Lufthansa, Malaysia, Mexicana, Philippine Airlines, Qantas, Singapore, Swissair, TACA, Thai, Varig

Terminal 4: American, American Eagle

Terminal 5: Aeromexico, Air Jamaica, China Southern, Delta, Spirit, Vanguard

Terminal 6: Continental, Copa Airlines, National Airlines, United Airlines, United Express

Terminal 7: United, United Shuttle, United Express

Terminal 8: United Shuttle

OTHER AREA AIRPORTS

Although Los Angeles International—about 34 miles from Disneyland—has by far the broadest selection of airlines and flights, you may be able to save time and

AIRPORTS NEAR LOS ANGELES

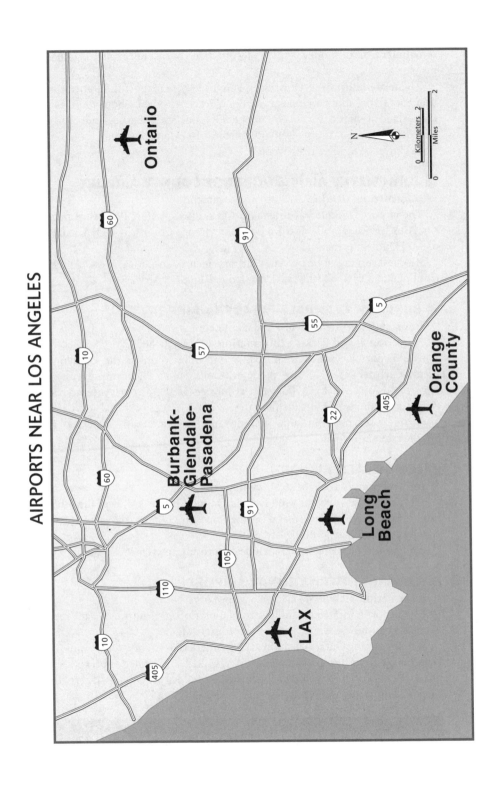

sometimes a bit of money by flying through one of several smaller regional airports.

The nearest airport to Disneyland is John Wayne Airport in Orange County near Santa Ana, about 13 miles away. Long Beach Airport is about 19 miles from Disneyland. Ontario Airport is about 35 miles from Disneyland. Burbank-Glendale-Pasadena Airport is 40 miles from Disneyland, and only about 6 miles from Universal Studios Hollywood.

■ JOHN WAYNE AIRPORT/ORANGE COUNTY AIRPORT

Information: (949) 252–5200. www.ocair.com.

The airport is located at Interstate 405 and MacArthur Boulevard in Santa Ana. Bus service is available from points in Orange County by OCTA; call (714) 636–7433 for information.

Airlines serving John Wayne Airport include America West, American, Continental, Delta, Northwest, TWA, United, and US Airways.

■ BURBANK-GLENDALE-PASADENA AIRPORT

Information: (818) 840–8847. www.bur.com.

Mass Transit and Parking Information: (818) 840–8837.

The airport is located in Burbank, one mile south of the Golden State Freeway (Interstate 5). The main entrance is at Thornton Avenue and Hollywood Way. An MTA bus stop is located at the airport entrance and a CalTrain station is just outside the gates.

Airlines serving Burbank include Alaska, American, America West, Southwest, and United.

■ LONG BEACH AIRPORT

Information: (562) 570–2600. www.lgb.org.

The airport is located at 4100 Donald Douglas Boulevard, near the intersection of Lakewood Boulevard and Spring Street in Long Beach. From Interstate 405, take the Lakewood Boulevard exit.

Airlines serving Long Beach include American, America West, and jetBlue.

■ ONTARIO INTERNATIONAL AIRPORT

Information: (909) 937–2700. www.lawa.org.

The airport is located two miles east of Ontario, on Airport Drive at Vineyard Avenue, near the Vineyard Avenue exit of Interstate 10.

Airlines serving Ontario include Alaska, America West, American, Continental, Delta, jetBlue, Northwest, Southwest, TWA, United, and United Express.

Omnitrans offers regularly scheduled bus service to Ontario International Airport. For routes and schedules, call (800) 966–6428.

LOS ANGELES REGION BUS AND TRAIN SERVICE

Here is a list of a few of the larger transportation services that connect LAX and other airports to the Greater Los Angeles area. Be aware that you may have to share your ride and take some side trips en route if you share a van with others. For direct service, use a taxi or limousine service.

Airport Bus. Between LAX and Disneyland-area hotels (adult round-trip about $22), between John Wayne/Orange County Airport and Disneyland-area hotels (adult round-trip about $16), and between LAX and John Wayne/Orange County (adult round-trip $32). (800) 772–5299 or (714) 938–8900.

Best Shuttle. Shuttle from hotels in Orange County to LAX and Orange County airports. (800) 606–7433.

FlyAway. Bus service between LAX and Van Nuys Airport Bus Terminal. (818) 994–5554.

Metropolitan Express. Vans to airports, Amtrak, harbors. (310) 417–5050.

Prime Time Airport Shuttle. Vans in Los Angeles and Orange County. (800) 262–7433.

Southern California Rapid Transit District. LAX to surrounding communities. (213) 626–4455.

Super Shuttle. Door-to-door service to LAX and area airports. (800) 258–3826 or (714) 517–6600.

■ LOS ANGELES COUNTY METROPOLITAN TRANSPORTATION AUTHORITY (MTA)

Information: (213) 626–4455. www.mta.net.

The MTA serves the Greater Los Angeles area from the San Fernando Valley to northern Orange County with bus, rail, and light-rail service on more than 200 routes.

Free shuttle service is provided to and from the Metro Green Line Light Rail's Aviation Station. Passenger pick up is on the Lower/Arrival Level under the LAX Shuttle sign.

Metropolitan Transit Authority (Los Angeles area) city bus information is available by telephone on the Information Display Board in the baggage claim area in each terminal. Board city buses adjacent to Parking Lot C by taking the "C" shuttle.

MTA buses connect to all Metro Blue Line and Red Line stations, Union Station, and Metrolink stations in Los Angeles County.

Buses run twenty-four hours a day, with limited service during late-night hours and on weekends and holidays.

■ THE RED LINE

In car-clogged Los Angeles, the idea of an underground subway system would seem to make a lot of sense. (Notwithstanding the fact that the tunnels run through a pretty active earthquake zone; that's something that Angelenos seem able to live with in everything they do.)

The $4.5 billion project was completed to Hollywood in 2000. The next challenge is to convince more than a few Angelenos to get out of their cars and into the underground. Operators hope for about 125,000 passengers a day during the week, which should leave plenty of room on the trains. (New York's sprawling

METRO RAIL SYSTEM

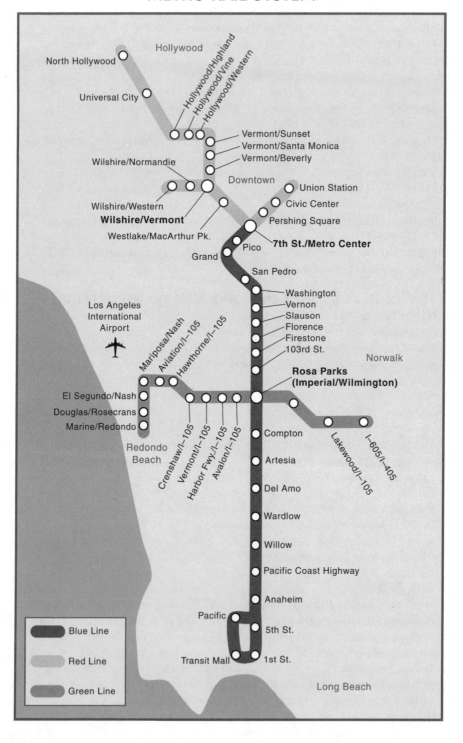

system draws more than three million users daily.)

Actually, the system may be of most use to tourists who can take the train to travel from downtown to Hollywood and Universal Studios in about fifteen minutes. The modern rubber-tired trains glide almost silently between clean and attractive stations. The base fare is $1.35 for adults for the Red and Green lines, plus 25 cents for each transfer to bus service. Self-service ticket vending machines can be found at each station.

The train stations themselves are worth seeing. The stop at Hollywood and Vine, in the heart of Hollywood, pays homage to the movies. A yellow brick road rises out of the red floor, leading upstairs to the street. The Vermont and Sunset station, nearby a hospital district, is decorated with medical symbols; the elevator to the street echoes the design of the Griffith Park Observatory's dome in the Hollywood Hills above it.

The Union Station end of the line has connections to Metrolink commuter rail trains and the Amtrak terminal, and is nearby to Chinatown, Olvera Street, and Little Tokyo. A station at the Tom Bradley Civic Center Station (First and Hill Streets) is near the Music Center; City Hall; Times Mirror Square; and several city, county, and government buildings. Travelers can transfer to the Metro Blue Line at the Pershing Square Station (Fifth and Hill Streets).

The Blue Line is a light-rail system of about 40 miles, with service from Los Angeles to Long Beach, from 5:00 A.M. to 11:00 P.M. daily.

Fares vary by distance traveled, and exact change is required. All buses and trains are wheelchair-accessible. Special family and tourist passes are available, usually limited to off-peak times.

For a timetable and route map, call MTA Information or write to: MTA Customer Relations, 425 South Main Street, Los Angeles, CA 90013–1393. For information, call (800) 266–6883 or consult www.mta.net.

▧ METRO TRAIN STATIONS

Red Line (Downtown Los Angeles, Wilshire Center, Hollywood)

North Hollywood. Lankershim and Chandler Boulevards. Academy of TV Arts & Sciences, El Portal Center for the Performing Arts.

Universal City. Lankershim Boulevard and Universal Terrace Parkway. Universal Studios Hollywood, Universal CityWalk. Shuttle bus to theme park.

Hollywood/Highland. Hollywood Boulevard and Highland Avenue. Egyptian Theater, El Capitan Theater, Hollywood Bowl, Mann's Chinese Theater.

Hollywood/Vine. 6250 Hollywood Boulevard. Hollywood Walk of Fame, Pantages Theater, The Palace.

Hollywood/Western. 5450 Hollywood Boulevard.

Vermont/Sunset. 1500 North Vermont Avenue.

Vermont/Santa Monica. 1015 North Vermont Avenue.

Vermont/Beverly. 301 North Vermont Avenue.

Wilshire/Western. 3775 Wilshire Boulevard.

Wilshire/Normandie. 3510 Wilshire Boulevard. Koreatown and Korean-American Museum.

Wilshire/Vermont. 3191 Wilshire Boulevard.

Westlake/MacArthur Park. 660 South Alvarado Street.

Seventh Street/Metro Center. 660 South Figueroa Street. (Red and Blue Line connection.)

Pershing Square. 500 South Hill Street.

Civic Center/Tom Bradley. 101 South Hill Street. Ahmanson Theater, Dorothy Chandler Pavilion, Los Angeles Children's Museum.

Union Station. 801 Vignes Street. Chinatown, Olvera Street, Little Tokyo.

Blue Line (Downtown Los Angeles to Long Beach)

Seventh Street/Metro Center. 660 South Figueroa Street. (Red and Blue Line connection.) Los Angeles Visitor Center, downtown hotels.

Pico. 1236 South Flower Street. Los Angeles Convention Center, Staples Center.

Grand. 331 West Washington Boulevard.

San Pedro. 767 East Washington Boulevard.

Washington. 1945 Long Beach Avenue.

Vernon. 4421 Long Beach Avenue.

Slauson. 5855 Randolph Street.

Florence. 7225 Graham Avenue.

Firestone. 8615 Graham Avenue.

103rd Street. 10100 Grandee Avenue. Watts Towers.

Rosa Parks. 11611 Willowbrook Avenue. (Blue and Green Line connection.)

Compton. 275 Willowbrook Avenue.

The Metro Blue Line's Pico station. *Photo by Jeff Hyman,* © *Corel Corporation*

Artesia. 1920 Acacia Avenue.

Del Amo. 20220 Santa Fe Avenue.

Wardlow. 2420 North Pacific Avenue.

Willow. 2750 American Way.

Pacific Coast Highway. 1798 North Long Beach Boulevard.

Anaheim. 1290 North Long Beach Boulevard.

Fifth Street. 598 North Long Beach Boulevard.

First Street. 108 North Long Beach Boulevard.

Transit Mall. 128 West First Street. Long Beach Aquarium of the Pacific, *Queen Mary,* Long Beach Convention & Entertainment Center.

Pacific. 498 Pacific Avenue.

Green Line (Norwalk to Redondo Beach)

Marine/Redondo. 2406 Marine Avenue, 5301 Marine Avenue.

Douglas/Rosecrans. 700 South Douglas Street.

El Segundo/Nash. 2226 East El Segundo Boulevard.

Mariposa/Nash. 555 North Nash Street.

Aviation/I–105. 11500 Aviation Boulevard. Los Angeles International Airport via free shuttle.

Hawthorne/I–105. 11230 South Acacia Street.

Crenshaw/I–105. 11901 South Crenshaw Boulevard.

Vermont/I–105. 11603 South Vermont Avenue.

Harbor Freeway/I–105. 11500 South Figueroa Street.

Avalon/I–105. 11667 South Avalon Boulevard.

Rosa Parks. 11611 Willowbrook Avenue. (Blue and Green Line connection.)

Long Beach/I–105. 11508 Long Beach Boulevard.

Lakewood/I–105. 12801 Lakewood Avenue.

I–605/I–105 Norwalk. 12901 Hoxie Avenue.

■ METROLINK

Information: (800) 371–5465.

Metrolink is a long-distance commuter train system that serves Los Angeles and area communities, including Burbank, Glendale, Riverside, and San Bernardino. There is also service to a station near Anaheim Stadium. Trains run from about 4:00 A.M. to 9:00 P.M. weekdays. Fares are based on distance traveled; free transfers to MTA lines are available.

■ AMTRAK

Information: (800) 872–7245. www.amtrak.com.

Amtrak connects Union Station (800 North Alameda Street) in downtown Los Angeles to points in California, including Orange County and San Diego, as well as cross-country service. There are Amtrak stations near Anaheim Stadium in Orange County as well as in Santa Ana, Fullerton, San Juan Capistrano, Irvine, Oceanside, Del Mar, and San Diego.

Union Station in Los Angeles, the terminal for long-distance Amtrak service. *Photo by Jeff Hyman, © Corel Corporation*

■ INTERCITY BUSES

Greyhound Bus Lines. The company has a terminal in downtown Los Angeles, and one in Anaheim at 100 West Winston Street. Information: (800) 231–2222. www.greyhound.com.

Orange County Transportation Authority (OCTA). (714) 636–7433. www.octa.net.

Metropolitan Transit Authority. Greater Los Angeles area, downtown, and airport service. **Information:** (213) 626–4455 or (800) 266–6883 in California. www.mta.net.

SHOULD YOU RENT A CAR?

Do you need to rent a car? In a word, probably. If you can arrange to stay at a hotel that offers shuttle bus service to and from one of the Los Angeles area airports (Los Angeles International, Orange County, or Ontario) and a shuttle to and from Disneyland, you may be able to do without a car. You'll be limited, though, in your ability to visit other attractions such as Knott's Berry Farm, Universal Studios, or Six Flags California.

An alternative is to hire a car service from your hotel to attractions and back; expect hourly rates of $40 to $80.

■ CAR RENTAL STRATEGIES

All the major car rental agencies, and a selection of smaller ones, have offices in Southern California. Most of the companies operate from the major airports, but a few also have pickup and drop-off sites in big cities and at some large hotels.

In 2002, prices for rental cars were on the climb, although they still represent a relative bargain. Think of the deal as borrowing $15,000 for a $35 fee to put things in perspective.

In general, you'll get the best deals on car rentals by booking in advance. Rental companies, like airlines and hotels, usually publish a limited number of deep-discount rates that they use to lure customers and when those are gone, you may end up paying a higher rate than the guy next to you at the counter for the same class of car.

However, as you fly across the country, read the airline's magazine in the seat-back pocket. There are often special car rental rates advertised for destinations served by the airline. It may be worthwhile to take the ad with you to the rental counter and ask for a better rate than the one you've reserved.

Your travel agent may be of assistance in finding the best rates; make a few phone calls by yourself, too. Sometimes you'll find significant variations in prices from one agency to another. Be sure to check online Web sites as well; sites such as www.expedia.com and www.travelocity.com allow you to directly compare rates from several rental agencies for the dates and locations you specify. You may also find lower rental rates at the Web sites of the rental car companies themselves. Join the agencies' priority clubs—usually free—to receive special offers.

If you fly into a large city like Los Angeles, be aware that the least expensive car rental agencies usually don't have stations at the airport itself. You'll have to wait for a shuttle bus to take you from the terminal to their lot, and you must return the car to the outlying area at the end of your trip. This may add about twenty to thirty minutes to your arrival and departure schedule.

Car rental companies will try—with varying levels of pressure—to convince you to purchase special insurance coverage. They'll tell you it's "only" $7.00 or $9.00 per day. What a deal! That works out to about $2,500 or $3,330 per year for a set of rental wheels. Of course the coverage is intended primarily to protect the rental company, not you.

Before you travel, check with your insurance agent to determine how well your personal automobile policy will cover a rental car and its contents. I strongly recommend you use a credit card that offers rental car insurance; such insurance usually covers the deductible below your personal policy. The extra

Fast Food

One advantage to bringing a car to a theme park is the chance to save a bit of money and get a more relaxed, better meal by ducking out at lunch or dinner and visiting a decent buffet or menu restaurant; come back to the park for some evening rides and the fireworks. (Be sure to get your hand stamped when you leave the park and hold onto your ticket stub—both are needed for readmission on the same day. Your parking receipt is also valid for reentry to any of the parking lots.)

auto insurance by itself is usually worth an upgrade to a gold card or other extra-service credit card.

The only sticky area comes for those visitors who have a driver's license but no car, and therefore no insurance. Again, consult your credit card company and your insurance agent to see what kind of coverage you have or what kind you need.

Pay attention, too, when the rental agent explains the gas policy. The most common plan says you must return the car with a full tank; if the agency must refill the tank, you will usually be billed a very high per-gallon rate and some-times a service charge as well. Other optional plans include one where the rental agency sells you a full tank when you first drive away and takes no note of how much gas remains when you return the car. Unless you somehow manage to re-turn the car with the engine running on fumes, you are in effect making a gift to the agency with every gallon you bring back. I prefer the first option, which re-quires making it a point to refill the tank on the way to the airport on getaway day.

Although it is theoretically possible to rent a car without a credit card, you will find it to be an inconvenient process. If the rental agency can't hold your credit card account hostage, it will most often require a large cash deposit—per-haps as much as several thousand dollars—before it will give you the keys.

And finally, check with the rental company about its policies on taking the car out of the state. Some companies will charge you extra if you're planning to take the car across a state line.

FROM HERE TO THERE IN LOS ANGELES AND ORANGE COUNTY

Getting from here to there in Los Angeles and Orange County mostly involves driving, and mostly on one of the famed California freeways. These free ex-pressways are among the wonders of the world—broad four- or even six-lane ribbons of concrete winding through valleys or arching over canyons.

The most important roads for readers of this book are the north-south free-ways, including Interstates 5 and 405, which run between Los Angeles and Orange County, and Highway 101, which connects Pasadena to Hollywood. The busy I–5 also serves visitors traveling between Disneyland, Knott's Berry Farm, Universal Studios, and Six Flags California.

There are two idiosyncrasies about California driving that may be confusing to out-of-towners. First is the fact that most of the highways have names as well as numbers, and some have more than one name for different sections. Second, many of the exit signs do not emphasize north or south but instead indicate a major destination point of the road.

Your rental car will come with a small map, which probably should be rele-gated to the glove compartment; pick up a Los Angeles map from AAA or a bookstore and give it a few minutes of study before you set out on a trip.

There are some times when you can drive at or near the speed limit, but from early morning through early evening, the roads coagulate with traffic. The drive from Disneyland to Six Flags California, for example, is about 63 miles, which should take just a bit more than an hour, which is probably possible at midnight. At 8:00 A.M. or 5:00 P.M., you will be in and among commuters, and the drive could easily take two hours. At midday, the drive should be somewhere between one and two hours.

Keep your radio on as you drive. Nearly every Los Angeles area station offers regular traffic reports, which may help you avoid traffic jams by taking detours. Major roadways also have electronic displays to alert drivers to delays.

■ TRIPTIKS

Los Angeles International Airport to the Disneyland Resort

Freeway route: From the airport, take Interstate 105 east to its end where it meets Interstate 605. Head south on I–605 about 5 miles to Highway 91 east to Buena Park where it meets Interstate 5. Take I–5 south about five miles to the Harbor Boulevard exit, which leads into Disneyland. About 45 miles, one hour and twenty minutes.

Fastest route: From the airport, take State Route 46 (Manchester Avenue) about 24 miles east through Inglewood, Huntington Park, Bell Gardens, and Downey to Interstate 5. Head south on I–5, 11 miles to the Harbor Boulevard exit, which leads into Disneyland. About 35 miles, one hour and six minutes.

Disneyland to Knott's Berry Farm

Take Interstate 5 north about 5 miles to SR–91 (Artesia Freeway) West. Exit on SR39 (Beach Boulevard) south to entrance. About 7 miles, ten minutes.

Disneyland to Los Angeles

Take Interstate 5 north 23 miles through Buena Park, Norwalk, Santa Fe Springs, and Pico Rivera. At East Los Angeles, turn off onto Highway 101 north into Los Angeles. About 27 miles, forty-two minutes.

Disneyland to Universal Studios

Take Interstate 5 north 23 miles through Buena Park, Norwalk, Santa Fe Springs, and Pico Rivera. At East Los Angeles, turn off onto Highway 101 north into Los Angeles. Continue on Highway 101 about 12 miles to Universal Studios exit. About 40 miles, sixty minutes.

L.A. Freeways

Directions refer to the path of the freeway through the Los Angeles area

NORTH–SOUTH ROUTES

5	Golden State/Santa Ana
101	Hollywood
110	Harbor/Pasadena
170	Hollywood
405	San Diego
605	San Gabriel River
710	Long Beach

EAST–WEST ROUTES

2	Glendale
10	Santa Monica/San Bernardino
60	Pomona
91	Artesia/Redondo
134	Ventura
210	Foothill

Disneyland to Six Flags California

Take Interstate 5 north 60 miles through Buena Park, Norwalk, Santa Fe Springs, Pico Rivera, East Los Angeles, and Newhall. Exit at Magic Mountain Parkway in Valencia. About 63 miles, ninety minutes.

Disneyland to Long Beach and *Queen Mary*

Take Interstate 5 south 3 miles toward Santa Ana. At Orange, turn off onto Highway 22 west toward Garden Grove and drive 8 miles. Turn right onto Interstate 405 north toward Long Beach. About 25 miles, forty minutes.

■ BUS SERVICE

Airport Coach. From LAX to Disneyland. (714) 938–8900 or (800) 772–5299.

Best Shuttle. On-call, to and from LAX and points in Orange County. (800) 606–7433 within Orange County.

L.A.Xpress Airport Shuttle. (310) 216–3336 or (800) 427–7483.

Prime Time Shuttle International. LAX, Orange County, Ontario, Burbank Airport, San Pedro Harbor. (800) 262–7533.

SuperShuttle. To Anaheim and Orange County from LAX. (800) 258–3826 or (714) 517–6600. www.supershuttle.com.

■ TAXI SERVICES

Yellow Cab of Orange County. Fixed-rate service to and from Anaheim for up to five passengers per cab. (714) 535–2211. www.californiayellowcab.com

■ BEACH, ATTRACTION, AND SHOPPING BUSES

Fashion Island Shopper. Connects to Fashion Island from various locations in Orange County. Call Beach Express Shuttle for information.

MainPlace/Santa Ana Shopper Shuttle. From Disneyland-area hotels to the shopping mall every half hour. (714) 547–7000.

PART II

THE DISNEYLAND RESORT

CHAPTER TWO

ONCE UPON A MOUSE

ONCE UPON A MOUSE, Walter Elias Disney sat down at the drawing board. The year was 1928, and the star of the cartoon short he created was named Steamboat Willie. His more familiar name, Mickey Mouse, came a bit later.

Everything else has been built upon the slender shoulders of this cute little rodent, along with his gal, Minnie, buddies Donald, Daisy, Goofy, Pluto, Snow White, and a cast of thousands of other cartoon and movie favorites.

Flushed with his early success in cartooning, Disney planned to set up a little park alongside his first movie studios in Burbank to entertain his employees and their families; part of the entertainment was to include an expansion of Disney's hobby, a small train system. World War II interfered with the plans for the humble park; when the postwar boom arrived, Disney was ready with a much more ambitious scheme.

Beginning in 1953 Disney conducted a search for a site of about one hundred acres somewhere in the Los Angeles area. He was looking for enough space to build a fantasy world with rivers, mountains, flying elephants, and a fairy-tale castle.

The land that Disney found was a 160-acre orange grove in rural Anaheim, near the new Interstate 5, a freeway that would eventually become the spine of California and the west coast, reaching from San Diego to Vancouver.

He called the place **Disneyland,** and he put his company into debt to commit every available dollar to the purchase of the land and construction of the park. The bottom line was about $17 million, a huge amount of money for an unproven entertainment concept at the time.

When Walt Disney opened his park on July 17, 1955, Anaheim was surrounded by orange groves. As the popularity of Disneyland grew, so did the city of Anaheim, to the point where the park was landlocked within a forest of motels and restaurants in a few years.

As Timur Galen, Walt Disney Imagineering General Manager of the Disneyland Resort notes, "If Disneyland had started as the only development in a sea of green, it was now the only green in a sea of asphalt."

Although a great deal has changed in the half-century since the first plans for Disneyland were drawn, the basic structure of the park, and all that has followed, is the same.

DISNEYLAND TODAY

Today, breathes there a man, woman, girl, boy, or mouse who has not dreamed of making a pilgrimage to Disneyland? The entertainment vision of Walt Disney—along with the incredible marketing skills of the company he left behind—has made Disney's parks and characters among the world's best-known popular icons.

You can see Mickey Mouse T-shirts on the streets of Moscow, Epcot towels on the beaches of the Caribbean, Minnie dresses on the boulevards of Paris, and Roger Rabbit hats in the alleys of Tokyo.

But if you haven't been to Disneyland since early 2001, you may not recognize the place, at least not until you are strolling up Main Street toward Sleeping Beauty Castle.

The Disneyland park itself is little changed, but everything around it has: almost magically, Disneyland has become the **Disneyland Resort.** The neon jungle of motels and restaurants around the park has been legislated into a buffer of greenery and palm trees.

The **Downtown Disney** shopping and entertainment district is now the sparkling gateway to the resort, an avenue of attractive restaurants and shops and entertainment for the grown-ups that jumps until late into the night.

And most importantly, the gateway leads to not one but two theme parks: **Disneyland** and **Disney's California Adventure.**

BEHIND THE SCENES AT DISNEY'S CALIFORNIA ADVENTURE

For five hundred years, California has been considered one of the world's great golden lands of opportunity. People came there from all over the world for gold, oil, oranges, and railroads. In more modern times, they came for freedom of expression and adventure.

California is the capital of the global motion picture industry, music, and television industries. It was also the birthplace of Mickey Mouse and Disneyland, the theme park that became the model for all others.

Walt Disney had been unable to buy enough land around his park to prevent the encroachment of outsiders or to allow enough space to expand his park; he took these lessons with him to Florida when he planned the massive Walt Disney

World, which spreads over some 40 square miles. According to the company, Michael Eisner began looking for a way to expand Disneyland soon after he became chairman of the company in 1984.

The goal was to expand Disneyland from a one-park, one-day attraction to a destination resort. At one point it appeared that a second park would be built in Long Beach or other nearby communities, but the plans were never finalized. Instead, Disney Imagineers came up with a scheme to build a second park in the parking lot of Disneyland.

Disney worked with the City of Anaheim to improve the appearance of the resort area and to create a whole new infrastructure to support expansion. The plan began with putting the Anaheim Mighty Ducks, an NHL hockey team, into the city-owned Arrowhead Pond in Anaheim. Disney next acquired the California Angels baseball team, renaming them as the Anaheim Angels and improving and transforming Anaheim Stadium into Edison International Field.

In 1990 Disney and the City of Anaheim began work on master plans for the Disneyland Resort and the Anaheim Resort Area, including expansion of the Anaheim Convention Center. A not-insignificant element of the plans was the creation of a new tourist district that encompassed the neighborhood surrounding Disneyland. The city enacted regulations that required the removal of large signs and advertising billboards, replaced with a standardized set of tasteful informational signs. Disney was not immune, taking down the venerable Disneyland marquee that had stood outside the original theme park for decades as well as the big blue neon tube letters from atop its own hotels. Disney bought several hotels and other businesses that were adjacent to its property and bought other land to be used for new parking lots and a massive parking structure.

When it opened, Disney's California Adventure left untouched a large surface parking lot in the southeast corner of the park, near the former original entrance to the Disneyland park. In 2002, work began on an expansion of the park that will feature a West Coast version of the **Twilight Zone Tower of Terror** that is a favorite at Walt Disney World in Florida.

And Disney also owns another large piece of land several blocks away, most recently used as a strawberry field; at a press event for the opening of Disney's California Adventure in 2001, Eisner acknowledged that there were tentative plans to add yet another theme park there in years to come. In May 2001, negotiations began with Anaheim city officials for zoning and planning approvals for a third park at the resort.

Millions Served

Disneyland welcomed its one-millionth guest six weeks after the park opened on July 17, 1955. On March 15, 2001, the resort notified one lucky guest who had just passed through the turnstiles that he was the 450 millionth guest. He was rewarded with a lifetime pass.

By the way, according to Disney, if all the people who have visited Disneyland since it was opened were lined up one behind another, they would circle the Earth more than seven times.

■ DESIGNING DISNEY'S CALIFORNIA ADVENTURE

The concept behind Disney's California Adventure was born in 1995. A Disney Imagineering team added new concepts to elements from other Disney parks around the world as well as pieces that had been developed for the company's unsuccessful attempt to build Disney's America in Virginia near Washington, D.C., and for an earlier concept for a new park in California, called Westcot.

"Disney's America in Virginia was a great idea and would have been a great park with a lot of great content," Eisner said in a meeting with reporters in 2001. "When it came time to find a more friendly place than Washington, a place that would embrace freedom of speech, we came back to California."

"First thing, we threw out the rulebook," said Barry Braverman, Walt Disney Imagineering Executive Producer for Disney's California Adventure Park. "This is a park that is very open in its views. You can stand at the park's entry plaza and see the gateway to Golden State; you can see the California Grizzly Bear icon high atop Grizzly Peak; you can see the gates to Hollywood; and you can see Paradise Pier's massive roller coaster, along with so much more. Here we have a park that embraces 'visual intrusion' and turns it into an attribute that draws guests into the environment and the excitement happening throughout.

"Usually we're working in a completely green field situation and we locate a site to fit the idea, much like what was done for Disney's Animal Kingdom at Walt Disney World in Florida," continued Braverman. "In this case, we knew where we were going to build it, and the space clearly has constraints such as size, configuration, and the fact that it was completely surrounded by an urban environment. We had to work our ideas inside that framework."

Construction commenced in 1997. By the time of its opening, Anaheim, Orange County, the State of California, various federal agencies, and The Walt Disney Company had invested nearly $4 billion to revitalize the Anaheim resort area and to expand The Disneyland Resort. In addition to Disney's California Adventure, Downtown Disney, and Disney's Grand Californian Hotel, the overall project included an expansion of the Anaheim Convention Center. Revitalization of the surrounding region brought new palm-tree-lined streets, repaved walkways, colorful boulevard banners, and lush landscaping throughout.

A parking structure, the largest in North America, now serves the new resort. Disney theme park guests heading north on the Interstate 5 freeway exit directly into the structure where parking for 10,250 cars is available. A pedestrian walkway leads from the parking structure to an escalator that leads directly to the tram loading areas. Convention Center and Downtown Disney guests travel on a separate roadway system. In addition, surface parking is available for 16,500 more vehicles.

With the opening of Disney's Grand Californian Hotel, the Disneyland Resort has a total of 2,243 guest rooms, including the existing Disneyland Hotel and Disney's Paradise Pier Hotel.

■ THE NEW PARK OPENS

On February 8, 2001, the gates were officially opened for the new park.

Disney chairman Eisner read the official dedication for the new park:

"To all who believe in the power of dreams, welcome! Disney's California Adventure opens its golden gates to you. Here we pay tribute to the dreamers of the past, the native peoples, explorers, immigrants, aviators, entrepreneurs, and entertainers who built the Golden State.

"And we salute a new generation of dreamers who are creating the wonders of tomorrow, from the silver screen to the computer screen, from the fertile farmlands to the far reaches of space. Disney's California Adventure celebrates the richness and diversity of California . . . its land, its people, its spirit and, above all, the dreams that it continues to inspire."

Also speaking was vice chairman Roy E. Disney, son of Walt Disney's brother, Roy.

"For countless years, the world has come to California in search of a golden dream and the chance to explore new frontiers," Disney said. "Some came to find freedom, others prosperity, but one pair of brothers—my Uncle Walt and my father Roy— had a dream like no other . . . ."

"We gather here today to continue that dream and to build upon those endless possibilities. As Walt Disney said over forty-five years ago, 'Disneyland will never be completed. It will continue to grow as long as there is imagination left in the world.'"

"My uncle and my father would be proud that we are holding true to that adventurous spirit. We stand at the dawn of yet another new dream and we invite the world to discover the newest adventure."

Special guests included celebrities who were on hand for the opening of Disneyland in 1955: Mouseketeers Bobby Burgess, Sharon Baird, and Tommy Cole; "Davy Crockett" co-star Buddy Ebsen; and TV host Art Linkletter.

Cutting the Lines

With great fanfare and much appreciation by guests weary of waiting in lines, Disney introduced the Fastpass system at all of its parks.

Here's how it works: you insert your ticket into a reader at special booths near attractions and receive a Fastpass ticket with an assigned time period. When you return, you'll enter into a special gateway to the attraction with a promise of no more than a fifteen-minute wait. On all but the busiest days of the year, you're allowed to hold only one Fastpass ticket at a time; when waiting time for a reservation extends to several hours, Disney allows ticket holders to make reservations at two different attractions.

CHAPTER THREE

FROM YOUR LAND TO THE DISNEYLAND RESORT

WHEN AND HOW—WE ALREADY KNOW WHERE AND WHY

Here are two hypothetical days spent at the Disneyland Resort:

July 4. It wasn't exactly the flight you wanted. However, you're grateful for the privilege of forking over $840 for a coach seat in the jammed cabin of the wide-body jet. All the rooms at the three official parks hotel—at $300 per night—are sold out, but you were lucky enough to pay just $100 for an extremely ordinary hotel room that's a twenty-minute, bumper-to-bumper drive from the parking lots.

You're directed to the very last space in what looks like the world's largest parking structure (it is). According to the driver of the tram that takes you on a journey to the entrance plaza, you are in the same county as the Matterhorn and Grizzly Peak, although you're not really sure.

When you get to the entrance, there's a thirty-minute wait just to buy your ticket. And as you get close to the counter, you see a sign posted by the window: "Disney reserves the right to halt the sale of tickets when Disneyland or Disney's California Adventure reach full capacity."

If you make it through the gates of Disneyland, you sprint to Tomorrowland to find that the line for the Indiana Jones Adventure includes what seems like the entire population of Boston. That's the good news; the bad news is that the first Fastpass tickets to skip the line at Space Mountain are for 6:00 P.M.

You might as well go out to lunch. You'd better plan on showing up at 10:45 A.M. to get the food and then make plans for a 4:30 P.M. dinner if you hope to find a table at even the lowliest overpriced burger stop.

DISNEYLAND AND SURROUNDING AREA

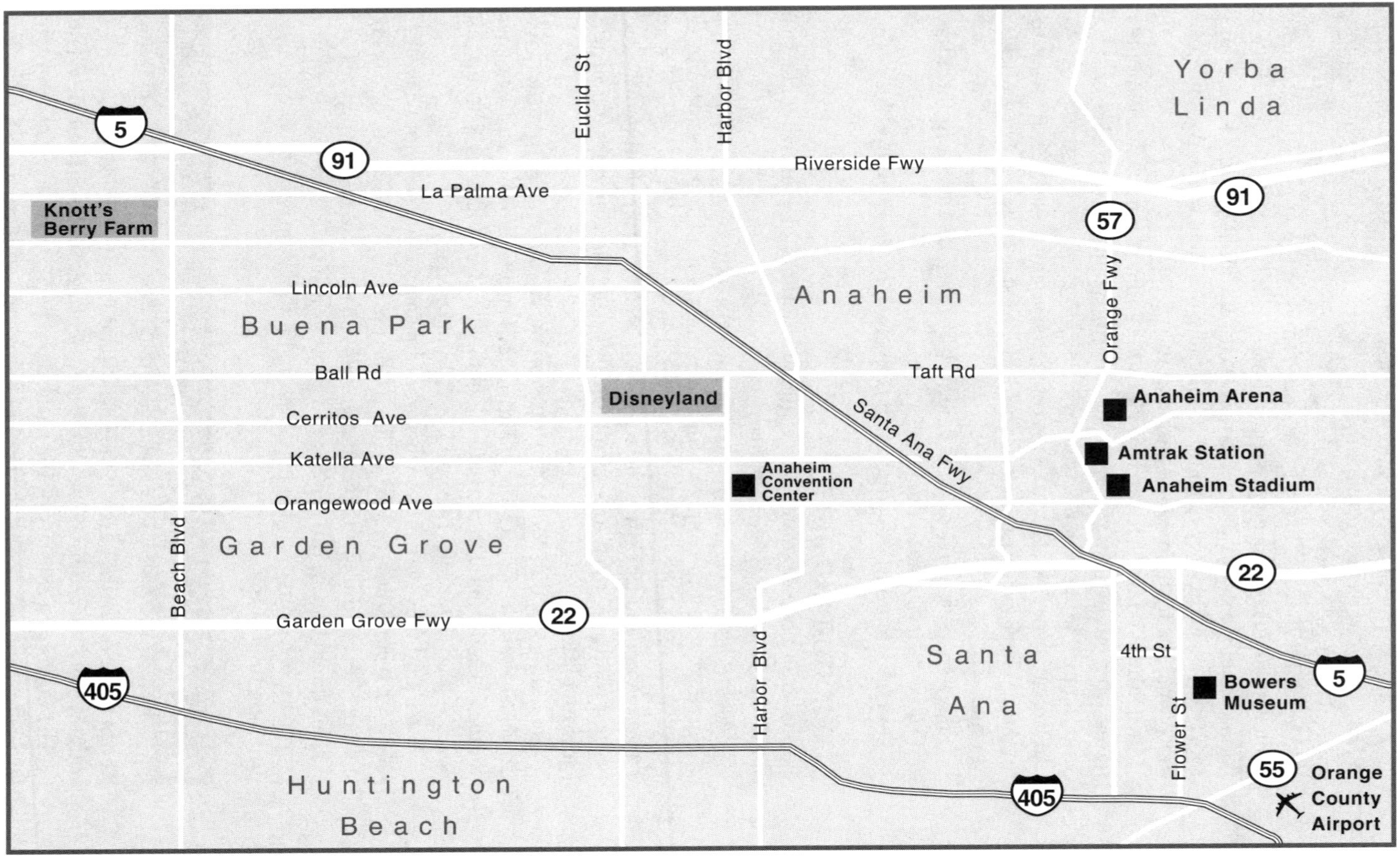

Yorba Linda

91

57

Anaheim Arena

Amtrak Station

Anaheim Stadium

Orange Fwy

22

Riverside Fwy

Anaheim

Taft Rd

Santa Ana Fwy

Harbor Blvd

Anaheim Convention Center

Disneyland

Euclid St

La Palma Ave

91

Knott's Berry Farm

5

Lincoln Ave

Buena Park

Ball Rd

Cerritos Ave

Katella Ave

Orangewood Ave

Garden Grove

Garden Grove Fwy

22

Beach Blvd

Harbor Blvd

Santa Ana

Huntington Beach

405

405

4th St

Flower St

Bowers Museum

5

55

Orange County Airport

If instead you've gotten into the new, smaller park, Disney's California Adventure, you may want to bring a good book to read while you wait for your spin on the Sun Wheel.

March 20. It seems like it's just your family and a crew of flight attendants stretched out across the empty seats in the warm sun at 30,000 feet. Even nicer, you were able to grab a deep-discount excursion-fare ticket for $298. Your hotel room cost you $39.95 (you could have rented one next to the park for just a bit more), and the highway to the park is empty.

At Disneyland, your leisurely walk to the Indiana Jones Adventure puts you into a ten-minute queue; later in the day you skate onto a rocket car at Space Mountain without breaking stride.

Over at Disney's California Adventure, the attendant asks if you want to ride the Sun Wheel by yourself or if you'd like to share the car with Mickey and Minnie.

Take your pick of restaurants, and feel free to take a break in the afternoon and run over to the hotel pool.

Do I have to point out which trip is likely to be more enjoyable?

■ OUR GUIDING RULE

The basic *Econoguide* strategy to getting the most out of your trip to the Disneyland Resort and Los Angeles is this:

Go when most people don't; stay home when everyone else is standing in line.

Specifically, try to come to California when school is in session and in the weeks between holidays. Come between Labor Day and Thanksgiving, between Thanksgiving and Christmas, between New Year's Day and Presidents' week, between Presidents' week and spring break/Easter, and after spring break until Memorial Day.

I'm not just talking about ways to avoid the crowds at the Disneyland Resort, Universal Studios, Knott's Berry Farm, Six Flags California, and elsewhere in Southern California. I'm also talking about the availability of discount airline tickets, off-season motel rates, and restaurant specials.

You'll find the lower prices when your business is needed, not when the "No Vacancy" lamp is lit. The best deals can be found in low-season, or during the shoulder-season midway between the least crowded and busiest periods.

This doesn't mean you can't have a good time if your schedule (or your children's) requires you to visit at high-season. I'll show you ways to save money and time, any time of the year.

A DISNEYLAND RESORT VACATION CALENDAR

The number of theme parks at the Disneyland Resort doubled in February 2001 with the opening of Disney's California Adventure. So did the potential crowds.

The maximum capacity of the Disneyland park is about seventy thousand, a level often reached during the Easter period, around Memorial Day, the Fourth of July, and from Christmas through New Year's Day.

At Disney's California Adventure, the maximum capacity is about thirty-five thousand with a similar attendance pattern. Although attendance levels in the first year of operation at the new park were lower than some expectations, in the long run you can expect Disney will work its marketing magic to pack the park, especially during the summer as crowds visit the Paradise Pier rides.

■ JANUARY TO MARCH

🚶 🚶 🚶 🚶 New Year's Day

🚶 Second week of January through mid-March

🚶 🚶 🚶 🚶 Presidents' Weekend in February and days surrounding

Headaches on New Year's Day and too much company for the weekend of Presidents' Day. January through mid-March is a semiprivate experience.

New Year's Day and a day or two afterward mark the end of the Christmas rush. But a day or two into January, the kids go back to school and most of the adults return to work, and attendance drops off sharply.

The period from the beginning of January through mid-March is usually among the least crowded times of the year, with weekday attendance at the Disneyland Resort of about ten to twenty thousand daily at each park; on weekends, the crowds usually double to a moderate to heavy level of twenty to forty thousand per day. Hotel room rates are generally at low-season levels.

Note that Disneyland generally closes early and does not offer nighttime parades or fireworks except during holiday periods.

■ MID-MARCH TO PRE-EASTER

🚶 🚶 Moderate crowds on weekdays

🚶 🚶 🚶 Lots of company on weekends

From mid-March until the first week of April, attendance begins to grow slowly.

Disneyland generally stays open until 9:00 or 10:00 P.M. during the week and until midnight on weekends, with *Fantasmic!* and fireworks offered only on weekends. Disney's California Adventure follows a similar schedule.

Weekday room rates are below peak rates.

■ EASTER

🚶 🚶 🚶 🚶 Week leading up to Easter Sunday

🚶 🚶 🚶 Week after Easter Sunday

The Easter Parade can get very thick.

The second and third weeks of April are among the most crowded times of the year, with Easter visitors and spring break students clogging the turnstiles to near-capacity levels.

Key to Calendar

🚶 = Semiprivate

🚶 🚶 = Moderate crowds

🚶 🚶 🚶 = Heavy crowds

🚶 🚶 🚶 🚶 = Elbow-to-elbow

🚶 🚶 🚶 🚶 🚶 = Too much

Both parks are usually open until midnight, with *Fantasmic!* and fireworks shows offered most nights.

Room rates are at high-season levels.

END OF APRIL TO PRE-MEMORIAL DAY

🧍 🧍 **Weekdays in early spring**

🧍 🧍 🧍 🧍 **Weekends in early spring**

A lovely time, with moderate attendance during the week and growing crowds on the weekends.

As the summer approaches, both parks begin with a schedule that calls for closing at 8:00 or 9:00 P.M., moving toward midnight later in May.

Room rates are between low- and high-season rates (called "shoulder" rates by travel agents), creeping into high-season rates near the end of May.

MEMORIAL DAY HOLIDAY PERIOD

🧍 🧍 🧍 **Weekdays leading up to Memorial Day**

🧍 🧍 🧍 🧍 **Memorial Day weekend**

🧍 🧍 🧍 🧍 🧍 **Memorial Day**

Lots of company for the holidays

Memorial Day marks the unofficial start of the summer holiday season, and by the time it arrives, the Disneyland Resort is ready to meet the public with operating hours running until midnight on the weekends. *Fantasmic!* and fireworks are presented most nights.

Room rates are at high-season levels.

JUNE, JULY, AND AUGUST TO PRE-LABOR DAY

🧍 🧍 🧍 🧍 **Summer weekdays**

🧍 🧍 🧍 🧍 🧍 **Summer weekends**

The crazy days of summer

Just after Memorial Day the throngs come. They stick around from the first week of June through the third week of August. Both parks are open late into the night, with nighttime parades and fireworks scheduled.

Room rates are at high-season levels for the entire summer.

LABOR DAY

🧍 🧍 🧍 **Labor Day Week**

🧍 🧍 🧍 🧍 **Labor Day Weekend**

The last gasp of summer

As Labor Day approaches, many visitors from elsewhere in the country head back home. At the same time, though, many Californians come to the park for one last fling before school and other lures take hold.

Room rates are discounted from peak levels.

▇ SEPTEMBER TO MID-OCTOBER

🚶 Weekdays in early fall

🚶 🚶 Weekends in early fall

Where have all the tourists gone?

On the day after Labor Day, the turnstiles slow to a relative crawl. The locals return on the weekends.

The parks generally close about 9:00 P.M.; there are some late hours on weekends, with parades or fireworks.

Room rates are at low-season levels.

▇ COLUMBUS DAY TO PRE-THANKSGIVING

🚶 🚶 Weekdays

🚶 🚶 🚶 Weekends

The holidays arrive early

The holiday season begins in mid-October with a Disneyfied observance of Halloween. In 2001 the Haunted Mansion is due to receive a Nightmare Before Christmas theme.

The run-up to Christmas begins about November 1 with special events and decorations. If the weather cooperates this can be a very pleasant time to visit with small crowds during the week and moderate levels on the weekend.

The parks generally close about 9:00 P.M.; there are some late hours on weekends, with fireworks.

Room rates are at high-season levels.

▇ THANKSGIVING WEEKEND

🚶 🚶 🚶 🚶 Turkey time

Merchants give thanks for huge crowds

Crowds build to near-peak levels, especially on the Friday through Sunday after Thanksgiving. Both parks are open until late in the night, with fireworks and shows.

Room rates reach high-season levels.

▇ POST-THANKSGIVING TO PRE-CHRISTMAS

🚶 Weekdays in late November and early December

🚶 🚶 Weekends in late November and early December

This is it: the secret season

Mickey can get lonely at times like these, especially during the week. From after Thanksgiving until the day Christmas vacation starts is the quietest time of the year for a visit.

The parks generally close at 8:00 or 9:00 P.M., and there are no nighttime parades or fireworks, except for weekends.

Room rates are at rock-bottom levels during the week, slightly higher on weekends.

👤 👤 Mid-December Weekdays

👤 👤 👤 Mid-December Weekends

'Tis the weeks before Christmas

■ CHRISTMAS THROUGH NEW YEAR'S DAY

👤 👤 👤 👤 👤 Every day is a holiday

Your sisters and cousins and aunts will all be in line—in front of you.

The Christmas–New Year's holiday is the most crowded, least time-efficient time to visit the Disneyland Resorts. You can expect the park to be open late, offer one or more nighttime parades, and fireworks.

Christmas is a special place at the Disneyland Resort with holiday decorations, celebrity appearances, and a Christmas parade usually scheduled to run from just before Thanksgiving until New Year's Day. You may even get a chance to be a part of the nationally televised festivities on Christmas Day—West Coast activities are usually taped a day or two ahead of time. The bad news is that if you visit Disneyland at this time of year, you will not be alone. If you must go, be sure to arrive at the parks early and follow the Power Trip plan for your best chance.

Hotel rooms are at or above high-season levels.

THE BEST DAY TO GO TO THE PARKS

At least half the typical crowd at the Disneyland Resort comes from local residents making a day trip. The proportion of out-of-town visitors goes up during school vacation periods. Disneyland helps regulate the flow a bit by excluding some classes of season-pass holders from both of the parks at the busiest times of the year.

Overall, Saturdays are usually the busiest day of the week; Tuesdays through Thursdays are usually the least crowded days to visit. Here are the days of the week, from least crowded to most crowded.

👤 Tuesday, Wednesday, Thursday

👤 👤 Monday, Friday

👤 👤 👤 Sunday

👤 👤 👤 👤 Saturdays and holidays

■ WEATHER OR NOT

Temperatures can go through a fairly broad range from cool mornings to hot afternoons and back to chilly evenings. And you can get a bit moist on Splash Mountain in Disneyland or soaked at Grizzly River Run at Disney's California Adventure. If the wind is blowing from the north, the mist from *Fantasmic!* can also dampen the crowd at Disneyland.

Think about bringing along sweatshirts and jackets and stowing them in a locker in the park; some visitors bring backpacks for the family. If there is a hint of rain in the forecast, you may want to bring along your own lightweight rain-coat. With the first drop of rain, Disney stores and pushcarts will quickly uncrate cases of throwaway plastic covers, which may or may not match your ensemble or please your pocketbook.

■ WHAT TIME DOES THE PARK OPEN?

It depends. On the busiest holiday weekends of the year, either of the parks may open to the public as early as 7:30 A.M. At the slowest times of the year, the parks often open at 9:00 A.M. Similarly, the park closes as late as midnight during the busy season and as early as 7:00 P.M. when crowds are small.

Guests at one of the three Disneyland Resort hotels may be offered early admission to certain sections of either park; at peak times, gates for guests with special passes open as much as ninety minutes before regular time.

Be sure to check with the Disneyland Resort the day before your visit to confirm operating hours. Call (714) 781–7290 or consult www.disneyland.com (go to the general information page).

YOU'VE GOT TO HAVE A TICKET

Ticket prices for Disneyland were in effect in mid-2002 and are subject to change. Prices are often adjusted (almost always upward) in early spring.

Note that in recent years Disney's definition of a child (you may have your own) declined a bit to ages three through nine.

From time to time Disney also sells other tickets, including **Ultimate Park Hopper** tickets available for extended periods to guests at Disney-owned hotels, and **Flex** tickets available at some nearby independent hotels. Visitors to major conventions in Anaheim can usually purchase special tickets, including an after-4:00 P.M. pass.

Disneyland and Disney's California Adventure Tickets

	ADULT	CHILD (ages 3 to 9)	CHILD (younger than age 3)	SENIOR (60+)
ONE-DAY PASS	$45	$35	Free	$41
Tickets are valid in one park on one day.				
THREE-DAY PASS	$114	$90	Free	$114
Pass allows park-hopping every day; pass must be used within fourteen days of first visit.				
FOUR-DAY PASS	$141	$111	Free	$141
Pass allows park-hopping every day; pass must be used within fourteen days of first visit.				
GUIDED TOUR	$16	$14	Free	$16
You'll also need to purchase an admission ticket. The four-hour tour visits every corner of the park, leaving you on your own to explore after the tour is over.				

Lines at the ticket booths can grow to unhappy lengths at the start of the day and stay that way on very busy days. Arrive early to buy the tickets or get them ahead of time to save the aggravation. Tickets can be purchased by mail from Disneyland Ticket Mail Order, P.O. Box 61061, Anaheim, CA 92803–6161. Call (714) 781–4043 to confirm current prices and handling charge; the same number can also be used to purchase by credit card.

Disney Stores around the country also sell daily tickets.

A PRIVATE TOUR

Guests can also rent a Guest Relations host or hostess for a private Premiere Tour of Disneyland. A group of as many as ten guests can walk with the guide; larger groups will require an additional guide. In 2002, the tour cost $75 per hour booked for a minimum of four hours. For information and necessary advance reservations, call (714) 781–7290.

MILITARY DISCOUNTS

Active members of the U.S. military and the Department of Defense can obtain discounted tickets through the Morale, Welfare & Recreation (MWR) offices. For information call (714) 781–4565.

ANNUAL PASSPORTS

Disney offers several types of annual passports including a premium pass valid every day and a deluxe pass with as many as forty-five excluded days. In years past annual passes were a great deal for visitors who come to the park for five or more days per year.

In past years Disneyland has offered substantial discounts to local residents for daily admission at slow times of the year, as much as one-third off regular ticket prices. Visitors must show a driver's license or utility bill. These tickets are available only at Disneyland ticket booths and only for the day of purchase. In years past, Californians were permitted to bring along a few friends; perhaps you can meet one in line.

MORE DISNEY DETAILS

Parking. Autos: $7.00. Trailers, campers, and recreational vehicles: $12.00.

Guests with Disabilities. For specific information, obtain a copy of the *Guidebook for Guests with Disabilities* from Disneyland. An audiotape tour and *Disneyland Braille Guidebook* are available at City Hall in the Disneyland park and at Guest Services in Golden Gateway at Disney's California Adventure.

Wheelchairs and electric convenience vehicles are available for rent just inside the main entrance of each park.

Strollers. Strollers are available for rent just inside the main entrances of both parks with a charge of about $7.00 per day.

Baby Care Centers. You'll find a bit of privacy for baby matters at the end of Main Street in Disneyland park and in the Pacific Wharf area of Disney's

California Adventure. Facilities are available for preparing formulas, warming bottles, and changing infants. The centers also offer diapers, formulas, bottles, and pacifiers for sale. Diaper machines and changing tables are available in most restrooms throughout the parks.

First Aid. Registered nurses are on duty at all times in the Disneyland park at the end of East Plaza Street, just off Main Street, and in the Pacific Wharf area of Golden State in Disney's California Adventure.

Kennel Club. Pets can be boarded for the day for about $10 at the kennels, which are located to the right of the main entrance of the Disneyland park. There are no overnight accommodations offered.

> **Y'all Come Back**
>
> If you want to leave the park during the day and return, be sure to have your hand stamped at the exit and hold onto your passport; you'll need to show both to get back in.

Money Matters. The Disneyland Resort will be happy to accept just about any form of payment for tickets including cash, checks, and most credit cards.

At Disneyland an automatic teller machine (ATM) can be found to the left of the main gate. Beyond the turnstiles, ATMs can be found at the Bank of Main Street Bank, at the Frontierland fort entrance marked "Paymaster," and at Fantasyland Theatre. You can cash a check for up to $20 at the Penny Arcade on Main Street or in the Starcade in Tomorrowland. At Disney's California Adventure, you'll find an ATM to the left of the main entrance. With appropriate identification, checks can be used to pay for purchases in shops within either park at the Disneyland Resort.

Lockers. Storage lockers can be rented at Guest Relations or Guest Services to the left of the gates to each park. Others can be found outside Disney Clothiers on Main Street, U.S.A., in Disneyland.

■ THE DISNEY CLUB

One way for serious Disney fans to save a bit of money is to join the Disney Club (successor to the Magic Kingdom Club).

Members receive a discount on multi-day tickets to any of the parks at Disneyland and Walt Disney World. In mid-2002, 3-Day Park Hopper tickets at Disneyland cost $104 for adults and $80 for children; 4-Day Park Hoppers sold for $126 for adults and $96 for children.

There are also discounts to Walt Disney World attractions including Disney Quest, Pleasure Island, Typhoon Lagoon, and Blizzard Beach. Based on availability and time of year, discounts at various Disneyland and Walt Disney World hotels range from 10 to 20 percent. Other benefits include a discount at Planet Hollywood and Rainforest Cafe restaurants in Orlando, the House of Blues at Downtown Disney in Anaheim, and other eateries.

You'll also receive a subscription to *Disney Magazine* and some of the benefits of the national Entertainment Club, which offers discounts at hotels across North America. The card is also worth a 10 percent cut on prices at many shops at Walt Disney World as well as at Disney Stores nationwide.

Suspended Animation

A recurring rumor about dear old Walt Disney is that he chose to be cryogenically frozen when he died of lung cancer in 1966, in hopes of a defrost in another day and age. Actually, according to the company, he went to the other extreme and was cremated before burial at the famous Forest Lawn Memorial Park in California.

An annual membership costs $39.95, with renewals $29.95; one membership can be shared among a family. If your average savings is 10 percent, the card would seem to make sense if you spend $400 or more on covered expenses per year.

Note that you may end up spending more money on a Disney room than you would outside one of the parks. And discounted rooms are limited in supply.

To join, call (800) 654–6347 or consult www.disneyclub.com.

As with any "deal," be sure to compare to the prices you could obtain by yourself. For example, the airfare discount generally applies to full ticket price and excursion fares may be cheaper; the hotel discounts may still be more costly than a direct booking at a lower-priced hotel, sometimes even another Disney property.

A DISNEYLAND RESORT PHONE AND ADDRESS DIRECTORY

Disneyland Resort recorded information line: (714) 781–4565. You'll hear a menu of options. From the first menu, press 1 for Disneyland, 2 for Disney's California Adventure, 3 for Disney hotels, 4 for Downtown Disney, and 5 for annual pass information.

Once you select one of the two theme parks, press 1 for hours, 2 for ticket prices, 3 for entertainment schedules, 4 for dining reservations, 5 for special events, and 6 for directions to the park.

To speak to a human being during business hours, call (714) 781–7290.

Disneyland operator: (714) 999–4560. Available Monday through Friday 7:00 A.M. to 7:00 P.M., Saturday and Sunday 7:00 A.M. to 10:00 P.M.

Disneyland Resort Web site: www.disneyland.com

Disneyland Hotel, Disneyland Grand Californian Hotel, Disney's Paradise Pier Hotel: (714) 956–6400.

Character Meal reservations at hotel restaurants: (714) 956–6406.

Disneyland Guest Relations, City Hall, Disneyland: (714) 781–4565.

The Walt Disney Travel Company: For information on travel packages, call (800) 225–2057.

Information is also available via mail by writing to Walt Disney Travel Company Inc., Travel Port Boulevard, 1441 South West Street, Anaheim, CA 92803.

You may also write for information on the park (at least three weeks in advance): Disneyland Guest Relations, 1313 Harbor Boulevard, P.O. Box 3232, Anaheim, CA 92803-6161.

THE DISNEYLAND RESORT WITH CHILDREN

Doesn't the title of this section sound ridiculously obvious? Well, yes and no: the fact is that for many kids a visit to the Disneyland Resort is the biggest thing that has ever happened to them—and although it almost always will be the most wonderful vacation they've ever had, there are special concerns for youngsters and their parents.

Here are ten suggestions to make a trip with young children go well.

1. Involve the children in the planning of the trip. Obtain maps and brochures and study them at the dinner table; read sections of this book together. Work together to come up with a schedule for the places you want to go on each day of the trip.

2. Draw up the "rules" for the visit and make sure each child understands them and agrees with them. The basic rule in our family is that our young children always have to be within an arm's length of mom or dad.

3. Study and understand the height and age minimums for some of the more active rides at the parks. Don't build up expectations of your 41-inch-tall child for a ride that requires you to be 42 inches in height. (Did we hear someone say something about lift pads in shoes? Just remember that the rules are there to protect children from injury.) And, alas, there have been more than a few accidents at Disneyland over the years, many of them related to youngsters wriggling out of harnesses or purposely breaking the rules. The following lists show the height requirements for rides in each park.

In 2002, Disneyland began experimenting with a system that adds a bit of fun—and takes away a bit of imprecision—when it comes to measuring the heights of youngsters.

The Disney system, tested at Disneyland at the top of Main Street, uses an ultrasonic beam to measure height. The beam bounces from a post to a paddle held over the guest's head and the system flashes a colored light. Wristbands are color-coded with Disney characters and matching signs at each attraction make it simple for short guests to determine if they can ride that attraction.

Disneyland

Autopia: Riders must be at least 52 inches to drive. Young children may ride with an adult at the wheel.

Big Thunder Mountain Railroad: 40 inches minimum

Chip 'n' Dale's Treehouse and Acorn Crawl: 49 inches maximum

Gadget's Go-Coaster: Riders must be at least three years old

Goofy Bounce House: 52 inches maximum

Indiana Jones Adventure: 48 inches minimum

Matterhorn Bobsled: Riders must be at least seven years old to ride alone, or three years old to ride with an adult

Space Mountain: 40 inches minimum

Splash Mountain: Three years old and 40 inches minimum

Star Tours: Riders must be at least seven years old to ride alone or three years old to ride with an adult

Mom and Dad, I Promise . . .

One of the best things about going to Disneyland or Universal Studios with kids is that a resourceful parent should be able to milk a few weeks of "If you don't behave right now, I'm not taking you to Disneyland" threats. My ever-more-resourceful son Willie came up with his own contract:

THE TEN THEME PARK COMMANDMENTS

I. Thou shalt not leave thy parents' sight.

II. Thou shalt not go on twister rides after a meal.

III. Thou shalt not complain about the lines.

IV. Thou shalt not fight with thy sister or brother.

V. Thou shalt not ask to buy something at the shops that costs more than the admission ticket.

VI. Thou shalt enjoy any of the boring things that Mom and Dad want to see.

VII. Thou shalt stand still so Dad can take at least one picture.

VIII. Thou shalt not pester the characters to talk.

IX. Thou shalt not sing "It's a Small World After All" more than sixteen times in a row.

X. Thou shalt go on at least one educational ride, even if it has a long line.

Disney's California Adventure

Jumpin' Jellyfish: 40 inches minimum

Grizzly River Run: 42 inches minimum

Mulholland Madness: 42 inches minimum

Redwood Creek Challenge Trail: 42 inches minimum

Soarin' Over California: 42 inches minimum

California Screamin': 48 inches minimum

Orange Stinger: 48 inches minimum

Maliboomer: 52 inches minimum

4. Come to a family agreement on financial matters. Few parents can afford to buy everything a child demands; even if you could, you probably would not want to. Consider giving your children a special allowance they can spend at the park. Encourage them to wait a day or two into the trip so they don't hit bottom before they find the souvenir they really want to take home.

5. When you arrive, and as you move through various areas, pick a place to meet if you are separated from your children. You should also have a backup plan—instruct your children to find a uniformed park attendant if they are lost, and plan on checking with attendants and security personnel yourself if you have misplaced a child.

You might want to attach a name tag to youngsters (available at Guest Services in the parks if you don't have your own) or put a piece of paper with your name and hotel in your child's pockets. Some parents even issue their kids walkie-talkie radios and keep one in their own pockets!

6. In summer and most any other time, keep your kids (and yourself) under hats and behind sunscreens, especially at midday. You may want to bring bottles of water for the entire family—it's a lot cheaper than soda at the snack bars, and better for you, too.

7. You are not supposed to bring food into the park. You'll probably be stopped if you arrive with a picnic basket, but we've never seen a paying guest searched for sandwiches less obviously stored in pockets or small backpacks.

8. A good strategy with youngsters, especially if you are staying at a Disneyland Resort hotel or nearby, is to arrive early and leave at lunchtime for a quick nap or a swim in the pool; return at dusk to enjoy the evening at the park. You'll miss the hottest and most crowded part of the day and probably enjoy yourself much more. Be sure to have your hands stamped when you leave the park and hold onto your tickets (including your parking pass) if you intend to return.

9. Although you can bring your own stroller, it is also easy to rent one for the day at the park. Park the stroller near the exit to the attraction so that it is waiting for you when you come out. Don't leave any valuables with the stroller.

10. Most restrooms (male and female) in the park include changing tables. You can also purchase diapers and even formula at baby services stations. There are also places set aside for nursing mothers.

■ A KID'S-EYE VIEW OF THE BEST OF DISNEYLAND

What are the best attractions for youngsters three to ten years old? Some youngsters find Haunted Mansion to be a real hoot, while others will have nightmares for weeks. You know your particular child's interests and fears better than anyone else, but here are some favorites and a few warnings.

Disneyland for Youngest Visitors

Autopia (Tomorrowland) *
Country Bear Playhouse (Critter Country)
Dumbo the Flying Elephant (Fantasyland)
Enchanted Tiki Room (Adventureland)
Gadget's Go-Coaster (Mickey's Toontown)**
It's a Small World (Fantasyland)
Jungle Cruise (Adventureland)***
King Arthur Carrousel (Fantasyland)
Mad Tea Party (Fantasyland)**
Mickey's House, Minnie's House (Mickey's Toontown)
Peter Pan's Flight (Fantasyland)
Pirates of the Caribbean (New Orleans Square)***
Roger Rabbit's Car Toon Spin (Mickey's Toontown)
Snow White's Scary Adventures (Fantasyland)***
Storybook Land Canal Boats (Fantasyland)
Tom Sawyer's Island (Frontierland)

Disney's California Adventure for Youngest Visitors

Bountiful Valley Farm
Golden Dreams
Grizzly River Run*
*It's Tough to Be a Bug!****
Redwood Creek Challenge Trail
Soarin' Over California**
Disney Animation
Hyperion Theater***
Jim Henson's Muppet-Vision 3D
Superstar Limo
Golden Zephyr**

Jumpin' Jellyfish
King Triton's Carousel
Mulholland Madness**
Orange Stinger**
S.S. *rustworthy*
Sun Wheel**

Notes: *Adult must accompany small children.
    **Can make some children dizzy.
    ***Loud noises and special effects (pirates, skeletons, beasts) may startle.

CHAPTER FOUR

THE WORLD OF DISNEYLAND

SURROUNDED BY CHANGE, Disneyland is the same.

The heart of Disneyland—Main Street, Sleeping Beauty Castle, Pirates of the Caribbean, the Matterhorn Bobsleds, Space Mountain, Haunted Mansion, and more—has been a comforting constant for nearly fifty years. Since it opened in 1955, more than 455 million people have made their pilgrimage there.

Today, Disneyland is the centerpiece of a new resort. Across the entrance plaza is Disney's California Adventure. Off its left shoulder is the lively Downtown Disney entertainment district. But within its gates, Disneyland is just as you remember it, and just as your children imagine it.

There are eight lands and districts at the park:

Main Street, U.S.A. Frozen in time in early twentieth-century America with the Disneyland Railroad at one end and the Central Plaza and Sleeping Beauty Castle at the other.

Adventureland. Home to Indiana Jones, Tarzan, and the impossibly corny Jungle Cruise and Enchanted Tiki Room.

New Orleans Square. Two of Disneyland's most cherished dark rides are the lure here: Pirates of the Caribbean and Haunted Mansion.

Frontierland. The slightly wild Big Thunder Mountain Railroad stands across the river from Tom Sawyer Island.

Critter Country. Splash Mountain, a raft ride with the Disney touch, is the big draw here.

Mickey's Toontown. Disney's classic cartoon characters have their homes here, and they welcome millions of visitors.

Fantasyland. This is Disneyland in a kid's mind's eye: Dumbo, Alice in Wonderland, Peter Pan, Snow White, and King Arthur Carrousel. Looking over it all is Disney's first mountain and still a classic ride: Matterhorn Bobsleds.

Tomorrowland. Everything new is old again in the spruced-up Tomorrowland, where you can blast off on Space Mountain, soar above a Jules Verne

MUST-SEES

Indiana Jones Adventure
(Adventureland)

Jungle Cruise
(Adventureland)

Splash Mountain
(Critter Country)

Pirates of the Caribbean
(New Orleans Square)

Haunted Mansion
(New Orleans Square)

Big Thunder Mountain Railroad
(Frontierland)

Fantasmic!
(Frontierland)

Tom Sawyer Island
(Frontierland)

It's a Small World
(Fantasyland)

Matterhorn Bobsleds
(Fantasyland)

Roger Rabbit's Car Toon Spin
(Mickey's Toontown; adults excused)

Space Mountain
(Tomorrowland)

Star Tours
(Tomorrowland)

Autopia
(Tomorrowland; new and improved)

Honey, I Shrunk the Audience
(Tomorrowland)

Innoventions
(Tomorrowland)

streetscape in an Astro Orbitor, or visit the moons of Endor in Star Tours.

MAIN STREET, U.S.A.

Walt Disney's memory of small-town America lives forever here. Main Street, U.S.A. is a place of friendly shopkeepers, mom-and-pop soda fountains, and horse-drawn trolleys. The streets are clean, the landscape neat, and a scrap of paper never lingers on the ground.

For most visitors at the start of the day Main Street, U.S.A. is a place to rush through on the way to somewhere else. That's fine: if you are following our advice, you will have arrived early at the park with a specific destination in mind. But be sure to come back later to browse, shop, or eat. When you do, marvel at the attention to detail of the storefronts and interior decorations of the shops.

Take a ride on a horse-drawn streetcar, a horseless carriage motorcar, an antique omnibus, or a vintage fire engine. Just before you pass through the tunnels under the railroad to enter Main Street, glance up to read the famous words of greeting: "Here you leave today and enter the world of yesterday, tomorrow, and fantasy."

A bit farther on, the 1955 dedication plaque on a flag pole reads, "To all that come to this happy place, welcome. Disneyland is your land. Here, age relives fond memories of the past, and here youth may savor the challenge and promise of the future. Disneyland is dedicated to the ideals, the dreams, and the hard facts that have created America . . . with the hope that it will be a source of joy and inspiration to all the world."

As you proceed up Main Street, stop from time to time and look up: most of the names on the second-story windows are those of former and present Disney employees responsible for creation or maintenance of the park.

And then grab a piece of sidewalk. Main Street is one of the best places to be if you are a serious parade fan. The entertainment moves toward or ends near the railroad station just inside the gates. (Other good spots include the Central Plaza at the top of Main

DISNEYLAND

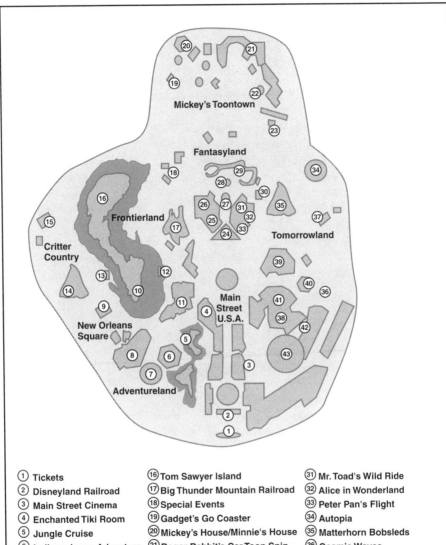

Mickey's Toontown

Fantasyland

Frontierland

Critter Country

Tomorrowland

Main Street U.S.A.

New Orleans Square

Adventureland

① Tickets
② Disneyland Railroad
③ Main Street Cinema
④ Enchanted Tiki Room
⑤ Jungle Cruise
⑥ Indiana Jones Adventure
⑦ Tarzan's Treehouse
⑧ Pirates of the Caribbean
⑨ Haunted Mansion
⑩ *Fantasmic!*
⑪ Golden Horseshoe Stage
⑫ *Mark Twain* Riverboat
⑬ Rafts to Island
⑭ Splash Mountain
⑮ Country Bear Playhouse

⑯ Tom Sawyer Island
⑰ Big Thunder Mountain Railroad
⑱ Special Events
⑲ Gadget's Go Coaster
⑳ Mickey's House/Minnie's House
㉑ Roger Rabbit's Car Toon Spin
㉒ Jolly Trolley
㉓ It's a Small World
㉔ Sleeping Beauty Castle
㉕ Snow White's Scary Adventures
㉖ Pinocchio's Daring Journey
㉗ King Arthur Carrousel
㉘ Dumbo the Flying Elephant
㉙ Storybook Land Canal Boats
㉚ Mad Tea Party

㉛ Mr. Toad's Wild Ride
㉜ Alice in Wonderland
㉝ Peter Pan's Flight
㉞ Autopia
㉟ Matterhorn Bobsleds
㊱ Cosmic Waves
㊲ Monorail Station
㊳ Starcade
㊴ *Honey, I Shrunk the Audience*
㊵ Astro Orbitor
㊶ Star Tours
㊷ Innoventions
㊸ Space Mountain

For years, a big crowd at Disneyland guaranteed big lines and long waits at the most popular attractions. There are few things less appealing to four-year-olds waiting in the sun for a ride on Roger Rabbit's Car Toon Spin, a teenager chilling out in the queue for Space Mountain, or an adult revisiting the ineffable charms of Pirates of the Caribbean.

In years past, we have offered detailed battle plans to our readers to help beat the waiting lines. We're happy to report that for the most part, Disney has come to the rescue with the introduction of Fastpass, a system that allows visitors to obtain a reserved time for a popular ride. Fastpass is not perfect, but it's a whole lot better than life without it.

In mid-2002 Fastpass was offered at nine Disneyland attractions: Autopia, Big Thunder Mountain Railroad, Haunted Mansion, Indiana Jones Adventure, Pirates of the Caribbean, Roger Rabbit's Car Toon Spin, Space Mountain, Splash Mountain, and Star Tours. In this book, look for the ≡*FAST* icon to spot Fastpass opportunities. (Among the popular rides not part of the Fastpass system: all of the kiddie rides in Fantasyland, plus Matterhorn Bobsleds, Astro Orbitor, and It's a Small World.)

So, our recommended Power Trip for Disneyland works like this: 1) start by coming up with a list of the attractions you most want to see; 2) divide the list into Fastpass attractions and waiting-line attractions; 3) get to the park as early as you can; and 4) begin your day by making a beeline to the first Fastpass attraction on your list and grabbing a ticket.

On busy days, weekends, and holidays the gates open about thirty minutes before the park itself; you will be able to stroll to a rope barrier at the top of Main Street. On extremely busy days, the park may open earlier than the officially announced time.

At busy times of the year, your first Fastpass reservation will tell you to come back in an hour or two; later in the day, the gap may extend to several hours. Going back to our Power Trip strategy: put the Fastpass in your pocket and head for the first stop on your non-Fastpass list. With a bit of luck, you can ping-pong back and forth between ride reservations and waiting lines.

Waiting times for the major rides are listed on a board near the Plaza Restaurant, which is just outside the entrance to Frontierland and Adventureland. Cast a quick eye on the waiting times as you enter to help adjust your Power Trip and check the lines any time you're in the neighborhood. Your goal: go where the crowds are not.

Moving beyond Fastpass, it's also important to understand the ebb-and-flow of traffic at the park. I've already suggested you arrive at the park early. You should also plan to eat lunch and dinner early to avoid lines and to take advantage of a break in the crowds when the rest of the world is chowing down. Another reduction in crowds at attractions comes during the daily parades, major shows, and fireworks.

Depending on how crowded the park is, you may want to repeat a few of the rides in the dark. My favorite after-dark excursions are on the Matterhorn and Big Thunder Mountain. You can also catch some of the story rides at Fantasyland, including Peter Pan, Mr. Toad's Wild Ride, and (for the hopelessly romantic or the hopelessly child-directed) It's a Small World.

In peak season and holidays, you can catch the late performance of the *Fantasmic!* show to end your day with a bang.

Street near Sleeping Beauty Castle and on the streets of Frontierland, both of which are nearer the major attractions of the park.)

■ DISNEYLAND RAILROAD

A pleasant way to tour the park, these real steam engines take passengers on a 1.5 mile, twenty-minute circuit of the park. A trip on the train is a great way to end up the day, or to take midday break.

Walt Disney was a railroad nut who ran a small-scale system in his own backyard. His first plans for a small amusement park for the employees of his studio were based around the trains.

The Disneyland line includes four engines, each one of them named for former executives of the Santa Fe Railroad. The oldest engine is the *Fred G. Gurley,* originally built in 1894 and used to haul sugarcane from plantations to the docks in New Orleans; it was rebuilt for Disney using original parts. The *Ernest S. Marsh* dates from 1925, originally built for a lumber mill in New England. The first engines at the park, the *C. K. Holiday* and the *E. P. Riley,* were designed and assembled by the Walt Disney Studios.

Each of the engines has a slightly different design. Pay attention to the number of wheels on each side of the engines and whether there are wheels beneath the tender (coal car). The locomotives no longer burn coal, by the way; all of the boilers have been converted to burn oil.

The trains run in a clockwise circle from Main Street to Adventureland, New Orleans Square, Frontierland, Fantasyland, Tomorrowland, and back to Main Street. They pass through the Zip-a-Dee Lady scene inside Splash Mountain, through the loading area for It's a Small World, and into the mass transportation corridor of Tomorrowland where the tracks for the steam train, the monorail, and Autopia cars come close together.

The train offers some views of areas that can only

Baby Biz

Walt Disney's baby picture adorns the wall at the Baby Care Center, where you can change diapers, nurse a baby, warm a bottle, and do all those other baby things.

The center is located next to the First Aid Station at the top of Main Street. Next door is the Lost Children Center. If you misplace a kid, contact the nearest cast member, who will spread the word throughout the park by radio and contact the center to arrange a proper reunion.

Disneyland Park's famous Main Street, U.S.A. *Photo by Corey Sandler. Used by permission from Disney Enterprises, Inc.*

be seen from the rails. After clearing the station in Tomorrowland, the train enters into a tunnel that holds two of Disneyland's less well-known attractions: the Grand Canyon Diorama and the Primeval World.

The Grand Canyon display re-creates a tiny bit of the South Rim of the canyon with a football-field-long painting and stuffed animals. Some of the original trees and plants were harvested from the canyon itself.

Primeval World, originally created for the Ford Motor Pavilion at the New York World's Fair in 1964–65, was in part inspired by Disney's animated classic *Fantasia*. The fair exhibit in turn helped set the tone for the considerably more detailed and realistic world of the dinosaurs installed at the Universe of Energy at Walt Disney World's Epcot.

If you ask nicely, you may be permitted to ride on the seat directly behind the engineer at the front of the train. First priority is usually given to visitors with special needs.

THE WALT DISNEY STORY, FEATURING GREAT MOMENTS WITH MR. LINCOLN

Here you'll find a most interesting mix of American heroes: Walt, Mickey, and Abraham Lincoln.

Within the doors of the Disneyland Opera House is a small museum dedicated to the life of Walter Elias Disney, without whom none of the rest of Disneyland would have been possible. Among the remembrances of Uncle Walt is his original office from Burbank, which he used for twenty-six years. On one side is his working office; on the other is his formal office where he held appointments with important visiting guests. Disney often sat at the grand piano with songwriters who stopped by to play their newly composed tunes or with famous singers trying out for parts in Disney films.

You'll see the announcement of Disneyland by Walt Disney and a speeded-up film of construction of the park, which opened on July 17, 1955. (In fairytale fashion the opening day was exactly a year and a day after work began).

Not particularly related to anything else but still interesting is a large and intricate model of the U.S. Capitol. It was carved out of caenstone in 1932, based on photographs and blueprints of the actual building.

Finally, there is a section of the hall that salutes Disney as a pioneer of animation. There are some drawings showing the combination of animation and live action pioneered by Disney and a description of how a multiplane camera works. You'll also see some drawings created in 1967 for the sculptures used in the Pirates of the Caribbean ride, including the familiar drunken pirate hanging onto a post.

After a short film about Disney, guests enter a larger theater where they are greeted by Audio-Animatronic Abe, who presents a speech drawn from Lincoln's own statements. The Disney film takes about seven minutes; Abe, about fifteen minutes.

Lincoln was one of the first animatronic figures created by the Disney Company, introduced at the Illinois pavilion of the New York World's Fair in 1964. Abe's appearance at Disneyland was updated in 2001. The new show immerses visitors in the first-hand perspective of a Union soldier on leave in Washington, D.C., in 1863. Period photographs and high-tech electronics paint an audio picture of a Civil War battle. The presentation climaxes with the robotic Lincoln's weary but emotional delivery of the Gettysburg Address.

Main Street Cinema

What else would you expect to be playing in the moviehouse on Disneyland's main drag but continuous Disney cartoons? Among the biggest treats are those that reach back to the dawn of Disney, such as

Disney Choo-choo

The fabulous theme-park empire that bears Walt Disney's name can trace its roots back to Disney's personal train set.

Train fanciers and Disneyphiles will want to visit the waiting room of the Main Street Train Station. There is an interesting display of photographs of Disney's private line, the Carolwood-Pacific Railroad, which he operated in the backyard of his Holmby Hills home. Disney was fond of taking his daughters, employees, family, and friends for a ride on the miniature line, which later served as a $\frac{1}{8}$-scale model for the full-size *C. K. Holiday* that has circled Disneyland since 1955. You will also see old pictures of Disney with his railroad system in his backyard seated on the little steam train.

A wooden display case exhibits a caboose from the Carolwood-Pacific Railroad built by Walt Disney himself. He hand-crafted all of its interior appointments, including bunk beds, clothes lockers, a magazine rack that has miniature newspapers, a desk, washstands, and a potbellied stove.

Lockers

You'll find a set of coin-operated lockers outside the gates of Disneyland all the way to the left, near a picnic area.

Inside the park, you'll find a bank of lockers on the right side of Main Street about midway between the Main Street Train Station and the Hub. Spots in this prime location often fill up on busy days. Another group of lockers can be found deeper within the park near the Fantasyland Theatre.

Steamboat Willie, the first Mickey Mouse cartoon, released in 1928.

The small theater has six small screens and no seats; it's rarely busy and is a great place to cool off on a hot day or dry off on a rare wet day. It's also a great meeting place if you and your party become separated.

Penny Arcade

Disneyland's marvelous collection of antique games and amusements includes penny hand-crank movies and some modern video games. The old nickelodeons in the front work on a penny, probably the only thing in all of Orange County available at that price; the new machines eat quarters and dollars.

Antiques include the Love Tester, a hand-squeeze meter that claims to measure your sex appeal. Some of the nickelodeon movies I've seen include Snitz Edwards in *Small Town Sheik,* and Ben Turpin in *Home Sweet Home.* Esmeralda, the Card-Reading Gypsy, stands in the position of honor right on Main Street.

Main Street Vehicles

Old-fashioned cars, a horse-drawn trolley, and fire engines move slowly down one end of Main Street to the other. (Following not far behind the horses are uniformed sanitation engineers with shovels.) Unless you can jump right on board one of the vehicles, it will usually be faster to walk the length of Main Street; at the end of a long day, though, a seated ride is mighty appealing.

The vehicles don't run during parade periods.

ADVENTURELAND

This is one of the quirkiest corners of Disneyland, home to the indescribably bizarre charm of the Enchanted Tiki Birds, the robotic alligators and the awful puns of the Jungle Cruise, the cement branches of the Tarzan's Treehouse (the former Swiss Family Treehouse), and the wild Indiana Jones Adventure, one of the most impressive theme-park rides anywhere.

MUST-SEE INDIANA JONES ADVENTURE ≡FAST

Whatever you do, don't look at the Forbidden Eye. You know, the one that's right ahead of you, the one that's pulsing brightly in front of your car full of explorers, the one that will make the walls of the temple crash down all around you if you sneak a peek. Oh no!

The Indiana Jones Adventure is a spectacular combination of a (slow) roller coaster and a simulator with some of the best special effects anywhere in

Disneyland or most anywhere else. The ride is based on the famous (and always exciting) explorations of Indiana Jones.

The Indiana Jones Adventure became one of the most popular attractions at the park when it opened in 1995. On a busy day, this is an attraction where you definitely want a Fastpass.

It seems that intrepid archaeologist Indiana Jones has made yet another fabulous find deep within a densely overgrown jungle. According to legend, the god Mara offers to all visitors one of three magical gifts: restoration from the Fountain of Eternal Youth, fabulous wealth from the Hall of Riches where all of the great treasures of history have been collected, or knowledge of all that is to come with the aid of a mystical amulet from the Observatory of the Future.

In fact, says the legend, Mara is so powerful that she can peer into your soul to choose the one gift that is best for you. But the legend also tells of a terrible curse for any visitor who is so foolish as to look directly into Mara's eye.

Unfortunately, funding for continued excavation is running out. To raise cash, Dr. Jones and his assistant Sallah have agreed to conduct tours. That's you, folks. Step right up!

As you approach the entrance to the temple, you'll pass through a reconstructed pre–World War II universe including trucks, generators, phones, typewriters, books, and more. You'll also see a loading dock stacked with treasures waiting to be picked up by one of the Jungle Cruise boats that pass nearby.

You'll make your way into the temple through an appropriately creepy torch-lit waiting area that includes caverns, an old well, and a makeshift movie theater where you'll learn details of the discovery of Mara's temple.

This is not a ride for the timid. If the waiting line doesn't scare you, consider that the ride includes skulls and skeletons, bugs, snakes, explosions, a crumbling bridge, explosions, fire, and a car that will give you the shakes. And the waiting queue is not for the claustrophobic; some of the areas are very narrow and cave-like.

On the busiest days the waiting line extends outside onto the plaza near the Jungle Cruise. When you enter into the building itself, if the queue ahead of you is full, you can expect a forty-five-minute wait.

About halfway through the waiting queue you will come to the Rotunda Room with a maze that circles a well—this point is about fifteen minutes away from the end of the line. The sign warns against pulling the

The Unhappy Kingdom

Look up at the store windows on Main Street for some neat surprises. Above the Cone Shop you'll see a dentist's office; listen carefully and you can hear some poor soul having a tooth extracted.

And speaking of pain, listen beneath the piano teacher's window for the sounds of a not particularly talented child receiving a piano lesson.

Sounds Like

More sounds on Main Street: there are some strange goings-on at the Hotel Marceline. (The hotel gets its name from Walt Disney's childhood home in Marceline, Missouri.) Listen in at the Detective's Office for the sounds of a snoring sergeant.

Private Digs

Proprietor Walt Disney built a private apartment over the Fire House on Main Street for special occasions when he stayed overnight at Disneyland. The lamp in the window is kept burning in his memory.

rope, but of course that is exactly what you are expected to do.

"Leave off the rope, old fella!" comes a yell from below; every once in a while the words are more extreme.

Another waiting area takes you through a screening room where you can watch a portion of the "Eye on the Globe" newsreel flashed up on the screen by a rickety old projector. You'll learn how celebrities have been flocking to visit Professor Jones's latest discovery; one of the segments of the newsreel tells of a celebrated but aging actress who visited the temple of Mara and received the gift of eternal youth. "No more matronly roles for her," the breathless announcer reports. If you listen very carefully, you will also hear how not all of the visitors seem to have escaped.

Finally, you're boarded onto a twelve-seater military transport. There are three rows of four narrow seats across in the vehicle. The leftmost passenger in the front row gets to hold on to the steering wheel—it does not steer the car, though.

In my experience, it seems that the wildest ride is given to the passengers sitting in the back row and the mildest to those sitting in the center row of the car. Then again, the front seat gives the best view, and that rider gets to spin and hold onto the (nonfunctional) steering wheel.

There are a total of sixteen transports, each nicely decorated to look dirty and beaten up. Vehicles are dispatched every eighteen seconds, and the ride can carry as many as 2,400 people per hour.

Free?

Here's the best bargain in the park. You can obtain a free pair of aspirin or Tylenol to cure a headache at the First Aid Station at the top of Main Street. The cup of water costs $10, though. Just kidding. There's a nurse on duty at the station, and arrangements can be made to store medication there. Over-the-counter medications can also be purchased at the Emporium on Main Street.

The ride handlers are very strict about enforcing the 48-inch minimum height requirement; adults shouldn't take the ride if they have back problems or other health issues, including pregnancy and heart conditions. Pay attention to the medical warnings: The ride is as wild as anything else at Disneyland, and severe enough that Disney has had to face a number of medical claims from visitors over the years. Be sure to buckle your seat belt and grab hold on the handlebars in front of you.

Beneath the shell of the transport is some of the highest technology of any ride at any theme park. Each vehicle has its own ride computer for sound and control. The troop transports use a Disney-developed technology known as Enhanced Motion Vehicle, which controls the movement of the transport forward and backward, up and down, and side to side, as well as the sounds and some of the special effects of the ride. Each vehicle can stop, back up, slow down, or go faster based on computer decisions. (The mechanism was adapted for use at Disney's Animal Kingdom at Walt Disney World in Orlando, where the vehicles run through Dinosaur!)

The ride is accompanied by John Williams's music from the Indiana Jones films, specially adapted and rerecorded by a ninety-piece orchestra. To tell you the truth, we can't remember hearing it, though; we were very busy holding on for dear life and watching the wild goings-on all around.

According to Disney there are something like 160,000 possible combinations of sounds, motion, and events on any particular journey through the temple, and no two consecutive rides will be identical. In reality, the difference from one ride to another is actually rather minor, but it is interesting to remember that you are in the electronic hands of a computer throughout.

Carved over the door to the temple is a warning in a strange language: It translates as "Beware of the eyes of Mara." (The characters are not that difficult to read once you realize they are like our standard alphabet with a few missing parts here and there.)

As your transport enters into the temple, you arrive at the Chamber of Destiny where you find three doors—one for each of the possible "good" gifts of Mara. Remember the warning against looking Mara in the eye, though.

You'll be offered the chance to decide together on the route you wish to take: the left door is labeled Knowledge, the center is Riches, the right is Youth. (We don't want to spoil the illusion by pointing out that the computer will ultimately make the decision for you, so we won't.)

Of course somebody in your transport just has to look in Mara's eye and things go wrong. As you turn the corner from the Chamber of Destiny, you'll meet Indy himself. "We've got a problem here," he might tell you. Or, crankily, "Tourists! You had to look."

The transport careens into and out of a series of caves, across a shaking suspension bridge, through clouds of smoke and sixty-mile-per-hour winds, alongside bubbling lava pits, steam vents, and more. The best effect of the ride is the final one when your vehicle comes face to face with a huge rolling ball; at the last moment the jeep ducks under and out of the way. And then Indiana Jones himself congratulates you on surviving the trip. Sometimes he's in a foul mood: "Next time you're on your own," he told us once. On another visit he was in a more congratulatory mood: "Not bad for tourists."

And then it's over . . . and if you've got the nerve you can get back in line.

In addition to the Indiana Jones Adventure, George Lucas has several other links to Disney, including Indiana Jones et le Temple du Péril, a roller-coaster adventure at Disneyland Paris; The Indiana

Going to the Dogs

You can't bring the family pet into the park—it might scare the mice, you know. And please don't be so cruel as to leave Bowser or Kitty in the car; temperatures in a glass and metal box in the sun can kill.

Disney offers a day kennel to the right of the main gate. The exercise area for dogs offers canines their own private fire hydrant.

Size Matters

In California, Disneyland occupies just eighty acres and Disney's California Adventure fifty-five acres. In Florida, the Magic Kingdom takes up 107 acres, the Disney-MGM Studios is spread over 135 acres, and Epcot covers 260 acres (including a 40-acre lake). The sprawling Walt Disney World resort includes 28,000 acres or some 43 square miles of land, making it about the size of San Francisco or twice the size of Manhattan.

Jones Epic Stunt Spectacular and Star Tours at Disney–MGM Studios in Florida; Star Tours at Disneyland and Disneyland Paris; Captain EO, formerly at Disneyland, and the ExtraTERRORestrial Alien Encounter at the Magic Kingdom of Walt Disney World.

Some of the original renderings for the Indiana Jones Adventure are on display at the Disney Gallery, located over the Pirates of the Caribbean in New Orleans Square. In addition to drawings that were eventually adapted for the ride as it now exists, you can also learn about some concepts that were not used, including a walk-through adventure and a high-speed mine car adventure within a temple. At one point, Imagineers considered using Jungle Cruise launches to shuttle guests to the new ride.

■ TARZAN'S TREEHOUSE

A "climb-through" experience that begins with a climb up a wooden staircase made of salvaged items from a shipwreck. On the other side of a suspension bridge is the moss-and-vine-covered tree that is the home of Tarzan's human parents and his ape foster mother Kala. Sketches by Tarzan's faithful companion Jane help explain the story of Tarzan's survival in the jungle.

On the other side of the bridge is a small hut that was once the heart of the family but is now obviously the scene of a terrible event. A canvas wall, ripped and shredded, testifies to an attack by Sabor, a vicious leopard; listen carefully and you may hear him growling nearby.

In the next room is a tiny overturned cradle that once belonged to the infant Tarzan. Jane's sketchbook shows how the baby was saved from the attack by a kindly ape named Kala, who then raised the boy as if he were her own.

At the base of the tree is an interactive play area where Jane has turned salvaged belongings into playthings and musical instruments. At times cast members bring live animals to the area to introduce them to young visitors.

The treehouse was the home of another shipwrecked clan, the Swiss Family Robinson, from 1962 until 1999. For the conversion, the tree was extended by 10 feet and nearly six thousand artificial leaves were applied to its 450 branches. If you listen very carefully you can hear "Swissapolka" playing from the old gramophone; it's a salute to the original attraction.

⦙MUST-SEE⦙ JUNGLE CRUISE

Another Disneyland classic, an escorted boat tour along the rivers of a wild kingdom that somehow stretches from the African veldt to the Amazon rain forest to the Nile valley and the jungles of southeast Asia. The cruise is one of the original entertainments from Disneyland's opening in 1955.

You are a somewhat willing participant in a trip with the Jungle Cruise Trading Company. The journey begins in the mist-filled rain forests of the Irrawaddy in Burma and continues up the Mekong River in Vietnam to Egypt's fabled Nile.

You'll see some of Disney's most famous special effects, such as the automated hippos lurking just below the water and the cavorting elephants that spray water from their trunks. The shores are lined with robotic zebras, lions, and giraffes.

The best part of the ride is the hokey, but still entertaining, patter of the tour guides in pith helmets. ("Be sure to tell your friends about Jungle Cruise," our guide told us on one trip. "It cuts down the lines." He also sincerely apologized to passengers for some of the worst [or best] one-liners in the patter: "I'd tell funnier jokes, but they have to be approved by Disney.")

You want more? "Welcome aboard," my deadpan host began. "If

A Jungle Cruise boat rounds a bend. *Photo by Corey Sandler. Used by permission from Disney Enterprises, Inc.*

you're here for fun and excitement, we got rid of that three years ago."

As we passed a slightly gruesome scene of wild animals feasting on a carcass, he cast a glance at some of the younger passengers on the boat. "Oh, look," he said, "A pride of lions protecting a sleeping zebra."

Some guides encourage riders to laugh at the line of people waiting their turn to enter the nearby Indiana Jones Adventure.

Amateur gardeners may be most thrilled by the amazing collection of unusual plants, flowers, and trees Disney's crew of groundskeepers keep alive. "On the right we have plants," the guide told us, pausing a beat for effect. "On the left we have more plants.

"Check out the gigantic bamboo plants. That's something you don't see every day. You don't, but I do."

The ride is just short of ten minutes; the line to get on board, alas, can sometimes wind around and around the corral for more than an hour. Go early or late on busy days.

◼ ENCHANTED TIKI ROOM

In the Tiki, Tiki, Tiki, Tiki, Tiki Room (you'll understand the reference after you sit through this exceedingly strange squawking show) you'll find a collection of

When It Rains

. . . you will get wet. Most of Disneyland is outdoors and many of the waiting lines are open to the skies. When the rains come, vendors magically appear selling bright yellow plastic ponchos decorated with Disney characters; they are usually good for a few wearings before they tear. If you fear the weather, you might want to shop before you travel or stop at one of the discount stores nearby Disneyland and purchase raingear there; you may save a few dollars, end up with something a bit more durable, and make a non-Disney fashion statement.

more than 200 wisecracking, flapping, automated winged creatures, along with a collection of chanting and singing flowers, totem poles, and statues in a somewhat interesting place decorated with wood carvings and a bamboo lattice roof. This is among the strangest attractions in the Disney realm, and you've got to be in exactly the right frame of mind to enjoy the show. Try tired and giddy, not wired-up and antsy.

The birds were among Disney's first attempts at Audio-Animatronics and represented the state of the art as it existed around 1963. We know some young children who have been absolutely enchanted by the birds; the very young and the very cynical need not apply. Adults might want to bring a Walkman.

CRITTER COUNTRY

You can take a gentle ride in a real Davy Crockett canoe, or make a wet and wild splashdown in the most enchanting log ride anywhere.

One thing you can no longer do is groan through the puns at the Country Bear Playhouse, the place that answered the question of what bears do on their vacations; here's Disney's answer: "A loaf of bread, a jug of wine, and seven thousand ants." The playhouse closed at the end of 2001, opening a spot for a new attraction, perhaps a version of The Many Adventures of Winnie the Pooh, a popular Walt Disney World dark ride.

▦ MUST-SEE ▦ SPLASH MOUNTAIN ≡FAST

This favorite, especially on a hot day, is a log flume ride that splashes together bits of Pirates of the Caribbean, It's a Small World, and Brer Rabbit.

Splash Mountain has several false drops—including one with a little hump in the middle—before the big one that plunges about 52 feet at a forty-five-degree angle and a top speed of about forty miles per hour. The big drop, visible to the crowds outside, makes it appear as if the log car has fallen into a pond. For the riders, though, the anticipation is much more intense than the experience itself—the drop is over in a few seconds.

Some of the best special effects take place within the mountain with a story based on Disney's classic Song of the South cartoon, made in 1946. The ride follows Brer Rabbit as he tries to outwit Brer Fox and Brer Bear on a wild journey to the Laughin' Place.

When you enter the Splash Mountain building itself, there are a few interesting exhibits, including a series of placards that tell the Brer Fox story: "Some crit-ters ain't never gonna learn" and "You can't run away from trouble. Ain't no place that far" among them.

More? "It was one of those Zip-a-Dee-Doo Days, the kind of day where you can't open your mouth without a song jumping right out." And, "Everybody's got a laughing place—the trouble is most folks won't take the time to go look for it. And where it is for one, mightn't be for another."

The interior waiting line for Splash Mountain is not a place for claustropho-bics; it's tight and dark in places, and on busy days it seems to last forever. You'll start by loading into your eight-passenger "log"; you may find the seats slightly wet. Be sure to protect cameras and other valuables from getting wet; traveling with a plastic bag to cover them is a good idea. In 2002, the logs were redesigned to include an over-the-shoulder harness.

The logs climb up into the mountain—you'll see the bottom of the big drop, and first-time riders will certainly be expecting a sudden sharp drop over the precipice they've seen from the ground. These are just teases. Instead of the great fall, your log will move gently through a beautiful, tuneful, and peaceful water world filled with more than a hundred Audio-Animatronic characters and lots of delightful details and insistently bouncy music. At the end of the first room there's a drop, but again it's not the big one. Eventually you'll come to the big one, the spectacular waterfall you've seen from the walkway below. You're over . . . and down in about four seconds.

There is one final surprise at the very end: a visit to a "Welcome Home Brer Rabbit" party. The Zip-a-Dee Lady paddleboat chugs alongside. This is the scene you can also spy from the Disneyland Railroad as it passes through a portion of the Splash Mountain building.

All told, Splash Mountain is one of the longer rides at Disneyland at nearly eleven minutes. Despite the brevity of the final drop, it does give you a lot more for your waiting time than Thunder Mountain or Space Mountain. If you can convince the kids (or the adults) to look past the short drop, they are sure to love the rest of the ride, which is pure Disney. Try the ride in the day and at night; the view of the park from near the top is worth the wait.

Splash Mountain is a watery place, and the log cars make a huge wave as they land at the bottom of the big drop, but you really won't get very wet on the ride. The two wettest places seem to be the very first row of seats and the last—the wave flies over the car. The front row has the best view of the drop; the last row has the most suspense.

On a busy day, you should use a Fastpass to avoid lines of ninety minutes or more.

There are Splash Mountains at Walt Disney World

Disabled Guests

Disneyland is pretty ac-commodating to visitors who have special needs; a list of attractions with wheelchair access is avail-able at Guest Relations. Wheelchairs can be brought into the park or can be rented. Disabled visitors, along with a lim-ited number of family members, can avoid wait-ing lines and enter directly onto certain rides.

and at Tokyo Disneyland; in California, guests sit one behind another while in Japan and Florida guests sit side-by-side. We think the Walt Disney World version is the most spectacular.

■ DAVY CROCKETT'S EXPLORER CANOES

Do you remember Davy Crockett? If you do, you're probably well over the average age around here.

The canoes are among the most realistic things in the park. These large vessels circle the Rivers of America around Tom Sawyer Island; in and among the river traffic of the Mark Twain Riverboat, the Mike Fink Keelboats, and the Sailing Ship; and across the path of the rafts to the island. The canoes, alas, are not operated every day and have been rumored to be headed for permanent dry dock for a number of years.

NEW ORLEANS SQUARE

A favorite spot for the hearty of heart, New Orleans Square is home of rollicking pirates and one of the world's largest collections of grim-grinning ghosts.

▦ MUST-SEE PIRATES OF THE CARIBBEAN ≡FAST

Yo, ho, yo, ho . . . one of Disney's very best, a cruise into the middle of a pirate raid on a Caribbean island town.

The ride begins with a calm journey across a dark bayou that is among the most realistic settings in all of the park, right down to the robotic fireflies and recorded crickets. As you move deeper into the Caribbean Sea, hidden underneath the park, you'll meet a rollicking crew of pirates. "Thar be no place like home," one declares, but then he warns: "Keep a weather eye! There be squalls ahead."

The best of those squalls is the moonlit battle between a pirate ship and a government fortress across the harbor; cannonballs seem to land all around you in the cool water as your boat passes through the mist. Pay attention, too, to the jail scene where a group of pirates tries to entice a mangy dog to bring them the key.

Everywhere you look you'll see members of the wondrous collection of more than 120 Audio-Animatronic humans and animals including robotic chickens and pigs.

The famous "auction" of women in chains to the pirates occupies another central scene of the ride. The sign still reads, "Take a Wench for a Bride." But a politically correct update removed the pirate who once held a piece of stolen lace and a woman hiding in the bushes in fear of the drunken pirates. In the central scene, a woman is still chased in circles by a pirate, but now she carries a big tray of food. A bit farther along, a woman brandishes a rolling pin at a pirate who has stolen a ham.

Even with the changes, the ride still paints a picture of some rather unpleasant pirates, an image that scholars say is relatively accurate. Some very young children may be scared by the simulated cannon fire and the skulls and bones that are liberally strewn about in some of the cave scenes.

The famed "Yo Ho" song is perhaps the second most recognizable ride song at Disneyland after "It's a Small World After All." The words here are a bit more threatening: "We kidnap and ravage and don't give a hoot. Drink up me 'earties, yo ho."

Lines can be quite long throughout the day, especially in the afternoon after serious thrill-seekers have finished with Indiana Jones, Splash Mountain, and Space Mountain. Use a Fastpass to avoid the lines or make your visit early or at the end of the day. The ride itself takes just short of fifteen minutes.

▮ THE DISNEY GALLERY

A quiet and cool respite where you can duck out of the madding crowds to absorb a bit of Disney culture and memorabilia. The entrance to the gallery is by a stairway above the Pirates of the Caribbean.

On recent visits the gallery has displayed models and sketches for Disneyland Paris, the Indiana Jones ride, and some of the original drawings for Disneyland itself showing places that had names such as the Mickey Mouse Club, Holiday Land, Frontier Country, the Hub, Fantasyland, Lilliputian Land, The World of Tomorrow, True Life Adventure Land, and Main Street. A scale model of the Disneyland Castle has a tiny mannequin of Walt Disney walking in.

The suite of rooms that is now the Disney Gallery was originally planned as a private apartment and reception room where brothers Walt and Roy Disney could entertain business associates and visiting dignitaries. Although the apartment was never completed as originally intended, certain touches remain, including the stylized initials WD and RD worked into the wrought ironwork of the balcony.

The Disney Gallery is also the site of the most elegant place to view the nightly *Fantasmic!* show. For about $30 per person, you can rent one of fifteen seats on the balcony of the gallery for the Fantasmic Dessert Buffet.

▦ MUST-SEE HAUNTED MANSION ≡*FAST*

Scare yourself silly in this masterpiece of an attraction that hosts some of the most sophisticated special effects at Disneyland. The experience begins in the graveyard waiting line; before the tombstones make you feel too creepy, stop and read some of the inscriptions. They're a howl!

Disney Imagineers continue to have fun with this venerable attraction; a recent addition was an old horse-drawn hearse parked out front. In recent years, a

---

One of a Kind

The following attractions are found only at Disneyland and not at Walt Disney World:

► **Alice in Wonderland** (Fantasyland)

► **Casey Jr. Circus Train** (Fantasyland)

► *Great Moments with Mr. Lincoln* (Main Street)

► **Indiana Jones Adventure, Temple of the Forbidden Eye** (Adventureland)

► **Matterhorn Bobsleds** (Fantasyland)

► **Mickey's Toontown**

► **Pinocchio's Daring Journey** (Fantasyland)

► **Sailing Ship** *Columbia* (Frontierland)

► **Sleeping Beauty** (Fantasyland)

► **Storybook Land Canal Boats** (Fantasyland)

sign out front reads: "Reservations accepted. Ghost Relations Disneyland. Please do not apply in person!"

When you are admitted to the mansion itself, you are ushered into a strange room that features an interesting visual trick: is the ceiling going up or the floor going down? Either way, the portraits on the wall are a howl. (Don't read this if you don't want to know. OK, you have been warned: at Disneyland, the floor moves down and the walls are stationary; at Walt Disney World, the ceiling moves up and the floor stays where it is. The stretching room was put into place in California as a way to get visitors to the loading level, which is on the other side of the railroad tracks. When the Florida house was built, there was no need to go down a level, but Imagineers wanted to keep the same illusion, even if it was accomplished in a different way.)

The attendants, dressed as morticians, are among the best actors in the park, almost always staying in character. They may tell you to "fill in the dead space" in the line. When the elevator at the start of the ride fills up they may announce, "No more bodies." They play their roles well—we've tried our best over the years to make them crack a smile, without much success.

You'll enter onto a moving set of chairs and settle in for a tour through a house that is in the control of the largest collection of spooks this side of the CIA. We've ridden the ride many times and see something different each time. Among the best effects are the dancing ghouls at the dinner party, the moving door knockers, and the face within the crystal ball.

This ride is probably the single best combination of Disney Animatronics, moviemaking, and scene setting. There are all sorts of dreadful details, enough to make it worth several rides if you have the time. Here are a few you might want to look for: the framed needlepoint that reads "Tomb Sweet Tomb," the legs sticking out from under the banquet table in the ghostly wedding reception, and the skull-shaped notes rising out of the top of the organ. Some very young children may become a bit scared, although most kids of all ages can see the humor among the horrors. To break the ice stop to read the inscriptions on the tombs at the exit.

Lines for this show vary greatly; the best times to visit are early or late in the day. The ride lasts about nine minutes, including a two-minute preshow.

The telegraph operator working in the train station at New Orleans Square is clicking away in Morse code; the text is drawn from Walt Disney's speech on opening day at Disneyland.

Disney has been subtly raising the scarification level of the ride over the years, perhaps in reaction to the overall explicitness of our society. The skeletons are now just a bit more real, the ghosts are just a bit more ghoulish.

Actually, though, the first plans for the Haunted Mansion were more gruesome than what was actually built. Because it was to be built near the New Orleans area of Frontierland, the idea was to make it look like an early 1800s Southern mansion; it actually ended up looking like an old home in Baltimore. Walt Disney himself vetoed a design that made the house appear to be derelict (Disney's first falling-down house would come some thirty years later with the construction of the Twilight Zone Tower of Terror at Walt Disney World).

The original plans also called for the tour to be a walk-through, with groups of about forty visitors escorted through the house by a butler or maid who would tell the story. The first story line was quite different, too, and not at all sugarcoated: It told of a wealthy sea merchant who built a fabulous mansion for his new bride but then killed her in a rage after she learned he was really a bloody pirate. Her ghost came back to haunt him and tormented him so much that he finally hung himself from the rafters, giving the mansion two unhappy spirits. About all that is left of that gruesome story is the weathervane in the shape of a sailing ship on top of the cupola of the mansion, some paintings with a seafaring theme, and a quick glimpse of a hanging body when the lights flash on in the "stretching room" in the preshow area of the ride.

The building was completed in 1963 but stood empty for nearly six years. The delay was in part caused by Disney's involvement in four major pavilions at the 1964–65 New York World's Fair, including Pepsi's It's a Small World—A Salute to UNICEF ride, General Electric's Carousel of Progress, the Illinois pavilion's *Great Moments with Mr. Lincoln*, and Ford's Magic Skyway ride.

The first three World's Fair exhibits were later recycled at Disney parks: It's a Small World came to Disneyland and became the model for similar and very popular rides at Walt Disney World, Tokyo Disneyland, and Disneyland Paris. The GE Carousel was moved to Walt Disney World; it was updated a bit in 1994 but remains essentially unchanged. Great Moments with Mr. Lincoln was Disney's first big success with his new Audio-Animatronic technology and was brought to Disneyland's Main Street.

The Haunted Mansion experience is accompanied by a decidedly strange soundtrack that is among the more literate writings anywhere at Disneyland. Here's part of the introduction from the stretching room:

When hinges creak in doorless chambers and strange and frightening sounds echo through the halls, whenever candlelights flicker where the air is deathly still, that is the time when ghosts are present, practicing their terror with ghoulish delight.

For Better or Verse

The tombstones and pet cemetery are located in the upper waiting area at the Haunted Mansion. If the lines are not long you may not even pass in front of them, but they're worth a side trip. Here is a selection of some of the very worst of the verse.

"Here lies Good Old Fred. Great big rocks fell on his head."

"Rest in Peace Old Cousin Hewitt. We all know you didn't do it."

Some of the named tombstones include those of M. T. Tomb, I. L. Beback. U. R. Gone, and Rustin Pece.

And then there are the heartbreaking stories behind some of the gravestones in the pet cemetery:

"Here lies long-legged Jeb, he got tangled up in his very own web."

"Rosie was a poor little pig, but she bought the farm."

And there is the last resting place of Old Flybait the frog, who croaked in 1859.

*Your cadaverous pallor betrays an aura of foreboding, almost as though
you sense a disquieting metamorphosis. Is this haunted room actually
stretching? Or is it your imagination? And consider this dismaying observation: this chamber has no windows, and no doors.*

*Which offers you this chilling challenge: to find a way out! Of course,
there's always my way.*

Says your Ghost Host: "We find it delightfully unlivable here in this ghostly
retreat. Every room has wall-to-wall creeps and hot and cold running chills."

You'll meet Madame Leota, a disembodied guide who will help you attempt
to make contact with the spirits within the mansion.

*Rap on a table, it's time to respond, send us a message from somewhere
beyond. Goblins and ghoulies from last Halloween, awaken the spirits
with your tambourine. Wizards and witches wherever you dwell, give
us a hint by ringing a bell.*

The best special effect of the ride is the wedding party scene, where guests
move from mortal coil to diaphanous spirit and back. After the party, you'll meet
the famous Grim Grinning Ghosts, captured within luminous globes. Through
dozens of rides at Walt Disney World's Magic Kingdom, Disneyland, and
Disneyland Paris we were completely unable to figure out what they were saying
until recently. Here's part of their song:

*When the crypt doors creak and the tombstones quake, spooks come out
for a swinging wake. Happy haunts materialize and begin to vocalize;
grim grinning ghosts come out to socialize.*

*Now don't close your eyes and don't try to hide, or a silly spook may sit
by your side. Shrouded in a daft disguise, they pretend to terrorize;
grim grinning ghosts come out to socialize.*

As the ride comes to an end, you'll be welcomed to hurry back; be sure to
bring your death certificate.

FRONTIERLAND

The world of the Old West that includes a nineteenth-century runaway mine
train, the *Mark Twain* paddle wheeler, and rafts to the kids' fantasies of Tom
Sawyer Island. Check out the quirky entertainment of the Golden Horseshoe
Stage and stick around or come back later for the fantastic *Fantasmic!* show presented on a watery curtain in the Rivers of America.

MUST-SEE BIG THUNDER MOUNTAIN RAILROAD ≡FAST

One of the best rides at the park is at the same time much more than and much
less than it appears.

Big Thunder is a Disneyfied roller coaster, one of only four "thrill" rides in
Disneyland (along with Space Mountain, Splash Mountain, and the Indiana
Jones Adventure).

As far as roller coasters go, it is fairly tame: It's got about a half mile of track

Big Thunder Mountain Railroad. *Photo by Corey Sandler. Used by permission from Disney Enterprises, Inc.*

and a three-and-a-half-minute ride, with a few short drops and some interesting twists and turns. But in the Disney tradition, it is the setting and the attention to detail that make this one of the most popular places to be.

You will ride in a runaway mining train up through a quaking tunnel, across a flooding village, and back down, around, and through an artificial steel-and-cement mountain.

The mountain is bedecked with real mining antiques that come from real old mines out West. Look, too, at the Audio-Animatronic animals, birds, and an old coot of a miner in a bathtub as you zoom by. The walls of the loading area are lined with actual gold-bearing rock.

The trains have been given adventuresome names. Look for *U. B. Bold, U. R. Courageous, I. M. Fearless, I. M. Brave,* and *U. R. Daring.* As they slow down to enter the loading station they pass through a small Western town, including the Big Thunder Saloon, an assay office, and the local newspaper, the *Big Thunder Epitaph.*

Picking the right time to visit the railroad can make a real difference at this very popular attraction; waits of more than an hour are common at midday in peak season. The shortest lines can be found early in the day or just before dinnertime. If you can, pick up a Fastpass on busy days.

Coaster fans say the best ride (meaning the wildest) can be had with a seat in the last row of seats. We also like the very front of any coaster ride because it gives you a view of the perils ahead, over the top of the engine in front. Thunder Mountain by night is another ride altogether. Like Space Mountain, the fun is increased because the darkness hides the track ahead of you.

Children younger than seven must be accompanied by an adult; no one under 40 inches is allowed to ride. Warn young children about the loud noises they will hear as their railway car is pulled up the first lift on the ride.

When you're through with the ride, listen to the talk coming from the bar in the little Western town, located above the ride next to the Mexican food place. At the Big Thunder Saloon: "Do you know your toupee's on crooked?" "No, but if you hum a few bars I'll try to fake it."

■ THE GOLDEN HORSESHOE STAGE

A longtime favorite, this is Disney's squeaky-clean version of a Western dance hall revue. The show includes pretty cancan girls, corny comics, and strolling musicians to entertain visitors of all ages.

Each performance is about thirty minutes in length. You'll need to arrive thirty to forty-five minutes before showtime to make your way to your seat and place orders for drinks or snacks, including chili, ice cream, and pickles (the food is strictly optional, although it may be difficult to prevent kids from badgering you for something at the table). In years past, admission to the show required a reservation made at the door, although in recent years the doors were thrown open on a first-come, first-seated basis.

The Golden Horseshoe can eat up as much as two hours of your busy day; it may not make sense to visit if you are pressed for time.

▦ *MUST-SEE* ▦ *FANTASMIC!*

The *Fantasmic!* show is like every other fabulous Disney entertainment, only more so. This is the highest tech singing, dancing, and pyrotechnical show we've ever experienced. A visit to Disneyland is not complete without a glimpse.

The twenty-five-minute show is performed at the south end of Tom Sawyer Island on the Rivers of America from Frontierland to New Orleans Square. Shows are usually presented twice nightly on weekends and every night during the summer and in holiday periods. During the winter and other off-season periods when the park closes early on many days, no show is presented. The show includes fog, fireworks, soaring flames, a trio of giant, 30-foot-tall by 50-foot-wide mist screens, and an audio system that engulfs listeners.

Like much of Disneyland, the story of *Fantasmic!* is a celebration of the power of imagination. Mickey Mouse appears on a stage at the end of Tom Sawyer's Island and summons forth a series of fabulous visions of fantasy creatures, including Dumbo's pink elephants and beauties of nature. But his reverie is interrupted by a band of Disney villains with such antifavorites as Maleficent from *Sleeping Beauty,* Ursula from *The Little Mermaid,* Monstro the Whale from *Pinocchio,* and the demon Chernabog from the "Night on Bald Mountain" segment of *Fantasia.*

It's up to Mickey to escape from his nightmare. Shortly before the happy conclusion (you figured that, right?) Maleficent transforms before your eyes into a 45-foot-tall fire-breathing dragon that sets the Rivers of America aflame.

The stunning finale includes a pirate ship (the specially decorated *Columbia* sailing ship) commandeered by Peter Pan, and the *Mark Twain* riverboat packed with happy Disney characters.

There are many places to watch including the waterfront near Splash Mountain, the bridge near the entrance to the Pirates of the Caribbean, the patios of the Cafe Orleans or the French Market Restaurant, and a tiered viewing area at the promenade at New Orleans Square.

The most elegant way to view the show is at the dessert and coffee buffet at the Disney Gallery near the Pirates of the Caribbean. Seats on the balcony sell for about $30 each. You can save a seat by registering at the Reservations Center on Main Street before noon or at the Gallery in the afternoon.

Crowds for *Fantasmic!* can be large, especially for the first (or only) show; later shows are usually more approachable. Sometimes parades are scheduled at the same time, splitting the crowd. If you beat a quick retreat from the *Fantasmic!*

Woodn't you?

The petrified tree in Frontierland along the Rivers of America in front of the Golden Horseshoe was a gift from Walt Disney to his wife, Lillian. Mrs. Disney gave it back to the park in 1957. It was taken from the Pike Petrified Forest in Colorado. According to the inscription, the section weighs five tons and measures 7.5 feet in diameter. The original tree, a redwood or sequoia, is estimated to have been 200 feet tall and was part of a sub-tropical forest fifty-five million to seventy million years ago in what is now Colorado.

show and move quickly back toward the Hub and toward Main Street, you should be able to catch the tail end of the parade as it heads toward the Disneyland Railroad Station.

If you are heading for a late show, here's the insider's plan: approach the viewing area from the Splash Mountain side as the previous show is coming to an end. This way you won't have to fight the thousands of departing guests clearing out through Frontierland.

In my opinion the best ground-level view of the show is along the river across from the entry to the Pirates of the Caribbean and facing the shack on Tom Sawyer Island. There's a "Kodak Photo Spot" sign along the river, just to the left of the prime spot.

Disney designers hide as much of the high-tech equipment as possible by lowering it into underground pits during the day. The elaborate multitrack audio system includes speakers located in front of and behind the audience; some of the speakers are disguised as lampposts, and two large boats in the lagoon carry additional speakers. Natural gas jets feed a wall of flame that erupts from the water around the island.

Disney gives credit to an outdoor history pageant in Vendée, France, for the development of the mist screen technology. Warning: some of the mist from the fountains in the show drifts back into the faces of the closest viewers. This can become a bit uncomfortable on a cool evening. The show will be canceled in very inclement weather or high winds.

▐MUST-SEE▐ TOM SAWYER ISLAND

Another essential, at least for the youngsters, is the raft ride over to this little island in the middle of the Rivers of America, based a bit on Mark Twain's classic book. You'll find dark caves, a waterwheel, a dungeon, a barrel bridge, and a bouncy rope bridge. At the western end of the island is Fort Wilderness, where kids can scramble around the parapets and fire air guns at passing riverboats, canoes, and rafts.

Parents will appreciate the space to let children burn off a bit of energy after standing in lines all day; be advised, though, that it is fairly easy to misplace a youngster in one of the simulated caves or on a trail. Choose a meeting place with your children in case you become separated.

You can go out on the front deck of Harper's Cider Mill to see some of the mechanisms for the *Fantasmic!* show. You can see spray heads in the water and underground lighting and projection platforms.

Around the bend is a working water-powered mill. Across from the pontoon bridge is the back side of Big Thunder Mountain Railroad. Here you'll find an abandoned mining train. Look closely at the cargo strewn about—robotic chipmunks poke up their heads every once in a while.

Lines for the raft rarely require more than ten minutes of waiting. The island closes at dusk and may not be open at all during the off-season or in bad weather.

The *Mark Twain* Riverboat passes by Tom Sawyer Island. *Photo by Corey Sandler. Used by permission from Disney Enterprises, Inc.*

■ *MARK TWAIN* RIVERBOAT

Reaching back to the birth of the Disneyland park, the original ⅝-scale paddle wheeler was built for the park. It has traveled uncounted thousands of miles without ever leaving the Rivers of America and without once deviating from its underwater track.

The ride is no great shakes, but it is a pleasant reprieve on a hot day. The Mike Fink Keelboats, Davy Crockett's Explorer Canoes, and the Sailing Ship *Columbia* make the same circle and see the same simulated Old West sights.

The ride takes about fifteen minutes; lines rarely extend beyond a full boat load, so your waiting time should be sixteen minutes or less.

Frontierland Shootin' Exposition

A durn-fancy shooting gallery, sort of a live video game, and not like any other shooting gallery you have seen at a county fair. For 50 cents, players aim huge buffalo rifles at a Disney replica of Boot Hill, a frontier town from the 1850s. The rifles fire infrared beams at targets on tombstones, clouds, banks, jails, and other objects; direct hits make the targets spin, explode, or otherwise surprise. Some of the signs tell a story: "Old Tom Hubbard died with a frown, but a grave can't keep a good man down." If you hit the skeleton of a steer, his horns will spin around.

Extra Admission

Got a spare $20,000 or so for a ticket to Disneyland? That's about the price of admission to the very private and little-known Club 33, located upstairs at 33 Rue Royale in New Orleans Square. Look for the green door with the number 33 just past the Blue Bayou restaurant; there is also an entrance between the pirate shop and the One of a Kind shop. What's inside? Well, there's a bar (the only place in the park serving alcohol) and some real nice chairs.

Club 33 was originally built as a private club for Walt Disney's guests; Disney was involved in its New Orleans design but died a few months before it was completed. In case you're interested, there is usually a several-year waiting list for the right to plunk down about $20,000 for a corporate membership, $10,000 for an executive membership, or a mere $5,000 for an individual pass. Then you get to pay about $1,800 per year in annual dues.

Within the door is an ornate grillwork elevator to the second floor. Upstairs are some equally impressive oldstyle appointments, including an oak telephone booth with leaded glass panels adapted from the one used in the Disney film, *The Happiest Millionaire*. The Lounge Alley is used for a buffet and sports a harpsichord decorated with a scene of a New Orleans harbor during the nineteenth century. The Main Dining Room is decorated in Napoleonic style, including three spectacular chandeliers.

The Trophy Room is the second dining room, a more informal place that has cypress-plank walls. Hidden within the chandeliers are microphones installed at Walt Disney's suggestion; according to Disney historians, the intent was to allow a vulture in the room to converse with guests during dinner.

French doors on the upper level open out onto a spectacular view of the Rivers of America, and it's a marvelous place to watch the *Fantasmic!* show . . . if you don't mind paying a bit extra for the privilege.

If you'd like to sign up, call Disney at (714) 781–4709.

More? "One last drink was in his hand, died a reachin', Red Eye Dan." Or: "Six-gun Tex lies in this grave, used his gun for a closer shave."

Sailing Ship *Columbia*

A full-scale replica (110 feet long, with an 84-foot main mast) of the three-masted merchant ship of the eighteenth century; the *Columbia*'s crew discovered and named the Columbia River in Oregon. The real vessel was launched in Plymouth, Massachusetts, in 1787 and made many trips around Cape Horn to the northwest. It disappeared on a voyage in the Orient.

The *Columbia* is definitely the classiest way to take a fifteen-minute tour of the Rivers of America. Below deck is a museum that depicts lifestyles of the sailors.

The vessel operates only during daylight hours and only on the busiest days.

Mike Fink Keelboats

Small riverboats follow the same circuit as the *Mark Twain*, the canoes, and the *Columbia;* they're a bit faster and a bit more personal with your own guide. Mike Fink, by the way, was a riverboat captain of legend who had an adventure with Davy Crockett. The small boats here, the *Bertha Mae* and the *Gullywhumper*, make a complete circuit in about ten minutes.

Because of the small capacity of the boats, I'd advise you to avoid joining a long line if there is one; we'd also suggest against duplicating a trip on the keelboats and one on the riverboat.

The keelboats run only during the day and may not operate at all on slow days.

FANTASYLAND

This is the stuff of young dreams: Dumbo, Peter Pan, Alice in Wonderland, Snow White, and the toy riot of It's a Small World. Fantasyland is a bright and cheerful place that's decorated in splashes of color and sprinkled with snippets of song. Looming over it all is Sleeping Beauty Castle.

▮ SLEEPING BEAUTY CASTLE

One of the emblems of Disneyland, more famous than most any real castle in the world, Sleeping Beauty Castle towers over the center of the park; well, it towers about 75 feet, but in true Disney fashion, the forced perspective design of the building makes it look taller than it really is.

The Sleeping Beauty Walk Through is a somewhat obscure corner of the park, located within the castle between the Castle Christmas Shop and Tinkerbell's Toy Shop. Climb the stairs to see animated dioramas of scenes from Sleeping Beauty. This display has been closed from time to time.

▮ PETER PAN'S FLIGHT

A mellow excursion into some of the scenes from Disney's version of the story of the little boy who doesn't want to grow up. Riders sit in a small pirate ship that suspends them a foot or so off the floor. Everyone's favorite scene is the overhead view of London by night, which does a pretty good job of simulating Peter's flight. Strictly for kids.

Closed!

Let's get this straight: we flew all the way across the country with two screaming kids, paid all that money, and ran all the way across the park, and Dumbo the Flying Elephant is closed for repairs? Yeah . . .

Because Disneyland is open every day, repairs and refurbishment have to be done while the park is in operation. Some minor jobs are done at night when the park is closed, but nearly every ride is closed for days, weeks, or even months every once in a while. Most of the closings take place during quieter times of the year; in other words, you can generally count on Indiana Jones Adventure, Space Mountain, Splash Mountain, and the Matterhorn Bobsleds being open around Christmastime and in the heart of the summer.

You can call (714) 999–4565 for information on refurbishment of rides before you travel.

Stop and listen beneath the window between the entrance and exit to the ride. You'll hear Peter Pan and Wendy discussing a trip to Never Land.

At Disneyland Paris, a jazzed-up version is one of the more popular attractions; not so at Disneyland, although lines can still reach to forty-five minutes or more on busy days for a two-minute ride.

■ MR. TOAD'S WILD RIDE

Not all that wild, but an entertaining ride based on one of Disney's more obscure films, *The Adventures of Ichabod and Mr. Toad,* which was in turn loosely based on the book *The Wind in the Willows.*

You will ride in an antique car on the road to Nowhere in Particular, crashing through fireplaces, into a chicken coop, and on a railroad track headed straight for an oncoming locomotive. It's light enough fare for most children, although the very young might become a bit scared by the Day-Glo devils and the somewhat loud sound effects. Adults will find this two-minute ride among the more ordinary at Disneyland; we'd recommend against joining a midday line unless a youngster is in charge.

■ KING ARTHUR CARROUSEL

One of the few mostly "real" things in this world of fantasy and probably the oldest antique in use in the park, the carousel was originally built in 1875. Disney reconstructed the ride with carved horses from Germany; no two are identical.

The lines for the two-minute ride ebb and flow; we'd suggest you wait for the times when you can walk right on board. And parents take note: the exit to the merry-go-round is in a different place than the entrance.

■ PINOCCHIO'S DARING JOURNEY

A trip to the scary side of Tobacco Road, the place where Pinocchio is sent when he disobeys Gepetto.

(Have you realized by now how many of our favorite fairy tales have a dark side? Are you beginning to get the idea that many of the attractions at Fantasyland emphasize the scary elements of the story?)

Later you'll enter Pleasure Island, which is a riot of Day-Glo colors, calliope music, and amusement-park rides. Eventually, we are rescued by Jiminy Cricket and reunited with Geppetto. At long last, we are reminded that "When you wish upon a star, your dreams come true."

The three-minute ride includes some of the more advanced technologies for the younger set, including fiber-optic fireworks and holograms. Lines are often slightly shorter than at other surrounding attractions in Fantasyland.

■ DUMBO THE FLYING ELEPHANT

Disney has taken an ordinary amusement-park ride and made it something special, at least for little visitors. Riders sit within fiberglass flying elephants that they can move up and down as they circle around a mirrored ball and a statue of Timothy Mouse, the little guy who becomes Dumbo's manager in the classic Disney movie.

This ride has always held a tremendous draw for young children, with lines of up to an hour for the ninety-second ride. If your kids insist on an elephant-back ride, head for Dumbo early or late in the day.

One of the Disney rites of passage, we suspect, is the day youngsters tell you they're willing to skip the lines for Dumbo in favor of a second pass at Space Mountain.

◾ ALICE IN WONDERLAND

A bit of this and a bit of that in a Disneyland version of the classic story: You'll climb into a four-seat cater-pillar vehicle for a four-minute journey down the rabbit hole in a chase after the White Rabbit. A merry time is had by most; get there early or late to avoid lines during busy times. There's not a lot to the ride; it's like a roller coaster without the roll.

◾ SNOW WHITE'S SCARY ADVENTURES

Read the sign over the door: see "Scary"? Now understand this ride can't hold a fading candle to the spooks in the Haunted Mansion across the way in New Orleans Square, but there are a lot more skeletons and witches than very young children might expect.

This ride emphasizes the grimmer parts of the Brothers Grimm fairy tale, as presented in Disney's 1938 animated movie.

Says the Wicked Witch: "One taste and the victim's eyes are closed forever." There's no real resolution to the threats presented in the ride except for a completely unexplained sign that reads: "And they lived happily ever after."

All that said, it's an interesting but short ride for children who can handle the dark side of the fairy tale; if your youngster is the sort who gets nightmares from Casper the Friendly Ghost, I'd suggest you go for two rides on Dumbo instead of one with Snow White.

▦ MUST-SEE ▦ IT'S A SMALL WORLD

Every little girl's wildest dream: a world of beautiful dancing dolls from all over the world. There is nothing to get your heart beating here, but even the most cynical—including little boys and adults—will probably find something to smile about in this upbeat boat ride; teenagers are hereby excused from a mandatory visit. This eleven-minute ride was first presented at the 1964–65 World's Fair in New York.

We especially enjoy the Audio-Animatronic cancan dancers. We only wish we could get the sugary theme song out of our heads.

Snow White is Watching

Lean into the wishing well in Snow White Grotto to the right of the castle at the entrance to Fantasyland to hear Snow White singing "I'm Wishing" from the Disney movie. The song was rerecorded for the fiftieth anniversary of the classic cartoon by the original Snow White, Adriana Caselotti. You'll also find statues of Snow White, the seven dwarfs, and various woodland creatures.

And so is the evil Queen. Keep your eye on the windows above the entrance to Snow White's Scary Adventures. Every once in a while the curtains will part and the evil Queen will glare out at the visitors below.

The boats are large and the lines move pretty quickly, but we'd advise coming to this attraction early or late in the day. Be sure to check out the mechanical-doll parade every quarter hour on the clock outside the building. The ride features an improved digital sound system and a rerecorded soundtrack with more instrumentals, originally produced for Disneyland Paris.

MUST-SEE MATTERHORN BOBSLEDS

The Matterhorn is one of the reasons why Disneyland is a magic kingdom. The Matterhorn Bobsleds is just a rather small and not-all-that-fast roller coaster that was one of the earliest attractions at Disneyland, but, like Space Mountain, which followed some two decades later, the Disney designers made it into something very special.

Here's the magic: these aren't roller-coaster cars. They're bobsleds about to make a sharp ascent up the interior of the famous pointed Swiss peak. Almost 150 feet into the air, the bobsleds start their rapid descent within the mountain and out onto exposed tracks that—if you look quickly—present some spectacular views of the park. (This is one of those rides worth riding in the daylight and again at night to experience the different views.) And do keep your eyes open for a quick glimpse of the Abominable Snowman.

The left (east) track, the one nearest the mountain at the turnstiles, has more turns and better views of the park, while the right (west) track has sharper drops.

Within the mountain, near the large ice crystals, look for a box marked "Wells Expedition." This is a tribute to Frank Wells, president of the Walt Disney Company, a renowned mountaineer who died in a 1993 helicopter crash.

Lines for the bobsleds can become quite long, although the Matterhorn is no longer the number one draw at Disneyland; that honor goes to either the Indiana Jones ride, Splash Mountain, or Space Mountain. In any case, get to Matterhorn early or late to avoid lines.

Speaking of lines, the Matterhorn Bobsleds are somewhat unique at Disneyland in that the twin waiting areas can be seen from the walkway; it should be fairly easy to gauge how long the wait will be. By the way, the line that heads toward Fantasyland holds fewer people than the one that heads toward Tomorrowland; if the two lines are about the same length, choose the queue toward Fantasyland.

Like Space Mountain, the Matterhorn is considerably tamer than a basic roller coaster at an amusement park; it's all in the setting. The best time to ride the Matterhorn (other than at the very start of the day) is during one of the parades. When crowds build, they usually set up two lines, one for each of the twin bobsled runs.

During parades the two lines are often combined into a single queue and routed away from the parade area. The single line looks long but moves twice as fast. When you are inside the final waiting area, turn to your right instead of the left for a slightly shorter wait.

If you're lucky, you'll see Mickey Mouse and Goofy climb up the mountain to join Minnie, who waits for them with a picnic lunch.

■ MAD TEA PARTY

A Disneyfied version of a basic amusement-park ride; circular cars move around a track and also spin around on platforms.

If it sounds dizzying, that's because it is: the very young and those with sensitive stomachs might prefer the carousel across the way. However, the riders do have some control over how fast the cups spin; to cut down on spin, grab hold of the wheel in the center of the cup and don't let go.

The ride is set in a scene from Disney's 1951 classic film, *Alice in Wonderland*. The ride itself takes only about ninety seconds; the wait can be much more than that, especially at midday. I'd recommend a spin only if lines are short.

Storybook Land Canal Boats

A kinder, gentler, smaller jungle cruise in and among some lovely miniatures taken from great fairy tales and Disney films, this is another of the early entertainments of Disneyland and a supposed favorite of Walt himself. Your journey begins with a trip into the mouth of Monstro the Whale, the giant beast of Disney's *Pinocchio*.

Guides point out some of the tiny scenes on a ten-minute tour, which has something for most everyone. The very young will enjoy spotting scenes from Alice in Wonderland, the Seven Dwarfs Mine, and more; adults will revel in the details, including tiny bonsai forests. As with the Jungle Cruise in Adventureland, some of the guides are about as lively as the bonsai while others put a bit of acting into their spiels.

Storybook Land has received some overdue attention in recent years, adding models of scenes from some of Disney's animated films, including *Aladdin, Beauty and the Beast,* and *The Little Mermaid*. A waterfall was added over the cave to Never Land. The improvements were derived from the Storybook area at Disneyland Paris.

Casey Jr. Circus Train

Climb into a circus animal cage or the caboose to circle Storybook Land on a three-minute train trip that your very daring youngsters may want to ride all by themselves. Adults can squeeze in, too, or can view the same displays from the Storybook Land Canal Boats.

MICKEY'S TOONTOWN

Disneyland, Walt Disney World, Disneyland Paris, Tokyo Disneyland, and the entire Disney empire were built upon the ears of the most famous rodent of all, but until recently Mickey Mouse didn't have a place of his own. At Walt Disney World, he got his own land (first a Birthday Party and then Mickey's Starland). At Disneyland, the Mickster shares the spotlight as emcee of Mickey's Toontown, a village based on some of the characters and locations of the Disney animated film *Who Framed Roger Rabbit*.

As you enter into Mickey's Toontown, check out the civic signs on the railroad overpass: there's a chapter of the DAR (the Daughters of the Animated Reel), the Loyal Knights of the Inkwell, the Optimists In Toon National, and the Benevolent and Protective Order of Mouse.

This section of the park is definitely for the youngest visitors; it's like Fantasyland but without the crossover rides like Matterhorn and It's a Small World. If you're not traveling with kids, you're excused.

Note that this is a rather small area and can become very crowded, leading to lines that will please neither you nor your youngsters. Get there early or late in the day to avoid the lines.

This is one place where you are almost certain to find one or more Disney characters walking about. Listen for bells, horns, and whistles from Toontown City Hall for the changing of the guard.

Other funny touches include the sign outside Goofy's Gas that asks, "Did we goof up your car today?" Goofy also offers: "If we can't fix it, we won't." The gas pump has fish floating around in the dispenser. Around the side of Daisy's Diner you will find The Third Little Piggy's Bank.

⁞MUST-SEE⁞ ROGER RABBIT'S CAR TOON SPIN ≡FAST

Training wheels for the up-and-coming thrill rider. Not for the easily dizzied, this ride is based on the wild taxicabs in Roger Rabbit's Toontown. Your cab goes out of control when one of the weasels throws a barrel of Judge Doom's toon-dissolving solution on the road. You're then off on a wild, spinning trip through special effects and Audio-Animatronic characters. Like the Mad Tea Party, you can control the speed of your spins by grabbing the wheel.

The lines for this three-minute ride can become quite long in midday; come early or late. The line you may see outside is only a hint at the interior queue that takes you through the back alleys of Toontown to your waiting cab. Figure on about thirty minutes from the entrance to the building until you are seated in a cab; if the line reaches to near the railroad underpass at the entrance to Toontown, the wait is at least one hour. Even better, pick up a Fastpass and come back later.

The waiting area, though, offers some entertainment of its own, as visitors can peek through holes in a fence to see the spinning cabs. You'll walk past Baby Herman's apartment, catch a glimpse backstage at the Ink and Paint Club, and learn about the invidious plot to literally wipe out the population of Toontown with a deadly concoction of paint solvents known as dip.

Along the way, you can even learn the formula for dip: one part acetone, one part benzene, and one part turpentine, mixed well. That actually is a real recipe for a solution that dissolves ink used by cartoon artists.

There are lots of other interesting details to be learned as you wait in line. Check out some of the license plates right inside the entrance: I M LATE, CAP 10 HK, 3 LIL PIGS, 1D N PTR, and 1DRLND among them. Whatever; all of the cars on the ride are called Lenny.

When you come to the door of the Ink and Paint Club, a hideous face will appear with one of several menacing messages, including "Beat it before I call a cop on you," or "Hey, who do you think you are, Mickey Mouse?"

You can also see Jessica Rabbit's very round shape passing by in silhouette on the window. There is a casting bulletin board outside of her dressing room announcing an audition for an upcoming Disney pic. They're looking for men, women, and animals; no giants, please.

Another sign: "Lost one magic feather. If found, please contact Dumbo c/o Timothy Mouse, Walt Disney Studio, Hollywood, CA."

More threatening is a "wanted" poster: "Wise Guy Weasel wanted in thirteen states for toon napping, assault with a silly weapon, petty larceny, grand larceny, and really grand larceny."

When you finally board your two-person taxi, you'll follow behind Roger Rabbit as he tears through town, pursued by Weasels who dump dip in the path of vehicles. You'll spin through Ferdinand's China Shop and an electrical storm in the Power Plant, and eventually you'll crash through the roof of the Gag Warehouse for a showdown with the Weasels.

The concept of the ride is supposed to allow drivers to control the spin of their cars as they move through the ride. We found the steering wheel a bit stiff and difficult to control and suspect that some young children will need the assistance of an adult in driving. You can spin the cars wildly or devote all of your energy to preventing the spin.

Mickey's House and Meet Mickey

If you have kids, or ever were one, there's not a whole lot of doubt about this: you've got to pay a personal visit to Mickey Mouse. What we've got here is a series of displays within the mouse's house (including some interesting memorabilia and lots of touch-me stuff) and a waiting area where you can see old MM cartoons. It all leads up to the big enchilada: an audience with the mouse himself. Groups of one or two families are ushered into the dressing room where Mickey will pose for photos, sign autographs, and stand still while he is hugged, poked, prodded, and otherwise inspected.

One thing he won't do, though, is talk. That's not in his job description.

Minnie's House

Next door is the home of Mickey's mouse-girlfriend; check out the strange stuff in her kitchen. Minnie herself, though, is not often in her own house; you'll more likely find her out walking the streets of Toontown. (No, she's not that kind of girl; she's just hard to tie down.)

Jolly Trolley

A slow trip around Toontown. Walking is faster, if less fun.

Gadget's Go Coaster

A very short and not-very-fast kiddie coaster. In Disney fashion, though, it's been made very attractive; the bad news is that lines can become unreasonable for a ride that lasts less than a minute.

The Jolly Trolley in Toontown. *Photo by Corey Sandler. Used by permission from Disney Enterprises, Inc. and Amblin Entertainment, Inc.*

If the line is more than a hundred kids long, I'd suggest you bribe the kids with an ice cream and skip any line longer than your kid's attention span or your willingness to stand around and do nothing.

Disneyland Railroad

The vintage railroad that circles Disneyland has a station near the entrance to Mickey's Toontown, a good way to deliver kiddies at the start of the day or extricate them at the end.

Chip 'n' Dale Treehouse

A Disneyfied climbing tree and slide and playground and a great place to let the kids burn off the energy while mom and dad collapse on a bench.

Goofy's Bounce House

Just like it says, a place to take off your shoes and bounce. A basic amusement-park play area that has a Goofy theme. Kids must be older than three years and less than 51 inches tall; keep an eye on the shoes they must leave behind. Lines can become quite long and move slowly at midday.

TOMORROWLAND

Every Disney visitor with a bit of spunk—and his or her mom and dad—has got to visit Tomorrowland at least once to catch a lift on the DL-200 Intergalactic Probe, also known as **Space Mountain.** And then there's the rare chance to journey into deep space with a rookie pilot in *Star Tours.* Other modes of transportation at Tomorrowland include submarines, monorails, and an old-fashioned steam train.

If you think about it, though, tomorrow is a place where we never arrive—it's always in the offing. So it seems appropriate that Tomorrowland should always be under construction.

Now Tomorrowland looks forward and backward at the same time: The setting is a Disneyesque salute to futuristic novelist Jules Verne, a concept first tried at Disneyland Paris and fine-tuned at Walt Disney World. You'll also see nods toward Leonardo da Vinci and H. G. Wells.

Tomorrowland's most recent update added an interesting retro-future mix. At the gateway near the Astro-Orbitor, the pathway consists of colored cobblestones; Imagineers replaced the cold chrome with warm brass, and white walls with greens and golds and rich velvets.

Space Mountain received a spectacular paint job in copper and electric green. Even more visible is the Astro Orbitor, which updated the old Rocket Jets to a phantasmagorical flight through moving planets and moons, based in part on sketches by da Vinci. (The old mechanism for the Rocket Jets was given a new life as a "kinetic sculpture" featuring satellite dishes.)

In one big step backward, Disneyland shut down the *Rocket Rods* system in 2001; the ride had been introduced with much fanfare just a few years before as the zippy replacement for the PeopleMover ride above Tomorrowland. Disney acknowledged the obvious, that the $25 million ride was subject to repeated mechanical problems and was shut down for extended periods of time. There was no word of a replacement attraction.

In the earliest plans for Disneyland, the area was dubbed "The World of Tomorrow." On opening day in 1955, there were three attractions: Autopia, Space Station X-1 (featuring a "satellite" view of America), and Circarama (the predecessor of CircleVision theater).

The TWA Moonliner stood outside the Rocket to the moon attraction when it opened a bit later in the year; the ride was updated to become Flight to the Moon, and later Mission to Mars. Now, Tomorrowland includes a rebuilt version of the Moonliner atop a soda stand near Space Mountain.

▪▪▪▪▪▪▪ MUST-SEE ▪ SPACE MOUNTAIN ≡FAST

The big enchilada, the highmost high, the place where hundreds of Disneyland visitors have dropped their eyeglasses, cameras, and hairpieces.

Space Mountain is a masterpiece of Disney Imagineering, merging a relatively small and slow (top speed of about twenty-eight miles per hour) roller coaster with an outer space theme. The small cars zoom around indoors in near-total darkness, the only light coming from the projected images of stars and planets on the ceiling.

The cars feel as though they are moving much faster than they are because you have no point of reference in the dark. And no, the cars don't turn upside down. But it is as close as most of us will get to space travel.

The waiting line wends its way through an imaginative maze designed to make the visitors feel as though they truly are embarking on an intergalactic journey. Television monitors that broadcast spoof ads and weather reports; Federal Express boasts about overnight delivery to anywhere in the galaxy; Crazy Larry, the used Weather Satellite dealer (with twenty-seven convenient locations around the universe) hawks his wares loudly; and there are promos for "Lifestyles of the Rich and Alien."

You'll walk through corridors decorated with satellite pictures of other planets, pass through beams of colorful pulsating light, and then descend a ramp to a walkway and a busy launching pad that is packed with technicians and engineers loading the DL-200 Intergalactic Probe.

Professional Space Mountain riders—and there are tens of thousands of them—will argue over which seat affords the best ride. The last row of seats seems to benefit from a "whip" effect as the cars make sharp turns; I prefer the very front row, where you don't have the back of someone else's head to mar the illusion of space travel, and there is a terrific blast of onrushing air as you move on the track. At busy times, you probably will not be able to cajole an attendant into allowing you to select the seat of your choice; your chances are better late at night or on the occasional slow day.

The latest tweak to the Space Mountain experience is the installation of stereo speakers in the headrests; your galaxywide experience is now accompanied by about as hard-rocking a musical soundtrack as anything at Disney. The music was performed by legendary surf guitarist Dick Dale. The reaction to the audio system is decidedly mixed, pretty much broken down by age group. My children think it's cool; my wife and I would rather experience the void of outer space in silence.

Children younger than three years old cannot ride Space Mountain, and those younger than seven years old must be accompanied by an adult; all riders must be at least 40 inches tall, and pregnant women and others with back or health problems are advised against riding.

The cars have two seats per row, with three rows per car and two cars in a train. Keep a hand on your personal belongings; wrap camera and purse straps around your feet and make sure that children are properly placed beneath the restraining bar.

Waiting lines can easily extend to ninety minutes or more on a busy afternoon. Get to the ride when the gates first open and you may be able to stroll right on board, or come back to the ride at the end of the day. Another somewhat quiet time is during the dinner hour or during major parades.

The ride is about two minutes, forty seconds in length. If both tracks are operating and the doors are open, a crowd backed up to the front door means a wait of about one hour; sometimes, though, attendants will build up the line outside while the inside queues clear out. This is often done at the end of the day to discourage huge crowds as closing hour approaches. Your best bet: pick up a Fastpass and return at your appointed time to stroll to your waiting rocket.

Space Mountain, along with other major rides including Big Thunder Mountain Railroad and Splash Mountain, offers a "switch off" arrangement if not all of the people in your party want to ride the coaster or if you are traveling with a child too young or too small to ride. Inform the attendant at the turnstile at the launching area that you want to switch off; one parent or adult can ride Space Mountain and change places with another at the exit.

Space Mountain is one of the most popular of all the attractions at other Disney parks. The Walt Disney World ride is similar but not identical; at Disneyland Paris a version named Discovery Mountain and based on Jules Verne's book *From the Earth to the Moon,* is a bit wilder, including a catapult launch to the top of the track and a 360-degree loop in the dark.

▓▓▓▓▓ MUST-SEE ▓ STAR TOURS ≡FAST

Whenever your plans call for intergalactic travel, say the Disney travel posters, consider flying Star Tours to the vacation moon of Endor.

Disney builds the atmosphere and excitement beautifully from the moment you walk beneath the huge space machine outside and continues building as you walk through the indoor waiting area that simulates a gritty space garage. Our favorite flaky robots, R2D2 and C3PO, are the mechanics.

Listen carefully to the announcements on the public address system. You'll hear a call for Egroeg Sacul (Star Wars creator George Lucas, spelled backward) and a summons to the owner of landspeeder THX-1138, which has been illegally parked in a "No-Hover" zone.

When your time comes, you will enter into a forty-passenger simulator cabin and meet your pilot, Captain Rex. The doors will be closed and your seat belts tightly cinched before he informs you that this is his first trip. Too late—you're off. You'll make an uneasy takeoff and then blast (accidentally) into and then through a frozen meteor, stumble into an active intergalactic battle zone, and finally make a wild landing at your goal, the vacation moon of Endor.

This is quite a wild ride, even in a simulator; it's a bit rough for the very young; pregnant women, and those with health problems are advised to sit this one out. The trip takes about seven minutes.

Much of the queue area is indoors, with waiting riders walking among artifacts from Endor. If the interior is filled to the doorway, you can expect as much as an hour on line. Remember the rule: Go early or late to the most popular attractions.

Children must be at least 40 inches to ride; tall youngsters younger than seven years old must be accompanied by an adult.

▓ ASTRO ORBITOR

Astro Orbitor is a basic amusement-park ride that has rotating rockets and an up/down lever, but in typical Disney fashion it seems like much more. The colorful five-passenger rockets (three single seats and one double) revolve in and around a fantastic, animated astronomical model of planets and constellations.

(Think of Astro Orbitor as a slightly faster and somewhat higher version of Dumbo the Flying Elephant.)

Nowhere near as threatening (to some) as Space Mountain and offering a nice view of Tomorrowland, Astro Orbitor nevertheless is not for people who have a fear of heights. Originally named Rocket Jets, this ride was renovated as part of the makeover of Tomorrowland. It is especially impressive at night.

⁞MUST-SEE⁞ AUTOPIA ≡FAST

Everything old is new again, including Autopia, one of the original attractions of Disneyland that dates back to 1955.

The popular miniature car track was revamped in 2000, combining the old Fantasyland Autopia and Tomorrowland Autopia tracks into a single course. Three car models are available: Cute Car, a cute VW-bug-like vehicle; Sports-car, low-slung with air intakes; and Off-Road, with big knobby tires. Cars are painted so they seem to be encased in an ever-changing palette of colors, a Disney creation called "ChromaLusion." Each can seat up to two adults or three children.

The experience begins before drivers reach the roadway, which is a good thing because this attraction has always had some of the longest lines in the park. The entrance to Autopia is through a central tower shaped like a giant piston. Guests cross an elevated walkway to "The Grandstand" where they can view the track and the passing cars; a stadium-sized video screen plays humorous animated in-terviews with vehicles.

As guests drive along the extended roadway, they experience the world through a car's perspective. Humorous billboards along the highway advertise directly to the vehicle. The track layout includes curves, bridges, a "car park" and an "off-road" driving experience.

Successful drivers are given a commemorative Autopia driver's license, a rec-ollection of the 1950s version of the attraction.

The best way to avoid the lines is to pick up a Fastpass.

⁞MUST-SEE⁞ *HONEY, I SHRUNK THE AUDIENCE*

A clever 3-D thriller that takes off where the two shape-altering Disney films (*Honey, I Shrunk the Kids* and *Honey, I Blew Up the Baby*) left off. In this case, the kids are all right; it's the audience that shrinks.

This is a theatrical performance that is simply not to be missed. We find our-selves as honored guests at the presentation of the Inventor of the Year award to Wayne Szalinski, played by actor Rick Moranis. Other members of the original film also appear in the Disneyland feature; they're joined by funnyman Eric Idle of *Monty Python's Flying Circus*.

As far as what happens next, we don't want to spoil the fun or play a cat-and-mouse game with you; oops, disregard that last hint.

The wild conclusion of the show comes when one of the machines goes berserk and ends up shrinking the entire audience down to toy size. "Stay in your seats and we will blow you up as soon as possible," says Wayne.

The auditorium conspires with the 3-D images to complete the illusion with moving seats, special lighting, and unusual effects that will tickle your fancy and sprinkle you with laughter.

⊞ MUST-SEE ⊞ INNOVENTIONS

The two-floor pavilion of technology uses the former Carousel Theatre's rotating theater base as a transport vehicle to various exhibits and showcases. Innoventions is divided into five major technology areas: Home, Entertainment, Workplace/Education, Recreation/Health, and Transportation.

Innoventions is like a permanent World's Fair, showcasing the latest in consumer and high-tech products from companies around the world; it debuted at Walt Disney World's Epcot Center. New exhibits in 2002 included Compaq's Space Training Center, which offered an electronic labyrinth, and interactive encounters that allow visitors to pilot their own ship, exploring the stars, and discover their weight on distant planets. Pioneer Electronics' futuristic Virtual Resort showcases the latest in high-definition plasma displays, recordable DVDs, and mobile and home entertainment; including an interactive aquarium. AT&T presented an exploration about interactive broadband television, personal computer, and phone technologies.

Guests board the slowly rotating building at various locations to receive introductions to a variety of show spaces. An Audio Animatronic, voiced by comic actor Nathan Lane, reprises the "Great Big Beautiful Tomorrow" song that was the theme of the old "Carousel of Progress" show. From there it's on to the upper level of the building, home to interactive presentations and hands-on displays, showcasing creative uses of tomorrow's technology.

For many visitors, the best action may be outside the pavilion, where cast members will be demonstrating the Segway human transporter, the high-tech scooter that inventor Dean Kamen hopes will revolutionize local commuting in cities and factories around the world.

■ DISNEYLAND MONORAIL

Yet another mode of transportation, but unlike all the others in this corner of the park, the monorail has a purpose: it is a quick and easy way to leave the park and zip over to a station at the head of Downtown Disney, across the road from the Disneyland Hotel and Disney's Paradise Pier Hotel and a short walk from Disney's Grand Californian Hotel. This is a great way to duck out of the park for lunch or dinner, too.

Glug, Glug, Glug

The Disney classic Submarine Voyage was scuttled after millions of circuits around a rather unimpressive artificial lagoon. The attraction was loosely based on the Jules Verne book *Twenty Thousand Leagues Under the Sea,* and in particular the 1954 Disney movie.

No plans have been announced for a replacement, but Disney insiders hint of a major water-themed attraction here and at the nearly identical and also closed version of the ride at Walt Disney World in Orlando.

The Disneyland monorail leaves the Tomorrowland station. *Photo by Corey Sandler. Used by permission from Disney Enterprises, Inc.*

When the monorail was first built in 1959 it was quite a novelty: the first full-time monorail transit authority in the country. (Walt Disney World has a much more extensive system with several tracks.)

The 2.5-mile trip gives some interesting views of Tomorrowland and Fantasyland as it crosses over the Golden Gate Bridge near the entrance to Disney's California Adventure. There are only two stations, though: at Tomorrowland in Disneyland and at Downtown Disney.

On an average day there are two monorail trains running; on an especially busy day controllers might add a third set of cars to the line, but the short track won't permit more than that. The trains are capable of going 70 miles per hour, but stay at 35 miles per hour or less.

If you leave the train at Downtown Disney, be sure to have your hand stamped and take your Disneyland passport with you so you can return to the park. You can also start your day by boarding the monorail at Downtown Disney if you have your passport.

For a minor thrill, you can maneuver yourself into one of the five seats in the front of the monorail with the driver; tell the attendant loading the monorail of your wishes and move to the first gate to wait your turn.

Cosmic Waves. Outside the entrance to Space Mountain is a lively fountain where guests can interact with "waves" and "mazes" of water shooting up from the ground in synchronized patterns. You can get as wet as you want to be. (There are bathrooms nearby at Space Mountain if you need to change into dry clothing.)

Starcade. It's a bit of a concession to the outside world, but then again Disney is not known for leaving too many nickels on the table; actually, we're talking half dollars, dollars, and more at this high-tech video-game arcade located on the lower level of Space Mountain. Every successful rocket rider has to pass the enticements of the machines.

You'll find just about every major arcade game here, but to Disney's credit, you won't find any first-person shooting games here or elsewhere in the park.

PARADES AND FIREWORKS

Throughout its history, Disneyland has celebrated the end of the day with a fireworks display. The show is presented on nights when the park is open late.

In 2002, Mickey Mouse, Donald Duck, Snow White, and more than forty other stars of Disney's animated films played lead roles in the "Disneyland Parade of the Stars," presented daily on Main Street, U.S.A. Casting a squad of Disney stars amidst fantastic images inspired by the work of classical artists, the parade presents stunning interpretations of scenes from *Beauty and the Beast, The Lion King, The Little Mermaid, Tarzan* and *Fantasia 2000,* among others.

When a parade is underway, there are only a few marked places where you can cross the traffic; crossing zones north of the Matterhorn are usually less congested than those near Main Street. With the closure of the Skyway, the only alternative is to take the Disneyland Railroad, which circles the park in a clockwise direction.

The best advice on getting a prime spot to see a parade is to get in place early, as much as thirty minutes or more before the start. One of the best spots is from the central plaza near the railroad station above Main Street; it's no secret, though, and this is usually one of the first places to fill up.

There's good and bad news about this, though. For the first parade of the day, the beginning of Main Street marks the end of the parade route, and it can take fifteen to twenty minutes for the entertainment to arrive; the second parade begins at Main Street and moves toward Fantasyland. Check the parade schedule listed in the Disneyland Today flyer you will receive as you enter the park.

On Friday and Saturday evenings and holiday periods, the park presented the pyrotechnics spectacular

Mouse Mouths

Walt Disney himself performed the voices of Mickey and Minnie in the earliest cartoons, including *Steamboat Willie,* which was the first Mickey Mouse cartoon with sound—but not the first movie starring the rascally rodent. That honor went to *Plane Crazy.* The current voice of the Mickster is Wayne Allwine, the third mouse mouthpiece.

What a Bunch of Characters

If you've ever wanted to see a child's eyes pop open like a cartoon character, watch carefully the first time a youngster comes face-to-face with a walking Mickey or Minnie Mouse.

The characters are scattered throughout Disneyland; if your child or you has a particular favorite, you can inquire at City Hall to check the day's schedule. You'll usually find them near the railroad overpass on Main Street, in and around the Castle, and in Toontown.

Don't be surprised if some very young children become frightened when their time in the spotlight arrives; the characters are large and usually surrounded by crowds. Cast members inside the suits (sorry to destroy the illusion) are pretty good at playing around with little ones, though.

Mickey, Minnie, Goofy, and most of the characters won't talk; they will, though, sign autographs if that is something you've always hoped for.

"Believe . . . There's Magic in the Stars." Low-level and high-level pyrotechnics are launched from multiple points to create a "layered" aerial effect that combines with innovative ways of adding music and audio effects into each performance.

DISNEY CHARACTERS

Face it: the real reason you flew a thousand miles and spent a thousand dollars and endured twenty thousand people in line was to get a picture of yourself with your arm around Mickey or Minnie, with Goofy's mouth engulfing your head, or with Roger Rabbit standing on your feet.

There are three ways to obtain the precious mementos: by chance, by investigation, or by plan.

The characters stroll about the park throughout the day, usually accompanied by handlers who help them navigate or help them escape from the occasional attacking hordes of children of all ages.

If you are willing to take things by chance, you can often find one or another character on Main Street near the railroad station and *Great Moments with Mr. Lincoln,* regular visits at the Hub near the castle, and strolling characters in Toontown.

If you're lucky, you may find yourself in the middle of what Disney calls a **Character Flood,** a sudden deluge of characters. On busy days, you can expect a double-decker bus full of characters to flood the Hub near the castle, often around noon.

If you're a planner, you can count on finding Mickey and friends in Mickey's House at Toontown, where His Mouseness meets his adoring public in small groups. One of Mickey's assistants is usually available to use your camera to take your picture, if you'd like.

On busy days there are (sorry to destroy any illusions) four Mickeys in Mickey's House, in different "movie sets": *Fantasia, The Band Concert, Steamboat Willie,* and *Through the Mirror.* You're not supposed to have a choice, although you may be able to sweet-talk one of the cast members into steering you to the particular room and the Mickey of your dreams.

Finally, you may be able to enlist the assistance of a cast member who has a walkie-talkie or a representative at City Hall who can tell you where some of the characters are scheduled to be that day.

EATING YOUR WAY THROUGH DISNEYLAND

It's my opinion that there are three types of restaurants at Disneyland: overpriced and bad, overpriced and barely acceptable, and overpriced and almost good. Well, OK, there are a few meals that are overpriced and good. In any case, I'd recommend that you not consider meals to be an important part of your experience at the park.

You do, though, have to eat. Disney has a rule against bringing your own sandwiches or other food into the park. The park provides lockers and a picnic area outside the gates, to the left of the entrance.

In years past, I used to say that I had never seen an attendant search a backpack or shoulder bag for tuna fish on rye; alas, in today's security environment, your small backpacks, shoulder bags, and purses will be searched for more dangerous items. I'd still expect that the guards are not likely to confiscate sandwiches, and you certainly can bring a baby's formula and a few candy bars for the kids.

If you don't pack your own, it is possible to pick and choose among the offerings at the park. Disneyland does offer a few more healthful choices, such as pasta salads, turkey hamburgers, and smoked turkey legs, at some of its stands. You'll also find fruit stands at several locations around the park, offering oranges, apples, bananas, and other real food. In Adventureland you'll find dill pickles. The stands sell plastic bottles of soda, which can be sealed up and stowed between rides.

Another very valuable strategy is to plan on taking an afternoon break and leaving the park to go to a real restaurant for lunch and then returning for a second visit in the evening. Your parking ticket allows you to exit and return on the same day, as does your park pass (with a hand stamp).

With the opening of Downtown Disney, lunch options are greatly improved. If the lines are not too long, consider jumping on the monorail and choosing from the impressive offerings at the new entertainment district. You can also walk to Downtown Disney from the front gate of Disneyland.

If you do eat in the park, you should try to avoid lines by eating early; arriving for lunch at 11:30 A.M. instead of noon can save an hour of your time.

Many restaurants offer a children's menu for about $4.00.

Gummed Up

You cannot buy chewing gum at any store in Disneyland. The idea of sticky rubber underfoot was too much for Walt Disney to bear, and it has always been banned. Cleaning crews regularly search the walkways for contraband.

■ MAIN STREET

Blue Ribbon Bakery. Through the windows of a show kitchen, you'll be able to watch all sorts of goodies in the making.

Carnation Cafe. You'll enter through a gazebo into an attractive shaded Victorian dining area for a breakfast of waffles, French toast, pastries, and more. Lunch and dinner include soups, salads, and sandwiches.

The eatery has gone a bit upscale in recent years. Specialties for lunch and dinner include shepherd's pie and chicken caesar, both priced at about $9.00.

Gibson Girl Ice Cream Parlor. Eight flavors of ice cream and six varieties of soft-serve frozen yogurt are served.

Plaza Inn. A longtime favorite on Main Street, redone in recent years as a large food court. Specialties include fried chicken, pot roast, pasta, and salads. Open for breakfast, lunch, and dinner.

■ ADVENTURELAND

Bengal Barbecue. Beef, chicken, and vegetable kabobs.

■ NEW ORLEANS SQUARE

Blue Bayou Restaurant. One of the prettiest spots in the park, this restaurant is set within the dark bayou scene at the opening of Pirates of the Caribbean. Dinner entrees, priced from about $20 to $26, include offerings such as Shrimp Creole and Blackened New York Steak with Cajun Butter. Lunch entrees range from about $10 to $17, including Caribbean Crab Cakes and Bronze Chicken. Lunch is served from 11:00 A.M. to 4:00 P.M. and dinner from 4:00 to 9:00 P.M. By the way, the Blue Bayou is one of two restaurants in the park, along with the Plaza Inn, to offer kosher food; inquire when making reservations.

Café Orleans. An informal eatery with lunch and dinner offerings priced from about $5.00 to $15.00 including prime rib and Cajun Boule (spiced chicken in a bread bowl). The menu also includes soup and salad choices.

French Market Restaurant. An attractive outdoor patio that has a view of the river and railroad and a simple buffeteria menu.

La Petite Pâtisserie. A somewhat hidden gem on Royal Street, this walk-up window serves decent turkey or ham sandwiches, pastries, and sweets and is usually not very crowded.

Mint Julep Bar. A little bit of New Orleans that offers just about everything except bourbon: libations include nonalcoholic mint juleps as well as espresso, cappuccino, fritters, lemonade, and ice cream novelties. Located next to the French Market dining patio, the bar is open seasonally.

Royal Street Veranda. Counter service for clam chowder and snacks.

Money Matters

The Main Street Bank is a bank on, uh, Main Street and it provides basic, uh, banking services to visitors on Main Street. You can also buy stamps, upgrade tickets, and buy "Disney Dollars" or gift certificates. There are also ATMs outside the park to the left of the entrance, on Main Street near the Penny Arcade, and in Tomorrowland and Frontierland.

FANTASYLAND

Village Haus Restaurant. Pizza, pasta, burgers, and salads.

CRITTER COUNTRY

Harbour Galley. In the shadow of the Haunted Mansion at the entrance to Critter Country, serving McDonald's French fries and drinks.

Hungry Bear Restaurant. Nestled amongst the pine trees on the Rivers of America, offering good ol' American food from burgers to chicken.

FRONTIERLAND

Golden Horseshoe Stage. Snacks, ice cream, and drinks, with regular entertainment by singing cowboys and dancing bargirls.

Rancho del Zocalo Restaurante. An attractive buffeteria serving tacos, enchiladas, and more.

River Belle Terrace. Near Tarzan's Tree House and Pirates of the Caribbean. Complete breakfasts of scrambled eggs, bacon or sausage, and potatoes for about $6.00; Mickey Mouse pancakes with bacon or sausage for about $4.55. Luncheon fare, priced from about $4.00 to $7.00, includes Huck Finn's chicken meal, Mississippi vegetable stew, the Showboat ham sandwich, and Aunt Polly's turkey sandwich.

Stage Door Cafe. Burgers, hot dogs, and chicken-breast sandwiches.

MICKEY'S TOONTOWN

Clarabelle's Frozen Yogurt. As advertised.

Daisy's Diner. Counter snacks, including pizza and salad.

Pluto's Dog House. Hot dogs and snacks.

TOMORROWLAND

Club Buzz—Lightyears Above the Rest. Fast food and fun. While you eat, you can enjoy "Calling All Space Scouts: A Buzz Lightyear Adventure," hosted by the space-age hero, Buzz Lightyear along with his costars Space Cadet Starla, the Little Green Men from outer space, and the nefarious Emperor Zurg.

Redd Rockett's Pizza Port. Quick pies.

DISNEY CHARACTER MEALS

Wanna chow down with Minnie Mouse, Chip 'n' Dale, or Goofy? Are your manners good enough to have tea with Mary Poppins? Then perhaps you should make plans for a character meal.

Prices range from about $12.00 to $20.00 for adults, and $8.00 to $13.00 for children. (The Practically Perfect Tea is the most formal and most expensive event.)

For information and reservations (necessary most days), call Disneyland Guest Relations at (714) 956–6755.

Breakfast with Chip 'n' Dale. Storyteller's Cafe, Disney's Grand Californian Hotel. Daily, year-round, from 7:00 to 11:30 A.M. All-you-can-eat buffet, including scrambled eggs, breakfast meats, potatoes, French toast sticks, waffles, cereals, and fruit. Adults, about $7.00; children (4–12 years old), about $5.00; infants (3 and younger), about $4.00. Various characters, but not Mickey. Parking validation available. Reservations suggested.

Classic Characters Breakfast. Plaza Inn, Disneyland. Year-round, on days when the park opens at 8:00 A.M. or earlier. Served from Park opening through 10:45 A.M. Various characters, but not Mickey and Minnie.

Goofy's Kitchen. Goofy's Kitchen, Disneyland Hotel. Lunch and dinner in summer and holiday periods; dinner only in off-season. Pasta, salads, breakfast items, and a build-your-own-sandwich and sundae bar. Goofy and friends attend.

Miss Minnie & Friends Breakfast. The Summertree, Disney's Paradise Pier Hotel. Daily. All-you-can-eat buffet with hot dishes, waffles, pastries, fruits, and a selection of Japanese offerings. Adults, about $10.00; children (4–12 years old), about $7.00. Minnie, Donald, and Daisy are regulars. Reservations suggested: (714) 956–6755.

Practically Perfect Tea. Tea Room, Disney's Paradise Pier Hotel. Saturdays 10:00 A.M., 12:30 P.M., and 3:00 P.M. Sundays 12:30 and 3:00 P.M. During the summer, weekday morning teas are also scheduled. Tea is served in a Victorian parlor by formally dressed attendants. Mary Poppins dispenses the odd teaspoon of sugar, with items including scones with sweet cream, crepes, quiche, and finger sandwiches. Picky palates can also select waffles or peanut butter and jelly sandwiches. Reservations suggested: (714) 956–6755.

CHAPTER FIVE

DISNEY'S CALIFORNIA ADVENTURE

DISNEY'S CALIFORNIA ADVENTURE: where they took down a parking lot and unpaved a paradise.

Visitors to Anaheim now have a choice between two wondrous Disney dreams. When you reach the ticket booths at the end of the Downtown Disney entertainment district, you can turn left to the world-famous original Disneyland park or head to the right and pass beneath a version of the Golden Gate Bridge and into the new theme park in town.

Disney's California Adventure is not Disneyland. It's a fabulous park filled with some of the most advanced simulators and thrill rides anywhere in the world, but it is meant to supplement and not compete with the classic original across the way.

The park—magically constructed in the former sprawling parking lot of Disneyland—is aimed at slightly older visitors and adults, with wild rides and a group of more thoughtful shows.

At Disneyland you'll find fairy castles, slow boats through a small world of dolls, animatronic pirates, burgers and nuggets, and Mickey Mouse.

At Disney's California Adventure you'll roll your way into a 360-degree loop on a coaster, zoom 180 feet into the air on a space shot, hang glide over Yosemite, meet the multicultural founders of the Golden State, sip on fine wine, and munch on sourdough bread baked in the park.

That doesn't mean you won't find Mickey Mouse at the new park; he's still the main guy around Anaheim. And it also doesn't mean that youngsters won't enjoy a visit to Disney's California Adventure, either; there are more than enough Disney-quality kiddie attractions and shows to make this place a must-see. In late 2002, the park unveiled **Flik's Fun Fair**, a play area based on *A Bug's Life*.

And the first major expansion of the park is now underway: in 2004, the **Twilight Zone Tower of Terror** will open in the Hollywood Pictures Back Lot; it

MUST-SEES

Soarin' Over California
(Golden State)

California Screamin'
(Paradise Pier)

Maliboomer
(Paradise Pier)

Sun Wheel
(Paradise Pier)

Grizzly River Run
(Golden State)

**Jim Henson's
Muppet*Vision 3D**
(Hollywood Pictures
Back Lot)

Golden Dreams
(Golden State)

It's Tough to Be a Bug!
(Golden State)

**Who Wants to Be a
Millionaire—Play It!**
(Hollywood Pictures
Back Lot)

will be a California version of the thrilling elevator ride that is one of the most popular attractions at Disney-MGM Studios at Walt Disney World in Orlando.

Disney has succeeded in adding a second attraction to its Anaheim empire, a first draw for teenagers and adults and a worthy second-place for the younger set. Although the park drew smaller-than-expected crowds in its first year, so did Disneyland when it first opened; we can expect a great deal of tinkering and Disney magic in years to come.

WELCOME TO DISNEY'S CALIFORNIA ADVENTURE

The park is made up of three lands: **Golden State** (including Condor Flats, Grizzly Peak Recreation Area, Bountiful Valley Farm, the Bay Area, and the Golden Vine Winery); **Paradise Pier;** and the **Hollywood Pictures Back Lot.**

Most visitors will enter from the main gate from the entry plaza that stands between Disneyland and Disney's California Adventure. From there, Hollywood Pictures Back Lot is to the left, Golden State straight ahead, and Paradise Pier deep into the park and to the right.

Guests at Disney's Grand Californian Hotel and Disney's Paradise Pier Hotel have their own entrances into the Paradise Pier section of the park.

GOLDEN GATEWAY

The main entrance to Disney's California Adventure, across the esplanade from Disneyland, is a giant picture postcard of California landmarks. You'll walk into the park through 11-foot-high letters spelling out CALIFORNIA. Overhead, the monorail passes across the Golden Gate Bridge. The gateway is framed by dramatic tile murals. Southern California icons are to the left as you enter; Northern California landmarks on the right.

Just past the bridge is **Sunshine Plaza,** dominated by a 50-foot "sun" made of gold-hued titanium inlaid with tiny glass particles; the sun seems to ride the crest of a wave in the fountain below. The huge solar icon speaks of sunny California; the face you see as you enter, though, is oriented to the north. That was no major problem for Disney Imagineers: they installed a set of six computer-controlled heliostats with large mirrors. The devices track the movement

DISNEY'S CALIFORNIA ADVENTURE

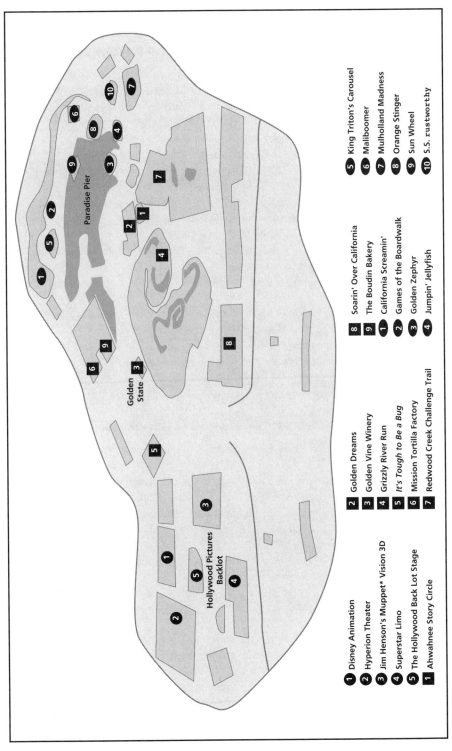

Paradise Pier

Golden State

Hollywood Pictures Backlot

1 Disney Animation
2 Hyperion Theater
3 Jim Henson's Muppet* Vision 3D
4 Superstar Limo
5 The Hollywood Back Lot Stage
1 Ahwahnee Story Circle

2 Golden Dreams
3 Golden Vine Winery
4 Grizzly River Run
5 It's Tough to Be a Bug
6 Mission Tortilla Factory
7 Redwood Creek Challenge Trail

8 Soarin' Over California
9 The Boudin Bakery
1 California Screamin'
2 Games of the Boardwalk
3 Golden Zephyr
4 Jumpin' Jellyfish

5 King Triton's Carousel
6 Maliboomer
7 Mulholland Madness
8 Orange Stinger
9 Sun Wheel
10 S.S. rustworthy

Power Trip #1: Thrill Riders

The big lures at Disney's California Adventure are the three major thrill rides deep in the park at Paradise Pier: **California Screamin', Maliboomer,** and **Sun Wheel.** Also at the top of the list for most excitement-seeking visitors: the oh-so-real simulated thrills of Soarin' Over California.

If you've got the need for speed or the want to go get high (in a Disneyfied family-friendly kind of way), arrive early with your track shoes on.

Pass through the Golden Gateway and bear to the right of Sunshine Plaza, between the sun icon and Grizzly Peak. Make a quick detour to pick up a Fastpass at the entrance to Soarin' Over California. Then return to the middle of the park and head for the lagoon (Paradise Bay), cross the bridge to Avalon Cove, and continue walking to the boardwalk.

Head directly for California Screamin'. Then move on to the Sun Wheel for a spin, and if the line is reasonable, shoot for the sky on Maliboomer. After you've done your time in Paradise Pier, head for Condor Flats and ride Soarin' Over California.

If you're a guest at Disney's Grand Californian Hotel, you can move a few steps ahead of other visitors by using the entrance from that hotel to the park; you'll set foot in the west side of the park near Grizzly River Run, about five minutes closer to Paradise Pier than the main entrance.

Power Trip #2: By Air and Water

For some visitors, the way to start the day is with a quick hang glider ride and a wild splashdown.

Arrive early and keep all the way to the right when you enter Sunshine Plaza. Head directly to Soarin' Over California. Grab a Fastpass and plan to come back later. Continue along the path to the entrance to **Grizzly River Run,** the wet and wild raft ride. After you've dried off, backtrack to Soarin' Over California and use your pass.

By this time, the lines will have built up in Paradise Pier; you can venture there and take a Fastpass for California Screamin' or join the line for the Sun Wheel.

of the California sun across the southern exposure and shine a golden glow on the icon from dawn to sunset. By night, the sun is handsomely lit by high-intensity orange, red, and yellow lamps.

The plaza is one of the prime viewing points for the daily parades of the park. To the right as you enter is a full-scale replica of a streamlined California Zephyr, a railroad train with Vista-Dome cars that brought millions of travelers to the state after World War II. Today it holds shops and restaurants. Disney Imagineers found the nose of a Zephyr in a Moline, Illinois, railroad yard. The cars were built as replicas.

Paradise Pier dominates the back of the park, just past the newest mountain in the Disney Range, Grizzly Peak. The tallest structure at the park is the Hyperion Theater.

GOLDEN STATE

Saluting the adventurous heritage of California and the immigrants who came looking for the golden dream, the park's Golden State includes:

Condor Flats
The setting is a test pilot landing field in the high desert; all around are weathered hangars left over from man's first attempts to break the sound barrier. The streets of the district are striped with airport runway markings.

Grizzly Peak Recreation Area
The newest mountain in the Disney Range is a granite peak shaped by nature (and the Imagineers) to liken the head of a growling grizzly bear. Grizzly Peak towers 150 feet over a High Sierra landscape of pine- and snow-covered slopes.

Disney Imagineers carefully created the mountain to resemble a natural rock configuration that just happens to look like a bear. The mountain began as a series of intricately sculpted models. Computer technology and a laser scanner then measured the models; the computer was later used to actually shape the underlying metal rebar to replicate the rock formations. The metal frame was then overlaid with wire mesh, which was then sprayed with plaster. The final plaster was hand-sculpted by artists, many of whom worked on the Tree of Life at Walt Disney World's Animal Kingdom.

On a real granite boulder on the side of the mountain you can learn a Native American legend about the peak. It seems that Ah-há-le, the coyote, called on the bear, Oo-so-ó-ma-te, to watch over and protect the land. The bear at first stood strong against those who threatened the animal realm. But when it seemed he could no longer resist, the coyote turned the grizzly to stone so that he could never be moved.

The legend of the mountain, "To this day people claim they can hear the great Bear's spirit in the wind that roars through the caverns and trees of Grizzly Peak."

Bountiful Valley Farm
In some ways all of California is a farm; the state is the nation's number one producer of at least 350 different varieties of farm products including citrus, dates, nuts, olives, artichokes, cotton, and grapes. Here at Disney's two-and-a-half-acre showplace you'll find displays of many of the products at the Farmers' Market, a tractor yard, and a water play Irrigation Station.

The Golden Vine Winery

Robert Mondavi brings a bit of the wine country to Anaheim with a small vine-yard of about 350 grapevines and hands-on demonstrations of the winemaking process. Out on the plaza is a wine-sampling bar and a high-end delicatessen; above is a gourmet restaurant serving Mediterranean fare . . . and wine.

A small screening room presents *Seasons of the Vine*, a short film about wine-making. How's this for civility: Adults are invited to bring a glass of wine to their seat.

The Bay Area

The small park here includes a 45-foot-high replica of the rotunda of San Francisco's Palace of Fine Arts. The real structure was built for the 1915 Panama-Pacific International Exposition and designed to look like a classical Roman ruin. A mural on the colonnade introduces the themes, characters, and stories that are told in *Golden Dreams* nearby.

::MUST-SEE:: SOARIN' OVER CALIFORNIA ≡FAST

You've got to ride this to believe it: your own hang glider for a virtual flight down the length of the Golden State. The amazing mechanism, a Disney first, lifts three rows of seats 40 feet into an 80-foot-high dome-shaped movie screen. With your legs dangling beneath you, you move up and into the picture, bank-ing with the hang glider as it soars from the Golden Gate Bridge in San Francisco to Mission Bay in San Diego and on to a special visit to a California icon that all started with a mouse.

The film swoops down so close to the ground and water you expect your feet to touch them and then soars up into the clouds. Your field of vision is nearly completely surrounded; Disney even adds a whiff of orange blossoms and pine trees in the farms and forests.

There is no narration to the film, and none is needed. The scenes of the film, from start to finish, include:

- Banking through clouds and then down over the Golden Gate Bridge and out to sea
- Winging down over rafters and fishermen in Redwood Creek
- Flying over farm hands tending grapes in Napa Valley vineyards
- Sailing out over the rugged coastline at Point Loma with fishing boats bob-bing on the surf below
- Swooping up the slopes of the mountains near Lake Tahoe, past oncoming skiers, and then skimming low over a tree-topped crest for a view of the lake it-self
- Banking a turn through Yosemite Valley past the falls and up toward Half Dome
- Passing through fragrant orange groves near Camarillo
- Flying into the rugged landscape of Anza Borrego State Park, the state's largest but relatively unknown park
- Encountering six jets from the Air Force Thunderbirds

- Passing closely across the aircraft carrier USS *Stennis* at San Diego and following close behind a Navy helicopter
- Surfing along the foaming crest of ocean waves at Malibu
- Cruising up the Harbor Freeway in rush-hour traffic and into downtown Los Angeles at nighttime
- Visiting a party at Southern California's most famous theme park

This attraction is one of the major draws at the park and includes a large outdoor waiting area as well as a hidden maze inside the building; if you see a crowd waiting outside, consider grabbing a Fastpass ticket and coming back later.

If you do end up spending time in the waiting queue within the building, you'll have the chance to learn about some of the famous and obscure heroes of aviation in California. A photo tells the story of John J. Montgomery, who in 1883, twenty years before the Wright Brothers, took a glider flight near San Diego. There's a display about Amelia Earhart, who made many of her pioneering flights to or from California, including her success as the first person to fly from Hawaii to the mainland in 1936. Other honorees include aviation industry figures Donald Wills Douglas, Allan Lockheed, and Howard Hughes.

When you make your way to the front, the line splits to fill two identical theaters. Each holds three banks of gliders, marked A, B, and C, with three rows in each. If you have the chance, choose the center glider (B) and take a seat in the front row. You'll be rewarded with a spectacular view of nothing but the screen.

By the way, the funny safety briefing before you enter the theater stars Patrick Warburton, Elaine's annoying sometime-boyfriend "Puddy" from the *Seinfeld* sitcom.

The lines for the ride can become quite long; this is a good place to grab a Fastpass. You can also shave quite a bit off your wait by entering the "singles" line, taking any available space on the hang glider.

▦ THE TECHNOLOGY BEHIND THE RIDE

To achieve the greatest clarity for Soarin' Over California, Imagineers used a 70-mm IMAX camera with a superwide angle lens and shot at forty-eight frames per second, double the standard rate; all the scenes were shot from a helicopter.

The film is projected from above onto an upside-down IMAX screen. The seats are mounted on a simulator base with its movements linked to the scenes in the movie.

Disneyland's Star Tours, an older attraction, creates a similar illusion using larger seat movements. Through trial and error Disney engineers discovered that much smaller movements, coupled with visual screen cues, could create the same illusion. Where Star Tours seats move as much as 12 feet and pitch forty-five degrees, the Soarin' Over California's seats move a scant 3 feet, with a six-degree pitch.

A critical design problem for the high-tech Soarin' Over California ride was solved with the aid of an old Erector set. The challenge was this: how to quickly load an audience of eighty-seven people into seats that would lift up and into a huge domed movie screen. Ride engineers had originally expected to construct three loading ramps, with each group entering at a different level, a slow process.

Imagineers Mark Sumner and Coulter Winn had worked before on creating the purposefully malfunctioning elevators for the Twilight Zone Tower of Terror at Disney–MGM Studios at Walt Disney World in Florida.

Sumner came up with a solution; to test it, he went to the attic of his garage and brought down his thirty-five-year-old Erector set. Sumner put together a model with the toy-size girders, nuts, and bolts and added cardboard seats. He brought the whole assemblage to work in a grocery bag.

The design allows all passengers to load on the ground floor, and then the three benches are raised into place to different levels, like a string puppet pulled into a standing position. The next challenge was to design a building to hold two of the ride systems. Winn put two theaters back-to-back and sunk the rooms 15 feet below grade so the building would not overwhelm other nearby structures in the park.

At a press event during the park's opening ceremonies, vice chairman Marty Sklar, head of Imagineering for Disney, said that all the other Disney theme parks were lobbying to get hold of the technology behind Soarin' Over California to create their own attractions.

The ride was dedicated by Dick Rutan and Jeana Yeager, who piloted Voyager on a nonstop trip around the world in 1986. The flight, completed in nine days, three minutes, and forty-four seconds, departed from Edwards Air Force Base in California.

⬛MUST-SEE⬛ FLIK'S FUN FAIR

New in late 2002, Flik's Fun Fair is a lively children's playland within **A Bug's Land,** inspired by characters and settings from the Disney-Pixar animated film *A Bug's Life.* The five new attractions give visitors a look at the world from a bug's point of view:

■ **Flik's Flyers.** A simulated bug-size hot air balloon ride.
■ **Tuck & Roll's Drive 'Em Buggies.** A drive-it-yourself bug car ride inside P.T. Flea's circus tent.
■ **Heimlich's Chew Chew Train.** A miniature railroad ride.
■ **Francis's Ladybug Boogie.** Spin-'em-yourself ladybugs.
■ **Princess Dot's Puddle Park.** A playground that surrounds a giant lawn sprinkler.

A Bug's Land includes the existing *It's Tough to Be a Bug* attraction and Bountiful Valley Farm.

⬛MUST-SEE⬛ GRIZZLY RIVER RUN ≡FAST

From the base of the mountain, a 300-foot-long gold ore conveyor lifts eight-passenger rafts to what Disney claims as the world's highest, longest, spin-ningest, and fastest river raft ride. More than 130,000 gallons of water roar down the flume each minute, spinning the rafts through swirling rapids 45 feet above the valley, and sending them into waterslides, caverns, and mineshafts and ending up in a wet plunge into a geyser field.

The six-minute ride marks the first time drops have been incorporated into a river rafting ride; the biggest plunge is 45 feet. In all, Grizzly River Run boasts two over-the-falls descents, one of which propels one after another spinning rafts over the rapids in a steep 22-foot fall. You will get slightly to very wet, depending on the wind, the weight and distribution of the passengers in the spinnable raft, and the luck of the splash.

The story behind the ride is this: the Eureka Gold and Timber Company mined and logged the mountain of all of its resources from the 1800s through the 1930s and then abandoned the area. Over time, the mountain reclaimed itself; trees grew back and the water rushed through once more. Now a group of young people have transformed it into a contemporary river rafting company that takes guests on the Grizzly River Run expedition.

Around the raft load areas are rusting ore crushers and donkey engines abandoned by prospectors and recovered from Sierra Nevada gold country.

Wet guests on Grizzly River Run head toward a geyser in front of Disney's Grand Californian Hotel. *Photo by Corey Sandler. Used by permission from Disney Enterprises, Inc.*

■ REDWOOD CREEK CHALLENGE TRAIL

Three fire ranger towers loom over vantage points at a child-size recreation and workout area with smokejumper cable slides, net climbing, and swaying bridges.

Check out the map posted at the entry so you're sure not to miss any of the highlights that include the Tunnel Tree Crawl Thru, the Hoot-n-Holler Logs, Pine Peril Bridge, Cliff Hanger, Hibernation Hollow, and the Sequoia Smokejumpers Training Tower.

Overlooking the campground are three ranger stations: Mount Lassen Lookout, Mount Shasta Lookout, and Mount Whitney Lookout where Disney park rangers in wide-brimmed hats, hiking boots, and hunter green uniforms tend watch.

At the Sequoia Smokejumpers Training Tower, kids can grab hold of a pulley system to zoom down an overhead cable. The Hoot-n-Holler Logs send guests sliding from an upper level of the recreation area to the wilderness floor, while the Cliff Hanger Rock Climb dares adventurers to traverse its rocky surface and make it back to the safety of the campground.

Down below in the redwoods, storytellers spin tales of nature and the forest on a stage within a downed redwood tree at the Ahwahnee Camp Circle.

There's a small stand of real redwood trees nearby, a young forest with hundreds of years of life ahead; the varieties (*aptos blues* and *soquil brown*) look like their northern California cousins but are better adapted to the warmer climate of Anaheim.

▓MUST-SEE▓ IT'S TOUGH TO BE A BUG! ═FAST

In an underground theater, an imaginative 3-D film show us humans who's really in charge. According to some scientist who has made a count, there are 10,000,000,000,000,000,000 (ten quintillion) bugs in the world. A handful of the most talented star in Disney's 3-D film, *It's Tough to Be a Bug!*

If you're lucky, you'll be personally greeted by Flik, who works the entrance to the show. Flik usually hangs around near a huge coral tree imported to the site; it will bloom in season.

You'll enter the "anty"-room of the 425-seat theater to pick up bug-eyed glasses. When the doors open, pick out a place to sit on a log and admire the tangled-root and vine architecture all around. The orchestra of creatures tunes up below while a buzzing can be heard from the wasp nest projection booth.

The show is ready to begin. The announcer has a request: Please refrain from buzzing, chirping, stinging, . . . or pollinating.

With your 3-D "bug glasses" in place, you're right in the midst of things. Flik, the ant master of ceremonies, welcomes visitors as honorary bugs and introduces us to some of the cast of millions.

"Take it from an ant. It's tough to be a bug," says Flik. "That's why we've developed some amazing survival techniques."

Assisted by a pair of acorn weevils equipped with a sling shot, Chile the Chilean Tarantula demonstrates his ability to throw poison quills. Yes, they're zooming out toward the audience.

Next, a belligerent acid-spraying soldier termite, "the Termite-ator," defends his mound by spraying intruders—that's us—in the seats below. The stinkbug soloist, Claire DeRoom, fills the room with her haunting yet malodorous performance.

But the big artillery arrives with a villainous grasshopper, a bug on a mission to wipe out the audience of intruders. "You guys only see us as monsters!" he says. "Maybe it's time you honorary bugs got a taste of your own medicine!" Suddenly we're under assault by a giant flyswatter, then a blinding fog of "Bug Doom" spray, and finally, a nasty hornet squadron.

I won't spoil the ending, but it does have a certain biting edge. When the butterfly curtain closes, the audience is reminded to remain seated while all the lice, bedbugs, maggots, and cockroaches exit first.

The film is loosely based on *A Bug's Life,* the animated feature from Disney and Pixar. The movie featured the voices of actors Dave Foley as Flik, Cheech Marin as Chile, and Jason Alexander as Acorn Weevil.

Try to sit in the middle of the theater—midway in from both sides and halfway back from the screen—for the best 3-D effects.

::MUST-SEE:: *GOLDEN DREAMS*

This marvelous film tells the California story through the eyes of her immigrants, including natives, Spanish explorers, a "picture bride" from Japan, a European-born moviemaker, and a dust-bowl farmer from Oklahoma. Disney considers the twenty-three-minute film the emotional heart of the park, bringing the history and heritage of California to life with drama and a bit of humor.

The narrator is Queen Califia, the namesake of the state. Spanish explorers, including Juan Rodriguez Cabrillo, among the first Europeans to see California in the sixteenth century, gave California its name based on a popular novel published in 1510 by Spanish author Garcia Ordóñez de Montalvo.

(Montalvo's book, *Las Seregas de Esplandian,* told of an island paradise called California near the Indies where beautiful Queen Califia ruled over a country of beautiful Amazon women possessed of great wealth in pearls and gold. Men were allowed to visit the island only one day a year, and only for the purposes of perpetuating the race. Explorer Hernando Cortez's men thought they found the island in 1535 when they found pearls near today's Mexico-California border.)

In the film, Califia is portrayed by actress and comedienne Whoopi Goldberg. Appearing first when a statue alongside the stage morphs into her image, Califia/Goldberg appears Zelig-like throughout the history of California, popping in and out of scenes in the costume of the period to help people like a fairy godmother.

The film is underlaid with historical accuracy. Disney brought together a group of California historians, sociologists, and culturalists as advisors. The panel included cultures from Native Americans to the variety of ethnic peoples who have immigrated to California.

By the Clock

Here's the official measurement of ride times for attractions at Disney's California Adventure. The clock starts running when the wheels start turning; sometimes the shortest ride times end up with the longest waiting lines.

► **California Screamin'.** 3.2 minutes

► **Golden Dreams.** 20 minutes

► **Golden Zephyr.** 4.1 minutes

► **Jim Henson's Muppet* Vision 3D.** 15 minutes

► **Jumpin' Jellyfish.** 2.4 minutes

► **King Triton's Carousel.** 5.5 minutes

► **Mulholland Madness.** 2.2 minutes

► **Orange Stinger.** 4.2 minutes

► **Soarin' Over California.** 7.4 minutes

► **Sun Wheel.** 9 minutes

► **Superstar Limo.** 4.4 minutes

Among the dramatic moments recreated in the film is a scene among the native Chumash who settled in California over thirteen thousand years ago. The scene was filmed at Montaña de Oro State Park near Morro Bay.

The arrival of the Spanish in 1769 brings a legacy of language, architecture, and rich colorful traditions. Califia meets Father Crespi and his band of Spanish missionaries just after an earthquake threatens their settlement.

You'll see a scene from the California Gold Rush of the mid-1800s that brought people from every corner of the globe to California.

Another scene shows William Mulholland opening the California aqueduct high in the mountains above Azusa to bring water from the mountains to Los Angeles. Because it had to look brand new, Disney had to build its own section of aqueduct for the shooting.

Another scene takes you to the immigration of the Chinese who built the first railroads that linked California to the rest of America. One of the most emotional scenes is the arrival of a Japanese "picture bride" who has come to meet her husband-to-be in 1913. Restrictions blocked new immigration except for immediate family, and so marriages were arranged through the exchange of photos. In the scene, a shy girl and her unexpectedly older fiancé are pelted with tomatoes by protestors. The scene was shot in Vallejo; an old steamboat blocks the view of the modern Mare Island shipyards.

We see scenes from the creation of Yosemite as a national park at the turn of the twentieth century and the 1936 mass immigration of thousands of farm workers when they left the dust bowl of the Midwest in search of a better life.

You'll see some history of the movie industry with a scene from the making of *The Wizard of Oz*. We meet Eastern European immigrant Louis B. Mayer, who arrived in California a poor man and went on to create MGM, one of Hollywood's most successful studios.

Another scene takes place during World War II when thousands of manual labor jobs were opened to women in the many aircraft factories and other military suppliers that flourished across the state.

In the fifties and sixties, you'll mingle with the beatniks and the hippies.

Union organizer Cesar Chavez is seen speaking with Mexican farm workers who have come to el Norte to work in the orange groves. From there it's on to the rise of the computer generation, including the introduction of Apple Computer by Californians Steve Jobs and Steven Wozniak, leading to the state's new gold strikes in Silicon Valley.

The film closes with the song, "Just One Dream," underscoring a montage of images representing the diversity of California's landscape. Included are characters from the film as well as famous modern-day figures from today's California. Among the faces that spin by quickly are those of Walt Disney, plus Ansel Adams, Gene Autry, Joan Baez, the Beach Boys, Sonny Bono, Johnny Carson, Cesar Chavez, Miles Davis, James Dean, Dianne Feinstein, Jodie Foster, Jerry Garcia, Danny Glover, Bob Hope, the Jackson 5, Billie Jean King, Sandy Koufax, Michelle Kwan, Bruce Lee, Richard Nixon, Carlos Santana, Charles Schultz, Tiger Woods, and Chuck Yeager.

Golden Dreams, shot in 70 mm, was directed by Polish filmmaker, Agnieszka Holland, who directed such acclaimed films as *Europa, Europa* and *The Secret Garden*. The film used a cast of thousands over the course of sixteen days of dawn to dusk shooting at sixteen locations around the state.

PACIFIC WHARF

In a setting reminiscent of Monterey's Cannery Row you'll find a trio of food factories that are themselves part of the story of California.

At **San Francisco's Boudin Bakery** on Fisherman's Wharf, you can learn about, watch the making of, and then enjoy the company's legendary sourdough bread.

Inside the bakery, comic and talk-show host Rosie O'Donnell and Colin Mochrie, the rubber-faced comedian from the show *Whose Line Is It Anyway?* star in a video that explains the unusual process of making sourdough bread. Among the details: Boudin (pronounced *BO-deen*) has used the same batch of starter yeast, called *lactobacillus San Francisco,* for nearly a century.

At **Mission Tortillas,** corn or wheat meal is made into fresh wrappers. The machine is a small version of a factory production machine, producing twenty-five tortillas per minute; the real thing at the Mission Foods plant in Rancho Cucamonga can crank out two thousand per minute. After you've watched the process you can go next door to **Cocina Cucamonga Mexican Grill** and enjoy tortillas with a variety of fillings.

Bakers turn out sweet treats at **Lucky Fortune Cookies.** Across the factory ceiling are a pair of 70-foot-long Oriental kites suspended from bamboo poles. Derrick, the younger kite, has a bright blue fabric body. Darian is made up of more than thirty three-foot red and yellow disks.

PARADISE PIER

The glory days of California's beachfront amusement piers—long before the dawning of the day of Disney—are recalled at Paradise Pier.

Dominating the skyline in this land is a mile-long roller coaster with a grand loop-de-loop through the ears of Mickey Mouse, a huge Ferris wheel with golden sun spokes, and a giant catapult that sends riders to the top of a Disneyfied version of a carnival strongman game. This section of the park is especially dramatic by night with the lights of the rides reflected in the lagoon at the base of the "pier."

At the north end of the lagoon, the **Boardwalk** recalls the classic roadside stands of Route 66: giant hamburgers, hot dogs, dinosaurs, and oranges. There's a real wooden boardwalk; Disney Imagineers worked to get exactly the right type of boards that would hold up to millions of visitors each year and still yield the distinctive echo of lumber. One of the patterns for the boardwalk was Santa Rosa's amusement pier, among the last remaining original woodies.

Lumber for Paradise Pier's boardwalk was crafted from a hearty hardwood from Paraguay and designed with authentic Coney Island boardwalk screw patterns. Landscaping includes tropical palms, sea grapes, and succulents.

MUST-SEE CALIFORNIA SCREAMIN' ≡FAST

In true Disney style, the ultimate wooden roller of Paradise Pier looks like an antique classic but is actually constructed with an ultra-modern steel superstructure.

Twenty-four-passenger cars scream from a standstill to 55 miles per hour in just under five seconds using high-tech linear motors in the track; there's no clickety-clack chain here.

Waves from the Paradise Pier lagoon crash against the jetty along the launch area at take-off time; the waves are generated by a high-tech wave machine positioned in the lagoon. Cars zoom out over the water at the edge of Paradise Bay and then climb by momentum 120 feet to begin a run of 6,072 feet.

The four-minute ride is the world's longest steel looping roller coaster. The maximum drop, 108 feet at an impressive fifty degrees, comes midway through the ride, not at first.

The steel design delivers an unusually smooth ride. And then there is the tight loop that passes through Mickey's ears; at night, the ears light up each time the train passes. At peak times, cars pass through every thirty-six seconds.

The cars have an on-board sound system. I have to admit I didn't hear the music the first time I rode; I was concentrating on the laws of physics as they applied to my particular fast-moving seat.

California Screamin' can be seen from almost every vantage point in the park.

A California Screamin' train races toward the Sun Wheel. *Photo by Corey Sandler. Used by permission from Disney Enterprises, Inc.*

"We knew we wanted a big backdrop to the park," said Imagineer and Paradise Pier designer Tim Delaney. "And the coaster was perfect. It's about a thousand feet across as your eye scans it from a distance."

The coaster was designed to mirror the wooden look of coasters of yesteryear but with twenty-first century technology.

"Scream tunnels" at several locations along the track provide a bit of extra excitement and help muffle the shrieks of riders climbing up, dropping down, and speeding across the steel reinforced track.

The induction motor system that powers California Screamin' is hidden beneath the ground in a concrete, earthquake-proof, climate-controlled bunker. Five-thousand-amp motors create traveling magnetic waves that thrust the vehicles forward as they glide along magnetic fields. As each car passes key points on the track, sensors gauge its speed and adjust the electromagnetic force to either speed it up or slow it down.

▋MUST-SEE▋ SUN WHEEL

Golden beams radiate from a grinning sun-god face at the hub of the massive Ferris wheel. Eight red, six-seat gondolas ascend to the top of the 168-foot-high structure; sixteen others—purple and orange—are attached to ellipsoid tracks within the wheel and slide forward and backward as it rotates. There are only two other wheels like this in the world: the venerable Wonder Wheel at Coney Island in New York, and another in Japan.

The cars seem to descend below the waters of the lagoon; the loading platforms are hidden in a well. Three cars load at once on the first slow rotation and then the wheel makes one more complete circuit before unloading begins.

The 5.8-million-pound Sun Wheel takes two minutes to make a complete revolution; a two-rotation ride including loading takes about eight minutes.

From the top of the wheel you can see most of Disney's California Adventure. To the east you can see some of the landmarks of Disneyland, including Space Mountain and the Matterhorn. To the west, on a clear day, is the coast and Catalina Island. By night, the Paradise Pier glows with neon and strobes.

A disappointment for some is the screen mesh that covers the windows of the cars; taking photographs from the Sun Wheel is a difficult challenge.

The Sun Wheel is a major draw at the park, but not part of the Fastpass system. The line for the red, non-sliding cars will usually be much shorter than the queue for the ones on the moving track.

▋MUST-SEE▋ MALIBOOMER

Here's your chance to ride a carnival strongman sledgehammer in a rocket to the bell at the top.

Three steel girder towers hold carriages that catapult riders an impressive 180 feet straight up in just two seconds and then let them fall and rise again like a bungee jump. Disney has put its own colors on a pretty common amusement park ride here; a similar tower exists at nearby Knott's Berry Farm.

The Maliboomer in mid-flight. *Photo by Corey Sandler. Used by permission from Disney Enterprises, Inc.*

One new Disney "feature": a clear plastic shield sits in front of the faces of the riders. Protection for the riders? For those walking below? Sound barriers for the neighbors? I'd guess all of the above.

The best views of Disneyland can be seen from the top of Tower 3; Tower 1 faces toward Anaheim. Me, I was looking at my feet.

■ MULHOLLAND MADNESS ≡*FAST*

An amusement park wild-mouse ride sends "woody-wagon" vehicles careening across a map of the Hollywood Hills and Santa Monica Mountains. The top of the ride is only 30 feet above ground and water and the drops are small . . . but the turns are very tight and fast.

■ S.S. *RUSTWORTHY*

A waterside playground on a wreck of a fireboat (the "T" of *Trustworthy* has rusted away) with all sorts of bells, whistles, and leaking water pipes. There are buttons to press, ropes to yank, water cannons to shoot, and other entertainments for kids and those lucky enough to come with them.

■ GOLDEN ZEPHYR

Looking like something out of a 1930s Buck Rogers science fiction adventure, zeppelin-shaped stainless steel spaceships are suspended by cable from a rotating 85-foot-high tower. Six vehicles hold twelve passengers apiece.

■ ORANGE STINGER

A giant California orange is peeled back to reveal another carnival favorite, a swing ride with just a bit of sting. Within the huge fruit are forty-eight single-seat "bees" suspended from a central tower that rises and falls and tilts as it spins.

Riders are accompanied by the sounds of bumblebees and a whiff of oranges in the air. The ride is wilder than it may appear; if you want to reduce the thrill a bit, choose a chair on the inner circle.

■ KING TRITON'S CAROUSEL

This is no ordinary merry-go-round. "Aquestrians" whirl around The Little Mermaid's undersea world; fifty-six creatures including hand-carved dolphins, sea lions, flying fish, sea horses, and otters circle to the sounds of surfer and beach songs pumped out on a classic band organ.

Selections include "Catch a Wave," "Surfin' Safari," "Sea Cruise," "The Tide is High," "I Get Around," and "Sea of Love."

■ JUMPIN' JELLYFISH

Young folk have their own scaled-down, gentler version of Maliboomer. Jellyfish-like capsules lurch up a 50-foot tower and then bounce down and back up again below a parachute. There are six two-passenger fish on each of the two towers.

The Orange Stinger. *Photo by Corey Sandler. Used by permission from Disney Enterprises, Inc.*

■ GAMES OF THE BOARDWALK (THE MIDWAY)

On the walkway that stands between California Screamin' and the Maliboomer is the Midway, a corndog, T-shirt, ice cream, pizza kind of place with a surfin' beat. Here you can try your hand at carnival games. Most cost a dollar or two per try; with luck you may win a stuffed animal worth about half what you paid.

■ **Boardwalk Bowl.** A Disney version of Skeeball.

■ **Shore Shot.** Think you can sink a basketball field goal? Maybe, but those hoops look a bit smaller than regulation size.

■ **San Joaquin Volley.** Softballs bounce into—and usually out of—the fruit basket targets.

■ **New Haul Fishery.** Dangle a magnetic lure into the moving river in search of a prize.

■ **Angels in the Outfield.** Knock down a doll with a hardball and walk home with a gift.

■ **Dolphin Derby.** As many as ten players compete to land a ball in a target and push their dolphin racers across the finish line.

■ **Cowhuenga Pass.** Land a ball in a milk can to make the cow moo.

HOLLYWOOD PICTURES BACK LOT

To much of the world, California is Hollywood, celebrated here with some of the icons of classic and modern-day television and movies.

The Grand Entrance to the back lot is through studio archways flanked by giant golden statues of elephants. The inspiration for the gateway dates back to 1917 when D. W. Griffith built a colossal set for *Intolerance* right in the middle of Hollywood Boulevard. The Babylonian palace courtyard set covered several blocks along the busy boulevard for many years.

Hollywood Boulevard recreates the feeling of great back lots constructed for major motion pictures. Klieg lights and cameras stand on scaffolding in front of Art Deco and Spanish landmarks of the real Hollywood Boulevard, including the Pantages Theater and the former Bullock's-Wilshire department store.

Behind the sets are shops, outdoor performance areas, soundstages, and studios for attractions.

Sometime in 2004, this corner of the park will become the home of **Twilight Zone Tower of Terror,** which is certain to become an instant classic in California.

`MUST-SEE` JIM HENSON'S MUPPET*VISION 3D ⟾*FAST*

Don't pass by this extraordinary multimedia show. If you don't have a kid with you, you can pretend you're with the ones in front of you in line.

The film, a masterpiece of corn and puns, was imported lock, stock, and whoopee cushion from the original show at Walt Disney World's Disney–MGM Studios. (The 3-D effects of the ten-year-old film are good, but nowhere near as impressive as those seen in a more current film, *It's Tough to Be a Bug!*)

Nevertheless, the film—and especially the preshow—is among the funniest presentations in the park. As you stand waiting to enter the theater, don't miss the overhead message board that alternately demands that you read various silly orders and then asks you to look away.

Spend the time to read the posters and signs around you within the Muppet 3-D FX Labs. Among my favorites: the 2-D department is a flat painting on the walls. Check out the supply of gags, including tongue inflators, volcanic ashtrays, and anvil repair kits. After a promised visit from Disney's corporate mouse, Rizzo the Rat appears with fake ears: "They're tourists. What do they know?"

We meet Sam Eagle who forthrightly explains the upcoming film as "a salute to all nations, but mostly America."

But the real fun is within the attractive 575-seat theater, which is decidedly more opulent than your neighborhood quintupleplex, although someone really should do something about those cracks in the plaster and the leak in the roof.

There's a robotic all-penguin orchestra in the pit (they took the job just for the halibut) and a private box at the front for Waldorf and Statler. The film in-

Behold the mysterious Hollywood Tower Hotel, a relic of Tinseltown's golden age gone full circle from California to Florida and back to Anaheim. It's an unusual place to visit, complete with a set of high-speed elevators guaranteed to fail on a regular basis.

The attraction at Disney's California Adventure is based on the original at Disney-MGM Studios at Walt Disney World in Florida, in turn based upon an episode of Rod Serling's classic television series, *The Twilight Zone*. Disney Imagineers were tweaking the design as this book goes to press; this preview is based on the Florida ride.

Even before you enter the lobby of the abandoned hotel, there are signs of danger high up on the side of the tall building—sparking electrical wires in a sign hanging above a gaping hole in the tower walls.

Legend says a full guest wing was once attached to that damaged wall. What happened to the wing? And more important, what happened to the people who were in the tower when it disappeared?

Once inside, the introduction begins in the darkened hotel library as a flash of lightning energizes a television in the corner. Our host, Rod Serling (long dead, but that doesn't matter in the Twilight Zone), tells the story of the dark and stormy night—Halloween of 1939, to be exact—when the guests disappeared from their elevator and stepped into a nightmare. "This elevator travels directly to . . . The Twilight Zone."

We learn that when the lightning bolt struck, all the main elevators of the building were lost; only the creaky old service elevator still functions.

And then the library doors open to reveal the entrance to the hotel's basement, a creepy world of boilers, generators, and electrical boxes. It even smells like a basement.

There's another waiting line down in the basement; the line splits into left and right queues that head to one or the other of the two elevator shafts in the building.

The ride begins with a launch skyward. There's a brief moment of panic when the cables of the elevator seem to snap in a shower of electrical sparks. The vehicle then plunges downward, falling faster than the force of gravity. Then it lurches back upward, only to fall again and again.

I counted seven plunges of various lengths and intensities, including a final drop that delivered a few moments of palpable weightlessness. I might have missed a few drops; it's not easy taking notes in a falling elevator.

The doors of the elevator will open on the first floor where you will see a happy family and bellhop suddenly struck by lightning; the view changes to a star field. Your car will move forward into the lights and the shaft.

When you arrive at the "fifth dimension" you will look out at what seems to be an elevator shaft. Wait a minute! Are you going up or sideways? And who are those people who seem to have hitched a ride in your elevator? They seem like ghostly doubles of you and those around you.

Finally, you are in the vertical elevator shaft in the most severely damaged part of the hotel; your cab rises up higher and higher. At the very top, you will reach the damaged elevator motors; they are sparking and flashing ominously.

In Florida, the doors open for a view of the park; guests watching from outside can catch a glimpse of the elevator cab hanging in space for a few seconds.

The elevator cab is actually driven downward by high-power motors so that it travels faster than it would in free-fall. The rest of the way down, the cab travels in what the engineers call "controlled deceleration." That means putting on the brakes.

cludes some marvelous 3-D special effects, as well as flashing lights, a bubble-maker, smell-o-vision, and a surprise from the skies.

WHO WANTS TO BE A MILLIONAIRE–PLAY IT! ≡*FAST*

Together for the first time, two of Disney's biggest stars: Mickey . . . and Regis Philbin.

Philbin handed the "keys to the hot seat" to a crew of theme park hosts charged with re-creating the drama delivered in the game show, *Who Wants to Be a Millionaire?*

Guests experience "Millionaire" in exacting detail, in a 600-seat replica of the high-tech set, complete with the dramatically lit hot seat. The one difference: guests play for points, not dollars, winning unique prizes along the way. Prizes range from collectible pins and hats to a grand prize trip to New York City to view a taping of the ABC-TV game show.

Like the television show, the fastest finger determines the first contestant to sit in the coveted hot seat. All audience members play along, using individual keypads as their scores are tallied throughout the session. They also get involved when players use the "ask the audience" lifeline. Other guests can be called upon for help with the "phone a complete stranger" lifeline. The "phone a stranger" phones are spread around the theme park.

HYPERION THEATER

At the end of Hollywood Boulevard is a thoroughly modern 2,000-seat theater inspired by the great movie palaces of the past. The façade and marquee recall the old Los Angeles Theater. As you walk up the road toward the entrance, stop for a moment to admire the amazing forced-perspective painting out front that expands the street scene up a skyscraper and into an amazingly blue California sky.

Visitors walk into a painted sky backdrop as they head toward the Hyperion Theater. *Photo by Corey Sandler. Used by permission from Disney Enterprises, Inc.*

The largest and tallest structure at the park, the theater includes orchestra, first-, and second-balcony seating in a semicircle. The balconies are close to the stage, but very high above it. The ultra-modern stage is 60 feet wide with spacious wings and a 90-foot fly space above for sets.

You'll choose your seating level before you enter the building; the outdoor waiting line branches into three separate queues. The balconies are well set back from the stage. All rows are steeply raked, with good sight lines. If the line for the orchestra is not too long, I'd suggest you go there. Almost every seat down low is better than one in the stratosphere.

In 2002, the theater was home to *The Power of Blast!*, a dancing, stomping, and pounding production based on the Broadway show *Blast!* The original show at the Hyperion was *Disney's Steps in Time*, a salute to Disney classics.

The theater's name is a tribute to Walt Disney's first studio on Hyperion Avenue in Los Angeles, where Mickey Mouse was born in 1928.

■ DISNEY ANIMATION

The Disney Animation pavilion is Hollywood Boulevard's most architecturally unique structure, designed in classic Art Deco style. The façade of the 30-foot-tall purple marquee atop the building is made of blue glass panels featuring a collage of classic animated characters.

Glass murals at the entrance evoke Hollywood landmarks including the famed Pantages Theater, Max Factor Make-Up Studios, and the Chapman Market.

Within the doors is the **Courtyard Gallery,** the most spectacular indoor space in the park, a total immersion into the world of animation with sixteen large-scale screens of moving and still images from classic films. The selections repeat every twenty-two minutes. Branching off from the center Courtyard

Lobby are the four animation attractions featured in the pavilion.

Parents: all of the attractions in the building exit back into the central courtyard, allowing kids to be set free to explore.

Within the pavilion is the **Sorceror's Workshop,** where visitors can lay their hands on some of the tools of the animator. The Magic Mirror Realm contains early animation devices including zoetropes, whirling drums, and turning cubes. At a workbench you can draw your own simple animation series and put it into one of the devices to bring it to life.

At **Enchanted Books** you can enter into the Beast's Library where you can take a computerized personality test hosted by Lumiere and Cogsworth from *Beauty and the Beast.* The test determines which animated hero or villain you resemble the most.

Spend a few moments here to appreciate some of the tricks of the Imagineers. The room itself comes to life about every four minutes; special effects change the environment of the room from the dark and somber mood of the library under the curse of the Beast to the bright and happy place it becomes when the curse is broken. Video flames flicker in a fireplace and projected petals fall from a rose under glass.

In **Ursula's Grotto,** you can play some Disney karaoke: choose a character from *The Little Mermaid* or another Disney classic and sing or speak the lines from a scene. When you're finished with your audition, sit back and listen to your effort as it is replayed.

At **Drawn to Animation,** an actor interacts with videos and the audience to portray the process or character development of an animated feature from concept through finished personality. Mushu, the reluctant dragon of Mulan (voiced by Eddie Murphy) disputes the artist's version of the story of his birth.

The set is an animator's work area, complete with crumpled balls of waste paper that missed the basketball hoop over the trash can. Among the things we learn is that Mushu's face was modeled on a camel, something that Mushu makes clear is not something he wants to know.

Outside of Drawn to Animation, the **Art of Animation Gallery** displays animation art from classic Disney films; the pieces are changed several times a year.

In 2002, the **Animator's Screening Room** began showing *One Man's Dream,* a marvelous biopic about Walt Disney.

The film *One Man's Dream* is introduced by Disney chairman Michael Eisner, decked out in his best Mickey Mouse tie. Some of the oldest images show Walt in a Red Cross ambulance unit in France during World War I. When he was hired as an artist in Kansas City, some of his first cartoons were based on drawings he made while in France. Included in the film is a glimpse of his first successful character, Oswald the Lucky Rabbit; Disney lost control of the rights in a contract dispute.

Disney Imagineers decided that no one could tell Disney's story better than Walt Disney himself. Many of the sound recordings were of poor quality, recorded in Disney's backyard by his daughter for a series of magazine articles she was writing; engineers had to work around chirping birds, the squeaky noises of the hammock Walt was sitting in, and passing airplanes and cars.

Twenty hours of recordings were distilled to about ten minutes of audio for the film. Imagineers also digitized and edited films and photos of Walt, some almost one hundred years old.

We see early incarnations of Mickey Mouse, and see Disney's important transition to the Silly Symphonies cartoons, a series of musicals without a central character. We learn how Disney put up the family fortune in 1935 to finance *Snow White*. With the profits of that film he built the studio that made the company a global success. In short order came classics *Pinocchio*, *Bambi*, and *Fantasia*.

Some of the images in the film show Disney's formative years on the farm in Marceline, Missouri; pictures on display at the exhibit include old images of Marceline that show how it influenced the design of Main Street U.S.A. at Disneyland and the Magic Kingdom.

■ SUPERSTAR LIMO

Even Mickey lays an egg every once in a while; this dark ride through Tinseltown in a top-down purple limousine was not much of a California adventure. In early 2002, the ride was closed for an indefinite time for a retooling.

The original concept made you a superstar on the way to your very own Hollywood premiere. The ride across town zipped through many of L.A.'s most famous neighborhoods. Rodeo Drive pops up first as the limo passes through the famous shopping boulevard, home of the rich and famous. Featured along the street are cartoon animatronics of Regis Philbin, his hands full of dollars ready to pay off TV's next millionaire, Melanie Griffith and Antonio Banderas sipping cocktails, and Cindy Crawford out for a stroll. Along Sunset Strip the sights include Tim Allen showing off his tool belt and Drew Carey selling maps to the homes of movie stars. In Bel Air, Jackie Chan leaps across two buildings.

Arriving at the Chinese Theater and the big premiere, painted set pieces of crowds line the route and flashbulbs pop. An oversized Whoopi Goldberg animatronic welcomes you to the opening where you've finally arrived as Hollywood's newest star.

PARADES AT DISNEY'S CALIFORNIA ADVENTURE

Everything old is new again; in this case the new park became home to **Disney's Electrical Parade,** a slightly updated edition of the famed Main Street Electrical Parade that was a longtime fixture at Disneyland and later traveled to other company theme parks. The parade brings many classic Disney animated features to life through three-dimensional floats covered with thousands of colorful lights. Among the most impressive scenes are the 23-foot-tall clock tower over Cinderella's Ball, complete with light-covered ballroom dancers, and the smoke-breathing, tail-wagging Elliott the dragon from *Pete's Dragon*. The parade is presented on Friday, Saturday, and Sunday nights, and on special holiday evenings.

Other entertainment includes "Goofy's Beach Party Bash," a wacky seaside spoof on the Hollywood Back Lot Stage; a cast of friendly Disney characters who entertain throughout the park; and Road Trip, a talented rock band that cruises as it plays.

At its opening, Disney's California Adventure debuted **Eureka! A California Parade,** celebrating many of the Golden State's cultures and lifestyles.

EATING AND SHOPPING YOUR WAY THROUGH DISNEY'S CALIFORNIA ADVENTURE

Everyone has to eat, but the overpriced junk at some theme parks is sometimes enough to put anyone on a diet. At Disney's California Adventure, the food offerings are a notch or two above ordinary. And you can also check out of the park to Downtown Disney for even finer fare.

▓ THE GOLDEN GATEWAY

Just inside the entrance is **Greetings from California,** the signature store at the park. The store is ready to meet your pressing souvenir needs as you arrive or as you drag yourself out the gate at the end of the day. **Engine-Ears Toys** offers playthings with a California and Mickey Mouse connection.

Nearby you'll find **Bakers Field Bakery & Coffee Roaster** and the **Bu-r-r Bank Ice Cream Shop.** The interiors of both stands were inspired by Los Angeles's Union Station; the tower outside is similar to one at the Santa Fe Depot in San Diego. While you're indulging your sweet tooth, check out some of the old photos of trains inside the bakery.

▓ GOLDEN STATE

In Condor Flats, the **Taste Pilots Grill** is housed in a Quonset hut-like hangar at the high-desert airfield. Food like that served to airplane mechanics and pilots just returned from a grueling test flight—or a few hours in a theme park—is cooked on a rocket engine grill. A replica of an X-1 jet, the first aircraft to break the speed of sound, pokes its nose through the sidewall.

Also in the area is **Fly 'n' Buy,** with Condor Flats souvenirs including jackets, caps, logos, and pins for the pilots and wannabes.

At the Grizzly Peak Recreation Area, **Rushin' River Outfitters** sells wilderness wear and sports gear; you can also purchase rain gear to take on the river raft ride.

Bountiful Valley Farm, a celebration of the agricultural abundance of the state, includes the Bountiful Valley Farmers Market, where you can choose from fresh California fruits and vegetables as well as hot baked potatoes and turkey legs. Also in the area is **Sam Andreas Shakes** (get it?), featuring date, citrus, and milk shakes. **Santa Rosa Seed & Supply** sells gardening supplies, flowers, and plants.

At Pacific Wharf, San Francisco's famed Boudin Bakery operates the **Pacific Wharf Cafe,** which features sandwiches on sourdough bread, seafood, and soup. You can combine all three with an order of clam chowder in an edible sourdough bowl.

Also along the wharf is the **Cucina Cucamonga Mexican Grill,** featuring meat dishes wrapped in corn or flour tortillas from the tortilla factory alongside. Less traditional offerings including tortillas wrapped around hot dogs or filled with peanut butter and jelly.

The **Lucky Fortune Cookery** serves Korean rice dishes, Chinese dim sum, and other Asian specialties.

Rita's Baja Blenders serves margaritas with a selection of tropic flavors. Golden Vine Winery offers a gourmet restaurant, **The Vineyard Room.** The eighty-seat mission-style eatery features hand-troweled plaster walls, terracotta risers, a wood beam ceiling, and *plein air* style mural. Outside on **Golden Vine Terrace** is a patio for wine tasting and al fresco dining.

Sample dishes at the Vineyard Room include seared ahi tuna with warm potato salad, bresaola with olive oil and lemon, artichoke caponata, and Gorgonzola Dolcelatte with roasted pears. Pasta dishes included butternut squash ravioli, saffron tagliatelle, and pappardelle with braised duck. And for a main course, offerings included gnocchi with Maine lobster, fennel-cured roasted pork loin, and braised beef short ribs with cippolini onions. A prix-fixe four-course dinner with wine costs about $42 for lunch or $50 for dinner; without wine, the bill came to about $28 for lunch or $36 for dinner.

A wine bar on the plaza offers samples of various Mondavi brands and varieties priced from about $5.00 to $8.00 per glass. You can also purchase whole bottles; they'll be sent to the gate to wait for your departure.

■ PARADISE PIER

The "under the sea" world of the **Avalon Cove** restaurant provides a picturesque setting for family dining that features spectacular views of Paradise Pier, appearances by the Disney characters, and a selection of specialty entrees for lunch and dinner.

The restaurant's architecture was inspired by the famous Avalon Casino on Catalina Island. A pair of conical towers are rimmed with hundreds of lights; inside, the decor features shells, dolphins, and lobsters.

The table-service restaurant is a favorite beachfront stop for Disney characters including Ariel, Minnie Mouse, Goofy, Pluto, and Chip 'n' Dale. The menu features three-course meals of family-friendly comfort foods, with inspiration drawn from foods traditionally served along the beachfront American boardwalk. Entrees include home-style meat loaf, crispy battered halibut, chicken potpie, and four-layer vegetable lasagna, as well as an assortment of soups, entree salads, sandwiches, and desserts.

The children's menu features the "Octadog," a hot dog sliced to resemble an eight-armed octopus guarding his bed of shell-shaped macaroni and cheese. Other dishes, including chicken nuggets, fish sticks, and mini corn dogs, are served in souvenir sand pails with the condiments placed in a souvenir sand shovel.

Guests are encouraged to become part of the show. Sand pails full of musical seashells and sand dollars are at each table, allowing everyone to shake, rattle or

Avalon Cove by night. *Photo © Disney Enterprises, Inc.*

jingle along with the music. During the signature song, "Under the Sea," everyone is invited to join the Disney characters and Avalon Cove Cast Members in a high-energy, follow-the-leader-style version of the song.

The restaurant originally opened as a gourmet eatery under the direction of famed California chef Wolfgang Puck; it was apparently too *haute* for the amusement pier theme of the area.

Along the boardwalk are a series of amusement park-style shacks. The dogs are out front at **Corn Dog Castle.** Malibu and Mexican burritos come together at **Malibu-Ritos.** The ultimate surfer beach shack is **Pizza Oom Mow Mow.** Chicken and sauces are on the menu at **Strips, Dips 'n' Chips.**

Burger Invasion recalls the California Crazy architecture of Route 66 roadside stands of the 1930s. Beneath the high Big Mac is a fanciful outpost of the McDonald's burger empire. Nearby is **Catch a Flave,** serving soft ice cream with fruit flavors swirled through.

As you would expect in a seaside amusement park (and a Disney theme park) there are many places to buy those essential T-shirts and Goofy hats. Shops along the boardwalk include **Dinosaur Jack's Sunglass Shack,** another architectural joke, topped with a giant reptile.

Treasures in Paradise is designed like a 1920s beachfront pavilion, a warehouse with an Art Deco spire. **Souvenir 66** would have been at home on Route 66. At **Point Mugu Tattoo,** you can purchase a temporary emblem.

■ HOLLYWOOD PICTURES BACK LOT

Near the Muppets show is **Hollywood and Dine,** a fast food restaurant with counters that salutes several once-famous Hollywood eateries including Dan the Beachcomber, Wiltshire Bowl Grill, and Villa Capri. At **Award Wieners,** a modern-style diner serves up haute dogs and french fries.

The quirky **ABC Soap Opera Bistro,** which featured "sets" from daytime dramas and a cast of waiters and waitresses who stayed within the sob stories of the shows, closed in late 2002. It will be replaced by **Playhouse Disney** in April of 2003.

Coming Attraction: *Playhouse Disney—Live on Stage!*

Kids will have another show of their own at Disney's California Adventure with the opening of *Playhouse Disney–Live On Stage!* in the Hollywood Pictures Back Lot in April of 2003.

The show, presented several times daily, will feature live performers, puppetry, and stories of friendship from popular Disney Channel *Playhouse Disney* programs such as *Jim Henson's Bear in the Big Blue House, Rolie Polie Olie, Stanley* and others.

CHAPTER SIX

DOWNTOWN DISNEY AND DISNEY HOTELS

THE NEW GATEWAY TO DISNEYLAND and Disney's California Adventure is a twenty-acre sprawl of shops, restaurants, and entertainment clubs in four districts.

Disney says the area is a California-modern phenomenon inspired by famous European shopping and theater districts and old-town walking streets such as Copenhagen's Strøget and Tivoli Gardens.

It's also worth crediting Universal Studios Hollywood with introducing CityWalk to southern California. Disney later created its own city in Florida at Walt Disney World's Disney West Side and Downtown Disney.

DOWNTOWN DISNEY

Starting at the central esplanade between Disneyland park and Disney's California Adventure park, the East Garden area takes its visual cues from the new Disney's Grand Californian Hotel with its early twentieth century Craftsmen architecture.

The La Brea Bakery, an outpost of an old artisan baker in Los Angeles, offers cafe dining and grab-and-go bakery treats, coffee, and espresso in a gatehouse to the hotel. Specialties include a coffee and espresso bar, breads, pastries, sandwiches, soups and salads, a food preparation station with items such as freshly grilled panini sandwiches and a crostini bar that serves open-faced, appetizer-size sandwiches using fresh grilled breads. A wine bar serves by the glass and offers microbrewery beers as well.

Naples Ristorante e Pizzeria offers casual Southern Italian cuisine in a Mediterranean setting; the attractive eatery is the second restaurant at Downtown Disney operated by chef Joachim Splichal. The 350-seat restaurant features a handcrafted wood-burning oven, an open kitchen, and trellises covered with bougainvillea.

Diners can watch skillful *pizzaiole* (pizza chefs) work at marble slabs, hand-patting the balls of dough and adding the fresh toppings such as imported vine-ripened plum tomatoes and fior di latte mozzarella. A conveyer system moves pizza pies between the kitchen and the two-story, wood-burning oven.

Naples also offers a selection of piccoli piatti. These small salads, similar to tapas, are offered on individual plates and include meats, seafood, and vegetables. Also on the menu are hearty pastas and other dishes prepared in the traditional Neapolitan cucina marinara style including pagnottelle, which are twice-baked sandwiches made from pizza dough.

An island in the center of the Wine District includes a vine-covered wine and tapas bar. The **Catal Restaurant & Uva Bar,** developed by chef Joachin Splichal, combines Art Deco and Westwood Village architectural styles in a two-story, 525-seat restaurant filled with the rich colors and streamlined aesthetics of the Jazz Age. The wine and tapas bar is located under a shaded champagne-flute trellis; as many as forty different wines will be sold by the glass. Uva is the Spanish word for grapes.

The menu features Mediterranean grilled seafood, poultry and vegetables, salads, and flavorful pastas. Dishes are infused with the fragrant herbs and olive oil that characterize the cuisine of the Mediterranean rim, including southern France, Greece, Italy, and Spain.

Joachim and Christine Splichal also own Pinot Bistro in Studio City, Pinot Hollywood in the heart of Hollywood's studio district, Café Pinot in downtown Los Angeles, Pinot Restaurant and Martini Bar in Pasadena, Pinot Blanc in Saint Helena, Pinot Provence in Costa Mesa, and Pinot Brasserie within the Venetian Resort in Las Vegas.

During morning hours it operates as a coffee bar, offering a variety of coffees and pastries.

The **Center Plaza,** the heart of the district, is surrounded by an unusual mix of major restaurants and showplaces.

Ralph Brennan's Jazz Kitchen brings a bit of New Orleans' Bourbon Street to Anaheim, featuring spicy Cajun cuisine and Dixieland music. The exterior of the 400-seat restaurant is straight out of the French Quarter with wrought iron balconies and gas lights.

A member of the Brennan family of Commander's Palace fame, Ralph Brennan's company includes Red Fish Grill, BACCO, Mr. B's Bistro, and The Storyville District, all part of New Orleans's French Quarter restaurants. For information, consult www.rbjazzkitchen.com.

The **House of Blues** is styled as a Carolina plantation estate house and seats as many as 500 for Delta-inspired cuisine. Live performances of blues, rock, rhythm and blues, and Latin music are planned.

The House of Blues Restaurant features an open-air kitchen serving fresh rotisserie items and Delta-inspired cuisine. Menu items include Memphis-style ribs, cedar plank salmon with watercress-jicama salad, and Voodoo Shrimp with rosemary cornbread. A specialty is the Sunday gospel brunch, which features performances by local and touring gospel groups, with a southern-style buffet. For information, consult www.hob.com.

Y Arriba! Y Arriba! A Latin dining and entertainment place hot as a jalapeño pepper, featuring live music and dancing every evening in a 600-seat tapas teatro. The restaurant includes elements of Cuban and Argentinian architecture; the founders of the restaurant also operate Club Tropigala at the Fontainebleu Hilton Resort in Miami Beach. The name comes from a line in Ritchie Valens's "La Bamba" that means "above and above."

The menu features tapas, the snack-size dishes that are a favorite throughout the Latin world, with a selection from every Latin country.

A cast of dancers performs from 11:00 A.M. to 2:00 A.M., augmented by a dance orchestra in the evening and occasional performances by major Latin stars.

Near the Disneyland Hotel at the West Side Garden, design themes return to Art Deco and celebrate the golden age of glittering Hollywood movie palaces in restaurants, theaters, and the Downtown Disney monorail station.

The **Downtown Disney Monorail Station** connects directly to Tomorrowland within the Disneyland park. As part of the development of Downtown Disney, the monorail station was moved across the street from the Disneyland Hotel. There is no station within Disney's California Adventure.

The **Rainforest Cafe** uses touches of Inca palace architecture merged with a concrete block house, "La Minatura," built in California in the 1920s by Frank Lloyd Wright. The central atrium is filled with hundreds of live jungle plants. Other Rainforest Cafes are located at Walt Disney World and Disneyland Paris. For information, consult www.rainforestcafe.com.

ESPN Zone is a sports entertainment bar and restaurant featuring satellite transmitters and receivers and more than 165 video monitors. The Studio Grill is inspired by sets from "ESPN SportsCenter" and other ESPN broadcast shows. The Screening Room is a theater to watch broadcast sports and live interviews of sports figures. The Sports Arena features interactive and competitive games, including a 30-foot Xtreme Glacier rock wall. ESPN is part of ABC, which is in turn owned by the Disney Company.

■ ENTERTAINMENT AT DOWNTOWN DISNEY

If the Disneyland park or Disney's California Adventure is not quite enough excitement for you, or if you're looking for nighttime entertainment aimed at adults, Downtown Disney offers jazz, blues, salsa, rock and roll, sports talk, and twelve screens of movies.

AMC Theatres. Twelve auditoriums with a total of 3,000 seats with modern amenities including stadium seating and high-tech sound systems. For show times and ticket reservations, call (714) 769–4262 or consult www.movietickets. com.

ESPN Zone. Guests can watch broadcasts and taping of ESPN radio and television talk shows as well as broadcasts of major professional and college sports. For schedules, call (714) 300–3776 or consult espn.go.com/espninc/zone/espn zoneanaheim.html.

House of Blues. Live musical performances several nights per week, plus the Sunday Gospel Brunch. For information and tickets, call (714) 778–2583 or consult www.hob.com.

Ralph Brennan's Jazz Kitchen. A house band and special guests perform. For information, call (714) 776–5200 or consult www.rbjazzkitchen.com.

■ SHOPPING AT DOWNTOWN DISNEY

And, of course, you can shop at Downtown Disney.

The flagship store here is the **World of Disney,** a full acre of Disney merchandise set amidst giant video screens and themed areas saluting classic films. More than 15,000 plush characters of various sizes and shapes fill one floor-to-ceiling display.

This is the second-largest Disney shopping experience on Earth; the monstrous store at Walt Disney World in Orlando is the largest.

It's all about retail, of course: The shop sells all manner of Disney character merchandise including backpacks, books, boxers, children's apparel, clocks, collectibles, costumes, dolls, figurines, gifts, hats, jewelry, luggage, photo albums, plush toys, sleepwear, slippers, socks, souvenirs, stationery, sunglasses, sweatshirts, T-shirts, ties, videos, watches, and more.

Other shops include **Compass Books & Cafe,** the west's oldest independent bookstore. For information, consult www.booksinc.net.

The French cosmetics and fragrances retailer **Sephora** has a store in the district; for information, consult www.sephora.com.

The **Lego Imagination Center** stocks more than four hundred Lego toy products. For information, consult www.lego.com.

Mainspring sells clocks and watches of all types.

Starabilias offers antique souvenirs and reproductions of Hollywood memorabilia. For information, consult www.starabilias.com.

Hoypoloi sells unusual glass and metal art pieces and lighting; the company's moniker plays off the name of its founder, artist Ron Hoy. For information, consult www.hoypoloi.com.

Department 56 sells its collectibles, Snowbabies, and home and holiday decorative products. For information, consult www.department56.com.

Illuminations is a national retailer of handmade candles and home decor items. For information, consult www.illuminations.com.

Parking for Downtown Disney guests is located off Disneyland Drive in areas just to the north of the Disneyland Hotel and just south of Disney's Paradise Pier Hotel. Cars are charged by the hour; the first three hours are free, with the movie theater and some restaurants offering two more hours to customers. Additional hours cost $6.00 per hour.

HOTELS AT THE DISNEYLAND RESORT

Several thousand lucky (and relatively well-heeled) guests can now stay in and around the theme parks in Disney-owned hotels.

■ DISNEY'S GRAND CALIFORNIAN HOTEL

The newest hotel at the park captures the spirit of the Golden State's coastal woodlands in a deluxe six-story, 751-room resort hotel. It brings the total number of rooms at official Disney hotels to about 2,300.

It is the first hotel with a direct entrance into any Disney park; a gate allows guests to come and go into Disney's California Adventure. It is also the first time the residential architecture of the Arts and Crafts movement has been applied to a structure as large as a major hotel. Reminiscent of old-style lodges such as the Ahwahnee Hotel at Yosemite or the Old Faithful Lodge at Yellowstone, the posh hotel is in many ways a West Coast version of the popular Grand Floridian Hotel at Walt Disney World in Orlando.

Planners chose the Arts and Crafts architecture that was popular for wealthy family homes in the California foothills. The style began in England in the late nineteenth century as a revolt against Victorian gingerbread and machine-made decor, and was embraced by noted architects such as Frank Lloyd Wright, Bernard Maybeck, and others. Designs strive to be in perfect harmony with the surrounding area. Each piece of wood was carefully chosen, each rock selected to be in perfect harmony with nature, and each piece of furniture was handcrafted by the artist. The best-known example of Arts and Crafts style in California is a Pasadena "bungalow" completed in 1908 by Charles and Henry Greene for Charles and Mary Gamble, of Procter and Gamble wealth.

Disney's implementation was designed by architect Peter Dominick, also responsible for Disney's Wilderness Lodge and the new Disney's Animal Kingdom Lodge at Walt Disney World in Florida.

A bungalow-style porte cochere greets guests arriving at the front entrance off Disneyland Drive. Large metal gates with a blue moon in the center guard the entrance to the hotel from Downtown Disney. Just inside the front entrance are large wooden trusses and stained glass light fixtures, recalling some of the elements of Northern California's first Craftsmen structure, the Swedenborgian church.

The star of the hotel is the impressive atrium lobby, 753 feet high with open timber trusses in the ceiling. Down below are large stone porches. The floor is decorated with fabric and stone in a floral pattern inspired by the work of British designer William Morris, one of the early leaders of the Arts and Crafts movement.

To complete the building Disney searched for artists and artisans to build elements. Spend the time to find:

■ A quarter-sawed oak grandfather clock with a hammered-copper face and cable-weight clockworks in the lobby

■ Large ceramic vases shaped like birds with human caricatures so unique they are called "grotesqueries"

■ A manhole cover with the face of the "north wind" in the pavement of the Court of Winds

Each room has its own balcony, with most of the rooms looking directly into Disney's California Adventure park or the Downtown Disney district. Surrounding the hotel is an evergreen forest and rock-post fences. (One somewhat incongruous element: the monorail breezing by overhead in the interior Courtyard of Winds, nipping through a corner of the building.)

The Grand Californian offers a supervised activity center, **Pinocchio's Workshop,** for younger children. Guests can leave their youngsters at the center while they go to dinner or explore the parks.

Within the hotel, the **Napa Rose Restaurant** celebrates the bounties of California from seacoast to farmlands, with a special emphasis on the vineyards. The 200 seats surround an open exhibition kitchen and a large wine cellar including some of the state's premium and boutique wines.

The wine list includes more than 600 California wines and sixty French champagnes. The menu places an emphasis on California produce and features foods that are in their prime season; for example, white asparagus in the spring, wild mushrooms in the fall, and fresh raspberries in the summer.

Large picture windows offer views of the park; other walls are decorated with stained glass grills and inlaid wood. Guests can watch twenty chefs and helpers at work in the kitchen; when meals are ready, a "runner" moves the dishes quickly to the table.

Storytellers Cafe is an informal setting for breakfast buffet and casual dining throughout the day. The restaurant's eight murals, done in the 1930s style of famed children's book illustrator N. C. Wyeth, celebrate the joys of reading. Disney characters including Chip 'n' Dale make regular appearances here.

Just off the lobby is the **Hearthstone Lodge,** serving gourmet coffee and baked goods in the morning and drinks and wine throughout the rest of the day. A stone fireplace is surrounded by handmade tile with century-old designs; a hand-carved redwood mural depicts an artist at work. What look like Mickey Mouse ears on some of the lamps are said to be reproductions of actual Arts and Crafts designs; we consider them hidden Mickeys, nevertheless.

The entrance to Disney's California Adventure is primarily for hotel guests, but can also be used by park guests after they have entered the main gates.

Rack rates start at about $300 per night; packages with admission tickets and meals are also offered. For reservations and information call (714) 956–6425 or consult www.disneyland.com.

■ DISNEYLAND HOTEL

The hotel across Disneyland Drive (formerly West Street) opened in 1955 and has grown over the years to become a small theme park of its own.

As part of the development of Downtown Disney and Disney's California Adventure, the hotel has been reborn again. The resort spreads across sixty acres of lush, tropical gardens and offers 990 guest rooms and sixty-two suites in three towers.

The centerpiece of the **Never Land** water play area, inspired by scenes from Peter Pan, is a large swimming pool with a winding "shoreline" that depicts the lagoon from the film, accented by the Hangman's Tree and a backdrop of the Misty Mountains. Rising from the pool is a sculpture of Tick Tock, the hungry crocodile always on the lookout for Captain Hook. Nearby is a spa themed after the Mermaid Lagoon, including a figure of a mermaid atop a fountain.

Guests can follow a trail that winds its way up the slopes of the **Misty Mountain,** across a wood-and-rope suspension bridge and to the 16-foot-high "headwaters" of the pool. The way down is a 110-foot-long water slide that rushes through the mountain range and plunges into the lagoon.

The Disneyland Monorail station is nearby, allowing easy access to Disneyland as well as a quick way out of the park for breaks at the pool or one of the restaurants. Day visitors to the Disneyland Resort can also use the restaurants at the hotel. The monorail does not stop within Disney's California Adventure; a tram links the main gate of the park to the hotel. Guests at the hotel can receive early admission to Disneyland on days when it is available.

Granville's Steak House offers steak, prime rib, lobster, and poultry specialties for dinner in a dark-wood American Southwest setting. After the lobster, steak, or seafood, see if you can polish off a Chocolate Fantasy Cake.

Hook's Pointe & Wine Cellar is a slightly upscale nautical theme restaurant offering mesquite-grilled specialties for breakfast, lunch, and dinner; dishes are prepared in a display kitchen. The below-deck wine cellar features more than two dozen California wines by the bottle or glass.

For a somewhat less sophisticated experience, **Goofy's Kitchen** features Disney character meals including an all-you-can-eat buffet as well as lunch and dinner from a menu prepared by Chef Goofy, Pluto, and other friends.

Rack rates for the hotel range from about $180 to $275 per night. Package plans with airfare and tickets are also available. There is no charge for children younger than eighteen sharing a room with parents.

The Disneyland Hotel is located at 1150 Magic Way in Anaheim. For reservations call (714) 956–6425 or consult www.disneyland.com.

▦ DISNEY'S PARADISE PIER HOTEL

Location, location, location: Disney's Paradise Pier Hotel is in one of the best spots in Anaheim. The fifteen-story high-rise—formerly the Disneyland Pacific Hotel—is a short walk from the Disneyland Hotel in one direction and the Anaheim Convention Center in the other.

But the clincher is the view from the upper floors of the east side of the hotel: Below you is the Paradise Pier section of Disney's California Adventure and beyond it is Disneyland. (Disney's Grand Californian is closer to the action, but only four stories tall.)

The 502-room hotel was purchased by Disney a few years ago and has undergone a complete renovation. It includes a swimming pool and spa, two restaurants, and access to the facilities of the Disneyland Hotel.

The building's towers are festively painted and decorated to reflect the California theme. With the purchase of park admission, hotel guests can enter Disney's California Adventure through a private gate leading directly into Paradise Pier; guests can save fifteen minutes or more over walking through Downtown Disney to the main entrance of the park and can easily return to the hotel for a break from the park.

The **Pacific Coast Highway** restaurant is among the better Disney restaurants, offering wood-fired specialty pizzas, unusual seafood such as sea bass marinated in sake, and a range of Pacific Rim entrees such as hoisin-grilled baby back ribs. In the morning the younger crowd takes over for breakfast with Minnie & Friends.

Disney's PCH Grill also hosts twice-monthly wine dinners featuring California wines that are paired with specially prepared five-course dinners. Winemakers from the featured winery are present to meet guests and answer questions.

Yamabuki, located next to the hotel's lobby, is Disneyland's only Japanese restaurant. Items include fresh sushi, tempura, sashimi, and teriyaki. A tatami room with both Japanese and Western-style seating is available for special occasions and small groups.

Up the grand staircase on the second floor is a traditional **English Tea Room.** The "Practically Perfect Tea" invites mothers and daughters, or the entire family, to step back in time. Victorian-era costumed servers, including Mary Poppins, serve tea and invite guests to play dress-up.

Rack rates for the hotel range from about $180 to $275 per night. Package plans with airfare and tickets are also available. There is no charge for children younger than eighteen sharing a room with parents. For reservations, call (714) 956–6425 or consult www.disneyland.com.

PART III

UNIVERSAL STUDIOS HOLLYWOOD AND UNIVERSAL CITYWALK

CHAPTER SEVEN

UNIVERSAL STUDIOS HOLLYWOOD

UNIVERSAL STUDIOS IS A PLACE of great history in the relatively short life of the motion picture industry. Its films and television shows have gone back in time to *Jurassic Park* and Bedrock, home of the Flintstones; to ancient Rome and Greece for *Spartacus* and Mel Brooks in a toga; to the classic antiwar theme of *All Quiet on the Western Front* and the slapstick *McHale's Navy;* to the chilling horror of *Psycho* and the technological terror of *Backdraft;* way into the future and then back again in *Back to the Future.* Each of these films and many more are celebrated at Universal Studios Hollywood with exhibits, rides, stage shows, and guided tours.

There are four main areas at Universal Studios Hollywood; plan on a full day to see them all. The entrance to the park evokes the great movie palaces and themes of the past and leads into the upper-level Entertainment Center, which is home to the stage shows—including *Waterworld*—and most of the park's eateries, as well as the astounding **Back to the Future . . . The Ride.**

Off to the right and down a long escalator is the loading area for the Back Lot Tram Tour. At the back left corner is the first of a series of four long escalators that take you down to the Studio Center for more rides, including the spectacular **Jurassic Park—The Ride.**

Finally there is the **Universal CityWalk,** a collection of unusual shops, clubs, and restaurants well worth a visit for lunch, dinner, or late-night entertainment. You don't even need an admission ticket to visit there, but if you're at the park it's a great place to duck out for lunch or dinner.

Universal Studios is about forty-five minutes by car from Anaheim, or fifteen minutes from downtown Los Angeles; driving times can more than double during the region's extended rush hours.

You can ride the Red Line of the Metro subway to a station at the base of the Universal City hill; Universal Studios Hollywood offers a free shuttle bus from the train to the park.

MUST-SEES

Terminator 2 3-D
(he's back . . .)

Jurassic Park—The Ride
(take a shower with the
dinos)

Earthquake
(Back Lot Tram Tour)

King Kong
(Back Lot Tram Tour)

**Back to the Future . . .
The Ride**

Waterworld—A Live
Sea War Spectacular

*The Wild Wild Wild
West Stunt Show*

Spider-Man Rocks!

Backdraft

E.T. Adventure

Special Effects Stages

Animal Planet Live!

**Shrek and Donkey's
Scary-Tale Adventure**
(Coming attraction)

A UNIVERSAL HISTORY

Universal Studios was established in 1912 with the founding of the Universal Film Manufacturing Company, started at the time of the nickelodeon in a cluster of tiny offices in New York. Under the leadership of Carl Laemmle the company became a major force in the industry.

When Laemmle decided to consolidate production facilities from both coasts to one site, he purchased a 130-acre chicken ranch in North Hollywood, and construction of what was to become Universal City began in 1914.

Because the property in Cahuenga Pass was far removed from what passed for the modern conveniences of Los Angeles at the time, the company installed its own power, water, and other facilities.

At the grand opening in 1915, Thomas Edison was on hand to officially start the studio's electrical equipment, and showman Buffalo Bill Cody was a special guest. Ten thousand sightseers were also there to view the dawn of the motion picture industry on the West Coast.

Almost immediately, Universal was the world's busiest motion picture studio; early filmmakers included the legendary John Ford, Eric von Stroheim, and Irving Thalberg.

A burst of expansion took place during World War II; government regulations prohibited excess profits during wartime, so the company poured cash into new soundstages and other construction.

In 1946 Universal expanded with a merger with International Pictures. In following years, the studio lured director Alfred Hitchcock and later Steven Spielberg and George Lucas. The Music Corporation of America (MCA) purchased the Universal studio facilities and land in 1959 and Universal Pictures itself in 1962. During the next two decades, MCA opened the Universal Studios Hollywood theme park, fourteen modern soundstages, the Universal Amphitheatre, and many other facilities including office buildings, hotels, shops, and restaurants.

Today Universal Studios is a part of CANAL+, the TV and film division of Vivendi Universal, a global media and communications company.

UNIVERSAL STUDIOS HOLLYWOOD

1. Universal CityWalk
2. Entrance
3. Back Lot Tram Tour
4. Stairway to Studio Center
5. Production Studios
6. Back Lot

Power Trip: The Jurassic Dash and the Terminator Trot

Jurassic Park—The Ride and **Terminator 2 3-D** continue as the major magnets at Universal Studios, and you can expect long lines there on busy days.

Our strategy: arrive early and head for the Terminator. After you've dodged laser beams for breakfast, act like a contrarian: go immediately to the escalators to Studio Center and head for the second-biggest draw, Jurassic Park. With luck, you'll miss the crush and sail on in. Dry yourself off and then visit **E.T. Adventure, Backdraft,** and the **Special Effects Stages.**

By now most of the other visitors will have taken the tram tour and will be heading your way. Grab an early lunch to avoid hungry crowds later, and then go against the flow, back up the escalator to the Entertainment Center. If the waiting line at **Back to the Future** is reasonable (half an hour or less), go on in; if not, go down the other side of the hill to the Back Lot Tram Tour and go back to Back, etc., later.

In early afternoon visit the shows including *Spider-Man Rocks!, Animal Planet Live!, The Rugrats Magic Adventure,* and *The Wild Wild Wild West Stunt Show.*

Just inside gates on the right side is the Daily Shooting Schedule that reports on movie and television projects underway in the studios and backlots. On a visit in the spring of 2002, work was underway inside closed studios on movies including *Red Dragon, The Hulk,* and *Minority Report.* The *Providence* television show was filming some scenes on the Colonial Street, and studio work was underway on *Crossing Jordan* and *Leap of Faith.*

It's a matter of pure luck whether you'll see a show being filmed, or run into a celebrity while on the back lot tram tour. Keep your eyes peeled as you are taken past the studios—watch for dressing room trailers and equipment trucks. From time to time, one or another star makes a point of waving to a passing tram, or more. According to studio lore, one day a crazed man dressed in a granny dress and waving an ax ran screaming out of the Bates Motel from *Psycho* in the back lot; it turned out to be Jim Carrey, taking a break from the filming of *The Grinch* to play with visitors.

UNIVERSAL STUDIOS HOLLYWOOD, TODAY

Since public tours were established at Universal Studios Hollywood in 1964, nearly ninety million guests have visited the former chicken farm as paying guests. Today, more than five million come to Universal Studios Hollywood each year.

Universal Studios Hollywood is located in Universal City between Hollywood and the San Fernando Valley, off the Hollywood Freeway (Interstate 101), at either the Universal Center Drive or Lankershim Boulevard exits.

The park is open daily except for Thanksgiving and Christmas. Operating

Universal Studios Hollywood Tickets

Prices were in effect in mid-2002 and are subject to change; prices do not include a 2 percent Los Angeles County tax. For general information, call (818) 622–3801 or consult www.universalstudioshollywood.com.

ONE-DAY PASS	ADULT	CHILD (ages 3 to 11)	SENIOR (60+)
	$45	$35	$39

Parking: $8
Preferred Parking: $13

DIRECTOR PASS	$69	$69	$69

Includes front-of-line privileges, reserved show seating, exclusive post-show demonstrations at The Wild, Wild, Wild, West Stunt Show and Waterworld, special session with the animals and trainers after the Animal Planet Live! show and commemorative photo.

FRONT-OF-THE-LINE PASS	$79	$79	$79

Priority entry privileges for an entire day on all attractions, limited to two times per attraction. Reserved seating at shows including Animal Planet Live!, Rugrats Magic Adventure (weekends only), and Waterworld—A Live Sea War Spectacular, plus a commemorative photo.

VIP EXPERIENCE	$125	$125	$125

Includes private trolley for a tour of front lot production facilities, including soundstages, sound mixing rooms, and the property warehouse, subject to production restrictions. The trolley then visits the back lot. Guests also receive front-of-the-line privileges at attractions.

HOLLYWOOD CITYPASS	$59	$39	$59

Valid for one admission to seven Hollywood attractions over a thirty-day period. Participating attractions are Universal Studios Hollywood, American Cinematheque at the Egyptian Theatre, Autry Museum of Western Heritage, Hollywood Entertainment Museum, Museum of Television and Radio, the Petersen Automotive Museum, and a two-hour bus tour of the homes of movie stars.

SOUTHERN CALIFORNIA VALUE PASS	$79	$59	$79

Unlimited admission to Universal Studios Hollywood and SeaWorld San Diego for fourteen consecutive days.

CELEBRITY ANNUAL PASSES			
Regular annual pass	$45	$35	$45

Regular annual passes are valid 333 days in a year, excluding holiday periods.

Deluxe annual pass	$69	$59	$69

Deluxe annual passes are valid every day in a twelve-month period.

hours in the summer are generally 8:00 A.M. to 10:00 P.M. and for the rest of the year from 9:00 A.M. to 7:00 P.M.

You can see all of the park in one very full day. In recent years Universal Studios has regularly offered **second-day free promotions** during low season; these allow you to come back to the park within seven days. A two-day visit is a good way to combine the park with the dining and entertainment venues at Universal CityWalk.

Groucho, or an actor who looks pretty much like him, drives through Universal Studios Hollywood with Chico and Harpo look-alikes. *Photo by Corey Sandler*

You may want to purchase special combination tickets, such as the **Southern California Value Pass,** which offers unlimited admission to Universal Studios and SeaWorld San Diego over a fourteen-day period, or the **Hollywood City Pass** with admission to Universal Studios plus seven museums and attractions in the area.

And you should also consider an Annual Pass; in 2002, a **Celebrity Annual Pass** valid 333 non-holiday days of the year was priced the same as a single one-day pass. A **Deluxe Annual Pass,** without any blackout days, cost less than two single day passes. They also offer some additional privileges including discounts on merchandise and dining.

By the way, a quick and easy way to save some money is to eat breakfast before you arrive or pack a meal to eat outside the gates. That is, unless you prefer paying $3.29 for a sticky bun and $2.50 for a tiny carton of orange juice. There are lockers near the exits of the parking garages at Universal CityWalk.

ENTERTAINMENT CENTER

MUST-SEE TERMINATOR 2 3-D

He's back . . . and with a vengeance. Universal's newest major attraction is a tour de force of film and computer special effects that puts the audience in the middle of an epic battle between and among the fearsome "cinebotic" robots, live actors, and the reunited stars of *Terminator 2*: Arnold Schwarzenegger, Linda Hamilton, Robert Patrick, and Edward Furlong, along with director James Cameron and special effects wizards from the movie series.

In this newest Terminator adventure—which begins in the present day and jumps to the Los Angeles of 2029 as depicted in the film—Cyberdyne Systems, the dreaded creators of Skynet and its fearsome Terminator cyborgs, has moved its corporate headquarters to Universal Studios Hollywood in the back corner of the Upper Lot, to the left of the entrance. And the sinister company is determined to showcase its advanced technologies to the world.

Guests twist and turn in their seats as menacing Cyberdyne Systems "T-70" cinebotic warriors train their sights on random targets, firing across the theater. The audience leaps back in three-dimensional shock when the T-1000 Terminator "cop" from *Terminator 2* morphs to life before their very eyes, then cheers with relief as Schwarzenegger's T-800 cyborg literally charges off the screen to save the day astride a 1,500-pound Harley Davidson "hog," which lands on the stage and then dives back into the screen and into the scene.

And I don't want to spoil the fun, but you'll want to hold on to your seats for the jaw-dropping finale. You'll understand what I mean when your feet are back on solid ground.

Lockup

A room full of lockers to store stuff you don't want to drag through the park can be found just inside the entrance gates on the right side; boxes rent for $1.00 and $1.50 for the day.

The show begins with a "super" entertaining preshow sales pitch by Kimberly Duncan, Cyberdyne's director of community relations and media control. "Imagine a world where butterflies run on batteries," Cyberdyne asks, expecting you to do so with happy anticipation, "where human error is a thing of the past. Our goal is complete control of global communication."

It's all really "super." Really.

The associate unveils Skynet, a computer-controlled defense system, and then suddenly something goes wrong with the promotional video: it seems that hackers have broken into the system to warn us against Cyberdyne.

Terminator creator James Cameron, who directed this third installment of the saga as well as the blockbuster *Titanic,* regards Terminator 2 3-D as a true sequel to the earlier Terminator films. "It's definitely the next film," he says. "The only difference is this film is only twelve minutes long and you can't see it in just any theater."

Because the audience is in the present day, the film script uses T-70 cinebots, a design of robots not seen in the movies, which take place several decades in the future. The six T-70s each stand 8 feet tall; they rise from hiding places along the walls of the theater with the aid of a sophisticated hydraulic system.

This film marks the first time interlocking three-dimensional images have been projected onto multiple screens, surrounding guests in 180 degrees of action. For the climactic third act, the film opens up from one center screen to simultaneous projection on three screens, arranged at sixty-degree angles from each other.

According to Universal Studios, the twelve-minute-long film is, frame for frame, the most expensive motion picture ever produced.

Live-action scenes for the film took place at Kaiser Eagle Mountain, an abandoned steel foundry in Desert Center, California; the area was rebuilt in spectacular fashion to resemble Los Angeles in the aftermath of a nuclear war. More than a hundred cars, trucks, and buses were hauled in from wrecking yards and strewn about the one-million-square-foot location set.

The background consisted not of mockups but of actual buildings that were blown up during two weeks of filming, lending a scale authenticity that surpasses many big-budget Hollywood action flicks.

Additional scenes were shot on a Los Angeles soundstage, where an elaborate 24-foot "miniature" of Skynet, the pyramid-shaped headquarters of Cyberdyne Systems, was constructed. Through the magic of cinema trickery it appears to be 800 feet tall on screen.

The best seats for the 3-D effects are from the middle to the back of the theater; the best seats to see the live action, including the arrival of the Harley on stage and the frozen breakup finale, are in the third or fourth row, center.

The Terminator show is nearly identical to one at Universal Studios Florida.

⊞ MUST-SEE ⊞ BACK TO THE FUTURE . . . THE RIDE

Dive into the world of the record-breaking movie trilogy *Back to the Future* in Universal's incredible simulator adventure. It's a roller coaster of an attraction that never moves more than a few feet in any direction.

It seems that weird Doc Brown is back home conducting new time-travel experiments. He has created his newest vehicle—an eight-passenger Time Vehicle that is faster and more energy-efficient than anything before . . . or since. That's the good news. The bad news is that Biff Tannen has broken into the Institute of Future Technology and threatens to end the universe as we know it! It's up to you to jump into your own DeLorean and chase down Biff.

Surrounded by images and sound and buffeted by the realistic motion of your flight simulator, you soar into Hill Valley in the year 2015, blast back to the Ice Age for a chilling high-speed encounter with canyons of sheer ice, explode into the Volcanic Era for a once-in-a-lifetime encounter with a Tyrannosaurus Rex, and then go through a volcano and over the edge of a molten lava fall.

Don't Say You Weren't Warned

Back to the Future is described as a "dynamically aggressive ride." Visitors suffering from maladies including dizziness, seizures, back or neck problems, claustrophobia, motion sickness, and heart disorders, or pregnant women, are advised to sit this one out. The ride also won't work for persons of a certain size or shape who cannot fit into the seats and safety harness. We suspect you know who you are.

This is a state-of-the-art attraction that combines a spectacular 70-mm Omnimax film with simulator ride vehicles. The 80-foot-diameter dome-like screens of the Omnimax theaters occupy all of the viewer's peripheral vision, making the screen seem to vanish by taking the viewer into the scene.

There are three levels of twelve eight-seater DeLorean cars in the theater dome. Universal insiders say the very best experience can be had by sitting in the front row of the center car on the second tier. This particular vehicle is in the absolute center of the movie dome, and you cannot easily see any surrounding cars that might distract from the illusion. If you are concerned about getting motion sickness, you may want to try to get onto the lower level of the ride. (I prefer a Dramamine in the morning and the middle car.)

The Institute of Future Technology in the waiting area features actual props from the *Back to the Future*

Doc Brown waits for volunteers at Back to the Future . . . the Ride. *Photo by Corey Sandler*

movie series including hoverboards (specially adapted skateboards without wheels) and the all-important flux capacitors for time travel.

Check out the bulletin board in the waiting area where you see the names of some of the visiting scientists who have offices in the building. They include Thomas Edison, Albert Einstein, and Francis Bacon.

Some of Doc Brown's inventions are found in the waiting area outside the simulators. Check out the Time Man Personal Time Travel Suit prototype. There are lots of clocks on the walls including ones for Greenwich, Moscow, Tokyo, Sydney, Hollywood, Hill Valley, Mexico City, and Orlando. Hill Valley is set about five minutes ahead of Hollywood.

When you enter into the holding room for the simulator, try to maneuver next to the door to get a seat in the front of the car. (Some visitors find the small waiting room a bit confining; you can ask the attendant to leave the door open if you feel it necessary. Trust us: a much more intense experience is coming.)

As you wait to board, pay attention to the short movie about the essentials of time-travel safety; we enjoyed watching crash dummies Fender and Bender at work. When you feel a rumble beneath your feet, you'll know your car has arrived.

Coming Attraction

If you have really sharp eyes and a good sense of balance, keep an eye out during your wild Back to the Future ride for the movie poster on the wall in Hill Valley; it advertises *Jaws 19*.

The preshow film and the movie shown in the ride itself were made specially for the simulator. Doc Brown (Christopher Lloyd) and Biff Tannen (Thomas Wilson) make special appearances, but Marty McFly (Michael J. Fox) has missed his date with destiny.

The director of the film used in the Back to the Future ride was renowned movie special effects designer Douglas Trumbull, who created special effects for hits including *2001: A Space Odyssey* and *Close Encounters of the Third Kind*. The four-minute, 70-mm movie portion of the ride took two years to make and cost as much as a feature film. Elaborate hand-painted miniatures were created for the filming.

The glass case in the preflight waiting rooms includes some juicy details for fans of the film. The cabinets include communication devices such as telepathic projectors, a multilingual translator, and a telekinetic projector; there are also emergency supplies including first aid, travel rations, and dog biscuits. You'll also find hoverboards being energized in case they are needed.

The DeLoreans themselves rise about 8 feet out of their garages at the start of the movie. When in the air four actuators—three for vertical movement and one for fore-and-aft movement—drive the car. Although it may feel as if your car is soaring and dropping hundreds of feet, the entire range of movement for the vehicle is about 2 feet.

To give the feeling of traveling through space, the cars are surrounded with a fog made from liquid nitrogen.

⋮MUST-SEE⋮ *WATERWORLD—A LIVE SEA WAR SPECTACULAR*

A seaplane crashes through a wall of jagged steel, exploding straight at terrified onlookers. Underwater warriors rise from the sea to battle invaders on jet skis. A fiery figure falls 50 feet, turning a lagoon into a blazing inferno.

And it's all presented live at Universal's *Waterworld* stunt show, based on the spectacular but flawed movie of the same name. We don't have to worry about the movie, though: We can enjoy the spectacular live stunt show they've made here, with some sixty stunts and special effects and water vehicles including jet skis, motorboats, and air boats. Don't pay much attention to the corny script, though; it only gets in the way of the stunts and pyrotechnics.

Visitors pass through a collection of some of the props in the movie into another century after the polar cap has melted and turned planet Earth into Waterworld. They'll find themselves seated with a view of the atoll, a floating island of boats, barges, driftwood, and debris; it's a dangerous day to pay a visit, though. Roving pirates of the future are swarming about the atoll, led by the Hellfire Gunboat.

Alarms sound. Nets drop. Flares explode in the sky. And high-pressure water cannons aimed at slaloming hovercraft and jet skis blast past the audience. A dive-bomber makes a low-level run, tearing off a chunk of the wall and showering the visitors with salt spray. Avoid the green-painted "wet seats" unless you are looking for a free shower with your clothes on. Special effects in the show include a submerged catapult that slingshots a jet skier from beneath the water and onto the watery stage.

Above it all, the Legendary Mariner and Deacon—the leader of the cutthroat pirates—struggle for the fate of the future in hand-to-hand combat that climaxes in a death-defying plunge and an explosive firestorm that destroys the set . . . at least until the next performance.

The 2,800-seat stadium eats up lines pretty quickly, and at busy times of the year there are as many as eight performances a day. Lines are at their maximum by midday; head for the show early or late to avoid the crowds. And be aware that the complex special effects and outside forces such as high winds can sometimes cause cancellation of some of the stunts; on one of our visits, the spectacular seaplane never got off the ground.

▣ MUST-SEE ▣ *THE WILD WILD WILD WEST STUNT SHOW*

Yee-ha! This is a very silly, very entertaining live show with some spectacular stunts, bad jokes, and enough gunfire and explosions to wake Spider-Man next door. The storyline goes something like this: the professional stunt coordinator rides onto the set aboard his trusty steed to introduce a demonstration of Western skills only to find that his cast of cowboys has been kidnapped by Ma Hopper and her mean and ugly sons. The Hopper family proceeds to wreak havoc with guns, dynamite, and gross and dumb jokes, culminating in a shootout that literally brings down the house.

The twenty-minute show is well worth a visit. Parents be warned: the explosions and gunfire may upset young visitors.

▣ MUST-SEE ▣ *SPIDER-MAN ROCKS!*

Live, on stage: singing, dancing, and web-slinging romance.

"Spider-Man Rocks!" recounts the comic book tale of Peter Parker, his school boy crush on the beautiful Mary Jane Watson and the infamous bite from a genetically altered spider that forever changed the high school student into one of the world's greatest superhero legends.

Capturing the essence of this classic Marvel Comic superstar, the stage performance is entwined with the danger and suspense wrought upon Peter Parker by his arch nemesis, the Green Goblin, and the ethical code by which Spidey lives his life: "with great power, comes great responsibility."

The show's highlights include pyrotechnics and high-flying stunts that literally propel the web-spinning Spider-Man more than 30 feet in the air over the audience.

The twenty-minute show live performance is presented at the Castle Theater (site of the old Beetlejuice show).

▣ FIEVEL'S PLAYLAND

It's a small outdoor playground where the kids can burn off a bit of energy on some interesting props and slides related to the cartoon feature *An American Tail*.

NICKELODEON BLAST ZONE

Children have a place of their own in the Nickelodeon Blast Zone, an adventure zone that includes an elaborate water play area based on programs such as "Sponge Bob Square Pants"; "Wild Thornberry's Adventure Temple," a ball play area with more than twenty-five thousand molten lava-colored foam balls; "Nick Jr.'s Backyard" for children under the age of six to slide, crawl, and climb through; "Blue's Clues"; "Little Bear"; and "Dora the Explorer." "The Rugrats Magic Adventure" is due to be closed at the end of 2002 to be replaced in mid-2003 by **Shrek and Donkey's Scary-Tale Adventure,** a show based on the movie *Shrek*.

Also in the zone is Animal Planet Live!

🏁 MUST-SEE 🏁 *ANIMAL PLANET LIVE!*

Animal stars, including more than a few rescued from animal shelters, take center stage at *Animal Planet Live!* The show brings Animal Planet television network's favorite shows together with the behind-the-scenes movie magic.

Animal Planet Live! features special video clips from such popular Animal Planet television shows as "Emergency Vets," "The Planet's Funniest Animals," "The Jeff Corwin Experience," "Wild on the Set," and the network's lively animal sports programs.

Many of the animal stars featured in *Animal Planet Live!* have credits in film and television production. Almost of all the dogs and cats were rescued from shelters and pounds.

🏁 MUST-SEE 🏁 *THE RUGRATS MAGIC ADVENTURE* (LAST CALL)

All singing, all dancing, and all Rugrats. This live music and magic show—due to close by the end of 2002 to make room for Shrek and Donkey's Scary-Tale Adventure—stars many of the stars of the popular *Rugrats* animated television series, including Angelica, Tommy, Chuckie, Phil, and Lil. OK, well maybe those are humans inside the large rubber heads, but they are Rugrats, nevertheless.

The show is based on an episode, "Angelica the Magnificent,"

The Nickelodeon Blast Zone. *Photo by Corey Sandler*

in which Angelica puts on a Las Vegas–style show in her backyard. Appropriately some of the illusions and stunts were designed by the designers who created illusions for David Copperfield and Siegfried and Roy. One of the tricks, of course, is a levitating diaper. The show replaced the *Totally Nickelodeon* stage show.

BACK LOT TRAM TOUR

Sit down and relax for a guided motorized tour through a large part of the famed back lot of Universal Studios, a place where many of the most celebrated movies and television shows of all time have been made.

Universal Studios Hollywood is unusual among theme parks in that the audience is delivered by chauffeured tram to the attractions for about half of its exhibits. There's just a single line to wait in; after you are loaded onto the large tram you'll be driven to and through sets and props for movies and TV shows, including *Back to the Future, Murder, She Wrote, Psycho, Jurassic Park,* and much more. And you'll go right into exciting re-creations of thrillers, such as *Earthquake* and *Jaws.*

The tram vehicles include high-tech LCD screens that display scenes from movies and television shows along with the occasional outtake. Tour guides, many of whom are wannabe actors anyway, get to mug for a camera that displays their face through the cars, too. The guides get to select from a library of more than a hundred video clips to match their patter and deal with any detours along the way.

On a recent visit, as the tram crossed Court House Square, the LCDs showed the set as it was used in the *Back to the Future* series. At Spartacus Square the screens showed scenes from the movie *Spartacus.*

The loading queue for the tram is located down the hill at the back of the main Entertainment Center level of the park. Lines are shortest when the park first opens, and usually again in early afternoon; the last tram departs about two hours before the park closes. The length of each tour can vary depending on how busy the park is and shooting schedules that may affect parts of the back lot; but each tour generally lasts about sixty to ninety minutes.

When you load onto the tram, try to avoid sitting too far forward or you will end up breathing a fair amount of diesel fumes on your journey. Despite what the guide might say, don't worry about a "wet" or "dry" side of the tram; not much water makes its way into the tram on the tour. For the record, the right side (facing forward) of the tram is closest to the cascading waters in the *Earthquake* set, and the left side is nearest the flash flood in the back lot.

Cameras are welcome throughout the tour; there are no rest room stops, and there is no way to get off the tram short of an emergency.

The introduction to the tour is from director and actor Ron Howard. As you descend from the loading area to the soundstages below, the tram passes a time-line of some of the 8,000 movies made on the Universal lot.

The order of the tour as presented here may be different when you visit the

Coming Attraction: Shrek and Donkey's Scary-Tale Adventure

A 4-D presentation . . . in OgreVision, no less, that continues the fractured fable of Shrek.

When it opens in the spring of 2003 at both Universal Studios Hollywood and Universal Orlando, **Shrek and Donkey's Scary-Tale Adventure** will mark the first time an Oscar-winning animated film has been developed as a film-based theme park attraction. The show will occupy the former home of **The Rugrats Magic Adventure.**

The show will be presented in dual-chambered theatrical settings designed to introduce OgreVision sensory immersion, including images, sound, a bit of touch, and a smidgen of smell.

The fifteen-minute film includes all-new animation, a spectacular swamp-dwelling, 700-pound ogre with poor hygiene, picking up the tale where the Academy Award-winning Best Animated Feature *Shrek* left off. The experience reveals the tale of Shrek's honeymoon with the beautiful Princess Fiona and their persistent companion, Donkey.

Shrek and Donkey's Scary-Tale Adventure will bridge the story between Shrek and the much-awaited DreamWorks Pictures sequel, *Shrek II.*

Guests will be ushered into a forbidding pre-show chamber based on the dark and dank recesses of Lord Farquaad's dreaded dungeons. Via multiple screens, they'll be greeted by the vertically challenged Farquaad himself, who, in his first posthumous appearance, will inform guests of his ghostly scheme to haunt Shrek, Fiona, and their donkey companion.

Once settled in specially designed seats in the main auditorium, guests will don OgreVision glasses and will be transported to the fairy-tale realm of Duloc, as the screen and the theater itself comes alive with the tale of the Shrek-Fiona honeymoon adventure. Surprising sensory elements will help propel the narrative experience through seats equipped with tactile transducers, pneumatic air propulsion, and water spray nodules and capable of both vertical and horizontal motion.

Shrek 4-D marks the first animation to be created for a theme park attraction by PDI/DreamWorks, whose invention of the Fluid Animation System was recognized with a technical achievement Oscar by the Academy of Motion Picture Arts and Sciences. The addition of three-dimensional depth to the animation by PDI/DreamWorks and the creation of in-theater effects by attraction designers at Universal Creative resulted in the introduction of the OgreVision multisensory experience.

In both Universal Orlando and Universal Studios Hollywood, the Shrek film will be housed in its own castle-like building with an hourly capacity of as many as 2,400 guests.

The original film was based on the children's book by William Steig. In the film, an ornery ogre named Shrek (voiced by Mike Myers) finds his solitude shattered by an invasion of annoying fairy-tale characters. Suddenly, there are blind mice in his food; a big, bad wolf in his bed; and three little homeless pigs in his personal space. All of them have been banished from their kingdom by the evil Lord Farquaad (John Lithgow).

Shrek strikes a deal with Farquaad to rescue the beautiful princess Fiona (Cameron Diaz) to be Farquaad's bride and get the unexpected visitors out of his hair. He sets off with the Donkey (Eddie Murphy) on a great expedition that reveals a deep, dark, and twisted secret.

park because of television or movie production schedules; sometimes entire sections have to be skipped because the cameras are rolling on the lot.

Front Lot Soundstages

Depending on shooting schedules and the time of year the back lot tour may give you a brief glimpse of part of the front lot—the soundstages. If you're lucky you may see a television or movie star strolling by, or perhaps grab a quick glimpse inside the open door of one of the large soundstages there; otherwise, you're going to see a lot of blank walls.

Universal's facilities are in almost continuous use for productions of television series and movies. Stage 27 housed Houston Mission Control for *Apollo 13*. Stage 28 holds the historic Paris Opera House set used in the classic *Phantom of the Opera* and many other films since. The Sultan of Strangeness Michael Jackson (and sister Janet Jackson) installed a flying saucer in Stage 24 for the "Scream" music video.

Colonial Street

Where else but in Hollywood could you expect to find a neighborhood that includes the homes of Beaver Cleaver, Herman Munster, Jessica Fletcher, the Hardy Boys, Elvis Presley, Casper, Ronald Reagan in *Bedtime for Bonzo,* Buffy in *Buffy the Vampire Slayer,* and many more? And where else would you find *The Best Little Whorehouse in Texas* at the end of the street? (The whorehouse was created within Stage 12 and the movie was filmed there; the set was later moved to its outdoor location.)

The official address is Colonial Street, and your tour guide will point out such sites as Frank and Joe Hardy's house from the *Hardy Boys* TV mysteries of the 1970s. Next-door to the Hardys is the home occupied by James Garner and Doris Day in *The Thrill of It All.* Just a bit farther down the road is an old

AAA S.O.S.

Card-carrying members of AAA can claim a 10 percent discount at most shops within Universal Studios.

A small-scale model used in the film *U-571* floats on a pond in the back lot. *Photo by Corey Sandler*

Colonial mansion that among other roles served as the sanitarium in James Stewart's beloved film *Harvey*.

At 1313 Mockingbird Lane is the home of the Munsters, nearby to one of Faber College's sorority houses from *Animal House*.

Then we're on to a portion of the town of Cabot Cove, made famous in the *Murder, She Wrote* series, one of Universal's most successful television projects. The brick building on the street has served as both the Cabot Cove Savings Bank and the Cabot Cove Town Hall; back in the '60s it was where the Beaver went to school in *Leave It to Beaver*.

Many of the homes on Colonial Street were used in the film *The Burbs* starring Tom Hanks and Carrie Fisher. And then the same street became Memphis, Tennessee, for an episode of *Quantum Leap* in which Sam leaps into the body of the King himself, Elvis Presley. Yet another remake made it one of the homes of Casper the Friendly Ghost.

Industrial Street
Many of the homes in this area are actual residences that were purchased for as little as $1 each and moved to the back lot to be used in the classic film *To Kill a Mockingbird* starring Gregory Peck and a then-unknown actor named Robert Duvall.

Old Mexico
In addition to standing in for some scenes in *Murder, She Wrote*, this area has been used for many old films and contemporary television shows. It was home of many scenes in the comedy *Three Amigos* with Steve Martin, Martin Short, and Chevy Chase.

Old West

Across the border from Mexico is the oldest section of the Universal Studios back lot, a filmmaker's re-creation of the Old West also known as Six Points, Texas. Many of the buildings, which appear to be made of brick or stone, are actually constructed of wood, chicken wire, and modern products such as foam rubber or fiberglass.

Note that some of the doors seem out of scale. Small doors were used to make small actors appear bigger and more threatening than they really were; oversize doors shrank tall cowboys and cowgirls down to size for the camera.

Old West was the home of stars including John Wayne, Tom Mix, Hoot Gibson, Audie Murphy, Ken Maynard, and others. Among the television series made there was *Wagon Train*. In more recent times, it was used in the United Artists' film *Wild Bill*.

At its height, there could be six films underway on the six streets at the same time; since the movies were silent, all the directors had to worry about was the possibility of an actor making a wrong turn from one film to another.

Old West's basic setup includes a hotel, bar, bank, and sheriff's office. In other words, a bad guy could stroll into town, get a drink, spend the night, rob the bank, and end up in jail.

Prop Storage

A prop on a movie set is just about anything that isn't nailed down. Some are small and some are huge; some are ordinary and some are one of a kind. More than a million of the studio's props are kept in the property warehouse at the back corner of the back lot, but many of the larger pieces are scattered outdoors. The tram tour does not enter the prop building; guests on the more expensive VIP Tour, though, are allowed an inside peek.

Along the course of the tram tour you'll pass by bits and pieces of the past and future from *Back to the Future*, fossils and props from *Jurassic Park*, and various vehicles from dozens of familiar movies.

In the middle of the props area is a tiny lake—more of a pond, really. This body of water served as the entire Pacific Ocean every week in the popular TV series *McHale's Navy*. The pond was also used for some of the shooting in the 1977 film *Midway*. Scale models of battleships and cruisers made war on the pond; some of the vessels were painted in Allied colors on one side and Japanese colors on the other so that they could serve double duty in the war.

When it rains . . .

you will get wet. Most of Universal Studios Hollywood is outdoors. The Back Lot Tram is exposed to the elements, and most of the shows are also uncovered.

Flimsy plastic rain jackets appear magically at shops, priced at about $6.95; umbrellas are priced about $16.95. If the skies are at all threatening, I'd suggest you make a stop at a discount store outside the park and pick up ponchos or umbrellas to bring with you. Some of the shows may be canceled because of rain.

In 2002, Universal Studios Hollywood introduced a "rain check" policy. Here's how it works: if it rains one-sixteenth of an inch or more before 2:00 P.M., visitors will be given a free ticket to return to the park anytime within the next 30 days.

After you exit Sound Stage 50 you'll have another view of the pond. It was also used as the home of *The Creature from the Black Lagoon* in 1954.

You will see a large metal tank that has been used in many underwater scenes including the original *Jaws*. The actors and props are placed within the tank while cameras and crew are outside, looking in through windows.

You may see some of the old wagons used in *Wagon Train* and *The Virginian*. Nearby on one of my trips was a gigantic football helmet and a huge shopping cart, both from the film *The Incredible Shrinking Woman* with Lily Tomlin. Another time the tram caught a glimpse of a chariot from *The Ten Commandments*.

Psycho House

Is there any house more famous than Mrs. Bates's pleasant Victorian up on the hill over the Bates Motel?

You'll approach the house alongside the small swamp used by Norman Bates (Anthony Perkins) to bury the car of Marion Crane (Janet Leigh) in the 1960 Alfred Hitchcock classic, *Psycho*. Later on in the tour you'll approach Psycho House a bit closer.

The house was built to three-quarter scale, which helped make Anthony Perkins look taller and more menacing as he posed in the foreground. When the house itself was pictured it was always shot from below to look larger.

The house is a shell with a complete outside but nothing within except for the beams that help keep it standing; well, OK, some wag did stick a dummy that looks like Norman's mom in the second floor window. It is a dummy, right? Indoor scenes were all shot on a soundstage.

Nearby is the Bates Motel, more or less as it was created for the original film. The archway entrance in front did not appear in any of the *Psycho* films but was added in 1986 for a television movie of the week called *Bates Motel*.

Spartacus Square

Parts of the classic film *Spartacus* were filmed in the section that is named in its honor; the same section was again used as ancient Rome in the great Mel Brooks spoof, *History of the World, Part I*.

Little Europe

This section of old buildings stood in for Greece in Brooks' *History of the World*. More recently it was Pamplona, Spain, for the opening sequence of *City Slickers*. Way back when, Little Europe was home of the classic antiwar film, *All Quiet on the Western Front*.

When Brenda and Donna left *Beverly Hills 90210* to go to France, they actually went just across town to Little Europe. Other television shows that have used this area include *Sea Quest DSV* and, of course, the ubiquitous *Murder, She Wrote*. The quirky television series *Moonlighting* filmed its takeoff of *The Taming of the Shrew* here.

Real film history can be glimpsed in the Court of Miracles, built in 1919 for the film *The Miracle Man* starring Lon Chaney. But it is most famous for the monster movie classics that followed, including Chaney in 1923's *The Hunchback of Notre Dame* and again in 1925 for *The Phantom of the Opera*. In 1930, Bela Lugosi was *Dracula* here; later classics included *Frankenstein, The Bride of Frankenstein, The Son of Frankenstein, Abbott and Costello Meet Frankenstein, The Wolf Man, The Mummy,* and *The Invisible Man*.

▪ MUST-SEE ▪ Earthquake

Quiet, now: You've got a green light to drive right into Stage 50, a real working soundstage. Well, it's sort of a real stage (and still in occasional use for special projects), but it's mostly given over to a spectacular re-creation of a scene from the 1974 disaster epic, *Earthquake*.

Bigger . . . (and certainly better) than the real thing, Universal's Earthquake unleashes an 8.3 temblor beneath your feet.

The earth falls out from under tramloads of visitors, trapping them in an underground subway station with sparking wires, out-of-control trains, and even a fuel truck that crashes through the ceiling and onto the tracks. Just to cap it all, water pipes let loose and trigger a 15-foot-tall wall of water in a 60,000-gallon flood.

Every detail of the simulation was based on the re-creation of real earthquakes. The soundstage was built with concrete pilings sunk 25 feet into the ground below the tram to withstand 600,000 pounds of force more than 200 times a day. The ceiling slab that falls into the subway station weighs 11,000 pounds.

The simulated earthquake is the equivalent of an 8.3 event on the Richter scale, which is the same level as the huge temblor that destroyed San Francisco in 1906. By comparison, the 1971 Sylmar quake measured 6.6, and the 1985 Mexico City disaster was an 8.1 event.

The simulation lasts for about two-and-a-half minutes. After your tram exits the soundstage, the entire set resets in fifteen seconds.

If it makes you feel better, engineers say the soundstage is built to withstand a genuine 8.3 quake, making it one of the safest places in the world to be during a real earthquake.

The *Earthquake* set was used for a scene in *Beverly Hills Cop 3*, which took place in a fictional amusement park. Just outside the *Earthquake* set is Stage 747, which includes full-size mock-ups of airplane interiors used regularly as sets in films and television shows.

Courthouse Square

The year is 1955. The date is November 5. And the time is 10:03 P.M. Down this road—with the aid of a great deal of movie magic—Marty McFly drove Doc Brown's time-traveling DeLorean at precisely 88 miles per hour hoping to catch the lightning bolt just in time to go back to 1985.

You'll see the Hill Valley courthouse more or less as it appeared in the film *Back to the Future* and its sequel, *Back to the Future 2*. It has also been used in many other films during the years.

▮MUST-SEE▮ King Kong

One of the most realistic sets at Universal Studios Hollywood can be found within a soundstage just past the Courthouse Square. It's a re-creation of lower Manhattan . . . and it smells suspiciously like bananas.

Your tram driver will take you and other passengers directly into an attraction that celebrates the spectacular 1976 version of the classic film, *King Kong*. The remake starred Jeff Bridges, Charles Grodin, and an unknown actress by the name of Jessica Lange, who went on to be an Academy Award winner.

King Kong rises out of the East River, towers over the Brooklyn Bridge, rips down power lines, attacks a hovering news helicopter, and then even tries to throw Universal's trams into the river as they move across the bridge. Kong comes within a few feet of the tram—so close you'll be able to smell the bananas on his breath.

Computers control twenty-nine facial movements from nodding his head to curling his lip to showing his vicious artificial teeth. (Movements are controlled mostly by pneumatic air pipes.)

The $6.5 million leading man really throws his weight around. He's seven tons of fur, steel, and computers and stands 30 feet high.

New York Street

Welcome to an all-purpose downtown home of scenes from *Columbo, McCloud, McMillan and Wife, Kojak, Ironside, The Rockford Files, The Streets of San Francisco, The Mod Squad, Baretta, The Night Stalker,* and many more.

In 1969 these streets were walked by Elvis himself for his final film role in *A Change of Habit*, also starring Mary Tyler Moore. Four years later New York Street became Chicago in the Academy Award–winning film *The Sting* starring Robert Redford and Paul Newman.

In 1977 New York Street was used to film scenes from the Warner Bros. classic movie *Dirty Harry* starring Clint Eastwood. A few years later it was turned into modern-day Chicago for *The Blues Brothers,* which starred John Belushi and Dan Aykroyd. It became London for *Wayne's World 2* and then transformed back to 1930s New York in many scenes from *The Shadow* starring Alec Baldwin.

Nearly all of New York Street was destroyed in a fire in 1991, but the re-creation of the Big Apple was re-created again.

On one of my visits a few years back many of the buildings were draped with fake icicles for a scene depicting the aftermath of a visit by Mr. Freeze in the movie *Batman & Robin*.

Collapsing Bridge

A bridge somewhat like this one was built in 1915 for a silent film. More recently it was used in television shows including *The Six Million Dollar Man* and *Quantum Leap*.

In the *Bionic Woman* series star Lindsay Wagner was shown jumping up from the water to the bridge. Actually a stuntwoman jumped backward from the bridge to the water and the film was reversed. If you ever see the scene, note the

A studio tour tram about to cross the reliably shaky collapsing bridge on the back lot. *Photo by Corey Sandler*

filmmakers' goof: her hair was not tied down and defies the law of gravity as she seems to fly upward.

These days the bridge has been fixed up so that it falls down . . . as the tram passes over the top. Don't worry, though: most passengers survive to make it to the souvenir shops.

Vehicles

The "boneyard" of the back lot includes dozens of vehicles from movies and television shows. You may spot one of several red Ferraris used in the television series *Magnum P.I.* starring Tom Selleck. Nearby on a recent visit was the much less impressive Mousemobile driven by John Candy as *Uncle Buck* in the film of the same name.

You may also see some small vehicles from *The Little Rascals,* DeLoreans used in *Back to the Future,* and some retro-military gear from *Waterworld.*

Bedrock and Jurassic Park

Still standing on both sides of the road is a piece of Bedrock, as it was constructed for *The Flintstones.* You'll see Barney and Betty Rubble's house and their car. Check out the welcoming sign with the town's claim to fame: "Bedrock: First with Fire."

Parked alongside the road just past Bedrock is the jeep that was nearly torn to pieces by a T. rex in *Jurassic Park.* Most of that film was filmed inside soundstages at Universal Studios Hollywood with just a small amount of exterior footage taken in Hawaii.

Jaws emerges from the lake to menace guests on a back lot tram. *Photo by Corey Sandler*

Flash Flood

The road that leads down toward Old Mexico was covered with dirt to become the Appian Way for *Spartacus* in 1960; hundreds of Roman soldiers marched right into ancient Rome.

Today's tour-goers, though, are given a watery treat as movie special effects are used to simulate a raging flash flood that roars down the hill on the left side of the tram. Some 10,000 gallons of water drop down from the top of the hill; it's all pumped back up for the next visitors. The flash flood scene was used in the film *Fletch Lives* in 1989.

MUST-SEE Jaws

Welcome to Amity Island, the reconstructed scene of some of the action from the classic 1975 fish-food movie, *Jaws*. Jaws Lake not only serves as the backdrop for the shark, but also stood in for Cabot Cove, Maine, in exterior scenes from (yes, again) *Murder, She Wrote*. The hairpin turn that leads past the lake is where Jessica Fletcher rode her bicycle every week at the beginning of the show.

Past the lake you come to the small home where Lansbury/Fletcher did her gardening. The same house has also been used in other productions including *Quantum Leap* and the mostly forgotten film *Shout* starring John Travolta.

Nearby is a light-colored house with green trim that was the home of Ben Matlock from the *Matlock* TV series. Next to Matlock's house is the home used in the classic Vincent Price horror film, *The House of the Seven Gables*.

Some of the scenes from the *Casper* movie were also shot near the lake.

Wilderness

As your tram begins to approach the wilderness area, you will come to a large log cabin that was used in *The Great Outdoors* and then later as an important element of the Paramount comedy *Naked Gun 33⅓.*

The wilderness, covered with fake snow, became the Antarctic for the remake of *The Thing.* A large painted backdrop behind a small lake was used for the splashdown scene for 1995's *Apollo 13.*

Just past the lake, your tram enters a tunnel . . . and into Gomorrah, a dizzying salute to the film *Scorpion King.* Over the years the same tunnel stood in for the Tomb of Imhotep from *The Mummy,* before then as a fiery hell for *Dante's Peak,* and before then as an icy avalanche zone. Whatever, if you're prone to dizziness, take the opportunity to close your eyes and take a short nap.

The tunnel was used in a scene from *The Six Million Dollar Man,* and according to studio legend, star Lee Majors became so dizzy he had a major problem staying upright long enough to get through his part.

STUDIO CENTER

The Studio Center is located down the hill from the Entertainment Center at the bottom of a series of three long escalators, a 200-foot drop down a 1,200-foot-long cascade of moving stairs.

The long trek down to the center is a good reason why you'll want to plan your day at Universal. It is not a minor thing to go from one area to another at the park. (There is, by the way, alternate shuttle transportation between the upper and lower parts of Universal Studios for disabled guests.)

▌*MUST-SEE*▐ JURASSIC PARK—THE RIDE

A spectacular ride millions of years (and $100 million) in the making: Jurassic Park—The Ride is the big splash of the lower level of the park.

The attraction, one of the most expensive and technologically advanced theme park adventures ever created, fulfills Universal Studio's promise to allow visitors to "ride the movies," in this case Steven Spielberg's version of Michael Crichton's bestselling novel and one of the most popular motion pictures of all time, ancient and modern.

You'll enter through the 35-foot-tall wooden gates of Jurassic Park. As you wait your turn to board your exploration raft, you'll see a multimedia preshow presented on massive video walls. The film features John Hammond, founder and owner of Jurassic Park; as in the movie, Hammond is played by distinguished actor Sir Richard Attenborough.

The journey begins as a gentle exploration of Jurassic Park's dinosaur habitat. The rafts explore the misty fog banks, brilliantly colored foliage, and exotic vegetation of "Herbivore Country," home of the vegetarians of the dinosaur world. Not to worry, though: The swift Velociraptors and the ferocious Tyrannosaurus rex are securely contained nearby in Carnivore Canyon behind a sparking 10,000-volt electrified fence.

A splash landing at Jurassic Park. *Photo by Corey Sandler*

The boats gently cruise through radiant Ultrasaur Lagoon with gentle waterfalls and clear tide pools. Just a finger away sits a gigantic 50-foot Ultrasaurus cooling off at the water's edge. The boat is nudged by what seems to be a rock below the surface, but it turns out to be a surprised baby Ultrasaurus, who eyes the riders curiously.

As the rafts glide out of the river two rambunctious Psittacosauruses frolic nearby, splashing water across the boat's bow. Erupting geysers spew billows of white steam as the boat arrives at Stegosaur Pond, where mother and baby Stegosauruses seem happy to have company. Small dinosaurs known as "Compys" shriek their greetings.

Riding an increasingly swift current, the boat moves into Hadrosaur Cove. Suddenly the waters begin racing and the raft is driven dangerously off-course into Carnivore Canyon, very close to the Velociraptor pen. And bad news: There's a jagged, gaping hole in the electrified fence. The vicious Velociraptors are nowhere to be seen, and signs of danger surround guests on the raft as it continues to veer out of control and deeper into unknown territory. A wrecked land cruiser dangles perilously from a nearby guardrail.

An empty abandoned raft drifts by; suddenly a "Spitter" rears his multicolored crown and bares his teeth in a sinister smile.

Jurassic Park's water pumping station is bedlam. Alarms blare as catwalks collapse and some of the station's pipes give way, spraying scalding water in the path of the raft. A pack of voracious Raptors spring forward and begin to pursue the runaway raft.

And then . . . well, we're not going to spoil all of the scary fun except to say that sooner or later the rafts plunge into an 84-foot drop in total darkness, splashing into the lagoon at speeds of nearly fifty miles per hour. (It's claimed to be the longest, fastest water plunge at any theme park.) To make things even more interesting, the drop includes a "vertical curve" (you might call it a bump) that makes riders feel that their boat is being lifted straight up before it nearly tips over and smashes to the lagoon below.

The ride technology includes some of the most advanced animatronic dinosaurs anywhere, using a new technique dubbed "compliant reactivity" to model the interaction of different parts of a body as it moves. Many of the dinosaurs are programmed to react to the presence of visitors, some attacking at speeds of up to 25 feet per second with the quickness of a striking rattlesnake.

Stars of the park include Ultrasaurus, tall as a five-story building; the armor-plated 18-foot tall Stegosaurus, 40 feet long from nose to tail; and the relentlessly pursuing Tyrannosaurus rex.

The twenty-five-passenger boats are the largest amusement ride watercraft ever built; they are free-flowing, not on tracks. The boats are paced by computer to travel at least thirty seconds behind the boat ahead, propelled along by 1.4 million gallons of rushing water.

The sixteen boats can move about 3,000 visitors per hour through the park for the ride, which lasts about five-and-a-half minutes. That still won't be enough to eliminate long lines from mid-morning through dinner; arrive early or late.

The minimum height to ride is 42 inches.

A restaurant, **Jurassic Cove Cafe,** and a retail shop, Jurassic Outfitters, are included in the compound. Look in the cement outside the restaurant for director Steven Spielberg's autograph and a special message to riders.

And I hope you've read down this far before riding: You can purchase inexpensive ponchos just outside the entrance to the ride. The front seats of the boats are usually the wettest.

The Starway escalators descend to the Lower Lot. *Photo by Corey Sandler*

The Park at Jurassic Park

The re-created world of *Jurassic Park* includes some spectacular greenery. There are some 353 palm trees of eleven species, including Sago, King, Queen, Kentia, and Canary Island Date. Gardeners put in 926 additional trees of thirty-three species, including Flame, Golden Rain, Orchid, Australian Tree Fern, Giant Bird of Paradise, and Dragon. Finally, there are 7,441 shrubs, plants, and seventy-six species of flowers, including Star Jasmine, Breath of Heaven, Rattlesnake Grass, Tasmanian Tree Fern, Shell Ginger, Mystery Gardenia, Sugar Bush, Bougainvillea, and Giant Burmese Honeysuckle. Scattered about are 300 bamboo plants of six varieties.

MUST-SEE BACKDRAFT

A back draft is a fire that has consumed all the oxygen in a room, leaving only superheated gas waiting for a fresh breath of air. *Backdraft* is also the name of a successful thriller by director Ron Howard, celebrated here in a spectacular demonstration.

You'll learn how the film included real blazes set in old warehouses in Chicago. Actor Scott Glenn tells about how flame-retardant underwear he wore in one important scene worked not quite long enough for comfort; he also exposes some of the secrets of the Ashmatic, a machine created for the movie that shot burning ash over the cast.

Backdraft includes a spectacular re-creation of some of the wildest scenes from the movie; in fact, the effects in this show are a lot more real than some of the movie magic seen in the film. As many as 200 times a day the Backdraft soundstage becomes a fiery furnace with ruptured fuel lines, superheated air, and scalding heat.

When you first enter the soundstage you'll watch a backdraft flame spinning wildly around the fictitious Nikolas Randall and Company chemical building. That is, of course, merely the overture: suddenly there's a massive explosion of fuel drums, which in turn causes overhead pipes to burst and spew their flammable contents toward the audience. The flames become a firestorm, reaching more than 2,000 degrees. The soundstage was built as a completely fireproof building; a special invisible "air curtain" protects visitors from the flames that march toward them.

There's a control room behind a glass window at the back of the Backdraft room where a technician supervises the show for safety purposes, as well as abundant fire extinguishers and other safety equipment in the room. Construction of the building required special dispensation from the Hollywood Fire Department.

MUST-SEE E.T. ADVENTURE

Climb aboard a flying bicycle, feel the wind in your face, and venture across the universe with E.T. in an effort to save his dying Green Planet in a spectacular, $40 million re-creation of the wondrous movie.

The attraction begins with a preshow film with director Steven Spielberg introducing E.T. and the ride that awaits you. "He must go home, and only you can help him," Spielberg says.

You're stopped soon afterward at a check-in station where an attendant asks you your name and gives you your Interplanetary Passport; hold on to it for later on.

Then you walk through one of the most imaginative, fully realized scene-setting waiting lines at any theme park, a forest where you can keep an eye on the searchers for the extraterrestrial all around you. If the ride is not too crowded, or if you're not in a rush, take your time and look around. Smell the smells, feel the fog.

Following an urgent plea from E.T.'s teacher Botanicus, E.T. and his new-found friends—that's you—escape government agents in a spooky forest and take flight on bicycles on a tour above Los Angeles. You'll go with him and eventually arrive at the Green Planet. Through a thick haze and a shower of volcanic ash E.T. extends his magic finger to help his friends Orbidon, Maagdol, and Tickli Moot Moots. Restored, they celebrate with you.

Special effects in the E.T. show include thousands of fiberoptic stars, fifty robots, a life-size redwood forest, and white billowy clouds.

At the end of the ride, E.T. thanks you for your help . . . by name.

As you exit the E.T. ride and emerge from the building, look to your left next to the escalator to see a re-creation of E.T.'s transmitter as used in the movie; it's constructed from a "Speak and Spell" toy, an old record player, a coffee can, and a tinfoil-covered umbrella.

The elaborate preshow area of the film received a spruce-up in 2002 as part of the commemoration of the twentieth anniversary of the original film.

Monitors display footage of the making of the film, featuring cast members Drew Barrymore, Henry Thomas, and Dee Wallace Stone, along with a bit of insight from director Steven Spielberg about his vision for the film. There's also a presentation by Search for Extra Terrestrial Intelligence (SETI) scientist Frank Drake, who comments on the film from a scientific perspective and demonstrates a sampling of radio frequencies picked up by radio telescopes that search for extraterrestrial life.

The E.T. Adventure at Universal Studios was envisioned by Spielberg as a continuation of the story told in the film. "The E.T. Adventure is the only place in the entire world where you can actually meet E.T.," says Spielberg in the introduction.

■ LUCY: A TRIBUTE

If you are a fan of Lucille Ball and everyone around her, you'll be enthralled at this collection of photos, scripts, memorabilia, and a continuous showing of episodes from her television show. Among my personal favorites is Lucy as part of a barbershop quartet.

There is a diorama showing how the original television show was filmed in front of a live audience. The show was shot on 35-mm black-and-white film on one large set; episodes were edited and combined for the final show.

You'll see part of the script from *Mame,* which in 1974 marked Lucy's final return to the big screen, and a display of her five Emmy awards. There's also a

Lucy, I'm home!

The original TV show was unusual in that the creators worked with three or four permanent sets that stood side-by-side in the studio, avoiding the flimsy-looking sets typical of television shows at the time. The permanent setting also allowed for more advanced lighting, allowing cameras to move quickly from one area to another. All of the sets were painted in carefully chosen shades of gray to control the contrast of the finished black-and-white film.

"Lucy" trivia quiz including questions like, "What was the biggest laugh in Lucy history?"

Here's a hint: the answer involves Lucy, Ricky, a bunch of raw eggs, and a wild and romantic dance. You figure it out.

On display are photos of Lucille Ball's home on Roxbury Drive in Beverly Hills where she lived for thirty-five years. Next-door neighbors were the Jack Benny family, and the Jimmy Stewart family lived across the street. There's also a selection of home movies narrated by Luci Arnaz and a collection of stereoscopic slides of Lucy's family taken in the 1950s.

Desi Arnaz was born Desiderio Alberto Arnaz y de Acha III in Santiago, Cuba, in 1917. The son of a Cuban senator, he lived in great luxury until the Cuban revolution of 1933 when the family left the country. Arnaz worked at various jobs, including cleaning birdcages for 25 cents.

Eventually he got a job in a band and soon became one of the top band leaders in New York. Signed to the lead in the New York musical "Too Many Girls," he played a Latin football player. When he went to Hollywood to play his role in the movie version of the musical, he met the studio ingenue Lucille Ball, and in late 1940 they began a bicoastal marriage.

After World War II, looking for a way to work together in Los Angeles, Lucy and Desi hired the writers of Lucy's radio show "My Favorite Husband" and produced a pilot for "I Love Lucy." Their company, Desilu Productions, became the largest television and film production company in Hollywood. Arnaz died in 1986. Lucy passed on in 1989.

■ SPECIAL EFFECTS STAGES

At Stage 1, visitors are introduced to a "virtual studio" showcasing green-screen compositing techniques and computer-generated imagery (CGI) such as was used to bring the *Jurassic Park* dinosaurs back from extinction. Two adult volunteers step into the movies, playing with a gigantic pussycat projected through a window, and sitting down to dinner with *The Nutty Professor*.

Stage 2 showcases Universal's historical "creature factory." Guests see some rare, behind-the-scenes footage of special effects pioneered by makeup artist Jack Pierce for *Frankenstein, Dracula,* and the original *Mummy*. There's also an introduction to the elaborate makeup techniques used to transform Jim Carrey into the Grinch, a process that took as much as four hours per day.

You'll learn some of the insider secrets of "stage blood." In black-and-white movies, like *Psycho,* Janet Leigh bled Hershey's chocolate syrup. For color films, technicians worked with colored corn syrup; some modern special effects departments use colored dish detergent, which has the added advantage of being easy to clean up.

Visitors also meet Fluffy, a "robotic" creature controlled by an audience volunteer—or so it seems. The attraction concludes at Stage 3, which features the art of Foley sound effects production, a technique pioneered by Universal's legendary sound man, Jack Donovan Foley in the 1920s. Guests participate in recreating sound effects such as those used in *U-571*, *Shrek*, and *The Scorpion King*.

Special Effects Stages replaced *The World of Cinemagic*.

EATING YOUR WAY THROUGH UNIVERSAL STUDIOS HOLLYWOOD

Soft drinks at Universal Studios are pricey at about $2.50 for a regular-size cup and nearly $4.00 for a large drink. You'll also find beer wagons at several locations.

In 2002, the **Saddle Ranch Chop House,** an Urban Cowboy–like eatery modeled after the original on Sunset Boulevard opened just outside the gates of the park.

■ ENTERTAINMENT CENTER

Carleon & Sons. Chicago-style pizza, hot dogs, ice cream, pies and pastries, salads, sandwiches, and espresso and cappuccino, with entrees priced from about $4.00 to $8.00.

Deli Variety. Breakfast deli sandwiches, pickles, burgers, French fries, handmade pretzels, and beer.

Doc Brown's Fancy Fried Chicken. Chicken dinners, biscuits, and corn on the cob. A three-piece basket of fried chicken is priced at about $6.00; a full dinner with potatoes and gravy is priced about a dollar higher. (Open in season only.)

Hollywood Cantina. Fajitas, tacos, burritos, nachos, enchiladas, and other Mexican favorites, priced from about $4.00 for soft tacos to $6.00 for fajitas. Platters, including rice and beans, sell for about a dollar more.

Mel's Diner. A remake of a 1950s diner reminiscent of the eatery in American Graffiti. Load up on burgers, fried chicken, hot dogs, and other fine fare, priced from about $3.00 to $6.00.

Ristorante Italia. Pizza by the slice from $2.95 for cheese, $3.25 for pepperoni, and $3.50 for barbecued chicken or vegetarian toppings. Also available are spaghetti, ziti, Italian sausage, and other dishes for about $5.00.

River Princess. Set inside a simulation of a riverboat with a wheelhouse above, the restaurant offers burgers, hot dogs, heroes, and cherry cobblers. Offerings priced at about $5.00 to $7.00 include barbecued chicken salad and a turkey and cheddar cheese sandwich on squaw bread. The super hero sandwich serves four to six people and is priced at about $18.

Mel's Diner on the Upper Lot. *Photo by Corey Sandler*

Roman Noodle #1. A Tuscan-style Italian cafeteria serving pizza, lasagna, fresh pasta, and garlic sticks. Entrees range from about $5.50 to $7.00.

■ STUDIO CENTER

Jurassic Cove Cafe. Bronto burgers, ribs, and salads . . . much fresher than the Jurassic period.

Margarita Bar. Margaritas, beer, and lemonade.

Studio Commissary. Philly steak sandwiches, tostada salads, and pizzas.

UNIVERSAL CITYWALK

In typical Hollywood fashion, Universal Studios saw a place where there should be a city—a clean, safe, and fun city—and so that was what they built. The concept for the development was for a street that was not an imitation of any particular place or time period, but instead a sort of architectural collage of the images and traits of Los Angeles without duplicating any buildings.

Universal CityWalk is an easy five- to ten-minute walk from the Entertainment Center of Universal Studios, making it an attractive alternative to the fast food of the theme park for lunch or dinner. See if you can convince the kids to save some of their souvenir money for the neat shops here.

Stores are open seven days a week from 11:00 A.M. to 11:00 P.M. with longer hours at peak times. By night Universal CityWalk comes alive with fabulous lighting that includes crackle-tube neon, cove and accent lighting, towers with theatrical lighting, and light-reflecting panels that splash color throughout the plazas. The Museum of Neon Art displays vintage neon signs along the street.

CityWalk has been a big success, and was nearly doubled in size in 2000 with new shops and restaurants and a multimedia sound and light system. CityWalk connects to the 6,200-seat Universal Amphitheatre, the eighteen-screen Universal City Cinemas, and the Universal Studios theme park.

You'll have to pay to park your car at Universal Studios; some of the clubs and theaters offer reimbursement or special deals for car owners.

■ ENTERTAINMENT AT CITYWALK

B. B. King's Blues Club and Memphis Restaurant. Authentic Southern cuisine and live blues music seven nights a week at the Los Angeles version of the original club on Beale Street in Memphis. (818) 622–5464.

Hard Rock Café Hollywood. Down-home American food seasoned with a bit of rock 'n' roll; includes occasional live performances. There is, of course, a gift shop. (818) 622–7625. www.hardrock.com.

Howl at the Moon. Dueling pianos.

Imax 3D Theatre. Six-story-high screen featuring high-tech projectors and Sonics Proportional Point Source Loudspeaker system.

Jillian's Hi Life Lanes. Multi-level rock 'n' roll bowling alley and interactive games room.

NASCAR Silicon Motor Speedway. A virtual racing experience.

Rumba Room. A multi-level Latin dance club featuring live salsa, Latin jazz, merengue, and rock español, accompanied by tapas and drinks.

Universal Amphitheatre. One of the hottest live performance venues anywhere with no curfew, no sound restrictions, and no seat more than 150 feet from the stage. (213) 252–9497. www.uniconcerts.com/uniamp.

Universal City Cinemas. Eighteen screens and more than 6,000 seats with the latest technology including DTS digital, THX, and Dolby sound systems. Highly popular among residents of the San Fernando Valley, it is one of the nation's busiest theater complexes. (818) 508–0711. www.loews cineplex.com/locations/ca/index.html.

Wizardz Magic Theatre. A close-up magic show with a three-course meal, or the other way around. The Theater of Illuzionz presents nightly performances featuring a laser light show and comedy, sleight of hand, and grand illusion. A luncheon buffet is available most days, and the bar is open in the afternoon with a magician working alongside the bartender. (818) 506–0066. www.wizardz magic.com.

■ RESTAURANTS AT CITYWALK

Buca di Beppo Restaurant. A quirky family-style Southern Italian eatery with an inside joke of a name: buca means basement, and Beppo is southern

Italian slang for Giuseppe, or Joe. So the meaning of the name is "Joe's Basement," a nod to the location of the first restaurant in this chain. You can dine in mock-splendor at the Pope's Table or at a kitchen table. (818) 509–9463. www.bucadibep po.com.

Cafe Tu Tu Tango. An eclectic menu of appetizer-size tapas dishes to be shared around the table. Designed like an artist's loft in Barcelona with brushes on the table and spontaneous performances by musicians and dancers. (818) 769–2222. www.cafetututango.com.

Camacho's Cantina. Andy Camacho, owner of the popular El Paseo Inn on Olvera Street in Los Angeles, brings authentic Mexican cuisine including many unusual dishes and a mariachi band. (818) 622–3333.

Daily Grill Short Order. High-tone short-order cooking favorites like pot pie, meat loaf, and Cobb salad. (818) 760–4448. www.dailygrill.com.

Gladstone's Universal. An outpost of a popular California seafood restaurant featuring live Maine lobsters as well as local fare. Fish doesn't get much fresher than this. The restaurant includes several huge saltwater tanks, an oyster tank, and sawdust on the floors. Out front is the San Pedro light buoy, which marked channels in and out of San Pedro Harbor from 1942 until its decommissioning in 1971. (818) 622–3474. www.gladstones.com.

Karl Strauss Brewery Garden. An onsite brewery serving handcrafted beers and American cuisine. (818) 753–2739. www.karlstrauss.com.

Shanghai & Mein. Casual Chinese food, featuring dim sum and noodles.

Tony Roma's. An open kitchen with a view of the ribs on the grill. (818) 763–7662. www.tonyromas.com.

Upstart Crow Cafe. A simple cafe alongside a friendly bookstore with sections for adults and children. The name of the place comes from a critical comment on the writing and acting abilities of William Shakespeare by a rival, one Robert Greene. (818) 763–1811.

Wasabi at CityWalk. Fresh sushi by day and disco by night. (818) 622–7224.

Wolfgang Puck Cafe. The celebrated chef brings his famous pizza as well as rotisserie fare to an outdoor cafe. (818) 985–9653.

■ FAST FOOD AT CITYWALK

Cafe Puccino. European-style bakery and cappuccino cafe, plus an Italian deli serving gourmet pizza, salads, and sandwiches. (818) 622–2233. www.cafe puccino.com.

Hollywood FreeZway. Pay no mind to the '57 Chevy bursting through the Hollywood FreeZway sign; the ice cream parlor features Häagen-Dazs just begging you to cruise on in. (818) 622–2653.

Jerry's Famous Deli. From matzo ball soup to pastrami on rye.

Jody Maroni's Sausage Kingdom. The king of the *haute* dog, a California favorite on Venice Beach and at Dodger Stadium. Specialties include hot and sweet Italian, Portuguese fig and pinenut, Bombay curried lamb, and chicken and duck with shallots and tarragon. (818) 622–5639. www.maroni.com.

Panda Express. Quick Chinese food.

A section of restaurants at Universal CityWalk. *Photo by Corey Sandler*

Pit Fire Pizza Co. Wood-fire-grilled pizzas.

Rubio's Baja Grill. Quick Mexican cuisine.

Smoothie King. Creamy fruit smoothies.

Tommy's Original World Famous Hamburgers. A venerated burger joint, specializing in chili-dripping burgers and fries.

Tropic Nut Company. Warm roasted nuts, trail mixes and honey served in a rustic Caribbean-style shack. (818) 622–6889.

Versailles Restaurant. Authentic Cuban food including garlic-drenched chicken and fried plantains.

Wetzel's Pretzels. Fresh-baked, hand-rolled in at least ten flavors.

▒ FASHION AT CITYWALK

Atomic Garage. Snowboard, skateboard, fashion apparel, and accessories.

Hollywood Harley Davidson. Motorcycle-theme apparel, merchandise, and collectibles.

Quiksilver Boardrider's Club. Men's and women's surfwear.

Skechers USA. Lifestyle footwear (some call them sneakers) and casual shoes.

UCLA Spirit. Books, clothing, and other samples of the college's Westwood campus. (818) 754–6719.

Universal Studio Store. Fashion, accessories, and character merchandise. (818) 622–8000.

Vans. Shoes from toddler to adult, as well as a full line of skateboarding equipment; there's a half-pipe skateboarding ramp inside the store.

■ GIFTS AT CITYWALK

Adobe Road. Native American jewelry, belts, skins, shirts, musical instruments, and wall hangings. (818) 622–3623.

All Star Collectibles. Autographed and authenticated sports memorabilia. (818) 622–2222.

Awesome Atom's. Scientific games and educational toys.

Cirque De Bijoux. Designer costume and body jewelry.

Dapy. Originating in Paris, offering a collection of unusual toys and gifts. Dapy is part of Spencer Gifts, which is in turn owned by Universal Studios. (818) 622–3279. www.spencergifts.com.

Fossil. Fashion watches. (818) 985–8209.

Glow. Glow-in-the-dark clothing, stationery, art, jewelry, paint, toys, and gifts. (818) 761–3270.

Hot Topic. Apparel, accessories, gifts, and music for teenagers.

Martin Lawrence Gallery. Arts and crafts. (818) 508–7867.

The Nature Company. An indoor rain forest at the entrance, and gifts, garden accessories, and educational playthings within. (818) 508–7867.

Out Takes. Computer-generated composite photography places visitors into famous movie or television scenes. (818) 752–1262.

Retro Rad. Vintage and nostalgic clothing and accessories.

Sam Goody Superstore. A 27-foot-high gorilla guards the doors to a huge collection of CDs, tapes, and videos and a rock 'n' roll stage. The piano-shaped coffee cafe serves cappuccino and music listening stations. (818) 763–4301.

Sparky's. Vintage and reproduction toys. (818) 622–2925.

Sunglass Hut. (818) 505–8446.

THEM! Science-fiction movie memorabilia.

Things From Another World. From Dark Horse Comics, all manner of games, aliens, creatures, and videos. (818) 622–8464.

The Wound & Wound Toy Co. Thousands of wind-up toys.

PART IV

KNOTT'S BERRY FARM

CHAPTER EIGHT

KNOTT'S BERRY FARM

IT ALL BEGAN WITH A BISCUIT AND JAM, thirty years before Walt Disney arrived in Anaheim. Today Knott's Berry Farm has more than 165 attractions, rides, live shows, restaurants, and shops spread across 150 acres—about the combined size of Disneyland and Disney's California Adventure about fifteen minutes away.

And a new corporate owner promises to invest millions to keep up with the neighbors in Anaheim and Hollywood. During the past few years the bodacious **Perilous Plunge** water ride made a big splash at the back of the park, while the front was transformed with the addition of **Ghost Rider,** a gigantic old-style wooden roller coaster. In the middle of the park came a spectacular space shot known as **Supreme Scream.** A completely new second gate, **Soak City U.S.A.,** opened across the road.

And, alas, there were two closures: the famous Parachute Sky Jump, a victim of old age, drops guests no more. The Windjammer coaster, a year-old new-comer, was shut down because of operational problems.

THE STORY OF KNOTT'S BERRY FARM

Knott's Berry Farm traces its history to 1920 when Walter and Cordelia Knott began farming twenty acres of leased land in Buena Park. They had spent the three years before unsuccessfully trying to homestead in the Mojave Desert.

Most of the family's savings went to purchase equipment and berry plants, and the business nearly died in the first year when a series of unusually heavy frosts nearly wiped them out. In the second year berry prices plummeted.

What saved the business was Walter Knott's decision to market his produce by himself. He built a roadside stand to sell his berries to summer vacationers who drove past the farm on Grand Avenue, now known as Beach Boulevard or Highway 39.

MUST-SEES

Xcelerator

Ghost Rider

Supreme Scream

Perilous Plunge

Timber Mountain Log
Ride

Jaguar!

Montezooma's
Revenge

Boomerang

Kingdom of the
Dinosaurs

Bigfoot Rapids

Mystery Lodge

Hammerhead

Camp Snoopy
(Unaccompanied adults
excused)

Soak City U.S.A.
(Second-gate water park)

There was competition, though, from other berry stands, so Knott combined his marketing skills with some agricultural engineering. In 1922 he read a newspaper article about an unusual berry that was larger than other berries; it was a cross between a dewberry and a loganberry, and it was named a youngberry. Knott tracked down the source to a farm in Alabama and imported them to Southern California for the first time, developing a business selling the berries to visitors and the plants to other area farmers.

By 1927 business was successful enough to allow Knott to purchase the land and build a home and a larger berry stand on the property. To make ends meet on their farm, Cordelia Knott began serving hot biscuits and homemade preserves to customers of the roadside berry stand.

The original berry farm stand was located at La Palma Avenue at Beach Boulevard, which today is in the first corner of the park you come to; the stand has been replaced by a statue of westward pioneers that's visible from the road.

About the same time Knott's growing fame as a berry farmer brought him in contact with Rudolph Boysen of Orange County, the city parks superintendent and an amateur botanist who had conducted experiments with a cross between a blackberry, a raspberry, and a loganberry. Boysen had abandoned his experiment, and it took some searching to find the last six surviving vines; they were brought back to life and eventually transplanted to Knott's farm.

They were named boysenberries, and they were an immediate success at the Knott's Berry Farm roadside stand. In June 1934 the momentous day came when Mrs. Knott decided to expand her menu to include fried chicken at 65 cents per full meal; the first day she served just eight meals on her own wedding china. By 1940 visitors were standing in line for hours to enjoy plates of Walter's boysenberries and Cordelia's chicken. Today the restaurant serves more than one and a half million meals per year.

As long as all those people were standing in line, why not find something else for them to spend their money on? In 1940 Knott built an Old West Ghost Town next door. The family started with an artistic cyclorama known as the "Covered Wagon Show," a detailed mural enhanced with real objects in the foreground; it

KNOTT'S BERRY FARM

Power Trips

FOR ADULTS AND OLDER CHILDREN

If you've got the nerve and stomach to ride **Xcelerator,** head there first or last. Knott's hot new coaster will be the biggest draw at the park for a few years to come.

The good news is that Xcelerator's arrival will take some of the early lines away from **Supreme Scream** and **Ghost Rider,** the two previous biggest draws. If you'd rather ride one of them, head there first.

Move on to **Boomerang, Montezooma's Revenge,** and **Mystery Lodge.** As it starts to get warm, move on to **Perilous Plunge** and then **Bigfoot Rapids.** You can dry off just a bit at the **Log Ride.** Use the afternoon to see some of the shows, including the **Stunt Show.** Visit **Kingdom of the Dinosaurs** and any other rides that strike your fancy.

The lines at Xcelerator will build through the day; come back at dinnertime or near the end of the day when the crowds will be elsewhere.

If you are going to stay into the night, think about ducking out for an early dinner (chicken, anyone?) and return to the park when others are heading for the feed lot.

FOR CHILDREN

The big draws for kids are in Camp Snoopy, which will become crowded by mid-morning. Arrive there early if you can.

Working counterclockwise from Camp Snoopy, visit whichever of the rides in Fiesta Village your youngsters can handle. These might include **Gran Slammer, Tumbler,** and **Sling Shot.** The **Carousel** is in Fiesta Village, too.

Amusement park rides that may appeal to some kids include **HeadSpin,** all but guaranteed to make adults dizzy. Most kids enjoy the **Bumper Cars** near the Charles M. Schulz Theatre. Adventuresome kids will love **Perilous Plunge;** bring a change of clothes or a rain jacket on a cool day.

Children are sure to enjoy the living fossils at **Kingdom of the Dinosaurs.**

Ghost Town will appeal to children of all ages. Youngsters will particularly enjoy **Big Foot Rapids** on a warm afternoon. So, too, a ride on the **Ghost Town & Calico Railroad** and the **Butterfield Stage.**

Very young children will probably not enjoy **Mystery Lodge;** save it for school-aged visitors.

depicted the journey of the Knotts to California. Knott found the Old Trails Hotel in Prescott, Arizona, and moved the 1848 structure to the farm to hold the cyclorama. He added a saloon (without alcohol) and soon expanded with other buildings, including a Kansas schoolhouse, a blacksmith's shop, and shacks from mining territories.

Knott's Berry Farm Tickets

Prices were in effect in mid-2002, and are subject to change.

	ADULT	CHILD (ages 3 to 11)	SENIOR (60+)
KNOTT'S BERRY FARM			
All-Day Pass	$42.00	$32.00	$32.00
Pass After 4:00 PM	$21.00	$15.00	$15.00
Annual Pass	$109.95	$49.95	$65.95
Parking: $7			
Annual Parking Pass: $35			
SOAK CITY U.S.A. BUENA PARK and CHULA VISTA			
All-Day Pass	$22.95	$15.95	$22.95
Pass After 3:00 P.M.	$13.95	$11.95	$13.95
Combo with Knott's Berry Farm (same day): $12.95 plus Knott's ticket			
Annual Pass	$59.95	$49.95	$59.95
Parking: $7			
Annual Parking Pass: $20			
PREMIUM ANNUAL PASSPORTS			
Admission to Knott's Berry Farm and Soak City U.S.A. Buena Park and Chula Vista			
Annual Admission Pass	$159.95	$99.95	$115.95
Annual Parking Pass: $35			

In 1952 Walter Knott purchased America's last operating narrow-gauge railroad, the Denver and Rio Grande, moving its rolling stock in its entirety to the farm. It originally traveled a 76-mile route from Denver to Colorado Springs. Installed at the park, the steam-powered train was renamed as the Ghost Town & Calico Railroad.

Over the years the ghost town grew into an important tourist attraction, and Knott's Berry Farm jams and jellies were packaged and sold across the country.

In 1954 the Bird Cage Theatre opened in Ghost Town as the home of the country's only daily melodrama troupe. A replica of the Bird Cage in Tombstone, Arizona, the theater was the training ground for many actors, including funnyman Steve Martin. The theater ended regular performances in 1996; it is now open only on holidays and special occasions.

In 1955, though, the local tourist economy was altered forever when Walt Disney opened Disneyland in Anaheim. According to their official biography, Walter and Cordelia Knott attended the July 17 opening ceremonies of Disneyland and returned to find the farm parking lot filled to capacity; their park went on to enjoy its best year ever.

Knott's Berry Farm and the Ghost Town continued to be an important tourist destination, though the park began to change with a cable car ride, a puppet theater, and a man-made mountain that had a simulated mine train ride within.

In 1960 Knott harvested the last berries from the Buena Park farm and began purchasing produce from other area farms.

A brick-by-brick re-creation of Independence Hall in Philadelphia, including a 2,075-pound replica of the Liberty Bell, was added in 1966. The reproduction is so exact you can see fingerprints in the brick, just as in the original. When the real Independence Hall was restored for America's bicentennial in 1976 its original blueprints could not be found; a reconstruction committee in Philadelphia contacted Knott's 'Berry Farm and asked to borrow the park's plans. In 1998 Knott's Independence Hall underwent an extensive remodeling and restoration project.

Cordelia Knott died in 1974 at the age of eighty-four; Walter died seven years later in 1981, just short of his ninety-second birthday.

Today every boysenberry plant in the world can trace its roots (pardon the pun) to Knott's Berry Farm. For old time's sake several boysenberry vines are still grown behind the **Original Berry Stand** in Ghost Town. (From 1920 to 1927, the stand was the farm's only structure.) All the produce for Knott's jams and jellies, though, are grown at outside farms.

Knott's Berry Farm allied itself with Charles Schulz and his beloved cartoon characters in 1983 with the opening of Camp Snoopy. Knott's Camp Snoopy opened in 1992 in Bloomington, Minnesota, at the Mall of America, the nation's largest shopping complex. The park, Knott's first outside of California, is also America's largest indoor entertainment park.

You'll find a discount coupon in this book. Other discounts are offered to non-ambulatory or pregnant guests, as well as to residents of Southern California. You should also ask at area supermarkets and fast-food restaurants for discount coupons. A Knott's spokesman said visitors can call before a visit to check on special offers.

In a welcome change from the usual policy at theme parks, visitors to Knott's are permitted to bring picnic lunches; however, bottles and glass are not allowed.

Call (714) 220–5200 for updated information on hours and special events. You can also consult www.knotts.com.

THE NEW ERA DAWNS AT KNOTT'S

Knott's watched as Universal Studios Hollywood and Six Flags California undertook major expansions with new attractions that had price tags as high as $100 million, and the Disneyland Resort added a whole new theme park, the $1.4 billion Disney's California Adventure.

The days of Knott's Berry Farm as a family-run operation came to a close at the end of 1997 when the company allowed itself to be purchased by Cedar Fair, which also owns the Cedar Point amusement park between Cleveland and

Toledo; Valleyfair near Minneapolis; Dorney Park & Wildwater Kingdom near Allentown, Pennsylvania; and Worlds of Fun in Kansas City, Missouri. The sale resulted in Knott's becoming the largest stockholder in Cedar Fair.

Knott's Berry Farm, bounded by La Palma, Western, Crescent, and Stanton Avenues, has developed only about thirty of its 150 acres.

Knott's purchased the 320-room Buena Park Hotel adjacent to the park, reopening it as the **Radisson Resort Knott's Berry Farm.** Renovated throughout, the hotel includes the Cuchina Cuchina restaurant. Half of one floor is set aside as a kid's world with Peanuts-theme rooms; Snoopy himself comes to turn down the beds each night and tell a bedtime story.

Cedar Park's other operations are not themed to the same extent as Knott's, relying instead on major thrill rides such as roller coasters. The new owners immediately boosted the thrill-ride quotient at Knott's with the introduction of Supreme Scream, touted as the "world's tallest, most intense vertically descending thrill adventure," and Ghost Rider, claimant to the title for the tallest, longest, most massive wood roller coaster in Southern California. Boasting 4,530 feet of track, the wooden giant towers 118 feet and delivers a spectacular 108-foot drop.

■ HOURS OF OPERATION

Summer hours: Open every day from 9:00 A.M. to midnight. (The summer season runs from about June 16 to September 3.)

Winter hours: Open 10:00 A.M. to 6:00 P.M. during the week, 10:00 A.M. to 10:00 P.M. Saturday, and 10:00 A.M. to 7:00 P.M. Sunday. Closed on Christmas. Extended hours during seasonal periods.

DRIVING INSTRUCTIONS TO KNOTT'S BERRY FARM

From West Los Angeles: Santa Monica Freeway (I–10) East to Santa Ana Freeway (I–5) South. Stay on Santa South to the Artesia Boulevard/Knott Avenue exit. Stay in one of the two right-hand lanes of the off-ramp. Go straight, making no turns. You will be on Knott Avenue, which leads directly into the park.

From Orange County and Disneyland Area: Santa Ana Freeway (I–5) north to Route 91 west to the Beach Boulevard exit, which leads into Knott's Berry Farm.

Here's an alternate route from Disneyland: Santa Ana Freeway (I–5) north to the Beach Boulevard exit. Bear right off the exit, and turn right (south) onto Beach Boulevard, which leads into the entrance to the park.

From Hollywood/San Fernando Valley: Hollywood Freeway (101) south to Santa Ana Freeway (I–5) south. Stay on Santa Ana Freeway south to the Artesia Boulevard/Knott Avenue exit. Stay in one of the two right-hand lanes of the off-ramp. Go straight, making no turns. You will be on Knott Avenue, which leads directly into the park.

GHOST TOWN

A rough-and-ready 1880s Old West boomtown of cowboys, cancan dancers, stunt fights, stagecoaches, a steam train, a log ride, old-time melodramas, and panning for real gold. Ghost Town is a fun place to walk about and explore.

Knott bought the California ghost town of Calico before he developed his own amusement park; the unofficial name for the ghost town is Calico because of that original purchase.

▓▓ MUST-SEE ▓▓ GHOST RIDER

The longest, tallest, most massive wooden roller coaster in Southern California, Ghost Rider sprawls over 4,530 feet of track, with a spectacular 108-foot drop. The modern woodie delivers a remarkably smooth ride, too.

Three trains of twenty-eight seats transport about 1,600 guests each hour. Towering 118 feet at its highest point, the coaster delivers a maximum G-force of 3.14.

A twisting drop on Ghost Rider. *Photo by Corey Sandler*

Ghost Rider's L-shaped track begins near the **Gold Mine,** soaring high above Grand Avenue to a former parking lot, making four high-speed passes over the road.

Built of yellow pine, the weathered look of the coaster blends nicely with Knott's Berry Farm's celebrated Old West atmosphere. Ghost Rider dominates the front of the park, its huge framework easily visible from busy Beach Boulevard.

According to insiders, designers at Knott's Berry Farm set out to create a wooden coaster that was longer and higher than the venerable Colossus at Six Flags Magic Mountain. Colossus's tower reaches to 115 feet, 3 feet short of Ghost Rider's peak.

Many roller-coaster fans believe that wooden coasters are preferable to modern steel designs because the former have more give. According to the designer of Ghost Rider, the structural flexibility of the classic wooden coaster intensifies the passengers' sensation of weightlessness. "Ghost Riders feel as if they are moving, shifting, and swaying with the structure."

▓MUST-SEE▓ TIMBER MOUNTAIN LOG RIDE

A Knott's Berry Farm classic, it was originally named the Calico Logging Company. When it opened in 1968 it was the first log flume theme ride in the country; today, it is still considered one of the best. Traveling in hollowed logs, guests float through animated scenes of the inner workings of an old-time sawmill.

There is a false drop in the dark, and then you are in a wilderness scene with wildlife; the room smells like a pine forest. The log moves out onto a track with a view of the outside world, very near to the tracks of **Jaguar!**

A Timber Mountain Log Ride boat heads for a splashdown. *Photo by Corey Sandler*

Eventually the logs reach the end of their tour within Timber Mountain and plunge down a 50-foot waterfall. Riders receive only a tiny splash; the ride was developed when most visitors came to the park to go to a chicken dinner and didn't want to get wet.

▓ GHOST TOWN & CALICO RAILROAD

Think the New York City subways are unsafe? The Knott's Berry Farm train line is held up by bandits more than 10,000 times a year. The train circles the park on a ½-mile tour that takes fifteen minutes (including a scheduled robbery).

The GT&C operates two locomotives: #41, *Red Cliff*, from the Rio Grande Southern, and #40, *Green River*, from the Denver & Rio Grande and the Denver & Rio Grande Western. Both were built by the Baldwin Locomotive Works in 1881, two of only twelve C-19 narrow-gauge freight engines built by Baldwin. Together, the engine and loaded tender weigh about 127,260 pounds. The engine's wheel configuration is 2-8-0.

Ghost Town & Calico Railroad. *Photo by Corey Sandler*

The stable of coaches for the GT&C includes:

- **Combine #351.** Built in 1880, and rebuilt in 1937 as a parlor-buffet car for service on the San Juan Express.
- **Closed Vestibule Coaches #310, #325, and #326.** Built by Pullman in 1887.
- **Parlor Car #105,** *Durango.* Built in 1880; one of only three narrow-gauge parlor cars still in operation.
- **Special Car B-20,** *Edna.* Used as a private business car for Otto Mears, president of the Rio Grande Southern. Originally lit by oil lamps, at one time it included mahogany-wood finish and crimson plush upholstery. Inside was sleeping space for six with a private bedroom with bathroom, kitchen, and dining room.

In January and February the two steam engines are regularly given time off, and service on the GT&C is provided by the *Galloping Goose,* a gasoline-fuel railway car built in 1931 for the Rio Grande Southern. Originally powered by a Pierce-Arrow engine, it now uses a GMC truck power plant.

Engineers conduct guided tours of the park's roundhouse; you can purchase tickets at the Train Junction shop in Ghost Town.

◼ SIEGE OF FORT KNOTT STUNT EXTRAVAGANZA

Join the audience to cheer on the ever-resourceful U.S. Agent Jebadiah Casy as he attempts to hold down the legendary Fort Knott from the gold-hungry likes of Welby Weed and his evil cohort, Frank Fargo.

Note that some of the seats are out in the sun; if you want to be sure of shade, arrive early and choose one of the covered stagecoaches that ring the top of the small amphitheater. There also are two stagecoaches and some seats on the stage itself; they are up close to some of the action but don't offer the best view for events going on at the other end of the stage.

The Old Trails Hotel

The first building erected in Ghost Town, the hotel was built in 1868 in Prescott, Arizona, and moved to the farm in 1940 to house the Covered Wagon Show, Knott's first attraction. The show was a cyclorama, a combination of costumed figures and artifacts with a painted backdrop; the exhibit is still in place and is open to the public for a few hours each day. Inside the hotel is a mirror backed with diamond dust and a key rack missing a hook for unlucky Room 13.

The Bottle House

All 3,082 empty wine and whiskey bottles that form the walls of the Bottle House face inward; if they didn't, they'd whistle in the wind. Built at Knott's Berry Farm in 1946, the Bottle House was inspired by similar structures in turn-of-the-twentieth-century mining towns throughout the West. While wood was scarce because it was needed in the mines, empty liquor bottles were plentiful.

Old School House

Everything in this old building—books, desks, chalkboard, and potbelly stove—is authentic and dates from about 1875.

Gold Mine

Take a pan to the sluice in Ghost Town and sift out a few grains of gold. Each year, guests take home more than $70,000 in real gold dust from Knott's Gold Mine in Ghost Town; more than $3 million has been taken from the stream since the park opened. The sluice is stocked with gold flakes each morning to increase your chances. In 2002 the fee was about $4.00.

Western Trails Museum

A most eclectic collection of things more-or-less Western. Some of the materials began from Walter Knott's own gatherings, but during the years many of the items in the Western Trails Museum were donated by guests.

The Gold Mine is one of the oldest attractions at Knott's Berry Farm. *Photo by Corey Sandler*

You'll see old china from the early mining ghost towns of Colorado and California, period photos of Bat Masterson and Annie Oakley, and many guns and knives. On the back wall, look for an unusual picture of the Rock Island Line train system; based on an original black-and-white photo from 1900, it was hand-colored on mother-of-pearl. The work was created in 1916 for E. J. Goreman, president of the railroad, for his office. Set near Colorado Springs, Pike's Peak is the snow-covered point at the right side of the range.

Another interesting exhibit is a display

of cigarette-box cards that offer a glimpse at what were considered naughty pictures at the turn of the century; there's nothing there to shock a modern-day visitor.

Butterfield Stage

The last regularly scheduled stagecoach line in America circles a portion of Ghost Town. Five of Knott's six stagecoaches are authentic and more than one hundred years old; many were used on the Oregon Trail in the 1880s and 1890s. The one replica, the Knott's coach, was built on the Farm in 1956. Knott's maintains a stable of more than fifty horses to pull the coaches around the park.

Medicine Show

Be on the lookout for Dr. I. Will Skinnem and his old-time medicine show; the fast-talking pitchman has a cure for whatever ails you.

Bird Cage Theatre

A meticulous replica of the Bird Cage Theatre in Kingston, Arizona, near Tombstone, it was claimed by Knott's as the oldest continually operated melodrama theater in the United States. The theater is open for special events only; check with the park for schedules.

Main Street Windmill

A one-hundred-year-old import from England, the windmill was originally intended by Walter Knott to serve as the boundary for the park. Today it stands in roughly the middle of Knott's Berry Farm. The mill was brought to California in the 1860s by an English syndicate that first laid out and subdivided Riverside.

Seated Statues

Knott's four sets of seated character statues—Handsome Brady and Whiskey Jim, the cancan girls in Ghost Town, the Mexican ladies in Fiesta Village, and the flapper girls in The Boardwalk—are favorite stops for visitors to the park. A fifth pair, Cecilia and Marilyn, sit in front of the Calico Saloon and were modeled after actual saloon performers of the 1850s. They have a recorded patter that is remarkably suited to the actions of some of the females and most of the males who sit down beside them.

At one time nearly all Kodak film was processed in one plant in Rochester, New York, and Knott's received phone calls from Kodak wanting to know who these guys were and why they kept turning up in thousands of photographs.

Old Betsey

Parked near the windmill, *Old Betsey* is a wood-burning engine that had been used in the early days of borax mining on the desert in Death Valley. The locomotive was a distinct improvement over the twenty-mule team that used to haul borax from the mines. The mineral borax has a number of industrial uses as a water softener and as part of the foundry process. The engine was retired to the park in 1941.

Handsome Brady and Whiskey Jim in Ghost Town. *Photo by Corey Sandler*

Berry Stand

In a nod to local history, the original stand that launched the Knott's Berry Farm empire is preserved as a refreshment counter.

Attached to the side of the stand are some old photos. Alongside is a Ford Model A, the vehicle driven by Walter and Cordelia Knott when they came to California. Out back is a small patch of boysenberry plants, the only berries still grown within the park.

Boot Hill

Most of the grave markers in this boneyard across the way from the Western Trails Museum are authentic relics of the Old West; the graves themselves were left behind. The painted backdrop to Boot Hill is the backside of the Good Time Theatre.

Check out the grave of Hyram McTavish. Legend has it the heart will beat again after one hundred years—any visitor who places his or her foot on the grave will feel . . . something. Our favorite epitaphs? "Butch Youngman 1857. Here lies Butch, we planted him raw. He was quick on the trigger, but slow on the draw." And, "Here lies Lester Moore. 4 slugs shot from a 44. No less and no more."

Alas, in 2001 the **Haunted Shack** faded away. The quirky, crooked residence of Shifty Sam and Slanty Sadie, a place where water ran uphill and the worst (or best) puns in the park took flight, was closed.

CAMP SNOOPY

The official home of the Peanuts gang, Camp Snoopy is a six-acre kids' paradise themed like a section of California's High Sierra. Camp Snoopy features thirty attractions for the youngest visitors.

Woodstock's Airmail is a smaller, gentler version of Supreme Scream, but I imagine it looks big enough to little eyes. Nearby is **Charlie Brown's Speedway,** a mini-NASCAR track.

Check out **Snoopy's Animal Friends** to get close to tame forest animals and birds, including a timber wolf, raccoons, and an owl. There's also a koi pond and pony ride.

Camp Snoopy's Bear-y Tales Playhouse is a just-for-kids world that includes winding corridors and all sorts of unusual surprises.

Other rides include the **Red Baron** planes, the **Twister** mini coaster, the **Ball Room,** the **Rocky Road** cars, and a kid-size Ferris wheel.

And children of all ages can take time out to learn at the **Thomas A. Edison Inventors' Workshop.** California's only collection of Edison artifacts and memorabilia, it includes early experimental lightbulbs and handwritten notes by Edison. There are ten hands-on exhibits demonstrating the invisible forces of electricity and magnetism.

FIESTA VILLAGE

A salute to California's Spanish legacy, Fiesta Village is also the prowling ground for Knott's **Jaguar!** adventure.

⋮MUST-SEE⋮ JAGUAR!

Knott's unusual roller coaster prowls through a large portion of the park like a cat stalking its prey, speeding up and slowing down as it threads the needle through thrill rides and circles the lake.

Passengers board the coaster at the Temple of the Jaguar, a five-story Mayan pyramid in Fiesta Village. The temple was inspired by the architectural style of the famed Tikal pyramid, which featured a decorative crown cap depicting a supernatural figure holding a jaguar mask.

According to Mayan and Aztec legend, there exists in this temple a deity who could transform himself into a mighty fire-breathing cat. As you make your way through the queuing area inside the Temple of the Jaguar, you will hear and see evidence of the cat and feel his presence.

The waiting line passes through detailed corridors and chambers as it moves its way toward the columned Hall of Egress. Still within the temple, passengers board sleek twenty-four-seat trains. As you board the trains, it becomes apparent that you have become the cat.

Immediately after departure riders climb 60 feet into the air and then dive back through the temple's crown tower to begin a twisting, spiraling expedition above Knott's Berry Farm. Jaguar! is a very quiet ride and actually travels very low to the ground in most places.

Halfway through your journey, trains return to the temple tower through fog, fire effects, strobe lights, and sound.

Along the way, Jaguar! passes right through the middle of the loop of another Knott's Berry Farm coaster, Montezooma's Revenge, and then careens within inches of the Timber Mountain Log Ride.

Before it is done, Jaguar! winds its way through all of Fiesta Village and parts of Camp Snoopy. The track crosses the path of the park-circling Grand Sierra Scenic Railroad in eight places.

The steel structure runs about 2,700 feet with a pair of 60-foot drops. There are no guardrails to block the view from the cars, which travel just fast enough to give a thrill in places; the cars do not turn upside down.

For much of its run, Jaguar! is more like an aerial tour of the park. The trip, about two-and-a-half minutes, is a ride that most everyone in the family will enjoy.

Three twenty-four-passenger trains can carry a total of 1,500 guests per hour. The wait for the ride can build to as much as an hour during the summer and on holidays; come early or on an off-season day to avoid the crowds.

▮▮▮▮ MUST-SEE ▮▮▮▮ MONTEZOOMA'S REVENGE

From zero to fifty-five miles per hour in just over three seconds, heading for two circles within a vertical loop, Montezooma's Revenge zooms riders through a 76-foot-high, 360-degree loop to the apex of a 148-foot tower; the train pauses at the top and then races backward through the loop and up a 112-foot tower at the opposite end of the track.

Calico Mine Train

Built in 1966 it was the first ride on Knott's Berry Farm and one of the first dark rides at any park. The walkway to the loading platform is decorated with old mining equipment. The scene is reminiscent of Disneyland's Thunder Mountain Railroad, but trust us: this is not a thrill ride.

The train chugs its way into the Calico Mine. Among the first sights is an old mine elevator like the ones used in the diggings of the west. You'll visit some interesting animated dioramas of miners at work and then arrive at the highlight of the trip: an otherworldly cavern of stalactites and stalagmites with a simulated cave organ as accompaniment.

The mine train cars seat about ten persons with five cars per train; traffic is pretty constant on a busy day.

Tampico Tumbler

Two cars revolve around a center pivot forward and backward as they rotate around the central column. At the same time, the entire ride climbs up and down the column. It sounds complicated, and it is, but all you've got to do is ride. This medium-wild experience is nearby to the entrance to Jaguar!

Dentzel Carousel

The oldest working carousel at any amusement park in the country, it was one of the first two-level carousels built. It was created by Gustav A. Dentzel in 1902 at G. A. Dentzel Steam and Horsepower Carousel Builder in Germantown, Pennsylvania. Before coming to Knott's in 1955, it entertained guests at Hershey Park in Hershey, Pennsylvania, and before then at Brady Park in Canton, Ohio.

Of the fifty-four animals on the ride, forty-eight are original, hand-carved works of art. Collectors have paid as much as $100,000 for original, hand-carved Dentzels. The animal menagerie includes lions, tigers, ostriches, camels, zebras, giraffes, pigs, cats, and horses that have real horsetail hair.

Music is provided by a pair of turn-of-the-twentieth-century organs, a Wurlitzer and a Gavioli band organ, which is capable of producing the sound of twenty-two instruments.

Church of the Reflections

Originally the First Baptist Church of Downey, California, the building was moved to Knott's in 1955 to provide a nondenominational respite for farm employees and visitors. More than one hundred weddings are performed in the small church each year. Bride and groom sometime ride off on a stagecoach; Snoopy is available as the best man.

Alongside the Church of the Reflections is a place of discomfort. Doctor Walker's dentist office was hauled in from the Ozarks in 1953. Dating back to the nineteenth century, the walls of the office include some frightening tools.

Reflection Lake

Between Fiesta Village and Ghost Town, the small pond is the site of the Incredible Waterworks Show, a sound, light, and water spectacle presented nightly in season.

THE BOARDWALK

Hear ye, hear ye: The Supreme Scream is in session. While you're in the neighborhood, you can also plunge over a watery cliff at Perilous Plunge, enjoy the looping action of Boomerang, the high-flying thrills of the Parachute Sky Jump, and the quaint Kingdom of the Dinosaurs.

▮MUST-SEE▮ XCELERATOR

Grab your leather jacket and cool shades; the wind will slick back your hair on Xcelerator, the '50s-themed roller coaster that arrived at Knotts in mid-2002. The high-octane coaster fires up its engines on the Boardwalk, dispatching a fleet of chrome-plated with flip-top, flame-decorated '57 Chevy cars across 2,202 feet of cool coral track.

Xcelerator trains are hydraulically launched to eighty-two miles per hour in just over two seconds, and up through a 205-foot ascent and immediate descent at a ninety-degree angle. That's right: straight down. The two trains have a capacity of twenty people each, carrying as many as 1,330 guests per hour.

The coaster occupies the former home of Windjammer.

┇ MUST-SEE ┇ PERILOUS PLUNGE

The name pretty much sums it up: you'll ride a boat up, up, up . . . and then over a cliff and into the water below.

The ride, which opened in 2000, is claimed as the highest, steepest, fastest, and wettest waterfall plunge in the world. The ride, unfortunately, lived up to its name in 2001 with a fatal accident; it was closed for nearly a year while safety issues regarding the safety harnesses were addressed.

Boats plunge down a record 115-foot drop at a seventy-five-degree angle, hitting a speed of fifty miles per hour and generating an amazing 45-foot, 180-degree splash.

The boats load in a sunny California setting of palm trees, beach, and oil derricks. The ride is open year-round; designers built in a system that allows operators to slow down the boats and reduce the splash on cold days.

Perilous Plunge. *Photo by Corey Sandler*

Three twenty-four-passenger boats travel a ninety-second track, accommodating 1,900 riders an hour. State-of-the-art water pumping technology pumps 40,000 gallons of water up the 121-foot lift per minute.

Universal Studios' Jurassic Park attractions in California and Florida drop guests 84 and 85 feet, respectively.

┇ MUST-SEE ┇ BOOMERANG

A high-speed, high-energy European-designed thriller, Boomerang turns riders upside down six times—three times forward and three times backward—in less than a minute.

The blue tracks of Boomerang take off from a loading station next to the Sky Jump. Riders sit two abreast, held into place by overhead restraints.

The train is pulled backward up a hill; at the top, the cars are suddenly released. The train races down the hill, back through the loading station and into a twisting turn one way and then the other, into a 360-degree double loop, and up another hill.

When you reach the top, you drop back through the same course, this time backward.

Boomerang's tracks are very close to the walkways of the park in The Boardwalk; passersby can get right up close to wonder why people would pay good money to subject themselves to such an experience.

Boomerang replaced Corkscrew, the first inverted 360-degree looping coaster in the country; Corkscrew was moved to a park in Coeur d'Alene, Idaho.

MUST-SEE SUPREME SCREAM

Supreme Scream is a "vertically descending thrill adventure"; what that means is that riders fall from a great height. The ride boasts a towering, 325-foot triangular steel structure, making it taller than any skyscraper in Orange County and 75 feet taller than Knott's landmark Sky Tower.

How does it feel? Think of jumping off the roof of a thirty-story building.

Each of the three towers accommodates twelve riders who are harnessed in outward facing seats with their legs dangling freely. They are sent soaring by a blast of compressed air; after a brief pause at the top, Supreme Scream plunges them straight down. But wait: another heart-pounding wallop awaits with an abrupt bounce halfway back up the tower before a final touch down to the launch pad.

The ride has a capacity of about 1,300 riders per hour. It replaced the anemic XK-1 ride.

The ride is a near-twin to the Power Tower, which opened in 1998 at the Cedar Point amusement park in Sandusky, Ohio. It is also similar to the Maliboomer at Disney's California Adventure.

MUST-SEE HAMMERHEAD

This ride just about defies description; we'll try anyhow. Designed by an obviously deranged Italian engineer, it's a cross between a Pirate Ship over-the-top ride and an egg beater. Riders take a seat in a set of stadium-like rows. The grandstand moves from right to left, rotating from top to bottom and upside down as it goes. Within seconds, riders are twisting and turning in 82-foot-high arcs. And then, mercifully, the ride comes to a halt . . . or at least it seems to. We don't want to spoil the surprise, but we can tell you this: it involves the fountain that bubbles innocently at the bottom.

Special Ks

Knott's Berry Farm's equivalent of Disney's "Hidden Mickeys" are the park's several dozen "Hidden Ks" that are woven into structures and decorations in the park. For example, look in the designs made out of twigs in the windows of the Art Gallery across from the Bottle House.

■ KINGDOM OF THE DINOSAURS

As your ride begins you find yourself within the lab of Prof. I. F. Wells in the 1920s. (This is obviously a guy who is a few initials left and right of fame.) Check out the details in the antiques and mementos, but don't let your mind drift too far—you are about to find yourself strapped into a time machine that will take you back into the day of the Tyrannosaurus rex.

You'll see a prehistoric world in battle with an ancient ancestor of the elk. Pterodactyls flap by overhead. And you'll even catch glimpses of Ice Age humans huddling for warmth in ragged furs.

The Supreme Scream takes off. Unlike a similar ride at Disney's California Adventure, seats are open to the rush of wind. *Photo by Corey Sandler*

There is a great deal of detail in the ride, beginning with the outfits worn by attendants who load you onto your car; they're in period dress, with argyle socks and knickers.

The massive fifteen-ton sculpture at the entrance to the Kingdom of the Dinosaurs was carved from Taiwanese marble by California sculptor John Cody. The dino's name, by the way, is Rocky.

When the ride opened in 1987 it was way ahead of Jurassic Park and Barney and the general dinosaur craze that followed; today, it's interesting but lagging behind thrill rides at Disney and Universal parks. Still it's a relaxing place out of the sun or rain, and young kids will love it.

Discovery Center at Kingdom of the Dinosaurs

As you exit the ride, the park's resident paleontologists are ready to answer questions about the wonders you have just experienced. A detailed chart shows stages in the earth's development. On display in the area are petrified wood, teeth, and tusks from prehistoric beasts, and priceless fossils—some as much as tens of millions of years old.

Slingshot

An old amusement park ride that still thrills; visitors sit in a swing suspended by chains from an overhead canopy. The whole apparatus spins, rises, and then tilts. Riders must weigh less than 230 pounds.

Sky Cabin

Knott's landmark Parachute Sky Jump, inspired by the classic Coney Island landmark, was closed at the end of 1999, the victim of old age. The ride lifted riders

235 feet into the air and then dropped to earth beneath a billowing parachute canopy. The Sky Cabin, a slowly revolving enclosed cabin, still climbs the tower.

Buffalo Nickel Arcade

Beneath the Kingdom of the Dinosaurs is a video arcade that neither is in Buffalo nor involves nickels (Buffalo design or otherwise) or pennies. You'll need lots of quarters to get through the modern electronic games and old-time skeeball alleys.

Charleston Circle Fountain

The unusual waterworks located in the circular plaza that opens to Ghost Town, the Charleston Circle Fountain was originally part of the set for the 20th Century Fox movie *Hello, Dolly!*, starring Barbra Streisand.

The Charleston Circle Fountain played a role in *Hello Dolly! Photo by Corey Sandler*

Charles M. Schulz Theatre

In the summer and at Christmastime, the stage (formerly known as the Good Time Theatre) features a

A Native American guide explains an ancient Aztec calendar at Indian Trails. *Photo by Corey Sandler*

live Broadway-style musical extravaganza with dazzling lights, spangled costumes, and special effects. Admission to shows is usually free and part of the general ticket for the park.

The Christmas entertainment usually features a Snoopy ice show. Summer performances have included an Elvis review and other rock performances.

HeadSpin
A spinning carnival ride; in late 1999 it was moved from within its dark building to an outdoor setting.

Wheeler Dealer Bumper Cars
A classic favorite, the ride is somewhat hidden past the entrance to the Kingdom of the Dinosaurs and near the Charles M. Schulz Theatre.

INDIAN TRAILS

Here is a celebration of the lore, legends, crafts, music, and dance of Native American tribes. The 27-foot Knott's Totem Pole at the entrance to Indian Trails is said to be the largest totem ever carved from incense cedar. The pole's figures include a Native American with child, buffalo, burro, turtle, owl, Knott's pioneer with covered wagon, grizzly bear, and eagle.

At Knott's Indian Trails, Native Americans produce intricate arts and crafts. The architectural styles include an authentic Big House and tepees of the Blackfoot, Nez Percé, Cheyenne, Crow, and Kiowa tribes.

The Big House is in the style of the Kwak'wala-speaking people. The building's facade and the hand-carved house posts near its entrance were created by Richard Hunt, a Kwak'wala artist from British Columbia.

Children's Camp at Indian Trails

Young visitors can create traditional honor bonnets as well as learn beadworking and sand painting. Native American storytellers recount living history, and kids can have their faces painted in authentic tribal fashion.

WILD WATER WILDERNESS

The Wild Water Wilderness recaptures the beauty of a California river wilderness park of the early 1800s. The trees, all indigenous to the Far West, include California black oak, coast redwood, and Torrey pines. Colorful wildflowers blossom throughout the wilderness, including poppies, bluebells, daffodils, larkspurs, and lilies.

`MUST-SEE` BIGFOOT RAPIDS

The whitewater river raft ride is a lot of fun if you don't mind getting a bit wet; depending on your luck, you may even get soaked. There: you have been warned. Now go and have fun.

(By the way, a sign at the Rapids tells visitors that garbage-bag raingear is not allowed. It seems that everyone wants to be a fashion critic.)

`MUST-SEE` MYSTERY LODGE

Legends tell of a magical place known as **Thunder Falls** that's located deep within the luxuriant green forests of the Northwest Coast. It's a place of miracles where grand waterfalls crash into a running river with such force that the canyon reverberates with the sound of thunder. Some say that the roar of the thunder brings forth mystic images of the distant past.

Visitors enter Thunder Falls through an ornate wooden archway, continuing across a re-creation of a traditional boardwalk like the ones that connect Northwest Coast tribal houses to the ocean.

The lights dim, and the sounds of a multimedia preshow set the scene. Suddenly lightning fills the sky, and guests are invited into the lodge to take refuge from the approaching storm.

Deep within the lodge a mystical old storyteller begins to spin his tale. It's a story of life, of birth and love and marriage and children and old age and the approach of eternal rest . . . and it presents a mystical calm to all who hear it. The

A Bigfoot Rapids raft spins through whitewater. *Photo by Corey Sandler*

message is that if we can share the mysteries of life with the wonder of a child, life will always be full of magic.

Master dancer Bill Cranmer, a hereditary Chief of the 'Namgis people and chairman of the U'mista Cultural Society, choreographed the traditional dance movements in the show, and he serves as the voice of the presentation. Kwak'wala musicians, including drummers and singers, perform the show's musical score.

I'm not about to destroy the illusions of the Mystery Lodge with an explanation of the magic, but I will tell you this much: The show combines a real actor on stage with spectacular lighting and special effects. The preshow and main lodge presentations total twenty-six minutes; the hourly capacity is 1,440 visitors.

The facade of Mystery Lodge, designed by Native American artists, includes images from the lore and legend of the Northwest People. The stonework includes four towering waterfalls dropping into Thunder Lake. At night bursts of fire, fog, and strange images issue forth from the building.

Aspects of the Mystery Lodge are based on traditions of the 'Namgis people of Alert Bay, Cormorant Island, British Columbia, Canada. The 'Namgis are one band of the Kwak'wala-speaking people, the native North American group who live on the northeastern coast of Vancouver Island, the central coast of mainland British Columbia, and the small islands in between.

Before contact with European settlers, the Kwak'wala-speaking people numbered about 7,000 persons. With the introduction of European diseases in the nineteenth century, the population was reduced to fewer than 2,000 by 1929. Today, the population is about 5,000 people.

Because of the groundbreaking work of the German-American anthropologist Franz Boas in the late 1800s, the Kwak'wala-speaking people's traditions are among the most fully documented of all North American Indian traditions.

Today the descendants of Boas's guide George Hunt are among the cultural leaders of their people, and the Hunt family of carvers produced some of the elements of Knott's Indian Trails area.

Skilled canoeists, fishers, and sea hunters, the Kwak'wala also excelled as carvers of totem poles, masks, and other ritual objects. They originated some of the most spectacular rituals of the Northwest Coast culture, including the potlatch ceremony.

Potlach means "to give" and is a ceremony common to all tribes in the area. Occasions for holding a potlatch include marriages, naming children, mourning the dead, and transferring rights and privileges from a retiring chief to his successors. Dancers dressed in dramatic masks and robes invoke theatrical magic to act out the legends and stories of their people in dances that are traditional to a particular family. The host distributes gifts as payment to his guests for witnessing the ceremony. By accepting the gifts, guests validate the host's claims to the dances.

Mystery Lodge Store and Museum

At the exit to the Mystery Lodge is an attractive shop offering a variety of handmade native crafts to view and purchase. A hand-carved Coast Salish canoe depicting a killer whale design hangs from the ceiling beams. The canoe was carved at Knott's Berry Farm during a canoe-making demonstration begun in 1992 to commemorate the opening of the Indian Trails area. Also on display are intricately carved house posts and other craftwork.

Items for sale include bentwood boxes made from a single piece of cedar and used to store blankets and prized family possessions; carvings in argillite, a slate-like stone; hand-woven baskets; and a selection of native silver jewelry.

Nature Center at Wild Water Wilderness

After your ride on Bigfoot Rapids, stop to ask park rangers about Sasquatch, the elusive creature known to some of his friends as Bigfoot. You'll see some photos and footprints that suggest that the huge beast really does exist. Rangers will also show displays of insects, tarantulas, scorpions, and native plants, plus a glassed-in apiary that puts you about as close as you ever may want to get to a buzzing beehive.

The ranger station is located in the old Maizeland School, the first school in the Rivera District constructed in 1868.

The Wilderness Dance Hall in Wild Water Wilderness once stood on the Burbank farm of Jim Jeffries, one-time American heavyweight boxing champion. Jeffries used the barn to train promising young fighters. Today, the barn is home to an antic assortment of entertainers, from bluegrass pickers to Smoky Mountain cloggers.

EATING YOUR WAY THROUGH KNOTT'S BERRY FARM

Mrs. Knott's Chicken Dinner Restaurant. The winner and still local champion is the sprawling eatery, which regulars and employees call the CDR. The restaurant seats more than 1,000 people in eight separate dining rooms and employs as many as 375 people during the summer.

The classic dinner, served from 11:00 A.M. until closing, is priced at a reasonable $11.45 and includes four pieces of fried chicken, cherry rhubarb, mashed potatoes and gravy, vegetable, soup or salad, as many buttermilk biscuits as you can eat, beverage, and boysenberry pie. You can also order broiled chicken breast, chicken and dumplings, chicken potpie, barbecued beef ribs and chicken, or chicken-fried steak for the same price.

Today, the CDR is the largest single-location chicken restaurant in the country and the single largest user of chickens in California. The part of the restaurant that faces Grand Avenue is the original restaurant that was built in and around the Knott's home. You can ask to sit in one of the straight wood-backed chairs under the paddle fans in the original dining room.

Check out the guest register on the wall in the waiting area. Among notable diners in early years were Eddie Fisher, Elizabeth Taylor, and Jane Russell.

The biggest days of the year are typically Mother's Day, Easter, and Thanksgiving. (The restaurant is closed on Christmas Day.) The biggest day on record at the restaurant was Mother's Day 1982, when 8,400 meals were served.

Auntie Pasta's Pizza Palace. Located in the California Marketplace, this restaurant features Italian fare.

Chicken to Go/Deli. You can buy a chicken and a boysenberry pie to go or pack up a picnic basket of fried chicken, sandwiches, or salads to take into the park. Located in the California Marketplace.

Coasters Diner. The Boardwalk area took a big step backward a few years ago with the opening of this 1950s-themed diner. Coasters combines neon, stainless steel, and glass block with cheeseburgers, French fries and extra-thick milkshakes. Several restored vintage or recreated cars and a 22-foot neon tower lure park guests to the restaurant's location at the back of Knott's Boardwalk area.

Fireman's Brigade Barbecue. Chicken, ribs, corn on the cob, and more, in Ghost Town. A stand offers huge dill pickles to properly top off your meal.

Hollywood Wok. You can chow on Chinese, Japanese, and Italian fast food items at this basic fast foodery in the back corner of the park near the Bumper Cars; it was formerly known as the Hollywood Beanery.

La Cocinita and Herdez Cantina. Mexican specialties in Fiesta Village.

Ghost Rider rises over the old Chicken Dinner Restaurant. *Photo by Corey Sandler*

SPECIAL EVENTS AND PRESENTATIONS

Independence Hall. A free exhibit outside the gates of Knott's Berry Farm. Within the reproduction is a replica of the Declaration-signing chamber; you'll see live performances by actors portraying Ben Franklin, Thomas Jefferson, Patrick Henry, and others.

There is an exact replica of the Liberty Bell, down to its crack. The only real difference lies upstairs where there is a large auditorium that is used for guest orientations, private parties, and special events.

Easter EggMazeMent. A hands-on family event with elaborate walk-through adventure mazes. Held each year for a two-week period on either side of Easter Sunday.

Independence Day. Annual fireworks show and special events.

Knott's Scary Farm. The park offers elaborate walk-through mazes that have ghastly storylines, live performances, and awesome special effects. Several rides are re-themed with disorienting special effects, music, and many monsters. Among the special live shows are The Hanging, an annual satirical send-up in Calico Square. More than 1,000 costumed and made-up performers haunt the park, mazes, and rides.

The Scary Farm is a special-ticket event not covered by general admission, and tickets sell out in advance each year. Tickets go on sale in August at Knott's, and at Ticketmaster outlets throughout the West. Not recommended for young children. Held weekends in October and Halloween night.

Knott's Scary Farm Halloween Haunt, first begun in 1972, is considered both the world's largest annual Halloween party and the largest annual event in the amusement park industry.

On the last two weekends of October, look for **Camp Spooky,** a daytime non-scare Halloween celebration for kids eleven and younger that includes trick-or-treating, costume contests, and other activities.

Knott's Merry Farm. The park is transformed into an 1880s Victorian Christmas shopping and entertainment village, complete with lavish decorations, dozens of artisans, special holiday foods, continuous Christmas shows, Santa's workshop, strolling carolers, choirs, and more. Held from about Thanksgiving to Christmas Eve. (The park is closed on Christmas Day.)

Classic Christmas Celebration. The annual party includes snow sledding on Beagle Hill, a holiday ice show, and other festivities.

SOAK CITY U.S.A.

Ocean waves now lap at the shores of Knott's Berry Farm at Soak City U.S.A., a thirteen-acre water park, opened in a former parking lot adjacent to Independence Hall, across Beach Boulevard from Knott's Berry Farm.

The park includes twenty-one water rides and attractions catering primarily to families and pre-teens, drawing on legendary South California beach towns such as Huntington, Newport, and Malibu for its decoration and theming.

Among attractions are sixteen high-speed tube and body slides, the **Tidal Wave Bay** wave pool, the **Shark Reef** lazy river, the **Zuma Express** family tube ride, and **Gremmie Lagoon,** a children's activity pool.

San Onofre Falls features three high-speed slides: **Blackball, Point Break,** and **Riptide; Malibu Run,** including four tube and two body slides named **Wipeout, Dropoff, Over the Falls,** and **Goofyfoot; Laguna Storm Watch Tower,** with three tube slides dubbed **Typhoon, Tornado,** and **Cyclone. Kowabunga Falls** offers a six-lane speed slide.

Soak City U.S.A. operates from May to September. Tickets are available for the water park, in combination with Knott's Berry Farm, and in packages including hotel accommodations.

PART V

SIX FLAGS CALIFORNIA

CHAPTER NINE

SIX FLAGS MAGIC MOUNTAIN

SIX FLAGS MAGIC MOUNTAIN is a thriller of a theme park, with roller coasters at every turn, and turns on every coaster like you'll not see anywhere else.

The park—about 34 miles north of Los Angeles or 62 miles from Disneyland—lays claim to the title of the world's "Xtreme Park."

The largest capital investment in the park's history in 2001 and 2002 brought forth the amazing **Déjà Vu,** the astounding **X,** and for the pint-sized crowd, the amusing kiddie coaster called **Goliath Jr.**

X is almost beyond description, which probably accounts for its name.

It's a place where the vital statistics for rides include their "G" rating, something that visitors will share in common with jet fighter pilots and astronauts. One G is a measure of ordinary earth gravity; 3 Gs, for example, mean that the forces pulling on a rider are three times normal. You may also experience zero Gs, or near to it, in drops.

Six Flags Magic Mountain claims the record for the most roller coasters at one park, with fifteen and a total of nearly 9 miles of track. Among the zoomers is the world's tallest and fastest roller coaster (**Superman: The Escape,** 415 feet and one hundred miles per hour, which blasts off from the Fortress of Solitude at the top of the mountain); the world's tallest and fastest super boomerang (Déjà Vu, 196 feet and sixty-five miles per hour); the world's tallest and fastest stand-up roller coaster (**The Riddler's Revenge,** 156 feet and sixty-five miles per hour); and the world's tallest looping coaster (**Viper,** 140 feet).

Just a year before, the park added **Goliath,** a massive steel coaster that comes face-to-face with the park's classic wooden coaster, **Colossus.**

These are just the latest additions to the park's world-class collection of roller coasters. Earlier members of the local flying Hall of Fame include the aforementioned Viper, the largest looping roller coaster in the world; **Flashback,** the world's only hairpin-drop roller coaster; **Psyclone,** a traditional boardwalk woodie; **Ninja,** a suspended roller coaster; **Gold Rusher,** the original thriller at the park; **Revolution,** a 360-degree looper; and the spectacular **Batman The Ride,** which almost defies description.

There's even the **Wile E. Coyote Coaster,** a mini-ride for the up-and-coming thrillseeker.

For younger visitors, **Bugs Bunny World** features sixteen rides and attractions with a new twist: kids and parents can ride together.

The **Looney Tunes Nites Parade** takes place nightly, except Tuesday, from mid-June to mid-August. Grab a spot to watch some forty cartoon superstars, including Granny and Tweety . . . with Sylvester not far behind, Wile E. Coyote, Foghorn Leghorn, the Tazmanian Devil, Yosemite Sam, Pepé Le Pew, and Daffy Duck. And there's also Superman and the Justice League of America and Batman.

The parade begins in Gotham City Backlot and concludes with a spectacular fireworks finale over Six Flags Plaza.

THE STORY OF SIX FLAGS

Land baron Henry Mayor Newhall bought the Spanish land grant known as the Rancho San Francisco in the mid-1800s. The Santa Clarita Valley was the site of California's first gold discovery in 1842 and of the state's first commercial oil well in 1875.

The amusement park opened its gates on May 29, 1971, a joint venture of subsidiaries of Seaworld and the Newhall Land and Farming Company. Intended as a draw for the housing developments in the area, Magic Mountain originally featured thirty-three rides, attractions, and shows as well as a local landmark, the 384-foot-tall Sky Tower. America's Bicentennial celebration in 1976 was the occasion for the introduction of the Great American Revolution—the world's first 360-degree looping roller coaster (now known as the Revolution).

In 1979 the park was purchased by the Six Flags Corporation of Arlington, Texas. Under the new management, Roaring Rapids was added in 1981—the West's first white-water rafting ride on a 2.5-mile-long, man-made river.

Six Flags was the dream of a Texas oil man who came back from a trip to

MUST-SEES

X
(the spot to be)

Déjà Vu
(you haven't been here before)

Goliath

The Riddler's Revenge
(a stand-up challenge)

Superman: The Escape

Flashback

Log Jammer

Colossus

Batman The Ride

Freefall

Dive Devil
(extra fee)

Psyclone

Ninja

Revolution

Roaring Rapids

Viper

Bugs Bunny World
(for kids and the adults with them)

SIX FLAGS CALIFORNIA

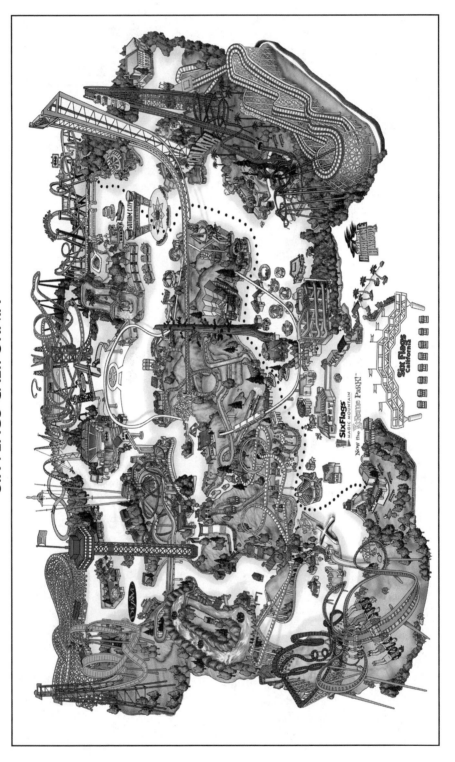

Power Trip: The Big Coasters for Breakfast

True thrillseekers are going to make a beeline for the new Déja Vu or X coasters, which may relieve some of the lines at the still-fabulous Goliath and Riddler's Revenge stand-up coaster, and from there on to Superman: The Escape and the venerable Batman The Ride.

Arrive at the park early, at least half an hour before the gates officially open.

PLAN A

Head directly for **Déja Vu** at the back of the park in Cyclone Bay. When you wobble off, take advantage of the fact that all the other coaster fanatics are heading your way. Here's your chance to jump on the older rides. Later in the day, the lines at **X** should be more manageable, and you can also ride Déjà Vu all over again. Catch lunch early or late and complete your tour of the park.

PLAN B

Head for the older coasters first and enjoy the shorter lines on **Riddler's Revenge, Superman: The Escape,** and the others. By lunchtime and early afternoon, the lines at **Déja Vu** and **X** will be a bit shorter. Catch lunch early or late and complete your tour of the park.

Disneyland in its early days, determined to create a mega-amusement park of his own. Angus Wynne, Jr., together with Hollywood director Randall Duell, created his first park in 1961: Six Flags Over Texas.

That first park, located between Dallas and Fort Worth, was divided into six "lands," which had the themes of the six national flags that had flown over Texas in its history.

Six Flags was subsequently purchased by Time Warner, whose properties included Warner Bros. Motion Pictures and Television (home of *Batman*), HBO, and *Time, People,* and *Sports Illustrated* magazines. This brought "cwazy wabbit" Bugs Bunny and his Looney Tunes cartoon compatriots to the park as mascots. The toon people have stuck around after Time Warner sold off its division in 1998.

Today, Six Flags claims the spot as the world's largest regional theme park company with more than thirty-seven parks in the United States, Europe, and Latin America. Among its properties are Six Flags Magic Mountain (Six Flags Magic Mountain and Six Flags Hurricane Harbor); Six Flags Over Texas and Six Flags Hurricane Harbor in Arlington, Texas; Six Flags Over Georgia in Atlanta; Six Flags St. Louis; Six Flags Astro-World and Six Flags WaterWorld in Houston; Six Flags Great Adventure and Six Flags Wild Animal Safari Park in Jackson, New Jersey; Six Flags Fiesta Texas in San Antonio; Six Flags Great America between Chicago and Milwaukee; Six Flags Worlds of Adventure in Cleveland, and Six Flags New England in Agawam, Massachusetts.

In 2001 the company added the La Ronde park in Montreal and Enchanted Village in Seattle to its roster.

Six Flags Magic Mountain Ticket Prices

Rates were in effect for the 2002 season and are subject to change. Note that general admission tickets apply to all visitors over 48 inches tall.

GENERAL ADMISSION: $44.99
Children (under 48 inches): $29.99
Seniors (55+): $29.99
Children (2 and younger): Free
Fast Lane Boarding Pass (4 one-time passes): $15 additional
Two-park combo ticket with Hurricane Harbor: $54.99
Parking: $8

SEASON PASSES
Season passes are valid for a calendar year, and can be used at any Six Flags theme park (excluding water parks) across the country.

Individual: $90
Family (family of four): $300
Additional member in family pass: $75
Magic Mountain/Hurricane Harbor combo pass: $120

VITAL INFORMATION

The park is set in the beautiful Santa Clarita Valley, about thirty minutes north of downtown Los Angeles, at the Magic Mountain Parkway exit off Interstate 5 in Valencia.

Six Flags Magic Mountain operates daily from late March through early October. For the remainder of the year, the park is open on weekends and during school holidays, including Christmas school vacation period through New Year's Day, with the exception of Christmas Day itself. Check for special offers at the park and at nearby merchants for deals.

Consult the section on Six Flags Hurricane Harbor for spring and summer operating hours for that park. Ordinary hours run from 10:00 A.M. to 6:00 P.M.; in the heart of summer and on holidays the park stays open to 10:00 P.M. or even midnight. Call (661) 367–5965 to confirm hours or consult www.sixflags.com/ magicmountain.

Special events include a Kids Fest in June with events for the smallest visitors of the park. There's also a major Fourth of July celebration.

On three weekends in October, Six Flags is transformed into a ghost town for Fright Fest, which features strolling skeletons, ghouls, and goblins, as well as creepy graveyards, mazes, and live entertainment.

In the busy summertime, the largest crowds are usually found from Wednesday through Saturday. Sunday is the least busy weekend day, and Monday and Tuesday are usually the quietest weekdays.

Fast Lane Boarding Pass. Time is money, even at a theme park; at Six Flags, visitors can purchase a pass that allows them to move to the front of the line at major thrill rides including X, Revolution, Arrowhead Splashdown, Colossus, The Riddler's Revenge, Roaring Rapids, Viper, and Goliath.

Here's the way it works: each pass costs $15, and allows four detours around waiting lines. The pass can be used at four different rides, or for four people at one ride, or other combinations. The park sells only a limited number of the passes each day.

SIX FLAGS PLAZA

Just past the entrance to Six Flags Magic Mountain is a mini-history of amusement parks in this century. To your left is a classic eighty-three-year-old merry-go-round; to the right is a modern, stomach-dropping stacked roller coaster. It's like that throughout much of the park, with old and new, machine and nature side by side.

MUST-SEE FLASHBACK

This is the world's only hairpin-drop roller coaster, with six head-over-heels dives and a 540-degree upward spiral. It's all packed into a relatively small area with 1,900 feet of track stacked above each other. The drops are severe, producing a freefall experience on the plunges; fast steel switchbacks connect the turns just before trains fly into the gravity-defying upward spiral.

Trains reach a maximum of thirty-five miles per hour, with a 3-G force on the one-and-a-half-minute ride. Flashback debuted in 1992.

MUST-SEE LOG JAMMER

A log-ride classic dating from the early days of the park and featuring a pair of straight-down drops.

GRAND CAROUSEL

A lovingly restored and maintained 1912 merry-go-round with moving wooden horses. Built by the Philadelphia Toboggan Company, it was operated at the Savin Rock Amusement Park in West Haven, Connecticut, for fifty years before it was brought to California. The carousel has sixty-six seats, including sixty-four horses and two carriages; rides last three minutes.

ORIENT EXPRESS

At the back left corner of the plaza is an inclined railway up the mountain to the rides and observation tower on Samurai Summit. The people mover is a much easier route up the hill than the stairs and ramps that lead from the back of the park.

PALACE GAMES

A skeeball and arcade game center. Nearby is the Palace Hoop Shoot, a basketball carnival stand.

Watch Your Back

Six Flags Magic Mountain is a thriller of an amusement park, and many of the rides carry with them important safety and health restrictions. Pregnant women and anyone with back, heart, or other health problems are advised against taking a trip on some of the wilder roller coasters and other rides. Some rides have height restrictions; these are intended to make sure passengers are safely held in place by safety bars, belts, or other restraining devices.

▶ **Must be at least 54 inches to ride**

Batman The Ride	Superman: The Escape
Goliath	Viper

▶ **Must be at least 48 inches to ride:**

Colossus	Psyclone
Déjà Vu	Revolution
Flashback	X
Goldrusher	

▶ **Must be at least 42 inches to ride:**

ACME Atom Smasher	Sandblasters
Freefall	Sierra Twist
Gordon Gearworks	Skycoaster
Ninja	Swashbuckler
Roaring Rapids	Tidal Wave

▶ **Under 48 inches must be accompanied by adult; children not permitted to sit on adult's lap:**

Goliath Jr.

▶ **Under 42 inches must be accompanied by adult; children not permitted to sit on adult's laps:**

Buccaneer	Arrowhead Splashdown
Circus Wheel	Jolly Roger
Grand Carousel	Log Jammer
Granny Gran Prix (must be over 48 inches to drive)	Yosemite Sam Sierra Falls

▶ **Must be at least 36 inches tall:**

Scrambler

HIGH SIERRA TERRITORY

One of the prettiest spots in a pretty park, the High Sierra Territory is beautifully landscaped with trees and plants of the mountains. All that said, the entrance to the area is through the General Sam Tree, a 140-foot-tall artificial Sequoia tree— a world-record holder for such replicated greenery, according to the park.

■ SIERRA TWIST
A fast-spinning sled ride on an inclined platter.

■ YOSEMITE SAM SIERRA FALLS
Splash down 760 feet of twisting, turning water slides aboard two-person rafts. Warning: You will get wet or even soaked. The heavier the riders, the more the water will fly.

■ METRO HIGH SIERRA TERRITORY STATION
A stop on the Six Flags aerial monorail system, connecting to stations at Colossus County Fair, Samurai Summit, or round-trip for a bird's-eye tour of much of the park.

BUGS BUNNY WORLD

The corner of the park devoted to the youngest thrillseekers has been completely revamped with more than a dozen rides and attractions. And for the first time parents can join their youngsters on the rides.

Goliath Jr.
Kiddies too small to ride Goliath, one of the park's signature rides, have their own downsized version here. The little coaster has a lift of 20 feet, reaching a top speed of ten miles per hour over a 350-foot-long track; that will still seem pretty awesome to young kids trying out their first thrill ride. Children under 48 inches must be accompanied by an adult.

Looney Tunes Lodge
An interactive fun zone filled with thousands of foam balls for throwing, cata-pulting, and blasting, plus slides and much more.

The Canyon Blaster
A roller coaster that offers pint-sized thrills for the kids (and their parents).

Daffy's Adventure Tours
A wild ride on an out-of-control bus, with Daffy Duck behind the wheel.

Sylvester's Pounce and Bounce is a kiddie-size version of Freefall. *Photo by Corey Sandler*

Elmer's Weather Balloons
Check the weather from these high-flying balloons with Mr. Fudd in charge.

Foghorn Leghorn's Barnyard Railway
A ride into Foghorn's barn on a real coal-burning choo-choo.

Merrie Melodies Carousel
Pick your favorite steed.

Pepé le Pew's Tea Party
Go for a ride as Pepé chases the love of his life in a whirling teacup ride.

Sylvester's Pounce and Bounce
Kids and their parents shoot to the sky and then bounce down to a smooth landing on this scaled-down version of the park's Freefall ride.

Tweety's Escape
Jump in a Tweety cage and watch out for Sylvester in the return of this classic ride.

Taz's Trucking Company
The best little bigfoot trucks in the west.

Yosemite Sam's Flight School
Take a lesson in high flying from the master of the air, Yosemite Sam.

Wile E. Coyote Critter Canyon
Here's your chance to take part in the time-honored pursuit of tame sheep, goats, ducks, and other critters you can pet. Display areas feature more than fifty species of rare and exotic animals.

Animal Action Show
Animals from exotic to household friends perform in a stage show presented in the Carrot Club Theater.

COLOSSUS COUNTY FAIR

MUST-SEE COLOSSUS

The county fair serves as the backdrop for the colossal Colossus coaster, one of the largest dual-tracked wooden roller coasters in the world with nearly a mile of track times two courses.

An old-style speed demon, the Colossus features cars that reach speeds of up to sixty-two miles per hour and experience G forces of up to 3.23 on the three-and-a-half-minute ride. (That's a long ride in roller-coaster terms.)

Colossus covers ten acres of land, climbing to 115 feet above the ground at its highest point. There are fourteen hills in all with two drops of more than 1,000 feet each (a world record at the time of its construction in 1978) and a climactic triple jump near the end.

There are two six-car trains on each of the two tracks; each car seats four riders. The maximum capacity of the ride is about 2,600 guests per hour. That's among the largest capacities of any thrill ride in the world. Colossus is a good place to head when lines are long elsewhere.

After dark, Colossus becomes a multicolored light show. A computer-controlled lighting system bathes the entire ride in color; as many as 128 different color combinations can be created.

MUST-SEE GOLIATH

Towering 255 feet above the earth, the massive steel superstructure has one of the world's tallest drops, and at eighty-five miles per hour it is one of the fastest roller coasters anywhere.

Combining traditional coaster thrills with a few new twists, the three-minute ride travels over 4,500 feet of track that includes

The modern steel coaster Goliath plunges alongside the classic woodie Colossus. *Photo by Corey Sandler*

sharp plunges, sweeping spirals, zero-gravity drops, and a 120-foot-long tunnel in total darkness.

Seated two-abreast in fire-orange trains, the cars climb high above the Colossus coaster and near the peak of Superman: The Escape. The sixty-one-degree first drop plunges 255 feet to the ground . . . and beyond into darkness of the black hole. Emerging from the tunnel, the trains race up into a giant sweeping turn where steel coaster technology meets a traditional woodie as the track soars 100 feet up and over the Colossus. From there it is into camelback hills and a high-speed spiraling curve, followed by a carousel dive outside the station.

Buccaneer
A rocking pirate ship swings back and forth, gathering momentum until it finally turns completely upside down.

Circus Wheel
Round and round you'll go; only the operator knows where you'll stop.

Swashbuckler
A spinning swing set.

Metro Colossus County Fair
A stop on the park-circling monorail, which also has stations at Six Flags Plaza and Samurai Summit.

Center Ring Games
Video machines, carnival games, and your chance to cut your own audio or videotape singing with a professional backup group.

GOTHAM CITY BACKLOT

The dark world of the Caped Crusader is recreated in Gotham City Backlot, the newest of Six Flags Magic Mountain's theme areas. You'll know you're in town when you hear the rumble of the awesome Batman ride and the screams of the visitors who paid good money to climb on board.

You'll enter through the portals of the city and into Bruce Wayne's beautifully landscaped Gotham City Park. As you move a bit farther into the park, though, you begin to hear some strange sounds and see some unsettling sights, including a crashed police car, a broken fire hydrant, and other indicators that all is not well with Gotham City. And then you are into the somewhat menacing tunnels beneath Gotham City, tunnels that lead up to Batman's newest crime-fighting device, The Ride.

⫶MUST-SEE⫶ BATMAN THE RIDE
You'll clamber aboard one of two sleek, black, ski-lift-style trains, each carrying thirty-two passengers sitting four across. Unlike standard roller coasters, though, the trains are missing something: the floor! You'll be locked into place with padded over-the-shoulder and belt-locking harnesses.

Traditional roller-coaster trains travel atop a track and inside of loops; Batman The Ride sends you soaring 360 degrees around the outside of a loop, a very different sensation. Passengers experience a maximum of 4 Gs on the 2,700-foot track. Reaching speeds of up to fifty miles per hour, the trains enter into two vertical loops (77 feet and 68 feet tall), two single corkscrews (each 40 feet long), and a one-of-a-kind, 224-foot "heartline" spin that delivers a zero-G weightless force with nothing but air below your feet.

The heartline spin comes after the first loop when riders go through a twisting spin centered around the middle of your body. It's a quick trip from a 4-G loop into a zero-gravity roll, which is something you don't do everyday unless you are a professional coaster rider.

Is Batman the ultimate in roller coasters? Well, the experts point out that there are faster, higher, and wilder coasters—including the Viper at Six Flags Magic Mountain—but Batman is unusual because the lower bodies of the riders are hanging free. Think of it as a ski lift gone crazy and you get the idea. Hardcore roller-coaster fans rank Batman The Ride among the most bodacious in America. I know it is on my personal list of terrors.

Six Flags also deserves credit for the good job of applying theme to the waiting areas for the ride. You'll walk through a crumbling neighborhood, past the steaming wreck of a police car, and into the decrepit innards of a factory on the way to your appointment with the ride.

(In the world of amusement park technology, the Batman ride is called an inverted coaster, whereas the Ninja is known as a suspended coaster because it has enclosed train cars hanging from an overhead track.)

The capacity of the Swiss-made ride is about 1,400 passengers per hour.

■ ATOM SMASHER

A whirling, wobbly turntable ride set within the industrial walls of the ACME factory.

■ GRINDER GEARWORKS

Let centrifugal force plaster you to the wall as the platform spins at a forty-five-degree angle. Riders stand up in a whirling cage that goes round and round and then turns on its side with prisoners, er, visitors stuck to the exterior by centrifugal force.

THE MOVIE DISTRICT

The Riddler is the star of the "ultimate backlot experience," the former Monterey Landing area of Six Flags Magic Mountain.

▓MUST-SEE▓ THE RIDDLER'S REVENGE

Turn on the superlative machine: among the latest and greatest at Six Flags is The Riddler's Revenge, the world's tallest and fastest stand-up roller coaster.

Looming 156 feet tall and reaching a top speed of sixty-five miles per hour and maximum G-force of 4.2, the coaster sends riders looping head-over-heels six times over nearly a mile of twisting, looping, and spiraling green steel track. Did we mention that riders stand up through the entire three-minute ride?

The ride's theme is based on the character Edward Nygma—The Riddler—from the Batman series. Guests are drawn through a glaring green neon question mark entrance into The Riddler's laboratory.

Standing four abreast and strapped in sleek green bullet-nosed trains, riders climb sixteen stories before plummeting almost straight down the first 146-foot drop. There are six inversions: a 360-degree vertical loop at a height of 124 feet, a 360-degree oblique loop, two over-the-top diving loops, and a pair of 150-foot-long barrel rolls. There's also a 250-foot-long, high-speed spiral.

The ride, designed by a Swiss company, has a capacity of 1,800 riders per hour. Guests must be at least 54 inches tall to ride.

▓▓▓▓ MUST-SEE FREEFALL

Here's an elevator ride you won't soon forget. Your car will rise to the top of a 98-foot tower, move out onto a platform . . . and then drop straight down. You'll reach fifty-five miles per hour in about two seconds and then zoom out on a curved rail at the bottom.

Each of the eight cars carries four passengers per trip; one car drops every twelve seconds. A state-of-the-art system applies brake pressure according to the weight of each car plus its passengers at forty different sensor locations along the slow-down pathway.

By the way, professional and amateur theme park enthusiasts consider this ride to be a roller coaster, albeit in a class of its own.

▓ GOLD RUSHER

The first roller coaster at Six Flags, this runaway mine train was built in 1971. By comparison to the big coasters, it's rather tame with a top speed of thirty-five miles per hour, but it still has its thrills. The ½-mile track is built into the hillside with its track very close to the ground; this is an excellent beginner coaster ride that lasts about two-and-a-half minutes.

▓ SANDBLASTERS

Every amusement park worth its name has a bumper car ride; if that's what you're looking for, here's a fine example.

▓ TIDAL WAVE

The wettest water flume that features twenty-passenger boats plunging over a 50-foot waterfall.

▓ *BATMAN & ROBIN LIVE ACTION SHOW*

Based on the film *Batman & Robin,* the *Batman & Robin Live Action Show* brings the hit movie to life with a behind-the-scenes look at big Hollywood stunts.

The explosive stage production features elaborate set designs, incredible stunts and special effects, plus athletic hijinks including in-line skating performed by Mr. Freeze's Icemen, and an assortment of unusual high-tech Bat-gadgets, including a souped-up Batmobile.

The action begins as the diabolical Mr. Freeze teams up with the lovely but deadly Poison Ivy to seize and freeze Gotham City. Poison Ivy, the result of a laboratory mishap, releases Mr. Freeze from the Arkham Asylum where he has been imprisoned; he promptly unleashes a new kind of frozen terror. However, Batman and Robin, along with superhero Batgirl, turn on the heat to melt Mr. Freeze's icy grip on the good citizens of Gotham.

Scrambler
This human eggbeater spins and rocks a two-seater car on an uneven platform.

Spin Out
As the cage spins faster and faster, the floor drops out below you.

CYCLONE BAY

A Southern California equivalent of a beachfront boardwalk and much more attractive than Coney Island in New York, this bay runs alongside the Psyclone wooden coaster.

MUST-SEE DÉJÀ VU
Wanna see the world's tallest and fastest suspended roller coaster with a super boomerang loop? Wanna see it again?

Strapped in ski-lift-style chairs suspended from the track above, riders plummet 196 feet and fly at sixty-five miles per hour over the outside of a vertical loop and into a 110-foot-tall boomerang turn with nothing but the sky above their feet. The first drop could not be any steeper: a ninety-degree free fall. The 1,203-foot-long track includes one vertical loop 102 feet in the air and a boomerang turn 110 feet up. Maximum gravitational forces reach a significant 4.5 G. The cars go through the track one time forward and one time backward: Déjà Vu all over again.

Each train carries twenty-four passengers, seated four abreast in a sleek V-shape design. The ride has a capacity of 1,100 riders per hour; expect long lines at midday. Guests must be at least 48 inches tall to ride.

MUST-SEE PSYCLONE
A traditional wooden coaster opened in 1991, Psyclone is a replica of the legendary 1927 Cyclone in Coney Island, New York. How realistic? Well, in addition to the feel of the steep drops and high-banked twists and turns, you'll also hear the somewhat unnerving sounds of creaking wood and screaming steel wheels.

There is more than ½ mile of steel track, eleven hills, and five high-speed banked turns; the track also drops into a 183-foot-long, pitch-black tunnel. Riders are treated to a maximum G force of 3.

Built in 1991 the ride required 450,000 board-feet of treated Southern pine, unpainted to emphasize the ride's natural beauty. It's held together with 16,000 pounds of nails and 125,000 pounds of bolts. One more useless but interesting factoid: The ride required something like 40,000 man-hours to build; if one carpenter had done the job by himself, it would have taken him twenty years to finish the job.

Psyclone features a 95-foot first drop angled at fifty-three degrees, ten additional steep hills, and average speeds of up to fifty miles per hour.

[MUST-SEE] DIVE DEVIL

A strange cross between a giant backyard swing, bungee jumping, hang-gliding, and skydiving, and you get to pay for the privilege!

The ride apparatus consists of a soaring 173-foot-tall steel arch from which four steel cables are suspended; alongside are a pair of launch towers. At the end of each pair of cables is an attachment for up to three flight suits.

The volunteer riders are placed in the suits and stretched out parallel to the ground, and then the fliers are pulled backward by cable behind the arch to the top of the launch towers, about 152 feet off the ground. When one of the riders pulls a ripcord, the fliers swoop down headfirst in free fall about 50 feet before they zoom past their starting point. When they reach the bottom of the fall, they are about 6 feet off the ground and moving about sixty miles per hour.

The forward motion of the fliers carries them about 90 to 100 feet up in the air in front of the arch, reaching a weightless free-fall stall in midair before they swing back in the other direction. The fliers swing back and forth about a dozen times before they come to a stop at the bottom.

To ride Dive Devil, you'll have to fork over an additional fee. For flights with three fliers in the harness, admission will be about $16 per flier; for two-person flights, the charge will be about $22; and for solo flights the fare will be about $28. Riders must be at least 42 inches tall.

■ ARROWHEAD SPLASHDOWN

A pleasant tour aboard a jet boat with a splashy 57-foot-plunge finale. Arrowhead Splashdown is less likely to soak riders than the Log Jam ride, but don't discount the possibility of the occasional damp touchdown. The loading platform for the ride is a circular turntable that is synchronized to the speed of the moving boats. Arrowhead Splashdown was previously known as Jet Stream.

Entertainment at Cyclone Bay includes Sharkey's Shooting Gallery and the Boardwalk Bandstand. Check the daily schedule for performances.

Muscle Beach Arcade

A video-game parlor.

SAMURAI SUMMIT

▓MUST-SEE▓ SUPERMAN: THE ESCAPE

Look, up in the sky: that roller coaster is accelerating from zero to a hundred miles per hour in just seven seconds and delivering six-and-a-half seconds of weightlessness. Only Superman: The Escape could perform such feats. In fact, Six Flags claims its unusual ride was the first to reach one hundred miles per hour.

We're not going to quibble over a few miles per hour or notches on the G-force belt; we do know that this ride is super-awesome.

The L-shape dual-track ride travels more than 900 feet (three football fields) from its launch pad on Samurai Summit on a track that suddenly curves into a climb straight up a 415-foot-tall tower.

The Superman adventure begins in the Fortress of Solitude, a crystalline ice cavern high atop the mountain ridge at Six Flags. Confronted by enemy forces inside the Fortress, the only escape for guests is to board fifteen-passenger aerodynamically designed vehicles. Electromagnetic motors blast the six-ton vehicles out of the Fortress through a special effects tunnel; the cars accelerate to one hundred miles per hour and 4.5 Gs and then climb the forty-one-story tower reaching near-total weightlessness when they reach the top and free-fall straight down the skyscraper.

The linear synchronous motors apply acceleration that has been compared to an F-18 jet fighter rocketing off an aircraft carrier.

The construction of the Swiss-designed ride—at a cost of about $10 million—changed the look of the park. Other alterations to the scene include a bridge over the lift for the venerable Gold Rusher coaster, which circles all around the loading station for the Superman ride.

▓MUST-SEE▓ NINJA

The Black Belt of coasters, this is the west coast's fastest suspended roller coaster. Trains swing 180 degrees side-to-side while hanging from an overhead track and traveling at speeds of up to fifty-five miles per hour. Riders are treated to a nearly 4-G positive gravity force in the second spiral.

Completed in 1988, the ride takes about two minutes to travel 2,700 feet of track. Each of three trains carries a total of twenty-eight riders sitting two abreast. The maximum capacity of the ride is about 1,600 riders per hour.

Metro Samurai Summit Station

A stop on the Six Flags aerial monorail system, connecting to stations at High Sierra Territory, Samurai Summit, or round-trip for a bird's-eye tour of much of the park.

Orient Express

The people mover down the mountain to Six Flags Plaza.

Sky Tower

The thirty-eight-story landmark offers a spectacular view of the entire park and much of the Santa Clarita Valley. The elevator ride to the top is part of the thrill.

RAPIDS CAMP CROSSING

▐MUST-SEE▐ ROARING RAPIDS

America's first man-made, white-water river. Twelve-passenger boats splash through waves, crosscurrents, and rapids.

Entertainment at Rapids Camp Crossing includes the Mining Town Arcade and Mining Town Games.

BAJA RIDGE

▐MUST-SEE▐ X

Welcome to the fourth dimension of roller-coaster technology, a trip where riders for the first time will travel in vehicles that can independently spin 360 degrees forward or backward as they move down the track. On X, once the train leaves the station, there is no up, down, left, or right.

The huge 20-foot-wide, wing-shaped vehicles each carry twenty-eight passengers seated four-abreast; the cars each weigh 10,000 pounds. Riders plummet 200 feet to the ground, head first and face down; then they race at seventy-six miles per hour, spinning through acrobatic head-over-heels loops along the course of the 3,600-foot twisting steel maze.

Stop for a minute and consider that first statistic: the trains are 20 feet wide. Riders sit two-abreast on each side of a large central control mechanism that rotates their seats. There are four rails beneath the huge trains; two hold the trains and the other two rotate the seats.

The first drop—the one that plummets 200 feet—produces a maximum 4 Gs. The track includes a twisting front flip, two back flips, and a pair of raven turns.

The ride has a capacity of 1,600 riders an hour; passengers must be at least 48 inches tall to ride.

▐MUST-SEE▐ REVOLUTION

You say you want a revolution? This giant looping steel roller coaster was the first of its kind when it was built in 1976. It included the world's first 360-degree vertical loop, 90 feet above the Grand Carousel.

The white steel track is built into the lush hillsides and features a fast-and-furious series of steep dips and serious dives inspired by old-fashioned wooden roller coasters.

The two-and-a-half minute ride travels over 3,457 feet of track; each train carries twenty riders in five cars sitting two abreast. The maximum capacity is about 2,000 riders per hour.

Revolution hugs the hillside. *Photo by Corey Sandler*

The Viper in Baja Ridge. *Photo by Corey Sandler*

Riders experience a maximum positive G force of 4.94 entering the vertical loop, which soars 90 feet high in a 45-foot diameter loop. The difference between the rider's lowest point at Valencia Falls and the highest point at the top of the lift is 113 feet.

⋮MUST-SEE⋮ VIPER

The largest looping roller coaster in the world, with a top speed of seventy miles per hour, three vertical loops, a double-barrel boomerang, and a classic corkscrew. Some roller enthusiasts consider the Viper among the most frightening rides on the planet.

Riders are turned upside down seven times and there are sixteen changes in elevation; the first drop is a gargantuan 188 feet, seven stories higher than the colossal Colossus.

The two-and-a-half-minute-long ride travels a 3,830-foot track; each of the three trains carries twenty-eight riders in seven cars, seated two across. The maximum capacity of the ride is about 1,700 riders per hour.

About those vertical loops: The first one rises and falls 114 feet, making it among the world's tallest; the second is a mere 90 feet in height, and the last 62 feet tall. The boomerang rotates riders upside down twice; it rises 60 feet from lowest to highest point. The corkscrew is 40 feet high and 200 feet long.

If you need a bit of reassurance before you strap yourself into the over-the-shoulder locking harness for the ride, consider that the construction of the Viper in 1990 required one million pounds of steel and 600,000 tons of concrete.

EATING YOUR WAY THROUGH SIX FLAGS MAGIC MOUNTAIN

Eateries at Six Flags run from the most basic of fast food—a McDonald's in Cyclone Bay—to a talking moose head to a sit-down family restaurant with a spectacular mountaintop view.

■ SIX FLAGS PLAZA

Chicken Plantation. Crispy fried chicken with all the fixings.

Plaza Cafe. A casual outdoor sidewalk bistro serving croissants, fruits, and specialty coffees alongside Valencia Falls in Six Flags Plaza.

■ HIGH SIERRA TERRITORY AND BUGS BUNNY WORLD

Mooseburger Lodge. The mooseburgers aren't really made from a moose, and the restaurant isn't really a hunting lodge in the High Sierras, but you could be fooled by both. This is an attractive, fun, family restaurant that features a trio of robotic moose heads who are aided and abetted by singing waiters and waitresses who will be glad to perform the Moose Muffle Shuffle just for you. In addition to the big burgers, you'll also find ribs, a buffet, and special desserts including (of course) chocolate mousse. Entrees range from about $7.00 to $10.00.

Wascal's. A kiddie-oriented burger and fries stand.

■ THE MOVIE DISTRICT

Eduardo's Grill. Mexican specialties.

Waterfront Commissary. A burger and fries and chicken strips eatery. Prices range from about $5.00 to $7.00, including a drink.

■ RAPIDS CAMP CROSSING

Katy's Kettle. Hamburgers, turkey burgers, and fries.

■ CYCLONE BAY AND SAMURAI SUMMIT

McDonald's. Perhaps you've heard of this burger joint?

Surfside Grill. What would you expect from a restaurant under a jumbo hot dog? Frankfurters, chili dogs, icees, and more.

■ COLOSSUS COUNTY FAIR AND PIRATES COVE

Carousel Grill. Philly cheesesteak, chicken club, and other specialties.

Food Etc. An indoor food court offering a wide range of delectables including Mexican food, pasta, pizza, and more.

■ GOTHAM CITY BACKLOT

The Pizza Vector. Like the sign says.

SIX FLAGS HURRICANE HARBOR

Whoosh! A hurricane of a water park swept into Six Flags in 1995 with the first season of Six Flags Hurricane Harbor. The park was expanded in 1996 and nearly doubled in size for 1997 with wet and wild new attractions.

The twenty-two-acre park tells the watery story of a lost lagoon in a forgotten world. Set amidst the fringes of a tropical jungle, you'll find the remains of a

Hurricane Harbor Ticket Prices

Rates were in effect for the 2002 season at Six Flags Hurricane Harbor and are subject to change.

GENERAL ADMISSION: $21.99
Hurricane Harbor/Magic Mountain combo ticket: $52.99
Children under 48 inches: $14.99
Children 2 and younger: Free
Seniors (55+): $14.99
Parking: $7

SEASON PASSES
Individual: $70
Family (family of four): $220
Additional member in family pass: $55
Magic Mountain/Hurricane Harbor combo pass: $120

disappeared civilization, hidden pirate treasures, playful sea creatures, ancient ruins, shipwrecks, girls in bikinis, guys in muscle shirts, kids in wave pools, suntan lotion, hot dogs, ice cream . . . you get the idea.

The water park is in the shadow of Colossus and Flashback, two of the biggest, baddest roller coasters at the park.

Six Flags expects that most visitors will spend a day at either Magic Mountain or Hurricane Harbor. Combination tickets for separate days are available. Some visitors, though, might choose to visit the water park in the day and cross through to the theme park at night. The parks share the same parking lot.

The operating schedule for Hurricane Harbor is dependent upon the weather, but plans call for it to be open on weekends only from early May and then daily from Memorial Day through Labor Day from 10:00 A.M. to 6:00 P.M.; the park will stay open until 8:00 P.M. on summer weekends. After Labor Day, Hurricane Harbor will remain open on weekends only through the end of September.

Be sure to call to confirm the schedule; call (661) 367–5965.

Rafts are required at Lightning Falls, Tiki Falls, Lost Temple Rapids, and the River Cruise. All visitors can use free tubes provided by the park; on busy days it may make sense to rent a personal tube for an additional charge.

⁞⁞⁞⁞⁞⁞⁞ *MUST-SEE* ⁞⁞⁞⁞⁞⁞⁞ BLACK SNAKE SUMMIT

The hot news at this cool park, the area features five speed slides, including the tallest enclosed speed slides in Southern California—two totally enclosed twisting slides, one almost vertical plunge, and two totally enclosed twisting tube slides.

The twin queens of this hill are Twisted Fang and Coiled Cobra, enclosed body slides each 500 feet long and dropping from the 75-foot level. Nearby is Venom Drop, an open slide that extends only 300 feet.

Sidewinder and Boa Constrictor are 59-foot-tall, enclosed tube slides that extend 650 feet.

▉ MUST-SEE ▉ LIZARD LAGOON

This just over three-acre activity area includes a 3.5-foot-deep pool that has basketball hoops, beach volleyball courts, a lizard slide, and the Reptile Ridge tower with five body slides.

REPTILE RIDGE

Five gentle body slides descend from the 35-foot-tall summit. There are two 130-foot-long enclosed twisting slides, Gecko Gully East and West, and Gator Gorge, a 70-foot-long enclosed straight drop. A pair of open flume body slides are the 230-foot-long twisting slide Iguana Ravine and the gentle Croc Creek, 255 feet long.

▉ MUST-SEE ▉ BAMBOO RACER

A six-lane racing slide from a 45-foot tower. Entrants plunge headfirst, side by side on water toboggans down 625-foot-long lanes.

▉ CASTAWAY COVE

Designed exclusively for the littlest swashbucklers (under 54 inches tall), Castaway Cove is one of the largest children's water play areas in California. Adventures include a variety of pint-size water slides, including a pair of cannon slides. Little visitors will also find waterfalls; a bamboo raintree; friendly sea creatures; an organ that squirts water as guests play the keys; hidden pirate treasures; and a kiddie fortress loaded with waterfalls, gadgets, swings, slides, and more. Youngsters can also splash in the secluded tide pools of Octopus Island, where a giant eight-legged creature stands guard.

▉ SHIPWRECK SHORES

The place where Red Eye the Pirate first dropped anchor is now a splashy lagoon that offers more than thirty-two family activities, including a huge skull that dumps thousands of gallons of water onto intruders every few minutes and weeping sails that shed continuous streams. Visitors enter through the rickety remains of Red Eye's ship, mysterious ancient ruins from a lost civilization. Around the shoreline are eight 11-foot-tall water-spraying statues and the old temple entrance to the volcano.

▉ GEYSER PEAK

Towering 45 feet above the harbor between Castaway Cove and Shipwreck Shores is the volcano where Red Eye the Pirate once hid his plunder.

▉ THE RIVER CRUISE

Guests board rafts that circumnavigate Castaway Cove and Shipwreck Cove on a 1,300-foot-long lazy river at the center of the park. The 3-foot-deep river moves at about two miles per hour, and a complete circuit takes about eight minutes. Along the river banks are nine 15-foot-tall tikis, replicas of the famous statues of Easter Island, as well as the Rainbow Reef, an overgrown tropical rain forest.

MUST-SEE FORGOTTEN SEA WAVE POOL

Hurricane Harbor's tide pool with a constant tide of 2-foot waves. The 480,000-gallon pool slopes down to a depth of 6 feet.

MUST-SEE TABOO TOWER

The park's showcase attraction—visible from Interstate 5—is the crumbled remains of an ancient temple; three speed slides, including a completely dark tube, are built into the 65-foot-tall ruins. They include the 300-foot-long Daredevil Plunge, with a forty-five-degree straight drop; the bumpy, 260-foot-long Escape Chute; and the Secret Passage, an enclosed 325-foot spiraling slide.

■ LIGHTNING FALLS

Three twisting, turning, 400-foot-long open tube slides named after island storms drop about 42 feet; look for Typhoon Tube, Tornado Twist, and Thunder Trough.

■ TIKI FALLS

Visitors splash through the mouths of Hurricane Harbor's three most famous tikis: Old Shut Eye, a 395-foot enclosed slide; Stone Face, a 385-foot closed-tube slide; and Bright Eyes, a semi-enclosed 400-foot tube.

■ LOST TEMPLE RAPIDS

A 560-foot-long, six-person family rafting adventure down the island's ancient aqueduct.

PART VI

SLEEPING AND EATING FOR LESS

CHAPTER TEN

NEGOTIATING FOR A ROOM

DON'T BUY A ROOM. Negotiate a room. Hotel rooms, like almost everything else, are subject to negotiation and change.

Here is how to pay the highest possible price for a hotel room: Walk up to the front desk without a reservation and say, "I'd like a room." Unless the "No Vacancy" sign is lit, you're going to pay the "rack rate," which is the published maximum nightly charge.

Here are a few ways to pay the lowest possible price:

1. Join associations and clubs that offer discounts to their members, such as AAA or AARP. And don't overlook direct offers from hotels and chains published in newspapers and magazines.

2. Get on the Internet and check out the Web sites for major chains and independent hotels. Be on the lookout for Internet specials that may be less than the price you will be quoted on the phone.

You can also make an Internet visit to travel portals—hotel booking and travel agency Web sites—that offer searches by location. Travel portals are usually more convenient, but in my experience, best prices are usually found by going direct to the hotel Web sites.

3. If you want to try to get an even better deal, pick up your telephone and call your best candidates directly. (Don't call the central booking number for hotel chains; they rarely have the best deals.)

Start by asking for the room rate. Then ask them for their best rate. Does that sound like an unnecessary second request? Trust us, it's not: we can't begin to count the number of times the rates have dropped substantially when we ask again.

[Here's a true story: I once called the reservation desk of a major hotel chain and asked for the rates for a night at a Chicago location. "That will be $149 per night," I was told. "Ouch," I said. "Oh, would you like to spend less?" the reservationist asked. I admitted that I would, and she punched a few keys on her keyboard: "They

Here's My Card

Membership in AAA brings some important benefits for the traveler, although you may not be able to apply the club's usual 10 percent discount on top of whatever hotel rate you negotiate. (It doesn't hurt to ask, though.) Be sure to request a Tour Book and a California map from AAA, even if you plan to fly to California; they are much better than the maps given by car rental agencies.

AARP members also receive a discount. Most hotels also offer senior discounts, accepting your driver's license or your gray hair as proof of age.

have a special promotion going on. How about $109 per night?"

Not bad for a city hotel, I reasoned, but still I hadn't asked the big question: "What is your best rate?" "Oh, our best rate? That would be $79," said the agent.

But, wait: "OK, that's good. I'm an AAA member, by the way." Another pause, and then the reservation agent said, "That's fine, Mr. Sandler. The nightly room rate will be $71.10. Have a nice day."]

When you feel you've negotiated the best deal you can obtain over the phone, make a reservation at the hotel of your choice. Be sure to go over the dates and prices one more time, and obtain the name of the person you spoke with and a confirmation number if available.

4. But wait: When you show up at your hotel on the first night stop, take a look at the marquee to see if the hotel is advertising a discount rate. Use your cell phone to make a few phone calls to neighboring hotels to check their rates. Many of the hotels in the Disneyland area adjust their prices based on attendance levels at the park. It is not uncommon to see prices change by $10 or more over the course of a day.

If the hotel you chose is still offering the best rate and you're going to stay, here's where you need to be bold. Walk up to the desk as if you did not have a reservation, and ask the clerk: "What is your best room rate for tonight?" If the rate they give you as a walk-up is less than the rate in your reservation, you are now properly armed to ask for a reduction in your room rate.

Weekly, Not Weakly

Are you planning to stay for a full week? Ask for the weekly rate. If the room clerk says there is no such rate, ask to speak to the manager. He or she may be willing to shave a few dollars per day off the rate for a long-term stay.

Similarly, if the room rate advertised out front on the marquee drops during your stay, don't be shy about asking that your charges be reduced. Just be sure to ask for the reduction before you spend another night at the old rate, and obtain the name of the clerk who promises a change. If the hotel tries a lame excuse like "that's only for new check-ins," you can offer to check out and then check back in again— that threat usually works. And you can always check out and go to the hotel across the road that will usually match the rates of its competitor.

5. Here is the way to play lowball roulette, in the low-season only: Come without a reservation and cruise one of the motel strips near Disneyland. Check the outdoor marquees for discount prices and make notes. Find a phone booth and make a few phone calls to the hotels whose rates you found attractive. Once again, be sure to ask for the best price. The later in the day you search for a room, the more likely you are to find a hotel ready to make a deal.

Except for the busiest periods of the year—the time from Christmas through New Year's and the heart of summer among them—you're not going to have any trouble locating a place to stay near Disneyland. In fact, the biggest problem facing most visitors is choosing among the various places to stay.

The opening of Disney's California Adventure in 2001 remade the hotel market in and around the Disneyland Resort. Disney's Grand Californian Hotel is a handsome new addition and is the first Disney-owned hotel with a direct entrance into a theme park.

Disney also upgraded the already-fine Disney's Paradise Pier Hotel (the former Disneyland Pacific Hotel) and the Disneyland Hotel.

With the opening of the new theme park in Anaheim, there are approximately 17,400 hotel rooms within a mile of Disneyland, an increase of 3,400 rooms from recent years. And several thousand more places to sleep are under construction or are planned to be built in the first decade of the twenty-first century.

Wrong Numbers

Be sure you understand the telephone billing policy at the motel. Some establishments allow free local calls, while others charge as much as a dollar for such calls. (We're especially unhappy with service charges for 800 numbers.) Be sure to examine your bill carefully at checkout and make sure it is correct. We strongly suggest you obtain a telephone credit card and use it when you travel; nearly all motels tack a high service charge on long-distance calls, and there is no reason to pay it.

ANAHEIM AREA

(Price ranges are approximate and are subject to change and adjustments in busiest seasons; ratings are relative for the area. Rates near the park are often the lowest in the area because of the intense competition, except during the busiest times of the year when the hotels may be sold out. You may have to stay in nearby communities, including Buena Park, Costa Mesa, Huntington Beach, Newport, Orange, and Santa Ana. Each is within about fifteen minutes of Disneyland; Buena Park is home of Knott's Berry Farm.)

The hotels listed here represent the best deals and best quality in the area; not every hotel is included. Properties marked with an Econoguide ★ are relatively better than others in the area.

Legend

$	Budget: less than $50
$$	50–$99
$$$	100–$149
$$$$	Luxury: $150 and more
★	Econoguide Bests
➋	Near Disneyland

Properties marked with a ⊳ icon are within five minutes of Disneyland.

⊳ **Anaheim Angel Inn.** 800 East Katella Avenue. (714) 634–9121 or (800) 358–4400. anaheimangel. tripod.com. Shuttle, pool. $–$$

★ ⊳ **Anaheim Carriage Inn.** 2125 South Harbor Boulevard.(714) 740–1440 or (800) 345–2131. www. carriage-inn.com. Continental breakfast, shuttle, pool. $–$$

★ ⊳ **Anaheim Desert Inn and Suites.** 1600 South Harbor Boulevard. (714) 772–5050 or (800) 433–5270. www.anaheimdesertinn.com. Continental breakfast, shuttle, pool. $$

★ ⊳ **Anaheim Desert Palm Inn and Suites.** 631 West Katella Avenue. (714) 535–1133 or (800) 635–5423. www.anaheimdesertpalm.com. Shuttle, pool. $$

★ ⊳ **Anaheim Fairfield Inn.** 1460 South Harbor Boulevard. (714) 772–6777 or (800) 228–2800. www. anaheimfairfieldinn.com. Shuttle, pool. $$

★ ⊳ **Annabella Hotel.** 1030 West Katella Avenue. (800) 887–1532. www.anabellahotel.com. Pool. $$$

★ ⊳ **Best Western Anaheim Inn.** 1630 South Harbor Boulevard. (714) 774–1050 or (800) 854–8175. www.stovallshotels.com. Shuttle, pool. $$

⊳ **Best Western Anaheim Stardust.** 1057 West Ball Road. (714) 774–7600 or (800) 222–3639. www.bestwestern.com. Shuttle, pool. $$

Best Western Courtesy Inn. 1070 West Ball Street. (714) 772–2470 or (800) 233–8062. www.bestwestern.com. Pool. $$

★ ⊳ **Best Western Park Place Inn.** 1544 South Harbor Boulevard. (714) 776–4800 or (800) 854–8175. www.stovallshotels.com. Continental breakfast, pool. $$–$$$

★ ⊳ **Best Western Pavilions.** 1176 West Katella Avenue. (714) 776–0140 or (800) 854–8175. www.stovallshotels.com. Shuttle, pool. $$

★ ⊳ **Best Western Raffles Inn and Suites.** 2040 South Harbor Boulevard. (714) 750–6100 or (800) 654–0196. www.bestwestern.com. Shuttle, pool. $$–$$$

⊳ **Best Western Stovall's Inn.** 1110 West Katella Avenue. (714) 778–1880 or (800) 854–8175. www.stovallshotels.com. Shuttle, pool. $$

★ **Candy Cane Inn.** 1747 South Harbor Boulevard. (714) 774–5284 or (800) 345–7057. Shuttle, pool. $$

⊳ **Carousel Inn and Suites.** 1530 South Harbor Boulevard. (714) 758–0444 or (800) 854–6767. www.carouselinnandsuites.com. Continental breakfast, pool. $$–$$$

★ ⊳ **Comfort Inn & Suites.** 300 East Katella Way. (714) 772–8713 or (800) 982–8239. www.comfortinns.com. Continental breakfast, shuttle, pool. $$

▣ **Comfort Inn Maingate.** 2200 South Harbor Boulevard. (714) 750–5211 or (800) 228–5150. www.comfortinn.com. Shuttle, pool. $–$$

▣ **Days Inn Suites.** 1111 South Harbor Boulevard. (714) 533–8830. www.daysinn.com. Pool. $–$$

★ ▣ **Disney's Grand Californian Hotel.** 1600 South Disneyland Drive. (714) 635–2300. www.disney.com. Pool. $$$$

★ ▣ **Disney's Paradise Pier Hotel.** 1717 Disneyland Drive. (714) 999–0990. www.disney.com. Pool. $$$–$$$$

★ ▣ **Disneyland Hotel.** 1150 West Cerritos Avenue. (714) 778–6600. www.disney.com. Monorail, pool. $$$$

★ **Embassy Suites Anaheim.** 3100 East Frontera. (714) 632–1221 or (800) 362–2779. www.embassysuites.com. Shuttle, pool. $$–$$$

★ **Four Points Sheraton Anaheim.** 515 West Katella Avenue, Anaheim. (714) 991–6868 or (888) 543–7878. www.fourpoints-anaheim.com. Pool. $$$–$$$$

★ **Hawthorn Suites Limited Hotel.** 1752 South Clementine Street. (714) 535–7773 or (800) 992–4884. Shuttle, pool. www.hawthorn.com. $$–$$$$

★ ▣ **Hilton Anaheim.** 777 Convention Way. (714) 750–4321 or (800) 222–9923. www.hilton.com. Shuttle, pool. $$$–$$$$

★ ▣ **Holiday Inn Anaheim at the Park.** 1221 South Harbor Boulevard. (714) 758–0900 or (800) 545–7275. www.holiday-inn.com. Shuttle, pool. $$

▣ **Holiday Inn Express–Anaheim Maingate.** 435 West Katella Avenue. (714) 772–7755 or (800) 833–7888. www.holiday-inn.com. Shuttle, pool. $$

★ ▣ **Howard Johnson Hotel.** 1380 South Harbor Boulevard. (714) 776–6120 or (800) 422–4228. www.hojo.com. Shuttle, pool. $$

★ **Hyatt Regency Orange County Disneyland Park.** Harbor and Chapman. (714) 750–1234 or (800) 233–1234. www.hyatt.com. Shuttle, pool. $$–$$$$

★ ▣ **Jolly Roger Inn.** 640 West Katella Avenue. (714) 782–7500 or (800) 446–1555. www.jollyrogerhotel.com. Pool. $$

★ ▣ **Marriott Anaheim.** 700 West Convention Way. (714) 750–8000 or (800) 228–9290. www.marriott.com. Shuttle, pool. $$$–$$$$

★ ▣ **Park Inn Anaheim.** 1520 South Harbor Boulevard. (714) 635–7275 or (800) 828–4898. www.parkhtls.com. Shuttle, pool. $$–$$$$

★ ▣ **Park Vue Inn.** 1570 South Harbor Boulevard. (714) 772–3691 or (800) 334–7021. Pool. $–$$$

★ ▣ **Peacock Suites Hotel.** 1745 South Anaheim Boulevard. (714) 535–8255 or (800) 522–6401. Shuttle, pool. $$–$$$

★ ▣ **Quality Hotel–Maingate.** 616 Convention Way. (714) 750–3131 or (800) 228–5151. www.cal-sunburst.com. Shuttle, pool. $$–$$$

★ ▣ **Radisson Hotel–Maingate.** 1850 South Harbor Boulevard. (714) 750–2801 or (800) 333–3333. www.radisson.com. Continental breakfast, shuttle, pool. $$

★ **Radisson Resort Knott's Berry Farm.** 7675 Crescent Avenue. (714) 995–1111 or (800) 422–4444. www.radisson.com. Shuttle, pool. $$–$$$$

▣ **Ramada Inn Near Disneyland Park.** 1331 East Katella Avenue. (714) 978–8088 or (800) 228–0586. www.ramada.com. Shuttle, pool. $$

▣ **Ramada Limited Main Gate South.** 921 South Harbor Boulevard. (714) 999–0684 or (800) 235–3399. www.ramada.com. Shuttle, pool. $–$$

Ramada Maingate/Saga Across from Disneyland Park. 1650 South Harbor Boulevard. (714) 772–0440 or (800) 854–6097. www.ramada.com. Continental breakfast, shuttle, pool. $$

▣ **Red Roof Inn.** 1251 North Harbor Boulevard. (714) 635–6461 or (800) 843–7663. www.redroof.com. $–$$

★ **Residence Inn Anaheim/Disneyland.** 1700 South Clementine Street. (714) 533–3555 or (800) 331–3131. www.marriott.com. Shuttle, pool. $$$$

★ ▣ **Sheraton Anaheim Hotel.** 900 South Disneyland Road. (714) 778–1700 or (800) 331–7251. www.sheraton.com. Shuttle, pool. $$$–$$$$

▣ **Super 8 Motel.** 415 West Katella Avenue. (714) 778–6900 or (800) 800–8000. www.super8.com. $–$$

Super 8 Motel–Buena Park. 7930 Beach Boulevard, Buena Park. (714) 994–6480 or (800) 800–8000. www.super8.com. $

▣ **Super 8 Motor Inn.** 915 Disneyland Drive. (714) 778–0350 or (800) 248–4400. www.super8.com. Shuttle, pool. $–$$

★ **Travelodge/Buena Park.** 7039 Orangethorpe Avenue, Buena Park. (714) 521–9220 or (800) 854–8299. www.travelodge.com. $–$$

★ **Travelodge International Inn.** 2060 South Harbor Boulevard. (714) 971–9393 or (800) 251–2345. www.travelodge.com. Continental breakfast, shuttle, pool. $–$$

▣ **Tropicana Inn.** 1540 South Harbor Boulevard. (714) 635–4082 or (800) 828–4898. www.bei-hotels.com. Shuttle, pool. $$

★ ▣ **Westcoast Anaheim.** 1855 South Harbor Boulevard. (714) 750–1811 or (800) 353–2773. www.westcoasthotels.com. Shuttle, pool. $$–$$$

LONG BEACH AREA

Long Beach is about thirty minutes away from Anaheim, although traffic delays can double the commute.

Best Western Golden Sails Hotel. 6285 East Pacific Coast Highway. (562) 596–1631 or (800) 762–5333. www.bestwestern.com. $$–$$$

Courtyard Long Beach Downtown. 500 East First Street. (562) 435–8511 or (800) 321–2211. www.marriott.com. Pool. $$$

★ **Hilton Long Beach.** 701 West Ocean Boulevard, at World Trade Center. (562) 983–3400 or (800) 445–8667. www.hilton.com. Pool. $$$

Holiday Inn Long Beach. 2640 Lakewood Boulevard. (562) 597–4401 or (800) 465–4329. www.holiday-inn.com. Pool. $$–$$$

★ **Hotel Queen Mary.** 1126 Queens Highway. (562) 435–3511 or (800) 437–2934. www.queenmary.com. Staterooms on the Queen Mary. $$$

★ **Hyatt Regency Long Beach.** 200 South Pine Avenue. (562) 491–1234 or (800) 233–1234. www.hyatt.com. Pool. $$$–$$$$

★ **Renaissance Long Beach Hotel.** 111 East Ocean Boulevard. (562) 437–5900 or (800) 228–2800. www.renaissancehotels.com. Pool. $$–$$$$

★ **The Westin Long Beach.** 333 East Ocean Boulevard. (562) 436–3000 or (800) 937–8461. www.westin.com. Pool. $$$–$$$$.

LOS ANGELES DOWNTOWN

Best Western Dragon Gate Inn. 818 North Hill Street. (213) 617–3077. www. dragongateinn.com. $$

Best Western Mayfair. 1256 West Seventh Street. (213) 483–1313 or (800) 821–8682. $$–$$$

Best Western Mid-Wilshire Plaza Hotel. 603 South New Hampshire Avenue. (877) 829–3230. www.bestwestern.com. $$

Days Inn Hotel. 457 South Mariposa Avenue. (213) 380–6910. $$

Figueroa Hotel—Convention Center. 939 South Figueroa Street. (213) 627–8971 or (800) 421–9092. www.figueroahotel.com. Across from Staples Center. Outdoor pool. $$$

★ **Holiday Inn City Center.** 1020 South Figueroa Street. (213) 748–1291 or (800) 465–4329. Outdoor pool. $$$

Holiday Inn Los Angeles Downtown. 750 South Garland Avenue. (213) 628–9900 or (800) 628–5240. www.holidayinnla.com. Outdoor pool, free parking. $$

★ **Hyatt Regency Los Angeles.** 711 South Hope Street. (213) 683–1234 or (800) 233–1234. www.hyatt.com. Outdoor spa. $$$–$$$$

InnTowne Hotel Los Angeles. 913 South Figueroa Street. (213) 628–2222. Outdoor pool. $$

Kawanda Hotel. 200 South Hill Street. (800) 752–9232, extension 608. www.kawandahotel.com. $$$

★ **Los Angeles Athletic Club.** 431 South Seventh Street. (213) 630–5264 or (800) 421–8777. www.laac.com. Continental breakfast, indoor pool. $$$

★ **Los Angeles Marriott Downtown.** 333 South Figueroa Street. (213) 617–6027 or (800) 325–3535. www.marriott.com. Outdoor pool. $$$$

★ **Metro Plaza Hotel.** 711 North Main Street. (213) 680–0200 or (800) 223–2223. www.metroplazahotel.com. Free parking. $$

Miyako Inn & Spa. 328 East First Street. (213) 617–2000 or (800) 228–6596. www.miyakoinn.com. Health spa. $$$

★ **Millennium Biltmore Hotel.** 506 South Grand Avenue. (213) 624–1011 or (800) 245–8673. www.regalbiltmore.com. $$$$

★ **The New Otani Hotel.** 120 South Los Angeles Street. (213) 629–1200 or (800) 421–8795. www.newotani.com. Japanese garden. $$$$

★ **Park Plaza.** 607 South Park View Street. (213) 384–5281. Indoor pool, free parking. $–$$

Quality Inn & Suites Downtown. 1901 West Olympic Boulevard. (213) 385–7141 or (888) 385–9889. www. qualityinns.com. Indoor pool, free parking. $$

Radisson Hotel Midtown. 3540 South Figueroa Street. (213) 748–4141 or (800) 333–3333. www.radisson.com. Outdoor pool. $$–$$$

The Millennium Biltmore in Los Angeles.
Photo by Jeff Hyman, © Corel Corporation

Radisson Wilshire Plaza. 3515 Wilshire Boulevard. (213) 381–7411 or (800) 333–3333. www.radisson.com. Outdoor pool. $$$–$$$$

Ramada Inn Commerce. 7272 Gage Avenue, Commerce. (562) 806–4777 or (800) 547–4777. www.ramada.com. Outdoor pool, free parking. $$

Ramada Inn–Los Angeles Downtown. 611 South Westlake Avenue. (213) 483–6363 or (800) 688–8389. www.ramada.com. Free parking. $$

Stillwell Hotel. 838 South Grand Avenue. (213) 627–1151 or (800) 553–4774. www.stillwell-la.com. $–$$

★ **The Westin Bonaventure Hotel and Suites.** 404 South Figueroa Street. (213) 624–1000 or (888) 625–5144. www.westin.com. Outdoor pool. $$–$$$

★ **Wilshire Grand Hotel & Centre.** 930 Wilshire Boulevard. (213) 688–7777 or (888) 773–2888. www.thewilshire grand.com. $$$–$$$$

★ **Wyndham Checkers Hotel.** 535 South Grand Avenue. (213) 624–0000 or (800) 996–3426. www.wyndham.com. Outdoor pool. $$$$

LOS ANGELES WEST SIDE AND BEVERLY HILLS

The Argyle Hotel. 8358 Sunset Boulevard, West Hollywood. (323) 848–6620 or (800) 225–2637. www.argylehotel.com. $$$–$$$$

★ **Avalon Hotel.** 9400 West Olympic Boulevard, Beverly Hills. (310) 277–5221. $$$–$$$$

Best Western Royal Palace. 2528 South Sepulveda Boulevard, Los Angeles. (310) 477–9066. www.bestwestern.com. $$

★ **Beverly Hills Hotel.** 9641 Sunset Boulevard, Beverly Hills. (310) 276–2251 or (800) 283–8885. www.beverlyhillshotel.com. $$$–$$$$

Beverly Hills Inn. 125 South Spalding Drive, Beverly Hills. (210) 278–0303 or (800) 463–4466. $$–$$$

Beverly Hilton. 9876 Wilshire Boulevard, Beverly Hills. (310) 285–1299 or (800) 445–8667. www.hilton.com. $$$–$$$$

The Beverly Plaza. 8384 West Third Street, Los Angeles. (323) 658–6600 or (800) 624–6835. www.beverlyplazahotel.com. $$–$$$

Bevonshire Lodge Motel. 7575 Beverly Boulevard, Los Angeles. (213) 936–6154. $–$$

Century Plaza Hotel. 2025 Avenue of the Stars, Los Angeles. (310) 277–2000 or (800) 937–8467. www.centuryplaza.com. $$$$

Courtyard Los Angeles Century City/Beverly Hills. 10320 West Olympic Boulevard, Los Angeles. (310) 556–3593 or (800) 321–2211. www.court yard.com. $$$

Crescent Hotel Beverly Hills. 403 North Crescent Drive, Beverly Hills. (310) 247–0505. www.beverlycrescenthotel.com. $$–$$$

DoubleTree Hotel, Los Angeles–Westwood. 10740 Wilshire Boulevard, Los Angeles. (310) 475–8711 or (800) 472–8556. www.doubletree.com. $$$

★ **Four Seasons Hotel at Beverly Hills.** 300 South Doheny Drive, Los Angeles. (310) 273–2222. www.fourseasons.com. $$$$

★ **Mondrian Hotel.** 8440 Sunset Boulevard, West Hollywood. (323) 650–8999 or (800) 525–8029. www.mondrianhotel.com. Outdoor heated pool. $$$$

Park Hyatt Los Angeles at Century City. 2151 Avenue of the Stars, Los Angeles. (310) 277–1234 or (800) 233–1234. www.hyatt.com. $$$$

Radisson Beverly Pavilion Hotel. 9360 Wilshire Boulevard, Beverly Hills. (310) 273–1400 or (800) 441–5050. www.radisson.com. $$$

Radisson Los Angeles Westside. 6161 Centinela Avenue, Culver City. (310) 348–4517. www.radisson.com. $$$–$$$$

Ramada West Hollywood–Beverly Hills. 8585 Santa Monica Boulevard, West Hollywood. (310) 652–6400 or (800) 272–6232. www.ramada.wh.com. $$$

★ **The Regent Beverly Wilshire.** 9500 Wilshire Boulevard, Beverly Hills. (310) 275–5200 or (800) 427–4353. www.fourseasons.com. $$$$

Renaissance Beverly Hills Hotel. 1224 South Beverwill Drive, Los Angeles. (310) 277–2800. www.renaissancehotels.com. $$$–$$$$

Sofitel Los Angeles. 8555 Beverly Boulevard, Los Angeles. (310) 278–5444 or (800) 763–4835. www.sofitel.com. $$$$

Sunset Marquis Hotel & Villas. 1200 North Alta Loma Road, West Hollywood. (310) 657–1333. www.sunsetmarquishotel.com. $$$$

HOLLYWOOD AREA

(Price ranges are approximate and subject to change and adjustment in busiest seasons; ratings are relative for the area.)

Banana Bungalow Hollywood @ The Gershwin West. 5533 Hollywood Boulevard. (323) 464–1131 or (800) 446–7835. www.bananabungalow.com. Budget hostel with dorms and private rooms. Free airport, bus, or train pickup. Beach and Disneyland shuttle available. $–$$

Best Western Hollywood Hills. 6141 Franklin Avenue. (323) 464–5181 or (800) 528–1234. www.bestwestern.com. Outdoor pool. $$

★ **Best Western Hollywood Plaza.** 2011 North Highland Avenue. (323) 851–1800 or (800) 232–4353. www.bestwestern.com. Outdoor pool. $$

★ **Beverly Garland's Holiday Inn at Universal Studios Hollywood.** 4222 North Vineland Avenue, North Hollywood. (818) 980–8000 or (800) 238–3759.

www.beverlygarland.com. Outdoor pool, lighted tennis courts. **$$$**

Days Inn. 5410 Hollywood Boulevard, Central Hollywood. (323) 463–7171. www.hotelinnhollywood.com. **$$**

Days Inn. 7023 Sunset Boulevard. (323) 464–8344 or (800) 329–7466. www.daysinn.com. Heated pool. **$$**

Econo Lodge Hollywood. 777 North Vine Street. (323) 463–5671 or (800) 446–3916. www.econolodge.com. **$$**

Econo Lodge Wilshire. 3400 West Third Street. (213) 385–0061 or (800) 266–0061. www.econolodgela.com. **$$**

Hilton Universal City and Towers. 555 Universal Terrace Parkway, Universal City. (818) 506–2500 or (800) 445–8667. www.hilton.com. **$$$–$$$$**

★ **Holiday Inn–Hollywood.** 2005 North Highland Avenue. (323) 850–5811 or (800) 465–4329. www.holidayinn.com. Heated pool. **$$–$$$**

★ **Magic Castle Hotel.** 7025 Franklin Avenue. (323) 850–7465 or (800) 741–4915. www.magiccastlehotel.com. **$$–$$$**

Hollywood Orchid Suites. 1753 North Orchid Avenue. (323) 850–7465 or (800) 537–3052. www.orchidsuites.com. **$$–$$$**

★ **Hollywood Roosevelt Hotel.** 7000 Hollywood Boulevard. (323) 466–7000 or (800) 950–7667. www.hollywoodroosevelt.com. Historic hotel, site of the first Academy Awards, restored in 2002. **$$$–$$$$**

★ **Le Rêve Hotel.** 8822 Cynthia Street, West Hollywood. (310) 854–1114 or (800) 835–7997. www.lerevehotel.com. Rooftop heated pool. **$$$–$$$$**

Ramada Inn Hollywood. 1160 North Vermont Avenue. (323) 660–1788 or (800) 272–6232. www.ramadahollywood.com. Pool. **$**

★ **Sheraton Universal.** 333 Universal Terrace Parkway. (818) 980–1212 or (800) 325–3535. www.sheraton.com. **$$$–$$$$**

Super 8 Motel–Hollywood. 1536 North Western Avenue. (323) 467–3131 or (888) 534–2293. www.stayanight.com/super8hlywd. **$$**

LAX AIRPORT AREA

Best Western Airpark. 640 West Manchester Boulevard, Inglewood. (310) 677–7378 or (800) 233–8060. www.bestwestern.com. **$$**

Best Western Airport Plaza Inn. 1730 Centinela Avenue, Inglewood. (310) 568–0071 or (800) 528–1234. www.bestwestern.com. **$$**

Best Western Suites Hotel. 5005 West Century Boulevard, Los Angeles. (310) 677–7733 or (800) 424–5005. www.bestwestern.com. **$$–$$$**

Crowne Plaza Los Angeles Airport. 5985 West Century Boulevard, Los Angeles. (310) 642–7500 or (888) 315–3700. www.crowneplaza.com. **$$$–$$$$**

Days Inn Airport Center. 901 West Manchester Boulevard, Inglewood. (310) 649–0800 or (800) 231–2508. www.daysinn.com. **$$**

Days Inn Airport South. 15636 Hawthorne Boulevard, Lawndale. (310) 676–7378 or (800) 231–2508. www.daysinn.com. **$$**

Embassy Suites. 9801 Airport Boulevard, Los Angeles. (310) 215–1000 or (800) 362–2779. www.embassysuites.com. **$$$**

Four Points Hotel Los Angeles International Airport. 9750 Airport Boulevard, Los Angeles. (310) 648–7007 or (800) 529–4683. www.fourpointslax. com. $$$

Hampton Inn. 10300 La Cienega Boulevard, Los Angeles. (310) 337–1000 or (800) 426–7866. www.hamptoninn.com. $$

Hilton Los Angeles Airport. 5711 West Century Boulevard, Los Angeles. (310) 410–4000 or (800) 445–8667. www.hilton.com. $$$–$$$$

Holiday Inn Los Angeles International Airport. 9901 La Cienega Boulevard, Los Angeles. (310) 649–5151 or (800) 624–0025. www.holidayinn.com. $$–$$$

Howard Johnson Hotel International LAX. 8620 Airport Boulevard, Los Angeles. (310) 645–7700. www.hojo.com. $$–$$$

Marriott Los Angeles Airport. 5855 West Century Boulevard, Los Angeles. (310) 641–5700 or (800) 228–9290. www.marriott.com. $$$–$$$$

Quality Hotel LAX. 5249 West Century Boulevard, Los Angeles. (310) 645–2200 or (800) 266–2200. www.qualityhotellax.com. $$–$$$

Ramada Plaza Hotel LA Airport North. 6333 Bristol Parkway, Culver City. (310) 484–7014 or (800) 321–5575. www.ramada.com. $$

Renaissance Los Angeles Hotel Airport. 9290 Airport Boulevard, Los Angeles. (310) 337–2800 or (800) 568–3571. www.renaissancehotels.com. $$$–$$$$

Sheraton Gateway Hotel Los Angeles Airport. 6101 West Century Boulevard, Los Angeles. (310) 642–4885 or (800) 325–3535. www.sheraton.com. $$$–$$$$

Travelodge Hotel at LAX Airport. 5547 West Century Boulevard, Los Angeles. (310) 649–4000 or (800) 421–3939. www.travelodge.com. $$

Westin Los Angeles Airport. 5400 West Century Boulevard, Los Angeles. (310) 216–5858 or (800) 228–3000. www.westin.com. $$$–$$$$

CHAPTER ELEVEN

AN ECLECTIC SELECTION OF RESTAURANTS IN ANAHEIM AND LOS ANGELES

THE SPRAWLING COUNTY of Los Angeles and the outlying areas of Orange County include a wide variety of gustatory options from funky California cuisine to fancy French food, from Pacific Rim to old Italy, and from down-home barbecue to the unusual zests of Vietnam, Thailand, and India.

In this chapter you'll find an eclectic selection of some of the best restaurants, selected for value and quality. Price ranges listed are estimates based on dinner entrees; lunch entrees are usually lower.

You'll also find listings of restaurants at Downtown Disney and Universal CityWalk.

Be sure to call to check on hours and to make a reservation, if needed, before heading out to any of the restaurants listed.

RESTAURANTS AT DOWNTOWN DISNEY

(For details, see Chapter 6)

Catal Restaurant & Uva Bar. (714) 774–4442

ESPN Zone. (714) 300–3776. espn.go.com/espninc/zone/espnzoneanaheim.html.

House of Blues. (714) 778–2583. www.hob.com.

La Brea Bakery. (714) 490–0233

Naples Ristorante e Pizzeria. (714) 776–6200

Rainforest Café. (714) 772–0413. www.rainforestcafe.com.

Ralph Brennan's Jazz Kitchen. (714) 776–5200. www.rbjazzkitchen.com.

Y Arriba! Y Arriba! (714) 533–8272

RESTAURANTS NEAR DISNEYLAND AND ANAHEIM

Following is an eclectic selection of the best or more interesting restaurants and the best deals in and around Disneyland and Anaheim. I've left out all the McDonald's, Denny's, Taco Bells, Red Lobsters, and other franchises you could ever want (or not); you'll find at least one of each within a mile or so of the park. See also the listings for restaurants at Downtown Disney and the three Disneyland resort hotels in Chapter 6.

Acapulco Restaurant. 1410 South Harbor Boulevard, Anaheim. (714) 956–7380. Family-style Mexican fare. $–$$

Anaheim White House. 877 South Anaheim Boulevard, Anaheim. (714) 772–1381. Northern Italian specialties in a landmark 1909 home. $$

Ashoka the Great Cuisine of India. 2021 South Harbor Boulevard, Anaheim. (714) 663–8501. Authentic cuisine, near the Anaheim Convention Center. $$.

Azteca Mexican Restaurant and Crooner's Lounge. 12911 Main Street, Garden Grove. (714) 638–3790. Mexican specialties, with an Elvis collection. $–$$

Benihana. 2100 East Ball Road, Anaheim. (714) 774–4940. Japanese steakhouse and teppanyaki dishes. $$–$$$

The Catch Seafood and Steakhouse. 1929 South State College Boulevard, Anaheim. (714) 634–1829. Local seafood favorite. $$

Cattleman's Wharf. 1160 West Ball Road, Anaheim. (714) 535–1622. Steak and fresh seafood. $$–$$$

Charley Brown's. 1751 South State College Boulevard, Anaheim. (714) 634–2211. Slow-roasted prime rib, steaks, chicken, seafood, and pasta dishes. $$.

Citrus City Grill. 122 North Glassel Street, Orange. (714) 639–9600. California cuisine in the heart of Old Town Orange. $$

Crazy Horse Steakhouse & Saloon. 11580 Brookhollow Drive, Santa Ana. (714) 549–1512. Corn-fed steaks, roasted prime rib, and fresh fish. $$–$$$

Fresca's Mexican Grill. 2085 East Katella Avenue, Anaheim. (714) 935–0666. Indoor and outdoor seating. $–$$

Gulliver's. 18482 MacArthur Boulevard, Irvine. (714) 833–8411. www.gullivers restaurant.com. Prime rib, Yorkshire pudding, creamed corn, and English trifle, as well as seafood specialties served in an Old English atmosphere. $$$

Hard Rock Cafe Newport Beach. 451 Newport Center Drive, Newport Beach. (714) 640–8844. www.hardrock.com. An outpost of the rock 'n' roll eatery. $$

The Hobbit. 2932 East Chapman Avenue, Orange. (714) 997–1972. High-tone contemporary/continental cuisine with a world-class wine cellar. Six-course prix-fixe dinner. $$$–$$$$

King's Fish House. 1521 West Katella Avenue, Orange. (714) 771–6655. Local seafood favorite. $$

Legend

Prices are for typical dinner entrees.

$	Entrees under $15
$$	Entrees $15 to $30
$$$	Entrees above $30

Koisan Japanese Cuisine. 1132 East Katella Avenue, Orange. (714) 639–2330. Traditional Japanese cuisine. **$$**

Market Broiler Restaurant. 20 City Boulevard, Orange. (714) 769–3474. Casual seafood eatery. **$$**

Mr. Stox. 1105 East Katella Avenue, Anaheim. (714) 634–3994. Continental fare, with a renowned wine cellar. **$$–$$$**

Mrs. Knott's Chicken Dinner Restaurant. Knott's Berry Farm, 8039 Beach Boulevard, Buena Park. (714) 220–5067. World famous fried chicken. **$$**

P.J.'s Abbey. 182 South Orange Street, Orange. (714) 771–8556. A renovated church, complete with stained glass windows. **$$**

Spaghetti Station Restaurant & Old West Museum. 999 West Ball Road, Anaheim. (714) 956–3250. www.spaghetti-station.com. Spaghetti, ribs, chicken, pizza, and more set among western arts and artifacts. **$$**

Spring Garden Restaurant and Sushi Bar. Ramada Plaza Hotel, 10022 Garden Grove Boulevard, Garden Grove. (714) 534–1818. Japanese and Korean specialties. **$$**

Thai and Thai Restaurant. 150 Katella Avenue, Anaheim. (714) 635–3060. Family-style authentic Thai cuisine. **$–$$**

Yamabuki. Disney's Pacific Pier Hotel, 1717 South West Street, Anaheim. (714) 956–6755. Fine Japanese dining. **$$–$$$**

Zorba's. 195 West Harbor Place, Anaheim. (714) 999–5075. Lively food and entertainment. **$$**

RESTAURANTS AT UNIVERSAL CITYWALK

(For details, see Chapter 7)

B. B. King's Blues Club and Memphis Restaurant. (818) 622–5464

Buca di Beppo Restaurant. (818) 509–9463. www.bucadibeppo.com.

Cafe Tu Tu Tango. (818) 769–2222. www.cafetututango.com.

Camacho's Cantina. (818) 622–3333

Daily Grill Short Order. (818) 760–4448. www.dailygrill.com.

Gladstone's Universal. (818) 622–3474. www.gladstones.com.

Hard Rock Café Hollywood. (818) 622–7625. www.hardrock.com.

Karl Strauss Brewery Garden. (818) 753–2739. www.karlstrauss.com.

Tony Roma's. (818) 763–7662. www.tonyromas.com.

Upstart Crow Cafe. (818) 763–1811

Wasabi at CityWalk. (818) 622–7224

Wolfgang Puck Cafe. (818) 985–9653

LOS ANGELES DOWNTOWN

Atlas Supper Club. 3760 Wilshire Boulevard, Los Angeles. (213) 380–8400. www.clubatlas.com. Eclectic fare in a setting from the twenties. **$$**

Azalea. The New Otani Hotel & Garden. 120 South Los Angeles Street, Los

Angeles. (213) 253–9235. www.newotani.com. California cuisine with continental and Asian influences. $$

Back Door Pub. The Milner Hotel, 813 South Flower Street, Los Angeles. (213) 627–6981. www.milner-hotels.com/milnerla.html. Casual Spanish-American specialties. $

Back Porch. Los Angeles Marriott Downtown, 333 South Figueroa Street, Los Angeles. (213) 621–1513. Casual California cafe. $

Bernard's. The Regal Biltmore, 506 South Grand Avenue, Los Angeles. (213) 612–1580 or (800) 245–8673. www.bernardsbistro.com. European and American country cuisine. $$$

Bonaventure Brewing Co. Westin Bonaventure Hotel, 404 South Figueroa Street, Suite 418A, Los Angeles. (213) 236–0802. www.bonaventurebrewingco. com. An indoor-outdoor beer garden high above the streets of downtown. $$

Brasserie. Hyatt Regency Los Angeles, 711 South Hope Street, Los Angeles. (213) 688–7777. American and Japanese bistro. $$

Cafe Pinot. 700 West Fifth Street, Los Angeles. (213) 239–6500. www.patina-pinot.com. Parisian bistro near the central library. $$

California Pizza Kitchen. 330 South Hope Street, Los Angeles. (213) 626–2616. Unusual pies. $$

Cardini. Wilshire Grand Hotel & Centre, 930 Wilshire Boulevard, Los Angeles. (213) 896–3822. www.wilshiregrand.com. Northern Italian fare in an elegant setting. $$

CBS Seafood Restaurant. 700 North Spring Street, Los Angeles. (213) 617–2323. Cantonese specialties and dim sum. $

Checkers Restaurant. Wyndham Checkers Hotel, 535 South Grand Avenue, Los Angeles. (213) 891–0519. Contemporary American. $$$

Ciao Trattoria. 815 West Seventh Street, Los Angeles. (213) 624–2244. www.ciaotrattoria.com. Italian in an Art Deco setting. $$

City Grill. Wilshire Grand Hotel & Centre, 930 Wilshire Boulevard, Los Angeles. (213) 627–4289. www.wilshiregrand.com. Light American fare. $

Ciudad. 445 South Figueroa Street, Suite 100, Los Angeles. (213) 486–5171. www.ciudad-la.com. Latin fare from Havana to Barcelona. $$

El Cholo. 1121 South Western Avenue, Los Angeles. (323) 737–7718 or (800) 789–2172. www.elcholocafe.com. Landmark Mexican restaurant. $

El Paseo Inn. 11 East Olvera Street, Los Angeles. (213) 626–1361. Authentic Mexican food in Old Los Angeles. $

Emerald Grill. Holiday Inn City Center, 1020 South Figueroa Street, Los Angeles. (213) 743–7618. Pizza, pasta, seafood. $

Engine Co. No. 28. 644 South Figueroa Street, Los Angeles. (213) 624–6996. www.engineco.com. Bar and grill in a century-old fire station. $$

Epicentre. Kawada Hotel, 200 South Hill Street, Los Angeles. (213) 621–4455 or (800) 752–9232. www.kawadahotel.com. Contemporary cuisine with an earthquake motif. $$

Fox Sports Sky Box. 1111 South Figueroa at Staples Center, Los Angeles. (213) 742–7345. www.staplescenter.com. Sports bar. $

Frying Fish. 120 Japanese Village Plaza Mall, 350 East First Street, Los Angeles, (213) 680–0567. Contemporary Japanese and sushi. $–$$

Garden Grill. The New Otani Hotel & Garden, 120 South Los Angeles Street, Los Angeles. (213) 253–9263. www.newotani.com. Teppanyaki and Japanese steakhouse. $$

Gill's Cuisine of India. Stillwell Hotel, 838 South Grand Avenue, Los Angeles. (213) 623–1050 or (800) 553–4774. www.stillwell-la.com. Clay oven Indian cuisine. $

Golden Dragon Restaurant. 960 North Broadway, Los Angeles. (323) 721–0774. www.chinatowncenter.com. Popular Chinese eatery. $

Grand Cafe. Hotel Inter-Continental, 251 South Olive Street, Los Angeles. (213) 356–4155. Fine dining in theater and museum district. $$

Harry's Bar & American Grill. 2020 Avenue of the Stars, Century City. (310) 277–2333. Venetian and Florentine specialties in a room modeled after the famous original in Florence, Italy. $$

Jyokamachi Japanese Restaurant. 404 South Figueroa Street, Suite 601, Los Angeles. (213) 629–9929 or (800) 888/629–2977. Teppanyaki, shabu-shabu, and sushi. $$

La Golondrina Café. W-17 Olvera Street, Los Angeles. (213) 628–4349. www.lagolondrina.com. Popular Mexican restaurant in 1850s brick building in Old Los Angeles. $$–$$$

La Vista Bonita. Holiday Inn L.A. Downtown, 750 Garland Avenue, Los Angeles. (213) 628–9900 or (800) 628–5240. www.holidayinnla.com. California and Mexican cafe. $

Les Freres Taix French Restaurant. 1911 Sunset Boulevard, Los Angeles. (213) 484–1265. www.taixfrench.com. Reasonably priced French country cuisine at a Los Angeles landmark. The Taix family are the third and fourth generations of a family of sheepherders and bakers from the "hautes-alpes" in southeastern France who immigrated to Los Angeles around 1870. The original Taix restaurant opened in 1927. $$

McCormick & Schmick's. The Library Tower, 633 West Fifth Street, Los Angeles. (213) 629–1929. www.mccormickandschmicks.com. Lush seafood shrine. $$

Moody's Bar & Grille. Los Angeles Marriott Downtown, 333 South Figueroa Street, Los Angeles. (213) 617–6023. New York-style bar and grill. $$

The Orchid Gardens. Best Western The Mayfair Hotel, 1256 West Seventh Street, Los Angeles. (213) 484–9789. hometown.aol.com/mayfairla/index.html. Art Deco restaurant popular for its lunch buffet. $$

Original Pantry Cafe. 877 South Figueroa Street, Los Angeles. (213) 972–9279. Landmark casual twenty-four-hour eatery. $

Pacific Dining Car. 1310 West Sixth Street, Los Angeles. (213) 483–6000. www.pacificdiningcar.com. Classic steak and seafood. $$$

Patinette at MOCA. 250 South Grand Avenue, Los Angeles. (323) 626–1178. www.patina-pinot.com. Light Mediterranean fare at the Museum of Contemporary Art. $$

Pavan Pacifico. Hyatt Regency Los Angeles, 711 South Hope Street, Los Angeles. (213) 683–1234. California cuisine with Asian influences. $

Philippe the Original. 1001 North Alameda Street, Los Angeles. (213) 628–3781. www.philippes.com. Simple family fare, famous for its French dip sandwich. $

Plum Tree Inn. 937 North Hill Street, Los Angeles. (213) 613–1819. Mandarin and Szechuan fare. $$

Rendezvous Court. The Biltmore Hotel, 506 South Grand Avenue, Los Angeles. (213) 624–1011. www.millennium-hotels.com. Lush setting of an indoor garden for lunch and high tea. $$

The Restaurant at the Standard. 550 South Flower Street, Los Angeles. (213) 892–8080. www.standardhotel.com. Eclectic fare at an agreeably bizarre hotel. $$–$$$

Saka-E. Radisson Wilshire Plaza, 3515 Wilshire Boulevard, Los Angeles. (213) 381–7411. Tempura, teppanyaki, and sushi. $$

San Antonio Winery & Restaurant. 737 Lamar Street, Los Angeles. (323) 223–1401. www.sanantoniowinery.com. Winery and historic landmark. $

Seoul Jung. Wilshire Grand Hotel & Centre, 930 Wilshire Boulevard, Los Angeles. (213) 688–7880. www.wilshiregrand.com. Korean barbecue. $$

Smeraldi's Ristorante. The Biltmore Hotel, 506 South Grand Avenue, Los Angeles. (213) 612–1562. www.millennium-hotels.com. Pasta and California specialties. $

The Sonora Café. 180 South La Brea Avenue, Los Angeles. (323) 857–1800. Mexican and Southwestern specialties. $$$

Tesoro Trattoria. 300 South Grand Avenue, Los Angeles. (213) 680–0000. www.calendarlive.com/tesorotrattoria. Tuscan specialties. $$

Three Thirty Three. Los Angeles Marriott Downtown, 333 South Figueroa Street, Los Angeles. (213) 617–1133. Fine dining piano bar. $$

Water Grill. 544 South Grand Avenue, Los Angeles. (213) 891–0900. Northwest seafood specialties. $$

Windows Steaks & Martinis. 1150 South Olive Street, Los Angeles. (213) 746–1554. Retro-sixties steakhouse high over downtown. Weekdays for lunch and dinner; Saturday lunch only. $$$

HOLLYWOOD

Bob's Big Boy. 4211 West Riverside Drive, Burbank. (818) 843–9334. A state burger-landmark restored to its 1949 heyday, complete with carhops. The eatery has appeared in several movies, including *Heat*. $

Cafe Sierra. Universal City Hilton and Towers, 555 Universal Terrace Parkway, Universal City. (818) 509–2030. Favored for its lunch buffets, Friday seafood buffet, and Sunday brunch. $$

Hard Rock Cafe Hollywood. 1000 Universal Center Drive, Suite 99, Universal City. (818) 622–7625. www.hardrock.com. Another gift shop with a menu. $$

Patina. 5955 Melrose Avenue, Los Angeles. (323) 960–1760 ext. 22. www. patina-pinot.com/. Flagship of Joachim Splichal's empire, serving regional specialties. $$$

Pink's Famous Chili Dogs. 709 North La Brea Avenue, Los Angeles. (323) 931–4223. Just like the sign says. $

Pinot Hollywood. 1448 North Gower Street, Los Angeles. (323) 461–8800. Bistro dining. $$

Theodore's. Hollywood Roosevelt Hotel, 7000 Hollywood Boulevard, Hollywood. (323) 466–7000 or (800) 950–7667. California fare for power lunchers and dinner dealers. $$

Yamashiro. 1999 North Sycamore Avenue, Hollywood. (323) 466–5125. www.yamashirola.com. Seafood, sushi, sashimi, and tempura with a panoramic setting. $$$

LOS ANGELES WEST SIDE

Cafe Le Parc. 733 North West Knoll Drive, West Hollywood. (310) 855–8888. www.leparcsuites.com. Mediterranean cafe. $$$

Cava Restaurant & Tapas Bar. Beverly Plaza Hotel, 8384 West Third Street, Los Angeles. (323) 658–8898. Spanish specialties including tapas. $$

Celestino an Italian Steakhouse. 8908 Beverly Boulevard, West Hollywood. (310) 858–5777. www.celestinodrago.com. High-tone Italian. $$$

Chaya Brasserie Restaurant. 8741 Alden Drive, Los Angeles. (310) 859–8833. French, Japanese, and Italian cuisine. $$

Citrus Restaurant. 6703 Melrose Avenue, Los Angeles. (323) 857–0034. www.larestaurant.com/citrus. Fancy Franco-Californian fare. $$$

The Dining Room. The Regent Beverly Wilshire, 9500 Wilshire Boulevard, Beverly Hills. (310) 275–5200 ext 5103. www.fourseasons. com. California specialties in a tony setting. $$$

Ed Debevic's. 134 North La Cienega Boulevard, Beverly Hills. (310) 659–1952. www.eddebevics.com. Classic short-order diner from the fifties. $

Gardens. Four Seasons Hotel, 300 South Doheny Drive, Los Angeles. (310) 273–2222. High-tone regional fare. $$

Griff's. The Beverly Hilton, 9876 Wilshire Boulevard, Beverly Hills. (323) 274–7777. American and continental. $$

Hard Rock Cafe. 8600 Beverly Boulevard, Los Angeles. (310) 276–7605. A gift shop with a menu. $$

House of Blues. 8430 Sunset Boulevard, West Hollywood. (323) 848–5100 or (800) 848–5194. www.hob.com. American regional fare with a bluesy setting. $$

Il Pastaio. 400 North Canon Drive, Beverly Hills. (310) 205–5444. www. celestinodrago.com. A favorite neighborhood trattoria. $$

Junior's Restaurant, Delicatessen & Bakery. 2379 Westwood Boulevard, Los Angeles. (310) 475–5771 or (800) 475–3354. www.deli.com. Classic Jewish deli. $

Lawry's the Prime Rib. 100 North La Cienega Boulevard, Beverly Hills. (310)

652–2827. www.lawrysonline.com. Seafood, steaks, and the signature prime rib, carved tableside. $$

McCormick & Schmicks–Beverly Hills. 206 North Rodeo Drive, Beverly Hills. (310) 859–0434. Seafood specialties. $$

The Palm Restaurant. 9001 Santa Monica Boulevard, Los Angeles. (310) 550–8811. Steak and seafood, in the lush style of the New York original. $$$

Pangaea Bistro. Le Meridien Hotel at Beverly Hills, 465 South La Cienega Boulevard, Los Angeles. (310) 247–2100 or (800) 645–5624. www.lemeridien beverlyhills.com. World cuisine with Asian influences. $$

The Polo Lounge. The Beverly Hills Hotel, 9641 Sunset Boulevard, Beverly Hills. (310) 276–2251. www.beverlyhillshotel.com. California fare with Asian accents in a fabled setting. $$$

The Restaurant at L'Ermitage. 9291 Burton Way, Beverly Hills. (310) 278–3344 or (800) 323–7500. www.lermitagehotel.com. French Provence and Italian Tuscan fare, with a touch of Asia. $$

Ruth's Chris Steak House. 224 South Beverly Drive, Beverly Hills. (310) 859–8744. www.ruthschris.com. Outpost of a national steak and seafood empire. $$$

San Gennaro Cafe. 140 Barrington Place, Brentwood. (310) 476–9696. Neighborhood Italian trattoria. $$

Spago Beverly Hills. 176 North Canon Drive, Beverly Hills. (310) 385–0880. A trendy "in spot" for celebrities since Wolfgang Puck's original place on Sunset Boulevard closed in early 2001. $$$

The Stinking Rose. 55 North La Cienega, Beverly Hills. (310) 652–7673. www.thestinkingrose.com. Regional and Italian fare, featuring lots of garlic. $$$

Terrace Il Ristorante. Century Plaza Hotel & Tower, 2025 Avenue of the Stars, Los Angeles. (310) 551–3359. Fancy Mediterranean fare. $$

The Tiara. Renaissance Beverly Hills Hotel, 1224 South Beverwil Drive, Los Angeles. (310) 772–2999. www.renaissancehotels.com. Pacific Rim and American specialties. $$

Trader Vic's. Merv Griffin's Beverly Hilton. 9876 Wilshire Boulevard, Beverly Hills. (310) 276–6345. Beef, seafood, and poultry in a South Seas setting. $$

BEACH CITIES

Allie's American Grille. LAX Marriott, 5855 West Century Boulevard, Los Angeles. (310) 641–5700. Fine dining, American-style. $$

Andiamo. LAX Hilton & Towers, 5711 West Century Boulevard, Los Angeles. (310) 410–4000. Elaborate menu of northern Italian specialties. $$

Andre's. 21333 Hawthorne Boulevard, Torrance. (310) 540–0500. www.hiltontorrance.com. California, Chinese, and continental specialties. $$

Benihana Japanese Steakhouse–Torrance. Village Del Amo, 21327 Hawthorne Boulevard, Torrance. (310) 316–7777. Teppanyaki and steakhouse specialties. $$

Benihana of Tokyo—Marina del Rey. 14160 Panay Way, Marina del Rey. (310) 821–0888. Teppanyaki and steakhouse specialties. **$$**

Border Grill. 1445 Fourth Street, Santa Monica. (310) 451–1655. www.border grill.com. Modern, bold Mexican specialties from chefs Mary Sue Milliken and Susan Feniger. **$$$**

Chelsea Restaurant. Queen Mary Seaport, 1126 Queen's Highway, Long Beach. (562) 435–3511. www.queenmary.com. Seafood specialties aboard the *Queen Mary* in Long Beach harbor. **$$**

Courtyard Cafe and Lounge. Courtyard by Marriott Marina del Rey, 1348 Maxella Avenue, Marina del Rey. (310) 822–8555. American fare near the beach. **$**

The Dining Room. The Ritz-Carlton Marina del Rey, 4375 Admiralty Way, Marina del Rey. (310) 823–1700. The Ritz-Carlton's signature French-Mediterranean–Pacific Rim restaurant overlooking Marina del Rey. **$$$**

Drago Ristorante & Bar. 2628 Wilshire Boulevard, Santa Monica. (310) 828–1585. www.celestinodrago.com. Another Italian gem from chef Celestino Drago. **$$$**

Gladstone's 4 Fish. 17300 Pacific Coast Highway, Pacific Palisades. (310) 454–3474. www.gladstones.com. Local favorite for seafood, with an ocean view. **$$**

Gotham Hall. 1431 Third Street Promenade, Santa Monica. (310) 394–8865. (800) 394–8865. www.gothamhall.com. California grill, with pool tables and a disco. **$**

Harbor House Restaurant. 4211 Admiralty Way, Marina del Rey. (310) 577–4555. Seafood and steaks at the marina. **$$**

Il Boccaccio. 39 Pier Avenue, Hermosa Beach. (310) 376–0211. www. ilboccaccio.com. Italian regional fare. **$$**

Jasmine's Steakhouse. 3635 Fashion Way, Torrance Marriott, Torrance. (310) 316–3636 ext. 6101. American steakhouse menu. **$$$**

JW's Steakhouse. Los Angeles Airport Marriott, 5855 West Century Boulevard, Los Angeles. (310) 641–5700. Classic steakhouse offerings. **$$$**

Landry's. Sheraton Gateway, 6101 West Century Boulevard, Los Angeles. (310) 642–1111. California cuisine. **$$**

Lavande. Loews Santa Monica Beach Hotel, 1700 Ocean Avenue, Santa Monica. (310) 576–3180. California and Mediterranean specialties, by the seashore. **$$$**

Library Steakhouse. Renaissance Los Angeles Hotel, 9620 Airport Boulevard, Los Angeles. (310) 337–2800. www.renaissancehotels.com. Steakhouse fare in a private club setting. **$$**

Marina del Rey Bar & Grill. Marina del Rey Hotel, 13534 Bali Way, Marina del Rey. (310) 301–1000. Harborside grill. **$$**

Palm Grill Restaurant. Four Points Hotel, 9750 Airport Boulevard, Los Angeles. (310) 645–4600. California and Pacific Rim specialties. **$$**

Rix. 1413 Fifth Street, Santa Monica. (310) 656–9688. Updated supper club offerings. **$$**

Rockenwagner. 2435 Main Street, Santa Monica. (310) 399–6504. www.rockenwagner.com. Fancy California and French offerings. **$$$**

Schatzi on Main. 3110 Main Street, Santa Monica. (310) 399–4800. www.schatzi-on-main.com. California and Austrian specialties at Arnold Schwarzenegger and Maria Shriver's place. $$$

Sir Winston's Restaurant. Queen Mary Seaport, 1126 Queen's Highway, Long Beach. (562) 435–3511. www.queenmary.com. California and continental menu onboard the Queen Mary in Long Beach harbor. $$$

Stones. Marina Beach Marriott, 4100 Admiralty Way, Marina del Rey. (310) 301–3000 ext. 6868. California grill. $

Waterfront Bar and Grille. Marina del Rey Hotel, 13534 Bali Way, Marina del Rey. (310) 301–1000 or (800) 442–8000. www.marinadelreyhotel.com. California and continental specialties at the marina. $

Wynsor's Grill & Bar. Wyndham LAX, 6225 West Century Boulevard, Los Angeles. (310) 670–9000. Elegant grill fare, featuring rotisserie duck and prime rib. $$

PART VII

BEYOND THE THEME PARKS

CHAPTER TWELVE

FESTIVALS

THE TOURNAMENT OF ROSES PARADE is a New Year's Day tradition. It dates all the way back to 1890 and then, like now, was meant as a proclamation to the world about southern California's temperate climate. Today the parade through the streets of Pasadena is broadcast around the world, and don't you think that makes the Chamber of Commerce happy?

Sponsoring groups and companies spend hundreds of thousands of dollars building their floats. Floats must be completely covered with flowers, greenery, or some other organic material, with an average float requiring up to 100,000 blossoms.

The whole shebang is accompanied by the traditional trappings of modern parades: marching bands, horses, television cameras, second-tier celebrities, and corporate logos.

The parade starts pretty early in the day, and many spectators spend the night or arrive at the crack of dawn to grab the best curbside viewing places. A limited number of grandstand seats are available for sale; they're usually spoken for well before the parade begins. Overnight parking on some Pasadena city streets near the route is permitted beginning at noon on the day before the parade; observe posted signs.

For information, contact the Tournament of Roses Association at (626) 449–4100 or (626) 449–7673, or write to the association at 391 South Orange Grove Boulevard, Pasadena, CA 91184.

Tickets for the parade and for some overnight parking spaces may be purchased—at a hefty premium—from companies that include:

A-1 Tickets, Inc. (800) 938–9929. www.aonetickets.com.

Al Brooks Rose Bowl Tours. (213) 626–5863. www.albrooks.com.

Sharp Seating Company. (626) 795–4171. www.sharpseating.com.

Southern California Ticket Service. (800) 888–7287. www.socaltix.com.

Ticket Time. (818) 783–1033

JANUARY

Annual New Year's Day Swim. San Pedro. The Cabrillo Beach Polar Bears go for a dip. (310) 833–1377. New Year's Day.

Chinese New Year. Celebrate the Lunar New Year with firecrackers, dragons, and a colorful parade in Chinatown. Contact the Chinese Chamber of Commerce. (213) 617–0396. www.lachinesechamber.org. Late January or early February.

Golden Globe Awards. Beverly Hills. The Hollywood Foreign Press awards for achievement in the television and motion picture industry. Spectators can watch on the sidelines or purchase bleacher seats. (310) 274–7777. www.golden globes.org.

Greater Los Angeles Auto Show. Los Angeles. (213) 741–1151. www.laauto show.com.

King Festival of the Arts. Exposition Park, Los Angeles. Arts and crafts. (213) 735–1261.

Rose Bowl Game. Pasadena. Champions of the Pac-10 and Big Ten Conference. (626) 449–4100. www.rosebowl.com. New Year's weekend.

Rose Parade Float Viewing. Paloma Street and Sierra Madre Villa Avenue, Pasadena. (626) 449–7673. January 1 and 2.

Tournament of Roses Parade. Pasadena. (626) 449–7673. www.rosebowl. com. New Year's Day.

FEBRUARY

Black History Month. Museum of Television and Radio. (310) 786–1000.

Feria De La Mujer. Los Angeles. Fashion show, cooking demonstrations, food booths, and other activities. (213) 468–5213. Mid-February.

Festival of the Whales. Dana Point. The annual migration of the California gray whales is celebrated with a parade, a street fair, whale-watching cruises, exhibits, lectures, and an art show. (714) 496–1555. www.dpfestivalofwhales.com. Late February to early March.

Presidents' Day Lawn Party and Road. 40 Presidential Drive, Simi Valley. Presidential look alikes, storytelling, music, singing, dancing, 5K run, and family fun run. (800) 410–8354. Mid-February.

Queen Mary Scottish Festival. Queen Mary, Long Beach. Pipe bands, highland dancing, parades, competitions, exhibits, performances, Scottish food, and drinks. (562) 435–3511. www.queenmary.com. Mid-February.

Santa Monica Pier Winter Music Series. Santa Monica Pier, Santa Monica. Music and dance. (310) 458–8900. pen.ci.santa-monica.ca.us/resource_mgmt/ pier. February through June.

Southern California Boat Show. Los Angeles. (714) 633–1427.

Whiskey Flats Days. An Old West festival in Kernville. (760) 376–2629 or (800) 350–7393. Mid-February.

Winter Wonderland. Brand Park, Glendale. (818) 548–2000. Sledding on mountains of manmade snow. Late February.

MARCH

Academy Awards. Kodak Theatre, Hollywood. Your chances of getting tickets for the ceremony itself are about as good as your chances of winning an Oscar, but there is a lot of excitement each March in the streets of Hollywood. Bleachers are set up near the award site itself for those who want to ogle the stars as they arrive. Late March.

Catalina Island Marathon. Catalina Island. (714) 978–1528. Mid-March.

Los Angeles Marathon. Los Angeles. World's largest running event, passing through many of Los Angeles's neighborhoods. (310) 444–5544. www.la marathon.com. Early March.

Los Angeles Marathon Bike Tour. 900 Exposition Boulevard, Los Angeles. Course begins and ends at Exposition Park, passing through Koreatown, Hancock Park, and Hollywood. (310) 444–5544. www.lamarathon.com. Early March.

Los Angeles Marathon Finish Line Celebration. Los Angeles. Huge block party with exhibitors of athletic gear, arts and crafts, live entertainment, and food. (310) 444–5544. www.lamarathon.com. Early March.

Return of the Swallows to Capistrano. A celebration of the miraculous return of thousands of swallows to the ruins of Mission San Juan Capistrano each March 19 (of course, some swallows also come on March 18 and March 20, but there's no party for them). (714) 248–2048. www.missionsjc.com.

APRIL

Earth Day Fair and Beach Clean-Up. 3720 Stephen White Drive, San Pedro. (310) 548–7562. Late April.

Easter Sunrise Service. 309 Esplanade, Redondo Beach. (310) 376–6911.

Easter Sunrise Service. Forest Lawn Memorial Park, 6300 Forest Lawn Drive, Los Angeles. (800) 204–3131. www.forestlawn.com.

Easter Sunrise Service at the Bowl. Hollywood Bowl, 2301 North Highland Avenue, Hollywood. (213) 896–1700. www.hollywoodbowl.org.

Feria de los Niños. Hollenbeck Park, Los Angeles. Hispanic folk festival for children. (213) 261–0113. Late April.

San Fernando Valley Street Fiesta. San Fernando Road and MacClay Street, San Fernando Valley. Games, carnival rides, food booths, arts and crafts, and live entertainment. (562) 495–5959. Mid-April.

Santa Anita Derby Day. 285 West Huntington Drive, Arcadia. Microbrew festival, 5K run, fan fest, and family fun day. (626) 574–7223. www.santaanita.com. Early April.

MAY

Carnival on the Beach. Ocean Boulevard, Long Beach. Carnival rides, food booths, arts and crafts. (562) 495–5959. Mid-May.

Cinco de Mayo at Macarthur Park. Wilshire Boulevard, Los Angeles. (562) 495–5959. Early May.

Cinco de Mayo Celebration. Dancing, singing, eating, and more in a movable Mexican feast around Los Angeles, including Olvera Street. Check newspaper coverage.

Memorial Day Parade. Canoga Park. Celebrities, floats, clowns, marching bands, antique and classic cars. (818) 884–4222.

Pasadena Cinco de Mayo Street Fest. 100 North Garfield Avenue, Pasadena. Carnival rides, food booths, arts and crafts, and entertainment. (562) 495–5959. Early May.

San Bernardino County Fair. Victorville. Old-style agricultural and crafts fair. (619) 245–6506. www.sbcfair.com. Mid-May.

Strawberry Festival. Village Green, Garden Grove. Strawberries, a parade, strawberries, music, strawberries, and more. Did we mention the strawberries? (714) 638–0981. www.strawberryfestival.org. Late May.

JUNE

American Film Institute Los Angeles International Film Festival. Various locations. (213) 856–7707. www.afionline.org. Mid-June.

Juneteenth Festival. William Grant Still Arts Center, 2520 West View Street, Los Angeles. Live concert performances featuring blues, jazz, and gospel music commemorating the end of slavery in 1865. (323) 734–1164. Mid-June.

Juneteenth Celebration. 4700 Western Heritage Way, Los Angeles. Demonstrations, reading of the Emancipation Proclamation, music, workshops, and lectures. (323) 667–2000. Mid-June.

Whale Festival. 3720 Stephen White Drive, San Pedro. Sand sculpture contest, children's activities, entertainment, and food. (310) 548–7562. www.sanpedro. com/spcom/festvals.htm. Early June.

JULY

Fireworks at Huntington Beach. Huntington Beach. (714) 374–1535. July 4.

Fourth of July at Queen Mary. 1126 Queen's Highway, Long Beach. Fireworks, carnival rides, game booths, and dancing to live bands. (562) 435–3511.

Fourth of July at Starlight Bowl. Lockheed View Drive, Burbank. (818) 545–3721.

Fourth of July Celebration. 2200 Crenshaw Boulevard, Torrance. Fireworks, games, food booths, carnival, train rides, and entertainment. (310) 618–2930.

Fourth of July Dance and Barbecue Dinner. 1 Casino Way, Avalon. Barbecue buffet dinner, music of the USC Marching Band, and fireworks over Avalon Bay. (310) 510–1520.

Fourth of July Fireworks Display. Marina del Rey. The fireworks display can be viewed from Burton Chace Park, Fisherman's Village, and waterside area restaurants. (310) 821–0555.

Fourth of July Fireworks Display. Sunset Boulevard and Temescal Canyon Road, Pacific Palisades. (310) 459–7963.

Fourth of July Parade. Avalon, Catalina Island. Golf cart parade featuring the USC Marching Band. (310) 510–1520.

Independence Day Picnic and Parade. Ontario. Marching bands, floats, street fair, arts and crafts, food booths, classic car display, and picnicking on the Guinness World Record's longest picnic table. (909) 395–2020. July 3 and 4.

Kaboom Celebration. McKinley Avenue, Pomona. Carnival, stage entertainment, chili cook-off, classic car show, pony rides, games, and fireworks. (909) 623–3111. July 4.

Malibu Summer Festival and Art Show. Malibu Civic Center, Malibu. (310) 456–9025. Late July.

Old-Fashioned Family Fourth of July. Presidential Drive, Simi Valley. Carnival games, storytelling, president look-alikes, face painting, pie-eating contest, and live music. (800) 410–8354. July 4.

Orange County Fair. Orange County Fair and Exhibition Center, Costa Mesa. Rides, exhibitions, and entertainment. (714) 708–3247. www.ocfair.com. Late July.

Pacific Palisades Americanism Parade. Pacific Palisades Park, Pacific Palisades. Floats, marching bands, celebrities, and politicians. (310) 459–7963. July 4.

Ramona Pageant. 27400 Ramona Bowl Road, Hemet. Asian-Pacific culture featuring entertainment, dragon boat races, flower show, art exhibits, children's activities, and ethnic food. (800) 645–4465. Mid-July.

Shakespeare Festival. Citicorp Plaza, downtown Los Angeles. (213) 489–1121. www.shakespearefestivalla.org. July and August.

Surf City Celebrates. Main Street, Huntington Beach. Marching bands, floats, and 5K run. (714) 374–1535. July 4.

Valley of the Stars and Stripes. Northridge. Car show, carnival rides, game booths, live entertainment, food, skydivers, and fireworks. (818) 368–3235. July 4.

AUGUST

African Marketplace & Cultural Faire. 5001 Rodeo Road, Los Angeles. Arts, crafts, games, soccer tournament, African business expo, and entertainment. (323) 734–1164. Late August and early September.

Model Boat Regatta. Long Beach. Youths race hand-built model boats. (562) 570–1725. Late August.

Nisei Week. Little Tokyo, Los Angeles. Parade and celebration of Japanese culture in America. (213) 628–2725 or (213) 687–7193. www.niseiweek.org. Early August.

Old Spanish Days. Santa Barbara. Weeklong celebration of Spanish culture. (805) 962–8101. www.oldspanishdays-fiesta.org. Early August.

San Fernando Valley Fair. Devonshire Downs, Northridge. Three days of exhibits, carnival rides, entertainment, and the Los Angeles County Beauty Pageant. (818) 373–4500. Early August.

SEPTEMBER

Annual Flea Market. Civic Center Way, Malibu. (818) 706–0233. Late September.

Annual Route 66 Rendezvous. Between Second and Fifth Streets, Los Angeles. Vintage cars, street rods, food booths, carnival rides, and live entertainment. (909) 889–3980. Late September.

Danish Days. Solvang. Parade, dance, and music. (805) 688–6144. www.solvangusa.com. Third weekend of September.

Festival of Philippine Arts and Culture. Cabrillo Beach. Dance, arts, and crafts. (213) 389–3050. vconline.org/fpac. Mid-September.

Grecian Festival by the Sea. Colorado Street, Long Beach. Dancing, music, food, and crafts celebrating Greek culture. (714) 220–0730. Early September.

Greek Festival. Santa Anita Racetrack, Arcadia. (626) 574–7223. Late September.

Korean Festival. Korean Community Center, Koreatown, Los Angeles. (213) 730–1495. Late September.

Los Angeles County Fair. County Fairgrounds, Pomona. The largest agricultural fair in the country, plus rides, racing, and entertainment. (909) 623–3111. www.fairplex.com. Second and third weeks of September.

Taste of Newport/Sandcastle Contest. Newport Beach. Food and art. (714) 729–4400. www.tasteofnewport.com. Mid-September.

OCTOBER

Autumn Sea Fair. 3720 Stephen White Drive, San Pedro. Swashbuckling pirates, dunk booths, carnival games, sandcastle building, live bands, and food. (310) 548–7562. Late October.

Calico Days. Calico Ghost Town, Yermo. (760) 254–2122. www.calicotown. com. Early October.

Halloween Carnival at Wilson Park. 2200 Crenshaw Boulevard, Torrance. Halloween games, costume parade, and food booths. (310) 618–2930. October 31.

Halloween on South Lake Avenue. Between Colorado and California Boulevards, Pasadena. Wicked witch, ghostly magic show, creepy crawly critter show, pumpkin hunt, and a costume contest. (626) 792–1259. October 31.

Knott's "Scary" Farm. Knott's Berry Farm, Buena Park. A Halloween conversion of the amusement park. See the chapter on Knott's Berry Farm in this book for information. (714) 220–5200. www.knotts.com.

Pier Days. Ocean Avenue and Colorado Street, Santa Monica. Antique car show, fireworks, sailing race, fishing derby, face painting, live bands, and more. (310) 458–8900. Early October.

Redondo Lobster Festival. Harbor Drive and Beryl Street, Redondo Beach. Eating contest, exhibit, displays, demonstrations, Maine lobster meals, food tasting from area restaurants, and live entertainment. (310) 376–6911. www.lobster festival.com. Mid-October.

Shipwreck Haunted Hull of Horrors. *Queen Mary*, Long Beach. The engine room of the *Queen Mary* is transformed into a maze with monsters, goblins, and gruesome creatures. (562) 435–3511. www.queenmary.com. Late October.

Silverado Days. William Peak Park, Buena Park. A carnival, a parade, entertainment, food, and arts and crafts. (714) 521–0261. Mid-October.

South Bay Greek Festival. Redondo Beach. Cultural booths, ethnic food, music, dance, arts, crafts, and costumes. (310) 540–2434. Early October.

West Hollywood Halloween Carnival. Between La Cienega and Doheny Streets, West Hollywood. Festival booths, live entertainment, costume contest, and parade. (323) 848–6547. October 31.

NOVEMBER

Doo Dah Parade. Holly Street, Colorado Boulevard, and Pasadena Avenue, Pasadena. A riotous spoof of the Tournament of the Roses parade, featuring more than 1,200 marchers that in past years have included synchronized briefcase drill teams, marching political pundits, midget gospel singers, and dogs in drag. (626) 440–7379. Third week of November.

Hollywood Christmas Parade. Sunset and Hollywood Boulevards, Hollywood. Celebrities, marching bands, and classic cars in a parade from Mann's Chinese Theatre. Grandstands seats available for a fee. (213) 469–2337. Sunday after Thanksgiving.

DECEMBER

Annual New Year's Eve Shipwalk Party. *Queen Mary*, Long Beach. Live music and entertainment and fireworks. (562) 435–3511.

First Night Fullerton. Downtown Fullerton. Music and arts. (714) 738–6575. New Year's Eve.

Hanukkah at the Skirball. 2701 North Sepulveda Boulevard, Los Angeles. Art workshops, children's sing-along, live music, candle-lighting, treasure hunt, special food, and more. (310) 440–4500. Date varies.

Holiday at South Lake Avenue. Colorado Boulevard and California Avenue, Pasadena. Santa arrives on a red fire engine plus strolling Dickens carolers and hay rides. (626) 792–1259. Early December.

Las Posadas. El Pueblo de Los Angeles Historic Monument, downtown Los Angeles. Candlelight procession depicting the journey of Mary and Joseph to Bethlehem. (213) 628–1274. Late December.

Los Angeles County Holiday Celebration. Dorothy Chandler Pavilion. Annual free festival on Christmas Eve, in and around the Music Center. (213) 974–1343. Late December.

Newport Harbor Christmas Boat Parade. Newport Beach Harbor, Newport Beach. More than 150 decorated and illuminated multimillion dollar yachts, kayaks, canoes, and small boats. (714) 729–4400. www.christmasboatparade. com. Late December.

New Year's Eve at Two Harbors. Catalina Island. Dinner and party. (310) 510–2800.

New Year's Eve Bash at the Beach. 17300 Pacific Coast Highway, Malibu. Dinner, laser show, and countdown. (310) 454–3474.

New Year's Eve on Catalina Island. Catalina Island. Black-tie gala with dancing to big band music. (310) 510–1520.

New Year's Eve on Pine Avenue. Long Beach. Music, street performers, street dancing, and confetti shower. (562) 437–7700.

Tree Lighting at *Queen Mary*. *Queen Mary,* Long Beach. Holiday sing-alongs, refreshments, and choir performances. (562) 435–3511. Early December.

CHAPTER THIRTEEN

GRIFFITH PARK AND LOS ANGELES MUSEUMS

GRIFFITH PARK

Griffith Park, a hilly green space in the foothills of the eastern Santa Monica mountain range, is the largest municipal park and urban wilderness area in the United States. The park, with elevations ranging from 384 to 1,625 feet above sea level, encompasses more than 4,100 acres of wild sage, manzanita shrubs, and California oak trees.

The park includes several major museums and attractions including the famed Griffith Park Observatory and Planetarium (currently under reconstruction and due to reopen in 2005), the Autry Museum of Western Heritage, the Travel Town Transportation Museum, the Los Angeles Zoo, and recreational facilities including a merry-go-round, pony and wagon rides, several golf courses, and an amphitheater. On the slopes below the planetarium is the site—off limits to the public—of the celebrated Hollywood sign.

Over the decades Griffith Park has been the setting for dozens of Hollywood movies with its valleys and hillsides standing in for locations around the world. The lower slopes of the park were once occupied by Native American tribes. The land was originally part of Rancho Los Feliz, a Spanish land grant given to scout and explorer Corporal Jose Vicente Feliz in 1796.

Today the park bears the name of its controversial former owner, Griffith J. Griffith. Born in South Wales in Great Britain, Griffith immigrated to the United States in 1865; he made a considerable fortune speculating on gold mines in California, parlaying some of the inside information he obtained as a newspaper reporter into investments. Griffith settled in Los Angeles in 1882 and purchased what is now the parkland, a property that stretched northward from the northern boundaries of the Pueblo de Los Angeles.

GRIFFITH PARK

GRIFFITH PARK

134

San Fernando Rd.

Colorado Blvd.

Los Feliz Golf Course

Griffith Rec Center

5

Riverside Dr.

Friendship Auditorium

Santa George St.

Griffith Park Blvd.

Griffith Park Dr.

Wilson Golf Course

Gene Autry Museum of Western Heritage

5

Train and Pony Rides

Los Angeles Zoo

Zoo Dr.

Merry-Go-Round

Vista Del Valle Dr.

Commonwealth Ave.

Roosevelt Golf Course

Hillhurst Ave.

Vermont Ave.

Commonwealth Canyon Dr.

Travel Town Museum

Griffith Park Dr.

Zoo Dr.

Mt. Hollywood Dr.

Tunnel

Greek Theatre

Western Canyon Rd.

Fern Dell Dr.

Griffith Observatory

Los Feliz Blvd.

Equestrian Center

Alameda Ave.

Riverside Dr.

134

Forest Lawn Dr.

Buena Vista St.

Hollywood Sign

Beachwood Canyon Dr.

Franklin Ave.

Hollywood Blvd.

101

Hollywood Reservoir

Described by his contemporaries as insufferably pompous (he insisted upon being called "Colonel Griffith" although there is no record he ever held a military title higher than major of riflery practice with the California National Guard), he gave his Rancho Los Feliz estate as a grandiose Christmas gift to the people of Los Angeles in 1896.

In 1903, though, he was put on trial for the attempted murder of his wealthy society wife, Christina Griffith. In perhaps the first of California's continuing string of celebrity trials, Griffith was portrayed as an alcoholic with a paranoid delusion that his wife was in league with the pope to poison him, steal his money, and commit treason against the nation. He was sentenced to two years in prison; while he was locked away, the city renamed the park's mountain from Mount Griffith to Mount Hollywood, the name it bears today.

Out of prison, Griffith tried to rebuild his standing, offering $100,000 to the city to build an observatory in 1912, and another $50,000 for the construction of a Greek Theatre in the park the following year. Politicians were besieged by petitions and rallies calling for them to reject the money from a morally suspect source.

It took more than twenty years—well after Griffith's death in 1919—before the city accepted the money. The Greek Theatre was built in 1930, and the Griffith Observatory and Planetarium was constructed in 1935.

The City of Los Angeles Department of Recreation and Parks maintains a Web site about Griffith Park, at www.laparks.org/grifmet/griffith.htm.

■ GRIFFITH PARK OBSERVATORY AND PLANETARIUM

One of the stars of Southern California has been dimmed for several years, but plans for the renovated **Griffith Park Observatory and Planetarium** promise a supernova at the top of Mount Hollywood when it reopens in mid-2005, the seventieth anniversary of its debut. During the three-year reconstruction, the entire area at the top of the mountain will be closed to the public.

If the observatory at the top of the south slope of Mount Hollywood in Griffith Park looks vaguely familiar, it may be because of its starring role in a number of motion pictures and television shows over the years. Plans call for every piece of the Observatory to be restored to its original grandeur and improved. Excavations under the building and part of its front lawn will allow a doubling of the interior space without changing the classic appearance of the structure. New features will include a presentation theater, two large exhibit areas, a restaurant, and an expanded bookstore.

The **Planetarium,** which museum officials acknowledge was world famous for having the most uncomfortable seats in the entire Milky Way Galaxy, will be completely renewed and will feature a new all-dome laser projection system, as well as a new Zeiss Mark IX sky projector . . . and better seats.

The main rotunda, noted for its massive **Foucault Pendulum,** custom marble, travertine, and mosaic work will be restored to its original architectural grandeur of the 1930s. The Hugo Ballin murals covering the ceiling of the main rotunda were damaged in an earthquake in 1994 and will be restored. The panels depict the scientific achievements of a variety of national groups, including the English, Italian, Chinese, Egyptian, Greek, Arab, and Mexican (Aztec) peoples.

The new 200-seat theater, the **Leonard Nimoy Event Horizon,** was partly funded by a $1 million gift by the actor and his wife.

When it returns, the Observatory will once again feature a rooftop observatory that has spectacular views of the city on all sides and the heavens above; that is, when the smog clears. The 12-inch Zeiss telescope is one of the largest public telescopes in the world.

The **Hall of Science** within will once again feature a collection of meteorites and geological specimens. A popular exhibit expected to return is a working World War II periscope, which was originally used on the USS *Blenny*. The six-power periscope extends 37 feet up, presenting a nearly 360-degree view from the top of the observatory.

To the right of the entrance to the observatory is a bust of James Dean, who died in 1955—the same year his most famous movie, *Rebel Without a Cause,* was filmed in and around the observatory. Over the shoulder of the bust is the famous Hollywood sign high up on the hills behind it. The observatory was also used as a setting in *The Terminator* and as a backdrop for many other films from classic to forgettable.

For information about the Observatory, call (323) 664–1191 or consult www.griffithobs.org. You can also call (323) 663–8171 to hear a recorded message about astronomical events.

MUST-SEE AUTRY MUSEUM OF WESTERN HERITAGE

In a corner of Griffith Park is a magical place that celebrates the history of the West from sixteenth-century Spanish armor to the Emigrant Trail and the fabulous growth of modern-day California.

The Autry Museum of Western Heritage features a significant collection of artifacts including possessions of some of the wagon train travelers who settled the West and the cowboys who worked the trails. Run as a nonprofit organization established by the Autry Foundation, the museum includes seven theme galleries with a permanent hands-on gallery for children. It's a hidden piece of Disneyland, too; Disney Imagineers helped create animated displays that celebrate and explain the real Old West.

Treasures include early guidebooks for westward travelers, such as a copy of the *Hastings Emigrant Guide,* which misled the Donner party to tragedy in the Sierra Mountains. You'll also find a gleaming brass Silsby Steam Pumper, purchased with community fundraising in 1874 in Carson City. And there's a huge mahogany Edison Multiphone coin-operated phonograph from about 1915 and a "Los Angeles" bar from the turn of the twentieth century that was used in a Montana saloon for nearly a century.

There's a collection of sheriff's badges, Belle Starr's revolver, and a Holdout Arm Cheating Device from about 1905 that hid a card up the sleeve. One case also contains Annie Oakley's gold-plated pistols, presented to her by her husband Frank Butler in about 1900; in 1875, at age fifteen, she beat professional marksman Butler in a local shooting match in Ohio. In 1885 she joined Buffalo Bill's Wild West Show where she starred for seventeen years.

The fine art collection features work by painters that include Frederic Remington and Seth Eastman. Remington's first sculpture, Bronco Buster, is also on display. A museum store offers jewelry, clothing, books, and posters.

Gene Autry, born in 1907 in Tioga, Texas, was a star of radio, music, Hollywood, and business. He began his radio career in 1928 as the result of a chance meeting with Will Rogers; his "Melody Ranch" show on CBS began in 1939 and ran for sixteen years. Autry appeared in ninety-five films and recorded more than 635 records, selling more than forty million copies. His most famous gold records include "Rudolph the Red-Nosed Reindeer," "Peter Cottontail," "Here Comes Santa Claus" (which he cowrote), "Tumbling Tumbleweeds," "Back in the Saddle Again" (cowriter), and "You Are My Sunshine."

Autry put some of his riches into business interests; he owned four radio stations in Los Angeles and Seattle, the California Angels baseball team, and other properties. He sold off majority ownership of the Angels to the Walt Disney Company in 1996. Autry died in 1998.

Located at 4700 Western Heritage Way in Griffith Park at the junction of the Golden State (Interstate 5) and Ventura (Highway 134) freeways, the Autry Museum is open Tuesday through Sunday from 10:00 A.M. to 5:00 P.M. On Thursday the museum is open until 8:00 P.M. Closed Monday except for certain holidays; closed Thanksgiving and Christmas.

Admission: adult, $7.50; senior (older than 60) and student (13–18), $5.00; and child (2–12), $3.00. Admission is free on the second Tuesday of each month. Parking is free. For information, call (213) 667–2000 or consult www.autry-museum.org.

■ TRAVEL TOWN TRANSPORTATION MUSEUM

This museum is a free and almost-secret treasure guaranteed to enthrall children of most ages. Come see the large collection of steam locomotives, retired Los Angeles street trolleys, antique railway cars, boxcars, cabooses, and old wagons; visitors can climb aboard most of the equipment, including a 110-ton Union Pacific locomotive.

One of the more spectacular engines is Engine No. 26 from the Western Pacific Railroad, which stands almost 12 feet tall. A set of steps leads you to the controls. You will also find a 1911 Metropolitan Transportation Authority streetcar and a 1902 Pacific Electric Electra car.

Located on Zoo Drive in Griffith Park, the museum is open weekdays from 10:00 A.M. to 4:00 P.M., and on weekends from 10:00 A.M. to 5:00 P.M. Parking and admission to the museum is free; there is a $1.75 fee for a train ride. For information, call (213) 662–5874 or consult www.cityofla.org/RAP/grifmet/tt.

Pony and Covered Wagon Rides

Crystal Springs Drive, near Los Feliz Boulevard in Griffith Park. (323) 664–3266. Three small pony tracks accommodate riders from one to one hundred pounds. Open Tuesday through Sunday from 10:00 A.M. to 5:00 P.M. Nominal fee.

Griffith Park Merry-Go-Round

A lovingly maintained 1926 wooden carousel located between the Los Angeles Zoo and the Los Feliz park entrance. The carousel hosts sixty-eight horses, all of them jumpers, with carved and jeweled bridles. The Stinson Military Band Organ plays more than 1,500 selections of marches and waltz music. Open daily from 11:00 A.M. to 5:00 P.M. in summer, and on weekends and holidays in winter. Nominal fee. For information, call (323) 665–3051.

LOS ANGELES–AREA ART MUSEUMS

World-renowned collections of ancient Greek, Roman, and Asian works highlight the art museums of Los Angeles.

⬛ MUST-SEE ⬛ J. PAUL GETTY MUSEUM AT THE GETTY CENTER

The Getty collection includes Greek and Roman marble and bronze sculptures, paintings, vases, and other objects from 3000 B.C. to A.D. 300. Major works include the Cycladic harpist from about 2500 B.C. and the limestone and marble *Aphrodite* from the end of the fifth century B.C.

The collection of drawings and paintings includes Rembrandt's *An Old Man in Military Costume* and other portraits; Thomas Gainsborough's *Portrait of Anne, Countess of Chesterfield*; Paul Cézanne's *Young Italian Woman at a Table*; Titian's *Venus and Adonis*; Peter Paul Rubens's *Andromeda*; as well as works by da Vinci, Raphael, Goya, Renoir, Munch, and van Gogh.

The spectacular museum consists of a cluster of two-story pavilions bridged by walkways on both levels with indoor and outdoor galleries and gardens. Visitors are delivered from the parking area to the hilltop facility by an automated tram; the cars are like a horizontal elevator, gliding ⅛ inch above the track on a cushion of air.

The Getty Center is located at 1200 Getty Center Drive in Brentwood, near the San Diego Freeway (Interstate 405) and the Santa Monica Freeway (Interstate 10). Take the Getty Center Drive exit from the 405 and follow signs.

The museum is open Sunday and Tuesday to Thursday from 10:00 A.M. to 6:00 P.M., Friday and Saturday from 10:00 A.M. to 9:00 P.M. Closed Monday and major holidays. Admission is free. Advance reservations are recommended for special events. Parking is $5.00; advance

Peristyle Garden: Getty Villa. *Photo by Alexander Vertikoff, Copyright © The J. Paul Getty Trust*

reservations for space required. For information, call (310) 440–7300 or consult www.getty.edu/museum.

Getty Villa, Malibu

The spectacular building in a gorgeous setting with a fabulous endowment was created by oil billionaire J. Paul Getty to hold his personal collection. It was closed to the public in 1997 for renovation and is set to reopen in 2003 as a re-search and cultural center.

The building is set in a re-creation of a first-century Roman villa, built on a cliff overlooking the Pacific Ocean; it is surrounded by manicured gardens. The design for the building is based on the Villa dei Papiri, which stood outside the ancient city of Herculaneum, overlooking the Bay of Naples.

The Villa's new mission includes the display of works of art from the Antiquities Collection, which now contains more than 50,000 objects. The collections will be displayed by themes such as religion and myth or on aspects of everyday life. The Villa will also have a number of galleries for temporary exhibitions of materials from other institutions and from the collections of the Getty Research Institute.

For information, call (310) 440–7300, or consult www.getty.edu/museum/villa.html.

⁞MUST-SEE⁞ HUNTINGTON LIBRARY, ART COLLECTIONS, AND BOTANICAL GARDENS

Another art-filled monument to old money, the extensive and wide-ranging collections of railroad magnate Henry E. Huntington are housed in a group of buildings in a two-hundred-acre botanical garden in the San Gabriel Valley. The estate was built in 1919. The library, built in 1925, contains more than half a million books and five million manuscripts, including a first folio of several of Shakespeare's plays, the Ellesmere manuscript of Chaucer's *The Canterbury Tales* from about 1410, and a Gutenberg Bible. The art gallery, built in 1910 as Huntington's home, showcases famous works such as Thomas Gainsborough's *Blue Boy.*

The estate's botanical gardens include a large Japanese garden with a koi fish pond; the Desert Garden is the largest such collection in the world with more than 5,000 desert plant species. Guided tours of the garden are available; call for details.

The museum is located at 1151 Oxford Road, San Marino, about 12 miles northeast of downtown Los Angeles and due east of Pasadena. Open Tuesday through Friday from noon to 4:30 P.M. and weekends from 10:30 A.M. to 4:30 P.M.; in the summer, the museum opens daily, except Monday, at 10:30 A.M. Admission: adult, $10.00; student, $7.00; senior, $8.50; children younger than 12, free. Admission is free to all on the first Thursday of each month.

For information, call (626) 405–2100 or consult www.huntington.org.

▦ MUST-SEE ▦ LOS ANGELES COUNTY MUSEUM OF ART

A sprawling collection of art from around the world including a fabulous collection of Tibetan, Indian, and Nepalese works, a gallery of Daumier prints, and a pavilion with one of the best gatherings of Japanese art outside of Asia.

The museum includes four main buildings: the Hammer Building (photography, prints, drawings, and late-nineteenth-century European art), the Bing Center, the Robert O. Anderson Building (primarily twentieth-century art), and the Ahmanson Gallery. The Ahmanson includes ancient Egyptian, Asian, Middle Eastern, pre-Columbian, and early American art and artifacts. The Bing Theater at the Bing Center offers a family film series on Friday and Saturday evenings.

The La Brea tar pits, one of the world's most important Pleistocene-era sites, are located directly behind the museum in Hancock Park.

The museum, at 5905 Wilshire Boulevard in Los Angeles, is open Monday, Tuesday, and Thursday from noon to 8:00 P.M., Friday from noon to 9:00 P.M., Saturday and Sunday from 11:00 A.M. to 8:00 P.M. Closed Wednesday, Thanksgiving, and Christmas. Admission is free on the second Tuesday of each month. Admission: adult, $7.00; student and senior, $5.00; and child (12 and younger), free. Admission is free to all on the second Tuesday of each month. Pay parking is available at Wilshire Boulevard and Spaulding Avenue, and at Wilshire and Ogden Drive. For information, call (323) 857–6111 or consult www.lacma.org.

▦ MUST-SEE ▦ MUSEUM OF CONTEMPORARY ART, LOS ANGELES (MOCA)

Like many of the pieces it displays, MOCA is a bit hard to get a handle on: To begin with, this is one museum with three locations.

The main building is known as **MOCA at California Plaza,** located at 250 South Grand Avenue, Los Angeles. In the best traditions of grand museums, the building that houses the collection of modern art at MOCA is a work of art by itself; designed by Japanese architect Arata Isozaki and opened in 1986, it includes spectacular pyramidic skylights and geometric angles. For information, call (213) 621–2766 or consult www.moca-la.org.

The more mundane **MOCA at the Geffen Contemporary** in Little Tokyo, which opened while MOCA was under construction, has been kept in service as home to traveling exhibitions and some of the works from the main museum. It is housed within a converted Los Angeles Police Department garage at 152 North Central Avenue, about a mile away from California Plaza. For information, call (213) 626–6222.

The most recently added piece of the pie is **MOCA at the Pacific Design Center,** at 8687 Melrose Avenue, West Hollywood. The small facility features contemporary architecture and design. For information, call (213) 621–1741.

All three of the museum buildings are closed Monday. Open Tuesday through Sunday 11:00 A.M. to 5:00 P.M. and until 8:00 P.M. on Thursday. Admission: adult, $8.00; student (12 and older), and senior, $5.00. Free admission on Thursdays from 5:00 to 8:00 P.M. One ticket is valid at California Plaza and the Geffen

Contemporary on the same day, and at the Pacific Design Center within 30 days of first use. Admission to MOCA at the Pacific Design Center only is $3.00.

▮MUST-SEE▮ NORTON SIMON MUSEUM OF ART

Only the best: modern nineteenth- and twentieth-century classics from Picasso, Monet, van Gogh, Renoir, Degas, Cézanne, Klee, and more, plus 2,000 years of Indian and Southeast Asian sculptures. At nearly every turn you'll see familiar works of art by famous artists.

Norton Simon, born in Portland, Oregon, in 1907, moved to Los Angeles and started a series of businesses. In 1929, at the start of the Depression, he invested $7,000 in a failing juice bottling company that became the highly successful Hunt Foods. His holdings eventually expanded to include Hunt-Wesson Foods, McCall's Publishing, Canada Dry, Max Factor, and Avis Car Rental.

Treasures include Botticelli's *Madonna and Child with Adoring Angel*, from about 1468; Peter Paul Rubens's *David Slaying Goliath*; Rembrandt's famed *Self-Portrait*; and Jean-Honoré Fragonard's *The Happy Lovers*. Modern masterpieces include Ansel Adams's famous photograph, *Moonrise, Hernandez, New Mexico*; Pablo Picasso's *The Ram's Head*, and Henri Matisse's *The Black Shawl*.

Located at 411 West Colorado Boulevard at Orange Grove Boulevard in Pasadena at the intersection of the Foothill (210) and Ventura (134) Freeways, the museum is open daily except Tuesday from noon to 6:00 P.M., and on Friday until 9:00 P.M. Admission: adult, $6.00; student with ID, free; senior $3.00; children (18 and younger) and students with current ID, free.

For information, call (626) 449–6840 or consult www.nortonsimon.org.

▮ PACIFIC ASIA MUSEUM

A somewhat incongruous sight in downtown Pasadena; housed within a replica of a Chinese imperial palace is an extensive collection of Pacific island and Asian costumes, ceramics, textiles, ornaments, and paintings. Located at 46 North Los Robles Avenue, north of Colorado Boulevard in Pasadena, the museum is open Wednesday through Sunday 10:00 A.M. to 5:00 P.M., and on Friday until 8:00 P.M. Admission: adult, $5.00; senior and student, $3.00; child (younger than 12), free. For information, call (626) 449–2742 or consult www.pacificasiamuseum.org.

▮ UCLA HAMMER MUSEUM

The twentieth-century industrialist and deal maker Armand Hammer's collection of Impressionist and Post-Impressionist paintings and caricatures by Honoré Daumier highlight the exhibition. Other stars of the collection include Claude Monet, Camille Pissarro, John Singer Sargent, Mary Cassatt, and Vincent van Gogh.

Nearby on UCLA's North Campus, the Franklin D. Murphy Sculpture Garden features more than seventy sculptures by such artists as Jean Arp, Alexander Calder, Claire Falkenstein, Barbara Hepworth, Gaston Lachaise, Jacques Lipchitz, Henri Matisse, Henry Moore, Isamu Noguchi, Auguste Rodin, David Smith, and Francisco Zuñiga.

Located at 10899 Wilshire Boulevard at Westwood Boulevard in Los Angeles, the museum is open Tuesday through Saturday 11:00 A.M. to 7:00 P.M., and Thursday until 9:00 P.M. Sunday 11:00 A.M. to 5:00 P.M. Admission: adult, $4.50; student and senior, $3.00; child (17 and younger), free. Admission is free on Thursday. For information, call (310) 443–7000 or consult www.hammer.ucla.edu.

■ UCLA FOWLER MUSEUM OF CULTURAL HISTORY

An eclectic collection of more than 750,000 objects representing prehistoric, historic, and contemporary cultures of Africa, Oceania, the Americas, and Asia. Admission: adult, $5.00; visiting students and seniors, $3.00. Parking $6.00. Located just west of Royce Hall on the UCLA campus, off Sunset Boulevard, the museum is open Wednesday to Sunday, noon to 5:00 P.M., and Thursday evenings until 8:00 P.M. For information, call (310) 825–4361 or consult www. fmch.ucla.edu.

■ BARNSDALL ART PARK

Architect Frank Lloyd Wright's first Los Angeles house was the Hollyhock House, built in 1918 for oil heiress Aline Barnsdall, who came West with hopes of developing a theater company. She donated the home and surrounding property to the city in 1927 as an arts center. Guided tours are offered Wednesday through Sunday at noon, 1:00 P.M., 2:00 P.M., and 3:00 P.M. Admission: adult, $5.00; senior, $4.00.

The park is located at 4800 Hollywood Boulevard, Los Feliz. For information, call (323) 913–4157.

Also on the grounds is the L.A. Municipal Art Gallery. Admission: $5.00. Hours are Wednesday through Sunday, 12:30 to 5:00 P.M. Open until 8:30 P.M. on Friday. For information, call (213) 485–4581.

■ LONG BEACH MUSEUM OF ART

An intriguing mixture of old and new with displays of modern art, sculpture, and videos in a 1912 mansion on a bluff overlooking Long Beach Harbor and the Pacific Ocean. Admission: free. The museum, at 2300 East Ocean Boulevard in Long Beach, is open Tuesday through Sunday 11:00 A.M. to 5:00 P.M., and until 8:00 P.M. on Friday. Admission: adult, student, senior, $5.00; children younger than 12, free. Admission is free to all on the first Friday of each month. For information, call (562) 439–2119 or consult www.lbma.org.

■ ORANGE COUNTY MUSEUM OF ART

Twentieth-century American art with an emphasis on 200 years of California culture. The museum is located at 850 San Clemente Drive in Newport Beach, about 45 miles southeast of Los Angeles or 15 miles south of Disneyland. It is open Tuesday through Sunday 11:00 A.M. to 5:00 P.M. Admission: adult, $5.00; student and senior, $4.00; child (16 and younger), free. For information, call (949) 759–1122 or consult www.ocma.net.

MUSEUMS OF SCIENCE AND CULTURE

In southern California, sometimes it's hard to separate science and culture; they seem inextricably bound up with each other in places like the La Brea Tar Pits and the International Surfing Museum.

⚎ MUST-SEE ⚎ LA BREA TAR PITS/GEORGE C. PAGE MUSEUM OF THE LA BREA DISCOVERIES

The La Brea Tar Pits are one of the most unusual elements of a downtown anywhere in the world, a little bit of the Ice Age in the shadow of the skyscrapers. The museum has within it more than a million fossils of plants and animals taken from the tar pits since their discovery in 1906.

Among the skeletal remains found in the tar are saber-toothed tigers, a mammoth, and the 9,000-year-old remains of a woman. Don't promise your kids a view of dinosaurs, though: the pits are only about 40,000 years old, and the big guys had been gone tens of millions of years before then.

As you enter **Hancock Park,** home of the La Brea Tar Pits, you can smell tar and asphalt in the air. The first historic reference to the tar pools was recorded in the diary of Gaspar du Portola in 1769; the area was originally a portion of the Rancho La Brea granted by Governor Alvarado in 1840.

The Lake Pit along Wilshire Boulevard fills a quarry where asphalt was mined in the nineteenth century; life-size fiberglass models of an imperial mammoth family stand at the east end of the lake, which is covered with an oily slick. Bubbles of methane burst through the surface of the lake regularly.

The pools of thick oil became unique death traps for countless Ice Age animals and birds, making La Brea the richest deposit of ice age fossils in the world. More than one hundred tons of fossil bones have been recovered.

The reconstructed Imperial Mammoth Bull alongside the Lake Pit is modeled after a nearly complete skeleton exhibited in the George C. Page Museum. The animal stood about 12 feet tall and weighed more than 10,000 pounds.

On a nice Sunday you will also likely find a collection of some of California's patented kooks. On one of my visits, I found a man exhibiting his pair of "psychic cats." If you held out a dollar bill, they would grab hold of it with their paws and push a lever on a cigar box to release a printed message.

The pits and museum are located at 5801 Wilshire Boulevard east of Fairfax Avenue in Los Angeles. Open Tuesday through Sunday from 10:00 A.M. to 5:00 P.M.; first Tuesday of the month is free. Admission: adult, $6.00; senior and student, $3.50; child (5–10), $2.00. Parking at the museum is $5.00 with validation.

For information, call (323) 857–6311 or consult www.tarpits.org.

⚎ MUST-SEE ⚎ LOS ANGELES COUNTY MUSEUM OF NATURAL HISTORY

A national treasure with dozens of major displays from the age of the dinosaurs to modern-day mammals and most everything in between. You'll find an insect zoo, a Hall of Birds, a sparkling collection of gems and minerals, and even a display of ancient Mayan artifacts.

Two world-famous habitat halls show African and North American mammals in their natural environments. The museum is also home to Megamouth, the world's rarest shark; the 14.5-foot-long male is one of only five of his species found since the first one was discovered in 1976. The Hall of Native American Cultures showcases more than 800 pieces from the museum's permanent collection, and the Marine Hall features intricate dioramas of sea life in California waters.

Located at 900 Exposition Boulevard in Los Angeles in Exposition Park, the museum is open daily from 9:30 A.M. to 5:00 P.M., and from 10:00 A.M. to 5:00 P.M. on weekends. Admission: adult, $8.00; child (5–12), $2.00; student and senior, $5.50. Admission free on the first Tuesday of each month.

For information, call (213) 763–3466 or consult www.nhm.org.

Within the museum is the Discovery Center, a hands-on, interactive gallery where visitors can dig for fossils, meet live reptiles, or observe insects at their own zoo. Call (213) 763–3239 for more information.

Next-door to the Natural History Museum is the Exposition Park Rose Garden, one of the largest displays in the country. Open daily. Admission: free.

■ LOS ANGELES MARITIME MUSEUM

The next best thing to a life at sea: a collection of more than 600 ship models, including a cutaway model of the *Titanic*, plus all manner of maritime equipment, including diving equipment and artifacts from the old whaling and shipping days to modern times. The museum is located at Berth 84, Sixth Street and Harbor Boulevard, San Pedro, in a former ferry building with a view of the harbor. Open Tuesday through Sunday 10:00 A.M. to 5:00 P.M. Closed Monday. Donation: adult, $1.00. For information, call (310) 548–7618 or consult www. lamaritimemuseum.org.

Nearby at Berth 94 is the SS *Lane Victory,* a restored cargo ship built in Los Angeles in 1945. The vessel served in the latter part of World War II, Korea (at the Chosin Reservoir operation), and in Vietnam. The ship was named after Isaac Lane, who rose from slavery to become a Bishop in the Methodist Episcopal Church and founded the Lane College in Jackson, Tennessee, in 1882.

The ship has been restored to near-pristine condition, with all of its naval guns and most of its equipment in place. It is open for tours throughout the year. The vessel is regularly employed as a set for films, televisions shows, and commercials; call ahead to confirm hours before a visit.

Six times a year during the summer the *Lane Victory* leaves its dock to cruise to Catalina Island, including a re-enactment of a World War II air battle. Organizers expect a donation of at least $100 per person for the all-day trip, including meals. For dockside visits, a donation of $3.00 per person is expected. Call (310) 519–9545 for information and schedules or consult www.lanevictory ship.com.

⚏MUST-SEE⚏ PETERSEN AUTOMOTIVE MUSEUM

A branch of the Natural History Museum of Los Angeles County, the permanent exhibit on the first floor traces the history of the automobile. The second floor contains five large, rotating exhibition galleries with state-of-the-art displays of race cars, classic cars, vintage motorcycles, concept cars, celebrity and movie cars, and automotive design and technology. The museum is housed in the former Ohrbach's Department Store in downtown Los Angeles and is named after benefactor Robert E. Petersen, a noted automobile enthusiast.

Located at 6060 Wilshire Boulevard, near Fairfax Avenue, the museum is open Tuesday through Sunday from 10:00 A.M. to 6:00 P.M. and is closed Monday except for holidays. Admission: adult, $7.00; child (5–12), $3.00; student and senior, $5.00. For information, call (323) 930–2277 or consult www.petersen.org.

▣ CABRILLO MARINE AQUARIUM

Saltwater aquariums, displays of sea plants, tide pools, and mud flats located in and around a 1920s bathhouse. The museum also sponsors educational lectures, whale-watching trips, and the annual Whale Fiesta in June and Autumn Sea Fair in October.

Located at 3720 Stephen White Drive in San Pedro, the museum is open Tuesday through Friday from noon to 5:00 P.M.; weekends from 10:00 A.M. to 5:00 P.M. Admission free; suggested donation adult, $2.00; child $1.00. Beach parking fee $6.50. For information, call (310) 548–7562 or consult www.cabrilloaq.org.

⚏MUST-SEE⚏ CALIFORNIA SCIENCE CENTER

A sprawling museum with hands-on explorations of science from medicine to outer space, second only in size to the Smithsonian in Washington. The two main theme areas are **World of Life** and **Creative World.** Check out the Life Tiles as you enter; art "morphs" from one image to another.

Guests who meet size and weight requirements can ride a high-wire bicycle hung 43 feet above the atrium floor of the Science Court. The bike is counterbalanced on a guide wire; you cannot fall, but you do have to overcome any fear of heights.

Suspended above the Science Court is a hyperbolic paraboloid sculpture, better known as Hypar, which is a fantastic blend of science and art made from 2,500 aluminum links. The sculpture grows from a compact cluster of 15 feet to 50 feet, maintaining its same shape.

The aerospace section includes historic airplanes, spacecraft, other exhibits, and the IMAX Theater with a 70-foot-high, 90-foot-wide screen for science, nature, and travel films in 2-D and 3-D formats. Call (213) 744–2014 for IMAX schedules. Admission to IMAX films: adult, $7.00; student, (13–17 and college students with ID), $5.25; child (4–12), $4.25; and senior, $5.25.

The museum is located in Exposition Park at 700 State Drive, next to the Los Angeles Memorial Coliseum; the area is often used for special events. There are many parking lots in the area; it is probably not advisable to park on the street. The museum is open daily from 10:00 A.M. to 5:00 P.M. Admission: free.

For information, call (213) 744–7400 or consult www.casciencectr.org.

JET PROPULSION LABORATORY

Exhibits include models of the Galileo and Cassini spacecrafts. Two-hour tours given by reservation only; call for information and hours. Children younger than 10 are not permitted. Call six to eight weeks in advance for a reservation. The laboratory is located at 4800 Oak Grove Drive in Pasadena. Call (818) 354–9314 for tour information. Information about the laboratory can be seen at www.jpl.nasa.gov.

HOBBY CITY DOLL AND TOY MUSEUM

More than 6,000 antique dolls and toys, with displays including a small-scale replica of the White House. Next door is **Adventure City,** an outdoor theme park for children under 13 that includes small-scale rides, a petting zoo, and play areas. Located at 1238 South Beach Boulevard, Anaheim, the museum is open daily 10:00 A.M. to 6:00 P.M. Nominal admission. For information, call (714) 527–2323.

HUNTINGTON BEACH INTERNATIONAL SURFING MUSEUM

Far out, dude: a collection of wicked surfboards, including a 1930 wooden behemoth that measures more than 12 feet and weighs 135 pounds. Other exhibits include posters, artwork, surfing music, and a Hall of Fame. Free surfer music shows in the parking lot Sunday afternoons; call for schedules.

Located at 411 Olive Avenue in Huntington Beach (exit I–405 at Highway 39–Beach Boulevard), the surfing museum is open daily in summer from noon to 5:00 P.M.; the remainder of the year open Wednesday through Sunday only. Admission: adult, $5.00; student, $3.00. Child (younger than 6), free.

For information, call (714) 960–3483 or consult www.surfingmuseum.org.

HISTORY MUSEUMS AND HISTORIC DISTRICTS

Historical museums and attractions in southern California explore the influences of immigrants from the East, from Asia, and Mexico and Central America.

AMERICAN MILITARY MUSEUM

An unusual collection of military equipment including tanks, jeeps, cannons, and other devices. Located at 1918 North Rosemead Boulevard, El Monte, within the Whittier Narrows Recreation Area, the museum is open Friday through Sunday 10:00 A.M. to 4:30 P.M. Closed in wet weather. Admission: By donation. For information, call (626) 442–1776 or consult hometown.aol.com/tankland/museum.htm.

CALIFORNIA AFRO-AMERICAN MUSEUM

Art exhibitions, a library, and theater celebrating African-American culture. Located in Exposition Park at South Figueroa Street and State Drive in Los Angeles. The facility was renovated in 2002, adding expanded exhibition space. Open daily except Monday 10:00 A.M. to 5:00 P.M. Admission: free. Parking $5.00. For information, call (213) 744–7432 or consult www.caam.ca.gov.

■ EL MONTE HISTORICAL MUSEUM

A small museum that celebrates El Monte's history as the end of the Santa Fe Trail, which extended some 780 miles from Independence, Missouri, to Santa Fe, New Mexico, and from there on to California. Hundreds of wagon trains made the forty- to sixty-day trip to New Mexico from about 1822 until 1880, when the Santa Fe Railroad reached the area.

The adobe-style building, a former WPA-built library, includes Victorian-era settings and a children's section with antique toys. Located at 3150 North Tyler Avenue, El Monte, the museum is open Tuesday through Friday from 10:00 A.M. to 4:00 P.M. and Sunday from 1:00 to 3:00 P.M. Donations are accepted. For information, call (626) 580–2232.

■ HERITAGE SQUARE MUSEUM

Eight Victorian-era and older buildings have been restored into a living museum with shops and displays; they are open for tours by costumed guides Saturday, Sunday, and most holidays. Buildings include the Palms Railroad Station, which has been restored and filled with railroad artifacts, plus several homes and a church from 1897. Special events include old-fashioned Fourth of July celebrations and Christmas festivals.

Located at 3800 Homer Street in Highland Park, guided tours on the hour from noon to 3:00 P.M. Open Friday 10:30 A.M. to 3:30 P.M., Saturday and Sunday 11:30 A.M. to 4:30 P.M. Admission: adult, $4.00; child (7–11), $2.00; senior and student (12–17), $3.00.

For information, call (626) 449–0193 or consult www.heritagesquare.org.

■ JAPANESE-AMERICAN NATIONAL MUSEUM

The story of Japanese immigrants to America told in artifacts, photos, art, and recordings.

The museum is located within the former Nishi Hongwanji Buddhist Temple, built by Japanese immigrants in 1925 as the first Buddhist place of worship in Los Angeles. The ornate structure mixes elements of a temple in Kyoto with other Japanese and Middle Eastern influences. A hub of religious and social life in thriving Little Tokyo, the structure was later used to store the belongings of Japanese Americans ordered to World War II internment camps. The temple eventually fell into serious disrepair and, in 1969, was sold to the City of Los Angeles. It was saved from demolition for use as the museum site.

Located at 369 East First Street at Central Avenue, Los Angeles, the museum is open Tuesday through Sunday 10:00 A.M. to 5:00 P.M. and until 8:00 P.M. on Thursday. Closed Monday. Admission: adult, $6.00; child (6–17) and students with ID, $3.00; and senior, $5.00. Free every third Thursday and every Thursday evening from 5:00 to 8:00 P.M. For information, call (213) 625–0414 or consult www.janm.org.

■ KOREAN FRIENDSHIP BELL

Angel's Gate Park, San Pedro, on Gaffey Street. What is said to be the largest bell in America was a gift from the Republic of Korea to the United States for the

1976 Bicentennial celebration. The one-ton bell is rung three times a year: on New Year's Day, the Fourth of July, and Korean Liberation Day, August 15. For information, consult www.sanpedrochamber.com/champint/korenbel.htm.

■ LUMMIS HOME

Writer and photographer Charles Lummis, who chronicled some of the early days of the Wild West, built his home—named El Alisal for a nearby stand of sycamores—between 1896 and 1910 from granite boulders, concrete, and telegraph poles from the Santa Fe Railroad. Inside are rare photos of Native Americans and other artifacts. Located at 200 East Avenue 43, Highland Park, near the Southwest Museum, the home is open Friday to Sunday from noon to 4:00 P.M. Admission: free. For information, call (323) 222–0546.

■ LOS ANGELES MUSEUM OF THE HOLOCAUST

A commemoration of the martyrs of the Holocaust including photographs, diaries, artifacts, and oral histories. Located at the Jewish Federation Council, 6006 Wilshire Boulevard, Los Angeles, the museum is open Monday through Thursday 10:00 A.M. to 5:00 P.M., Friday 10:00 A.M. to 2:00 P.M., and Sunday noon to 4:00 P.M. Open Tuesday until 8:00 P.M. Closed Saturday. Admission: free. For information, call (323) 852–3242 or consult www.jewishla.org/html/l.a._holo caust_museum.htm.

■ MUSEUM OF TOLERANCE, SIMON WIESENTHAL CENTER

Never again: exhibits on twentieth-century genocide, war, and oppression, from the Holocaust to the fighting in Rwanda and the Neo-Nazi movement. Some of the exhibits can be rather intense, including the Whisper Gallery where visitors walk through an audio gauntlet of racial and ethnic slurs, and the Hall of Testimony, where you will hear stories of survival and sacrifice from the Holocaust in Europe.

Simon Wiesenthal, trained as an architect, survived the Nazi death camps of World War II. After the war he became a hunter of former Nazis. The Simon Wiesenthal Center was founded in 1977.

Located at 9786 West Pico Boulevard at Roxbury Drive, Century City, the museum is open Monday through Thursday 10:00 A.M. to 4:00 P.M., Sunday 10:30 A.M. to 5:00 P.M., and Friday from 10:00 A.M. to 3:00 P.M. summer, and until 1:00 P.M. in the winter. Closed Saturday and Jewish holidays. Admission: adult, $9.00; student and youth (3–10), $5.50; and senior, $7.00. For information, call (310) 553–8403 or consult www.wiesenthal.com.

■ SKIRBALL CULTURAL CENTER

Jewish history and art from around the world and across time, with a performing arts center. Located at 2701 North Sepulveda Boulevard, Los Angeles, the center is open Tuesday to Saturday from noon to 5:00 P.M., Sunday 11:00 A.M. to 5:00 P.M. Admission: adult, $8.00; student and senior, $6.00; child (12 and younger), free. For information, call (310) 440–4600 or consult www.skirball.org.

■ SOUTHWEST MUSEUM

An impressive collection of artifacts and crafts of Native Americans of the West, as well as elements of the Spanish colonization of California. Located at 234 Museum Drive, near Highland Park in Los Angeles, the museum is open Tuesday through Sunday 10:00 A.M. to 5:00 P.M. Closed Monday. Admission: adult, $6.00; child (7–17), $3.00; senior and student, $4.00. For information, call (323) 221–2163 or consult www.southwestmuseum.org.

■ WELLS FARGO HISTORY MUSEUM

A history of the rough side of development of the West including stagecoaches, the Pony Express, mining equipment, gold nuggets, and a replica of a nineteenth-century Wells Fargo office. Visitors can try their hands at a telegraph key and examine early photos and documents that trace the history of Wells Fargo Bank from its founding in 1852 into the electronic age. Located at 333 South Grand Avenue at Third Street in the Wells Fargo Bank Center, Los Angeles, the museum is open weekdays from 9:00 A.M. to 5:00 P.M. Admission: free. For information, call (213) 253–7166 or consult www.wellsfargo.com.

■ WILLIAM O. DOUGLAS OUTDOOR CLASSROOM

Nature center, family and children's hiking trails, and special educational and ecological programs. Located at Franklin Canyon Ranch, north of Beverly Hills. Admission: free. Center open sunrise to sunset daily. For information, call (310) 858–3834.

CHILDREN'S MUSEUMS

■ CHILDREN'S MUSEUM OF LOS ANGELES

The mother of all child museums in Los Angeles will reopen in two new facilities in 2003 and 2005. The first new facility, the **North Valley Campus,** is on an acre of land in the Hansen Dam Recreational Area located in the northeast San Fernando Valley. The museum structure will include activities for children to learn, explore, and discover all sorts of neat stuff. Plans call for a grand opening in late 2002 or early 2003.

The second half of the museum will be within the **Art Park** located adjacent to the Geffen Contemporary Museum of Art and next to the Japanese American National Museum and the Union Art center. The Art Park site will include a 100,000-square-foot building celebrating the urban environment and the performing and visual arts.

The former facility, at 310 North Main Street, closed to the public in 2000.

For information, call (213) 687–8800 or consult www.childrensmuseumla.org.

■ KIDSPACE

Children try on some of the roles of adulthood in this innovative museum that insists that visitors touch the exhibits. Children can visit a television weather set, climb on a real fire truck, and much more. Children must be accompanied by an adult, and the other way around. Located at 390 South El Molina Avenue, Pasadena, the museum is open Tuesday from 1:30 P.M. to 5:00 P.M., Wednesday through Friday 1:00 P.M. to 5:00 P.M., Saturday 10:00 A.M. to 5:00 P.M., and Sunday 1:00 P.M. to 5:00 P.M. Admission: adult and child, $5.00; child (1–2), $2.00; senior, $5.00. For information, call (626) 449–9143.

■ LA HABRA CHILDREN'S MUSEUM

A converted train depot with hands-on exhibits including a real big city bus, a minimarket that has a cash register and scales, a dino-dig, and a model train village. Check out the dino topiaries at the entrance. Located at 301 South Euclid Street, La Habra, the museum is open daily from 10:00 A.M. to 5:00 P.M. and Sunday from 1:00 to 5:00 P.M. Admission: adult and child (2–16), $4.00. For information, call (562) 905–9793 or consult www.lhcm.org.

TRANSPORTATION MUSEUMS

■ LOMITA RAILROAD MUSEUM

Step back to the turn of the century and explore a 1921 Southern Pacific locomotive, an old train station, an antique caboose, and other equipment. Located at 2135 250th Street, at Woodward Avenue, Lomita, the museum is open Wednesday through Sunday 10:00 A.M. to 5:00 P.M. Admission: adult, $2.00; child (12 and younger), $1.00. For information, call (310) 326–6255 or consult www. lomita-rr.org.

■ MUSEUM OF FLYING

Located at the Santa Monica Airport, this is a working museum of aviation home to more than forty vintage aircraft, including the 1924 Douglas World Cruiser biplane New Orleans, the first aircraft to fly around the world; World War II planes; and modern jets. A theater shows films about aviation. Located at 2772 Donald Douglas Loop North at Twenty-eighth Street, Santa Monica, the museum is open Wednesday through Sunday 10:00 A.M. to 5:00 P.M. Closed Monday and Tuesday. Admission by donation: adult, $8.00; senior and student, $6.00; child (3–17), $4.00. For information, call (310) 392–8822 or consult www.museumofflying.com.

■ THE AIR MUSEUM–PLANES OF FAME

Rare aircraft from World War I to the space age. The collection includes more than a hundred aircraft and displays spanning the history of manned flight; there are more than forty historic "warbirds" in airworthy condition. Monthly flying events the first Saturday of every month. Located at Chino Airport, 7000 Merrill Avenue, the museum is open daily 9:00 A.M. to 5:00 P.M. Admission: adult, $8.95; child (younger than 12), $1.95. For information, call (909) 597–3722 or consult www.planesoffame.org.

ENTERTAINMENT INDUSTRY MUSEUMS

▣ HOLLYWOOD BOWL MUSEUM

The history of the Hollywood Bowl in a small but rich museum. Located at 2301 North Highland Avenue, Hollywood, the museum is open Tuesday through Saturday 10:00 A.M. to 8:30 P.M. in summer and until 4:30 P.M. the rest of the year. Admission: free. For information, call (323) 850–2058 or consult www.holly woodbowl.org/museum.

▣ HOLLYWOOD HERITAGE MUSEUM (THE DEMILLE BARN)

Memorabilia, costumes, and equipment from the early days of moviemaking. The museum is located in the barn where Lasky's Feature Play Company, with Cecil B. DeMille as director, produced *The Squaw Man,* the first feature-length film made in Hollywood. Objects on display include the chariot from *Ben Hur.* Reopened in 1998 after damage from a fire. Located at 2100 North Highland Avenue, Los Angeles, near Hollywood Bowl, the museum is open weekends from 11:00 A.M. to 4:00 P.M. Admission: adult, $3.00; senior, child (6–12), and student, $1.00. For information and operating hours, call (323) 874–2276.

▣ HOLLYWOOD WAX MUSEUM

Get up close and personal with more than 200 of Hollywood's greatest stars; just don't expect them to give you an autograph. The museum also features a Chamber of Horrors with residents including Frankenstein's Monster, Dracula, the Wolfman, Pinhead, Elvira, and the Phantom of the Opera, and a movie theater that shows films celebrating the old hometown. Located at 6767 Hollywood Boulevard, Hollywood, the museum is open daily from 10:00 A.M. to midnight. Admission: adult, $8.95; child (6–12), $6.95; senior, $7.50.

Combo tickets may be purchased for the Wax Museum and the Guinness Book of World Records Museum across the street.

For information on the Hollywood Wax Museum, call (323) 462–8860 or (323) 462–5991 or consult www.hollywoodwax.com.

SPECIAL TOURS

▣ LOS ANGELES FIRE DEPARTMENT OPEN HOUSE

On the second Saturday of May, all 102 Los Angeles fire stations are open to the public for their annual tours and demonstrations. Admission: free. For information, call (213) 485–5162 or consult www.LAFD.org.

▣ LOS ANGELES TIMES

Located at First and Spring streets, Los Angeles. The newspaper offers half-hour tours of the newsrooms and printing plant, Monday through Friday at 11:15 A.M. Children age 10 and older only. Reservations required. Admission: free. For information, call (213) 237–5000.

CHAPTER FOURTEEN

HOLLYWOOD MOVIE AND TELEVISION STUDIOS

ON ANY GIVEN DAY IN LOS ANGELES, a film or television crew is likely to be shooting scenes on the streets or within a public building. They're not difficult to spot: A film crew usually travels with a phalanx of several dozen trucks with equipment, mobile dressing rooms, caterers, and carloads of technicians, production assistants, and more. They are also often accompanied by police cars.

On one of my trips, there were no less than two movies being filmed in and around my hotel room at the Westin Bonaventure Hotel in downtown Los Angeles. In the lobby, a crew worked on *Nick of Time,* a political kidnapping story. Outside my window, Al Pacino and Robert DeNiro ran up and down the street with machine guns as a huge crew shot action scenes for *Heat.*

One way to find filming locations is to visit the **Los Angeles Film and Video Permit Office,** across from Mann's Chinese Theatre; for about $10, you can buy a list of any current projects that require permits from the city. The office is at 7083 Hollywood Boulevard, Fifth Floor, Hollywood. For information, call (323) 957–1000.

Moviemaking takes place mostly behind closed doors or in remote sets. But several major studios offer tours from simple peeks behind the curtains to elaborate theme-park-like attractions such as Universal Studios. Fans of television, from game shows to sitcoms to talk shows, may have good luck in obtaining tickets to television studios.

MUST-SEE PARAMOUNT STUDIOS

This historic movie studio—where classics include *The Godfather,* the Bob Hope and Bing Crosby *Road* pictures, many of Elvis Presley's "vehicles," and hundreds more—is now mostly used for television production. The Paramount empire includes the holdings of the former Desilu Production Studio, formed by Lucille Ball and Desi Arnaz, and RKO-Pathé (home of many of the Fred Astaire–Ginger Rogers films).

Paramount Studios is not a theme park; the two-hour Paramount Tour is a real visit to working parts of the historic movie and television factory, including soundstages, sets, and production departments.

Most film sets are closed while in production, but you may be able to take a peek at the stages when they are quiet. Television shooting for a series is usually done on Tuesday and Friday with audiences, but additional action can be scheduled for any day. *Entertainment Tonight* is usually in production daily, while talk shows are usually taped in clusters, with several episodes shot on one day.

The entrance to the tour is on Melrose Avenue where you'll walk through a reproduction of the famed Paramount Gate. The real thing is a block east; guests will visit it on the tour. Hollywood superstition still calls for young would-be stars to hug the wrought-iron gate, stare at the Hollywood sign in the distance, and declare the famous line from *Sunset Boulevard,* which was filmed on the lot: "I'm ready for my close-up, Mr. DeMille." Atop a soundstage at Melrose and Gower you can see the remains of the famous RKO globe and transmitter tower.

To your left as you enter is the Lubitsch Building, which was used as the high school in *The Brady Bunch,* and with the change of a flag and a few potted plants as the embassy broken into weekly in *Mission Impossible.* Ahead is Stage 4, former home of *Wayne's World* and *Coming to America.*

Some of the other soundstages you will pass include Stage 30, where parts of *Forrest Gump,* including the famous Oval Office scene, were shot; Stage 28, home of *Entertainment Tonight;* and Stage 32, where many of the classic dance-musicals were made, including *Top Hat.* Stage 25, once the home of *Here's Lucy,* and later the *Cheers* set, is now used for *Frasier.* Stages 19 and 20 were used for much of the shooting for both *Addams Family* films; the television sitcom *Wings* used part of the stage.

When Desilu Studios owned the RKO lot, Desi Arnaz's office overlooked a little park designed to look like Lucy and Desi's upstate New York vacation home. Near a kiosk at the park are the unauthorized but still appreciated handprints and names of *Cheers* stars Ted Danson and Woody Harrelson, added in 1989.

Across from the Marlene Dietrich Building is a small trophy case that displays some Academy Awards, Emmys, Golden Globes, and other trinkets. Among the most historically noteworthy is the 1927 Academy Award for the classic motion picture *Wings;* it was the first Best Picture winner.

Nearby is Production Park, a small, grassy area once used by Bing Crosby and Bob Hope as a putting green; in a well-remembered episode of *Cheers,* Diane Chambers (Shelley Long) played croquet on the grass as she recovered from a nervous breakdown.

A large parking lot near the Production Park doubles as a "tank" for water shots; walls around the lot can hold several feet of water, and there are deeper pits that can be opened for special effects. A blank wall at the back of the tank can be painted as a backdrop or used as a blue screen for video productions. In 1995 the tank was used for some of the scenes from *Waterworld* and *Congo.*

The Property Department is like a gigantic attic, holding bits and pieces of props from thousands of movies and television shows. In one corner is a room full of creepy artifacts from *The Addams Family;* around the corner you may spot Marcia Brady's debating team plaque.

Within the Bing Crosby Building is Paramount's Scoring Stage, where musical soundtracks are recorded.

The best time to visit is from mid-summer through mid-April when television sitcoms and dramas are in production. Feature films can be shot at any time and may be inside on soundstages or on an outdoor set. The tours are conducted by studio pages and are limited to fifteen persons at a time; the tours involve a great deal of walking, and there is little shelter in bad weather. Cameras and video equipment are not permitted on the tour.

Paramount Studios is located at 5555 Melrose Avenue, south of Santa Monica Boulevard, Hollywood. Tours are held Monday through Friday 9:00 A.M. to 2:00 P.M. every half hour. Tickets were priced at $15 in 2002; visitors must be 10 or older. For information, call (323) 956–1777 or consult www.paramount showtickets.com.

SONY PICTURES STUDIOS

The Sony Pictures Studio offers a small tour with a great deal of history on the former MGM lot in Culver City. Two-hour walking tours include glimpses of the sound stage where the Yellow Brick Road once wound through Munchkinland in *The Wizard of Oz,* the stage where agents from *Men in Black* battled aliens, and the *Jeopardy* game show set. The studios are in heavy demand for film and television production.

The tour concentrates on Columbia and Sony projects, although the studios themselves are redolent with MGM history. There are very few remaining large outdoor sets.

The studios are located at 10202 West Washington Boulevard in Culver City. Tours begin at Sony Pictures plaza on weekdays from 9:00 A.M. to 3:00 P.M. Admission is $20 per person; all visitors must be 12 or older. For information, call (323) 520–8687.

UNIVERSAL STUDIOS

From the very start of the studio in 1915, when filmmaker Carl Laemmle charged 25 cents to watch movies being made, Universal has welcomed visitors.

Of course, in true Hollywood style, things have gotten a whole lot flashier and more grandiose over the years. Universal Studios Hollywood is now a major theme park, mixing glimpses of working elements of the studios with re-creations of some of recent filmdom's greatest hits, including *E.T., King Kong, Back to the Future,* and *Backdraft.* See Chapter 6 on Universal Studios Hollywood for more information.

Universal Studios is located in Universal City, off the Hollywood Freeway (U.S. 101) at Lankershim Boulevard. For information, call (818) 508–9600 or consult www.universalstudios.com.

▓ MUST-SEE ▓ WARNER BROS. STUDIOS VIP TOUR

Follow in the footsteps of Humphrey Bogart, Bette Davis, and Jimmy Cagney; walk down the same dirt road trod by Gary Cooper and Maverick, and step into the soundstage that once housed *The Old Man and the Sea, My Fair Lady, Camelot,* and part of *Jurassic Park.*

In 2002 television shows in production on the lot included *Friends, Drew Carey, ER,* and *West Wing.*

The two-and-a-half-hour Warner Bros. tour is a real chance to go behind the scenes at a working studio. No two tours are the same because of production schedules; with a bit of luck, visitors will get to see a film in production or see a rehearsal or taping of a television sitcom or series. The twelve-passenger trams, led by a knowledgeable guide, go through the famous back lot of the 110-acre studio and visit some of the soundstages.

The summer shooting schedule at the studio is usually very slow and not much actual production may be under way at that time; in any case, the summer is the busiest time for the tour, and reservations may be necessary several weeks in advance. The tour begins at the Visitor Center, inside Gate 4 at the corner of Hollywood Way and Olive Avenue.

Tickets are $32 for all visitors. Children younger than 8 are not permitted. Free parking is available at the Visitors Center, at the corner of Olive Avenue and Hollywood Way in Burbank. For information and reservations, call (818) 972–8687 or consult www.studio-tour.com or wbsf.warnerbros.com/home.html.

The tour is offered weekdays on the hour from 9:00 A.M. to 3:00 P.M.; in the summer, trams leave every half hour. The studio is closed on holidays and weekends. Reservations are required; they are accepted by telephone several weeks in advance.

Photography but not video cameras is permitted on the back lot—the famous outdoor sets—but not allowed at the soundstages.

You are invited into the small theater by the recorded voice of announcer Gary Owens, welcoming you to "beautiful downtown Burbank." The short film—updated regularly—is an entertaining collage of some of Warner Bros. most famous stars and some of the best-loved punch lines from classic films. You'll see James Cagney, Henry Fonda, Clint Eastwood, Bette Davis, Ronald Reagan, Jodie Foster, and many others at work and play. Strung together are Michelle Pfeiffer's Catwoman "meow"; a very young Mickey Rooney as Puck in *A Midsummer Night's Dream* declaring "What fools these mortals be"; Jack Nicholson's "Here's Johnny!"; a brief conversation between Tom Hanks and Meg Ryan from *You've Got Mail;* and Bugs Bunny's "What's up, doc?" Among the favorite lines is the one delivered by doe-eyed starlet Bette Davis: "I'd like to kiss

Warner Bros. Studio VIP Tour. *Photo courtesy Warner Bros. Studio VIP Tour*

you, but I just washed my hair." The biggest laughs come from an assemblage of outtakes and flubs by famous stars.

■ THE WARNER BROS. STORY

Warner Bros. Studios is among the oldest motion-picture centers to be continuously occupied by the same company. Warner films have earned more than one hundred major Academy Awards, including six Best Picture Oscars for the films *The Life of Emile Zola* (1937), *Casablanca* (1943), *My Fair Lady* (1964), *Chariots of Fire* (1981), *Driving Miss Daisy* (1989), and *Unforgiven* (1992).

The studio was originally built for First National Pictures on farmland purchased from Dr. David Burbank, a dentist and rancher after whom the city of Burbank was named. The Warner brothers acquired the property in 1929, two years after they had revolutionized movies with their release of the first "talkie," Al Jolson's *The Jazz Singer*. Soon they were turning out movies at a feverish pace—eighty-six features in 1929 alone.

By the late 1930s Warner Bros. had built nine new soundstages (all of which are still in use today) with Darryl F. Zanuck as head of production and Busby Berkeley bringing his musical extravaganzas to theaters.

The studio also developed its own zany brand of animation at a rundown Hollywood annex somewhat affectionately known as "Termite Terrace," and after 1940 at the main studio. From the drawing boards of Tex Avery, Chuck Jones, and Friz Freleng sprang such classic and enduring characters as Bugs

Bunny, Daffy Duck, Yosemite Sam, Sylvester and Tweety, the Road Runner, and Pepé le Pew. All voices for the original characters were performed by Mel Blanc.

The 1940s saw the studio add three more soundstages and many more classic titles, including *Yankee Doodle Dandy* and *The Treasure of the Sierra Madre*.

During the 1950s Warner became the first studio to switch part of its operation to television. At first Jack Warner tried to fight the advent of television with the major film hits *A Streetcar Named Desire, A Star Is Born,* and *Mr. Roberts.* But by the 1950s Warner had become the most successful major producer of series television in Hollywood, creating shows that included *Maverick, The Lawman, 77 Sunset Strip, Cheyenne,* and *Hawaiian Eye.*

The studio was purchased by the Kinney National conglomerate in 1969, and the whole company became known as Warner Communications Inc. In 1972 Warner Bros. and Columbia Pictures joined forces to create a single production facility named The Burbank Studios. The studio now was like a small city with its own fire department, mail service, parks, bank, and bicycle shop. (In 1990 Sony purchased Columbia Pictures and moved the company off the Burbank Studios property.)

In 1980 Warner Bros. purchased the Samuel Goldwyn Studios in Hollywood, renaming it Warner Hollywood Studios. In 1988 the company acquired Lorimar Products and moved it to the Burbank lot. Finally, in 1989, Time-Life merged with Warner Bros., creating Time Warner Inc., one of the largest and most powerful media companies in the world. Time Warner has subsequently become part of AOL.

■ EXTERIOR SETS

Midwestern Street. Welcome to Smalltown, USA, complete with village green, gazebo, and town square. The residential section was built in 1941 for *King's Row* with Ronald Reagan, and the storefront section was constructed in 1945 for *Saratoga Trunk* with Gary Cooper and Ingrid Bergman. Later the set was used for television series including *The Dukes of Hazzard, Growing Pains,* and *Sisters.*

The street still includes the gazebo where Robert Preston declared there was trouble in River City in *Music Man.* And Paul Newman was arrested nearby for cutting down parking meters in *Cool Hand Luke.* Scenes from *Contact* with Jodie Foster and *Conspiracy Theory* with Mel Gibson were shot here. For many visitors, there's this: The street was used in the final episode of *Seinfeld.* Yada-yada.

New York Street. Around the corner from the Chicago set is New York, used in many famous scenes. The New York of the 1920s was seen in *The Great Race* and in *The FBI Story* with Jimmy Stewart. On the road was the courthouse used in the 1960s *Batman* television series. It was also decked out in neon for the futuristic main drag of *Blade Runner* and later for scenes in *Batman Returns.* Robin Williams and Billy Crystal worked on each other in *Father's Day* here.

Hennesy Street. Designed by Dale Hennesy for *Annie,* it was transformed into Kansas of the 1930s for *City Heat* and was also seen in *Dick Tracy, Pee-wee's Big Adventure,* and the television series *Scarecrow and Mrs. King.*

Nearby to Hennesy Street is the exterior of the emergency room entrance to the county hospital of *ER.* Overhead is a simulated stretch of elevated train tracks. Depending on the shooting schedule, you may also see Doc Magoo's Diner, the greasy spoon eatery visited from time to time by the *ER* cast; the diner is on wheels and is moved into position when that particular set is needed.

Laramie Street. This stretch of road and sagebrush was built in 1941 for Westerns and served as the location for some of the best-loved films of all time including *High Noon* with Gary Cooper. A very different kind of classic, Mel Brooks's *Blazing Saddles,* was also shot there. Television series that used Laramie included *Bonanza* in its last five years, the original *Maverick* series, *F Troop, Kung Fu,* and *Little House on the Prairie.*

The buildings on the Western set are constructed at ⅞ scale, allowing filmmakers to exaggerate the height of cowboy-actors; camera operators have to shoot from a low angle anyway to avoid including power lines and skyscrapers located just outside the Warner Bros. lot.

1930s Set. Built in 1938 for *Angels with Dirty Faces* with James Cagney and Humphrey Bogart, the area has been maintained since for a long string of gangster movies and stories never envisioned at the time. For example, it was used as Gotham City for the *Batman* movies; in *Batman Forever,* it was where Robin stole the Batmobile and took it for a spin through the street. It has also served as Metropolis for *Superman* movies, as Atlanta for the TV series *The Client,* and as Chicago for *Sisters* and *ER.*

The set is made up almost entirely of facades; only a few structures have any interior spaces. With some special set dressing, the same streets stood in for Tokyo in *Karate Kid Part II,* and as Havana in *The Mambo Kings.*

Kings Row. Used for the Ronald Reagan classic of the same name, it also was featured in *Rebel Without a Cause.* On the same street you'll find the home of Marion the Librarian from *The Music Man,* the *Gremlins* house, the heart of Hazzard County, and the place where Elvira, the Mistress of the Dark, filmed some of her high-camp scenes. The area also played a part in *Grumpier Old Men* with Walter Matthau and Jack Lemmon.

The Jungle. The forested area was created in 1930 and was the home of *Tarzan.* It also served as Sherwood Forest for Errol Flynn as *Robin Hood* and for parts of *Camelot* and *Finian's Rainbow.* Scenes from the *Fantasy Island* television show were shot there, and a small pond in the jungle was Walton Pond in *The Waltons.* More recently the jungle was Vietnam in the television series *China Beach;* it was also used in films *Hot Shots Part Deux,* and *Six Days, Seven Nights* with Harrison Ford.

And a moment of high drama from the *ER* series was also shot in the small pond; it was here that actor George Clooney struggled to pull a small boy out of a drainage pipe while floodwaters raged all around him.

Costume Warehouse. The huge Costume Warehouse on the back lot is an occasional stop of the tram tour, depending on shooting schedules on the lot. The building includes no less than 8 miles of hanging rack space and 3.5 miles of shoes. One section holds enough wedding gowns to open a bridal shop. There are aisles of straw boaters and fedoras, Roman gladiator outfits, and maternity and fat pads.

There's a small museum at the warehouse that on one visit included part of the *Batman Forever* wardrobe. The producers of that film spent $6 million on costumes; a great deal of that money went for latex rubber suits worn by Batman and Robin; examples of the expensive duds were on display.

■ INDOOR SOUNDSTAGES

Warner Bros. has thirty-seven soundstages, which is the largest collection in Hollywood. Thirty-two are on its lot and five others are down the street. Most were built in the 1930s. Warner Brothers built its first new soundstage since 1945 on the lot; its first major feature was *Space Cowboys* with Clint Eastwood. Most of the stages do not have dressing rooms; movable trailers are parked outside most of the buildings.

The operating rooms for *ER* are within Stage 11. Next door, in Stage 10, *Family Matters* was home for many years. Nearby is the Little Brown Schoolhouse, used by school-aged children involved in productions on the lot; state law requires young actors to attend four hours of school per day.

Stage 16. The tallest full-time soundstage in the motion picture industry, it was raised to its present height of 98 feet in the 1930s by William Randolph Hearst, who had moved his production company to the lot in hopes of creating pictures for Marion Davies.

Stage 16 was later used for films that included *My Fair Lady, Camelot, Key Largo, Gremlins 2,* and *Batman Returns.* Also known as the "lake stage," it can hold an entire "sea" of water, as seen in *The Old Man and the Sea* and *PT 109.* Steven Spielberg installed a waterfall for a scene for Universal's *Jurassic Park* shot at the stage.

A glass-and-chrome office building was constructed within for the rise and fall and rise of Michael Douglas and the rise and fall of Demi Moore in *Disclosure.* Scenes for a revived *Wild, Wild West* were done there as well.

Stage 19. The home of the spectacular dancing scenes from *Yankee Doodle Dandy,* it was also used in *The Story of West Point* with Jimmy Cagney, *Gypsy,* and a number of Doris Day musicals including *Calamity Jane.*

Stage 4. Used to shoot the popular television sitcom *Murphy Brown,* it was where Bette Davis filmed *Now, Voyager.* The stage was also home to the musical *Mame* with Lucille Ball, and was transformed into the fifth floor of the Washington Post for *All the President's Men.*

Stage 9. This stage once held the entire set of Rick's Café Americain for *Casablanca.* It was also used for the famous egg-eating scenes in *Cool Hand Luke* and served for ten years as home to the television comedy *Night Court*. In 1996 it was the home of the *Hanging with Mr. Cooper* show.

Stage 8. Most recently used for the television series *Sisters,* this stage also housed memorable scenes from *Who's Afraid of Virginia Woolf?* with Richard Burton and Elizabeth Taylor.

Stage 24. The home of *Friends,* which despite its name, is not very accommodating to visitors. Tickets to tapings of the show are among the most difficult to obtain in Hollywood.

OTHER FILM STUDIOS (NOT OPEN TO PUBLIC)

Burbank Studios (Warner Bros. and Columbia). 4000 Warner Boulevard, Burbank. "Gower Gulch" is named after the would-be actors who would gather outside the gates in hope of gaining a job in one of the many classic silent Westerns shot there in the 1920s. The original Columbia lot is now known as Sunset-Gower Studios and is used primarily for productions by ABC Television.

Culver Studios

9336 West Washington Boulevard, Culver City. Among various owners was Cecil B. DeMille. It later became RKO-Pathé. *King Kong* was filmed here; the studio's white mansion on Washington Boulevard was used for some of the scenes for *Gone with the Wind.* Today the studio is used mostly for television productions.

Hollywood Center Studios

1040 North Las Palmas Avenue, Hollywood. At one time the home of Harold Lloyd's production company, it was used by Howard Hughes for his 1927 silent movie *Hell's Angels* featuring the debut of Jean Harlow. Shirley Temple made her debut here as well, and the first episodes of *I Love Lucy* were made here in 1951. More recently, it was the location of Francis Ford Coppola's Zoetrope Studios. It now rents out its facilities to production companies.

Lorimar Telepictures

3300 Riverside Drive, Suite 405, Burbank. The one-time Metro-Goldwyn-Mayer studios, former home of Clark Gable, Greta Garbo, Katharine Hepburn, the Marx Brothers, and dozens of other icons of the day.

Raleigh Studios

650 North Bronson Avenue, Hollywood. Mary Pickford and Douglas Fairbanks made their films here in the 1920s and 1930s. They went on to use this location to form United Artists. Films made here included *Mark of Zorro, Hopalong Cassidy, Guys and Dolls,* and *The Best Years of Our Lives.* It was also the home of television's original *Superman* series.

20th Century–Fox Film Corporation

10201 West Pico Boulevard, Los Angeles. The much-reduced Fox Studio still includes major sets, such as the New York City set employed in numerous films including *Hello, Dolly!* It has also been used as an all-purpose downtown in many other films; you can see part of the set from the street. Films made at the lot include *The Sound of Music, Butch Cassidy and the Sundance Kid*, and the original *Planet of the Apes.*

TELEVISION STUDIOS

There are three principal ways to obtain tickets to see a television taping or live broadcast: connections, planning, or luck. Connections with someone in the industry may work at any time. Planning a few months ahead of time may give you tickets for specific shows; the very lucky may be able to walk into a show on the day of taping.

ABC Television Network
4151 Prospect Avenue, Los Angeles. (310) 577–5700. Handles tickets for tapings of various ABC shows and dress rehearsals.

Audience Associates/TV Tickets
7471 Melrose Avenue, #10. Tickets to ABC, CBS, Disney, Fox, KTLA, NBC, Paramount, Sony, and Universal productions. Up to ten free tickets per request; call at least one day in advance but not earlier than one month before the date of your visit. For information, call (323) 653–4105 or consult www.tvtickets. com.

Audiences Unlimited
100 Universal City Plaza, Building 153, Universal City. (818) 753–3483. An agency that supplies audiences for more than fifty network shows produced at studios in Hollywood, Burbank, Culver City, and at Universal Studios Hollywood. Call to check on scheduled shows; send a self-addressed stamped envelope for up to six free tickets (Zip code 91608). Allow several weeks for delivery. To order by phone up to sixty days in advance, call (818) 753–3470 or consult www.tvtickets.com.

Audiences Unlimited also operates a same-day ticket booth at Universal CityWalk and within the gates of Universal Studios Hollywood.

CBS Television Network
7800 Beverly Boulevard, Los Angeles. (323) 852–2458. CBS and independent productions.

KCET Studio Tour
Public television station KCET offers a free tour of its historic facilities, located at 4401 Sunset Boulevard. The studio was the former home of Monogram Pictures and Allied Artists. Monogram made famous low-budget films including the *Charlie Chan* detective series and the *Bowery Boys.* For information, call (323) 953–5289.

KTLA-TV

5800 Sunset Boulevard, Hollywood. Independent and Warner Bros. productions. The original home of Warner Bros. Studios. Al Jolson made the first "talkie," *The Jazz Singer,* here in 1927. Tickets available through Audiences Unlimited.

NBC Television Network

3000 West Alameda Avenue, Burbank. (818) 840–4444 or (818) 840–3537. The studio offers seventy-minute guided tours of some of its stages and production facilities, including the home of *The Tonight Show* and a soap opera set. Tours depart at regular intervals weekdays from 9:00 A.M. to 3:00 P.M. Closed Easter, Thanksgiving, Christmas Day, and New Year's Day. Admission: adult, $7.00; child (5–12), $3.50. For tours, call (818) 840–3537 or consult www.studio audiences.com/tvstudios/nbcburbank.shtml.

Studio Audiences

For a listing of a wide variety of available television tapings, consult the Web site for this company at www.studioaudiences.com.

TV Time

A one-hour television show requires about eight long days to shoot; filming usually takes place only on weekdays. Half-hour sitcoms take four or five days for each episode.

Visitors on the tour sometimes get to see rehearsals for shows. Tour guides can sometimes arrange for tickets to television tapings on the day of your visit. Most regular series go on "hiatus" from mid-spring through mid-summer, resuming production in July and August.

The Tonight Show

Jay Leno took over the mantle as the King of Burbank when he took the helm of *The Tonight Show.* For much of the year he tapes his nightly talk and entertainment show from his custom-designed studio there.

If you want to be in the audience for taping of *The Tonight Show,* you can try for tickets at the NBC kiosk on Universal's CityWalk on the day of the show. (The booth may also have tickets for other shows.) You can call (818) 840–3537 for a recorded announcement of the taping schedule and upcoming guests.

Or if you have a few weeks' advance notice, send your request by mail to NBC Tickets, 3000 West Alameda Avenue, Burbank, CA 91523; include the day or days you hope to see a show and the number of tickets you need along with a stamped, self-addressed envelope.

Taping takes place about 5:00 P.M. Monday through Friday; with tickets in hand, you must be in line by 4:00 P.M.—even earlier if there is a particularly popular guest booked that night. Like it or not, the studio gives out more tickets than there are seats; on a typical day thirty to fifty people are turned away.

There is no parking lot for the studio, but early arrivals should find spaces around the corner at a location you could find only near Hollywood: Bob Hope Drive, across from Johnny Carson Park.

The slow and disorganized waiting line is annoying, but you might want to keep your eye out for strolling members of the crew looking for audience members to use in skits; on the night of one of my visits they were planting questions for "Iron Jay," Leno's dim-witted weightlifter alter ego. You may also be offered tickets to the taping of sitcoms while you wait. The only way to avoid standing in line is to pull whatever strings you can to obtain invited VIP tickets; these tickets guarantee entrance to the show but not necessarily the best seats in the house.

The Tonight Show studio seats just 320; there are only thirty seats on the "floor" of the studio. Lucky guests here are usually personally greeted by the host at the start of the show. The show is recorded straight through; in television terms that means it is "live on tape."

PART VIII

SPORTING ACTIVITIES

CHAPTER FIFTEEN

BEACHES, WATER PARKS, PARKS, AND ZOOS

STROLLING THE MAKE-BELIEVE STREETS of the Disneyland Resort, Knott's Berry Farm, Universal Studios Hollywood, or the concrete canyons of Los Angeles, it is sometimes hard to remember that you are within swimming distance of the Pacific Ocean and some of the most famous beaches on the West Coast.

There are dozens of swimming, surfing, and sunbathing strands along the 75-mile coastline from above Malibu to Newport Beach.

LOS ANGELES AREA BEACHES

Los Angeles County Beaches and Harbors Information Center. (310) 305–9545. beaches.co.la.ca.us/BandH/Main.htm.

■ NORTHERN SECTION

The beaches between Point Mugu and Malibu are among the less crowded in Southern California and offer excellent swimming, surfing, water sports, and fishing. There are public campsites at **Leo Carrillo** and **Point Mugu State Park;** there are also some spectacular hiking trails that lead into the foothills.

Leo Carrillo Beach. 36000 Pacific Coast Highway, Malibu. There's something for everybody at this 1,600-acre beach named for actor Leo Carrillo (best known as Pancho on the television series *The Cisco Kid*). It's a fine swimming, surfing, and snorkeling beach (including a "clothing optional" section); there's also a nature trail that leads to tide pools and rock formations, and Sequit Point, which contains sea caves and a natural tunnel. (818) 880–0350 or (805) 488–5223. cal-parks.ca.gov/default.asp?page_id=616.

Zuma Beach. 30000 Pacific Coast Highway, Malibu. Like wow, man: a handsome beach carpeted with valley girls and surfer dudes. The surf can get rough.

LOS ANGELES AREA BEACHES

At the paved side of the beach are playgrounds, showers, restrooms, and concession stands. (310) 457–9891.beaches.co.la.ca.us/BandH/Beaches/Zuma.htm

Point Dume. South of Zuma and a little less well known, it is still an excellent swimming and surfing site. From November to May the Point Dume Headland is a prime vantage point to observe migrating California gray whales just offshore. (310) 457–9891. calparks.ca.gov/default.asp?page_id=623.

Malibu Surfrider Beach. 23200 Pacific Coast Highway, Malibu. This is the one you're thinking of, the one you've seen in the *Gidget* movies, the surfing competitions, and your dreams of hanging ten. There's nearly a mile of beach alongside the hulking Malibu Pier. There's also a marine preserve and a nature center. (310) 457–9891. cal-parks.ca.gov/default. asp?page_id=835

■ CENTRAL SECTION

Las Tunas Beach. Below Malibu toward Santa Monica. A small beach with an offshore reef popular for diving and fishing.

Topanga Beach. Another mile-long sandy beach between Topanga Creek at the end of Topanga Canyon Road, popular for surfing and swimming.

Will Rogers Beach. 16000 Pacific Coast Highway, Los Angeles. Donated to the state by the famous author and commentator, this three-mile beach offers moderate surf, a playground, and gymnastics equipment. (310) 578–0478.

Santa Monica Beach. Pacific Coast Highway at Colorado Boulevard, Santa Monica. A broad, attractive beach that has relatively gentle surf, it flanks the Santa Monica Pier, which includes a turn-of-the-twentieth-century carousel, arcades, restaurants, and gift shops. The pier is also used for fishing. (310) 578–0478.

Venice Beach. 1531 Ocean Front Walk, Venice. The beach is quite nice, but the real attraction here is the **Venice Boardwalk,** the world capital of West Coast weird. The boardwalk is lined with food stands and shops; the roadway is populated with street performers and roller-bladers, and in and among the palm trees is the famous outdoor gym, **Muscle Beach.** You can rent roller skates or bicycles and join the circus. (310) 578–0478. www.venicebeach.com.

■ SOUTHERN SECTION

Dockweiler Beach. Vista del Mar Boulevard, Playa del Rey. This is not the beach of your dreams, but it is a very lively local favorite for some reason. It lies in the approach path of LAX and is alongside a sewage treatment plant and an oil refinery. There's a beach for swimming and surfing, a playground, and a bicycle trail. (310) 379–8471.

Santa Monica Pier

An out-to-sea amusement place that includes a Philadelphia Toboggan Company carousel built in 1922 and maintained and restored to its original splendor. The march of the hand-carved horses is accompanied by the incomparable sounds of an antique Wurlitzer organ. The pier also features some other more modern kiddie rides. (310) 458–8900. www.santa-monicapier.org.

Manhattan Beach. Highland and Manhattan Boulevards. A fishing, swimming, surfing, and snorkeling beach with two miles of broad beachfront. There are more than one hundred volleyball courts. At the back of the beach is the Strand, a concrete promenade crowded with skaters, skateboarders, and joggers. (310) 379–8471.

Nearby is **Sand Dune Park,** at Thirty-third Street at Bell Avenue, Manhattan Beach. The park is just what it sounds like: a colossal, steep sand dune that kids can climb, slide on, and carry home in their bathing suits. There's also a playground and picnic area. Run by the Manhattan Beach Parks and Recreation Department. Open daily. Admission: free. (310) 802–5409.

Hermosa Beach. A relatively quiet mile-long beach with a fishing pier and concession stands.

Redondo Beach. Esplanade at Knobhill Avenue, Redondo Beach. A wide beach extending from the Redondo Pier with restaurants, gift shops, and concession stands. Excursion and fishing boats depart from the pier. (310) 379–8471.

Torrance Beach. A popular diving, surfing, and swimming beach with facilities including a bathhouse and playground.

Malaga Cove. Paseo del Mar at Via Arroyo, Palos Verdes. A gazebo on the bluffs gives a great view of the cove; a path leads down to the sandy beach. (310) 379–8471.

Abalone Cove. 5755 Palos Verdes Drive South. On the Portuguese Bend of the Palos Verdes Peninsula with a view of Catalina Island. No lifeguards. (310) 379–8471.

Point Fermin Lighthouse. The lighthouse, built in 1874, sits on the bluff with a view of Catalina Island; trails descend to the beach below. There's a playground and a small amphitheater.

Cabrillo Beach. A generally calm waterfront with a playground and snack bar. Nearby is the Cabrillo Marine Museum.

LONG BEACH AREA BEACHES

Long Beach City Beach. The 7-mile beach is within the harbor breakwater and therefore generally offers calm water. The Belmont Pier offers fishing locations. East of Long Beach City Beach, the Alamitos Bay Peninsula reaches almost a mile into Alamitos Bay with calm waters on the bay side and surf on the ocean side. (562) 570–6555.

ORANGE COUNTY BEACHES

Newport City Beach. Another one of the picture-perfect Southern California beaches. There's a famous sand castle contest each summer. The Dory Fleet returns each morning to sell its catch on the west side of Newport Pier. (949) 722–1611.

LOS ANGELES AREA PARKS

Griffith Park. This is the true back lot of Los Angeles and Hollywood, some 4,100 acres of mostly undeveloped hilly land in the eastern Santa Monica Mountains. The park ranges from 384 to 1,625 feet above sea level and includes semiarid foothills and heavily forested valleys.

The park includes hiking trails, picnic areas, the first-class Griffith Observatory and Planetarium, the Los Angeles Zoo, a railroad and transit museum, the SR-2 simulator ride, a western heritage museum, and the Greek Theatre (an outdoor amphitheater).

The park is regularly used by Hollywood filmmakers for location shooting, with some of the most famous scenes including parts of *Rebel Without a Cause* and *King Kong.* A wilderness area that includes a former rock quarry was the location of the Batcave in the television and film versions of Batman.

When weather conditions are right—which in Los Angeles, unfortunately, is not very often—it is well worth the short trip up the hill to the park to see the view of the city below. Take appropriate big city precautions if you make a visit to the park at night.

See Chapter 13 for more details on cultural activities.

Arriving by car, you can use any of eight entrances: Commonwealth Avenue, Ferndell Drive, Forest Lawn Drive, Riverside Drive, North Vermont Avenue, Interstate 5 (Griffith Park Drive or Zoo Drive exits), and Highway 134 (Victory Boulevard exit). MTA buses 96 and 97 connect downtown to the park.

The park is open from 6:00 A.M. to 10:00 P.M. daily; horseback and hiking trails and mountain roads close at sunset. The speed limit within the park is twenty-five miles per hour and is strictly enforced. (323) 913–4147. The City of Los Angeles Department of Recreation and Parks maintains a Web site about Griffith Park, at www.laparks.org/grifmet/griffith.htm.

REGIONAL PARKS

California Department of Parks and Recreation. For information on state parks, call (818) 880–0350 or consult parks.ca.gov/default.htm.

National Park Service. For information, call (818) 597–9192. For MISTIX Campground Reservations, call (800) 365–2267.

U.S. Forest Service. Angeles National Forest. (626) 574–5200. www.fs.fed.us. National Forest Recreation reservations: (877) 444–6777.

Angeles National Forest. If Griffith Park is the back lot of Los Angeles, then the Angeles National Forest is the outback. It's a gigantic preserve—some 695,000 acres—that sits like a shield over north Los Angeles, incorporating within it the San Gabriel Mountains.

The forest has nearly 600 miles of hiking and horse trails, nearly 200 miles of fishing streams, 400 miles of off-road trails and sixty-four campgrounds. Several lakes are available for swimming, fishing, and boating. The park rangers offer a variety of programs in the summer.

Entrances to the park include Highway 2 from Pasadena, which becomes the Angeles Crest Highway that traverses most of the park from west to east; Highway 39, which enters from near Azusa and proceeds north to Crystal Lake; Big Tujunga Canyon Road from Sunland; and Mount Baldy Road from Glendora. (626) 574–5200 or (626) 335–1251. www.r5.fs.fed.us/angeles.

For further information, you can also call one of the visitors centers of the park:

- **Chantry Flat Visitors Center.** Open weekends only from mid-November through mid-May. (818) 355–0712
- **Chilao Visitors Center.** (626) 796–5541
- **Crystal Lake Visitors Center.** (626) 910–2848

Ernest E. Debs Park. Part of Arroyo Seco Canyon, this is an interesting piece of near-wilderness in northeastern Los Angeles. The 300-acre park includes a fishing lake, hiking trails, and picnic areas. Enter the park off Monterey Road, north of Huntington Drive. (213) 847–3989.

Henninger Flats Museum. A small environmental museum on a fire road in the foothills of the San Gabriel Mountains near Altadena. (626) 794–0675.

Kenneth Hahn State Recreation Area. The park includes an Olympic Forest planted with trees and shrubs representing each of the nations that competed in the 1984 Olympics in Los Angeles. Recreational facilities include playgrounds, picnic areas, lake fishing, and hiking trails. Located on the western edge of Los Angeles, at 4100 South La Cienega Boulevard between Rodeo Road and Stocker Street. (323) 298–3660. www.parks.ca.gov/default.asp?page_id=21767.

San Gabriel Canyon Entrance Station. At the northern end of the mountains that lie east of Los Angeles is a range of peaks, many more than 9,000 feet tall; the biggest is Mount San Antonio, better known as Mount Baldy. For information about the San Gabriel Canyon call (626) 969–1012. To contact the **Mount Baldy Visitors Center** call (909) 982–2829.

Santa Monica Mountains National Recreation Area. A spectacular seaside preserve stretching 55 miles from Santa Monica to Point Mugu and including favorite beaches such as Leo Carillo State Beach, Zuma Beach, Point Dume, and Malibu Surfrider Beach.

The **J. Paul Getty Museum** is also within the park. *See the section on beaches and the chapter on museums for more details.*

Many miles of hiking and walking trails are marked; there are some 500 miles of trails in the park. For information stop by the Visitors Center off Highway 101 at 401 West Hillcrest Drive, Thousand Oaks. Open Monday through Friday 8:00 A.M. to 5:00 P.M., Saturday, Sunday, and holidays from 9:00 A.M. to 5:00 P.M. Closed Christmas, New Year's, and Thanksgiving. (805) 370–2329. www.nps. gov/samo.

Satwiwa Native American Indian Cultural Center. Via Goleta Road, Newbury Park, within the Santa Monica Mountains National Recreation Area. Open Saturday and Sunday from 10:00 A.M. to 5:00 P.M. (805) 375–1930. www.nps.gov/samo/fos.

Will Rogers State Historic Park. 1501 Will Rogers State Park Road. The famous humorist and former cowboy's home and 187-acre estate were given to the public following his death in a plane crash in 1935. The home includes remembrances of Rogers's career and life; his private polo field is used for weekend games, and visitors are welcome. The park is open daily from 8:00 A.M. to sunset; tours are conducted from 10:30 A.M. to 3:30 P.M. every hour on the half-hour. Admission: free. Parking, $6.00. (310) 454–8212.

HISTORIC RANCHES

Paramount Ranch. Cornell Road, Agoura. Not quite the real thing . . . this 760-acre ranch was once used by Paramount Pictures to film some of its classic Westerns; it was later used for early television horse operas. The remains of a false-front Western town from the TV years still stand, and there are hiking and nature programs available. The town was used for six years as the home of *Dr. Quinn, Medicine Woman.*

Nearby is the Peter Strauss Ranch, at 30000 Mulholland Highway, Agoura. Originally developed as a lakeside resort, it was later owned by the actor whose name is now attached to it. There are hiking and nature trails and infrequent theatrical presentations and concerts at an outdoor amphitheater. (805) 370–2301 for Paramount Ranch and Peter Strauss Ranch.

William S. Hart Park. 24151 North San Fernando Avenue, Newhall. The cowboy world of former Western film star William S. Hart, about an hour north of Los Angeles and near the Six Flags California theme park.

The collection includes saddles and gear, weapons, and artifacts. The 250-acre ranch is home to farm animals and a herd of buffalo; the animals were a gift to the public by Walt Disney. The Spanish colonial Revival-style mansion contains original furnishings, a collection of Western art, Native American artifacts, and mementos of early Hollywood.

William S. Hart was born in Newburgh, New York, in 1864 and began an acting career in his twenties; at the age of forty-nine, Hart came west to Hollywood to start his movie career. During the next eleven years, he made more than sixty-five silent films, the last being *Tumbleweeds* in 1925. He lived at the ranch nearly twenty years until his death in 1946; in his will, Hart gave the Horseshoe Ranch to the County of Los Angeles.

The park is open daily; tours of the house are offered from mid-September to mid-June on Wednesday through Friday from 10:00 A.M. to 1:00 P.M. with the last tour at 12:30 P.M., and Saturday and Sunday from 11:00 A.M. to 4:00 P.M., with the last tour at 3:30 P.M. In the summer, tours are offered Wednesday to Sunday from 11:00 A.M. to 4:00 P.M., with the last tour at 3:30 P.M. Admission: free. (661) 259–0844, park; (661) 254–4584, museum. www.hartmuseum.org. On weekends you can visit the adjacent Saugus train station, restored to turn-of-the-twentieth-century realism. For information, call (661) 254–1275.

ZOOS AND ANIMAL PRESERVES

Los Angeles Zoo. 5333 Zoo Drive, Griffith Park, near the junction of the Golden State (I–5) and Ventura (Highway 134) freeways.

The zoo includes more than 1,200 rare and exotic animals from around the world, along with a magnificent set of botanical gardens. It is divided into geographical continents; a safari shuttle transports visitors from area to area for an extra charge of $3.50 for adults, $1.50 for children 2–12, and $1.00 for seniors.

An exciting area at the zoo is **Chimpanzees of the Mahale Mountains,** named after a thriving wild troop in Tanzania. It is the first phase of the zoo's planned Great Ape Forest; the second phase, the Red Ape Rain Forest, opened in mid-2000 and showcases orangutans.

When the Los Angeles Zoo opened in 1966 it was the third zoo to serve the city. The privately run Selig Zoo opened downtown in 1885. It was supplanted by the Griffith Park Zoo—largely a collection of former circus animals—in 1912. By 1956 the citizens of Los Angeles realized their city had outgrown the small zoo and passed a bond measure to help build a new one.

Open daily from 10:00 A.M. to 5:00 P.M.; closed Christmas Day. Admission: adult, $8.25; child (2–12), $3.25; senior (65 and older), $5.25. Strollers and wheelchairs are available for rent. (323) 644–4200. www.lazoo.org.

America's Teaching Zoo at Moorpark College. Moorpark College, Campus Road, Moorpark. A small collection of exotic animals. Saturday and Sunday, 11:00 A.M. to 5:00 P.M. Show times are noon, 1:00 P.M., 2:00 P.M., and 3:00 P.M. Carnivore feeding time is 4:00 P.M. Admission: adult, $5.00; child (2–12), $3.00. (805) 378–1441. www.vcnet.com/gwhiz.

W. K. Kellogg Arabian Horse Farm. California State Polytechnic University, 3801 West Temple Avenue, Pomona. Purebred Arabian horses on display daily; shows presented first Sunday of each month from October to June. Admission for show: adult, $5.00; child (6–17) and senior, $3.00. (909) 869–2224. www.csupomona.edu/~equine/Kellogg.htm.

Santa Ana Zoo. Prentice Park, 1801 East Chestnut Avenue, Santa Ana. Smaller mammals and birds plus a Children's Zoo with petting section and playground. The Zoofari Express train operates from Friday to Sunday on a track around a section of the original children's zoo.

Open daily, weather permitting, from 10:00 A.M. to 5:00 P.M. Admission: adult, $4.00; child (3–12) and senior, $2.00. (714) 836–4000. www.santaanazoo.org.

ARBORETUMS

Descanso Gardens. 1418 Descanso Drive at Verdugo Boulevard, La Cañada Flintridge. A wonderland of camellias, roses, azaleas, clivias, irises, lilies, and other flowers and plants. Camellias are in blossom during the winter, from October to March; lilacs are at their best in April; and roses and other glories own the summer months.

Guided tours by tram are offered Tuesday through Sunday at 1:00, 2:00, and 3:00 P.M. The gardens are open every day except Christmas from 9:00 A.M. to 4:30 P.M. Admission: adult $5.00; student and senior, $3.00; and child (5–12), $1.00. Guided tour by tram $2.00 all tickets. (818) 952–4401. www.descanso.com.

The Arboretum of Los Angeles County. 301 North Baldwin Avenue near Colorado Boulevard, Arcadia. More than 30,000 plants from around the world outdoors and in greenhouses on the historic Rancho Santa Anita. Also on the 127-acre grounds are a former Santa Fe Railroad depot from Santa Anita, replicas of Indian homes, and a historic Queen Anne cottage.

Baldwin Lake, hidden within a stand of huge palm trees, was the setting for many of the original Tarzan movies. At the far side of the lake is a restored adobe, dating from 1839.

Guided tram tours are conducted on Wednesday beginning at 11:00 A.M. Open daily 9:00 A.M. to 4:30 P.M. except Christmas. Admission: adult, $5.00; student and senior, $3.00; child (5–12), $3.00. (626) 821–3222. www.arboretum.org.

WATER PARKS

Raging Waters. In San Dimas where I–10, I–210, and Highway 57 meet, about twenty-five minutes from Disneyland and thirty minutes from downtown Los Angeles.

The largest water theme park west of the Mississippi, there are two dozen rides and slides, including the **Volcano FantaSea,** a smoking volcano with water slides descending to a blue lagoon. Other attractions include a raft ride, a river ride, and a wave pool.

Another thrill: **High Extreme,** a 600-foot head-first plunge. A recent addition was **The Wedge,** a sort of half-funnel, four stories high. A three-person tube drops to the bottom, rises up again, and drops once more.

Open weekends from mid-April through Memorial Day, daily from about June 1 to mid-September, and weekends from mid-September to the end of the month. General admission, $26.99; junior ticket for children less than 48 inches tall, $14.99; seniors $16.99. Children 2 and younger enter free. (909) 802–2200. www.ragingwaters.com.

Wild Rivers. 8800 Irvine Center Drive, Laguna Hills, off Interstate 405 at the Irvine Center Drive exit. An artificial mountain of water slides and tube rides, plus the **Thunder Cove** wave pool and the **Explorer's Island** play area for children. Open daily from 10:00 A.M. to 8:00 P.M. from mid-June to early September; from 11:00 A.M. to 5:00 P.M. weekends and holidays from mid-May to early June and in mid-September until early October. Admission: $25; children less than 48 inches tall, $18. (949) 768–9453. www.wildrivers.com.

Magic Mountain Hurricane Harbor. *See the section about Six Flags Magic Mountain in Chapter 9.*

Soak City U.S.A. *See the section about Knott's Berry Farm in Chapter 8.*

CHAPTER SIXTEEN

SPORTING NEWS

MAJOR LEAGUE BASEBALL

The Anaheim Angels and the Los Angeles Dodgers play major league baseball in a regular season that runs from April to early October.

ANAHEIM ANGELS

At Edison Field there are Angels in the outfield and (for the moment) Disney in the boardroom. Disney bought a majority interest in the American League team in 1996 and spent nearly $80 million to convert Edison Field to a modernized "retro" baseball park, including asymmetrical outfield dimensions with a family zone in left field, a gushing geyser and a rock garden in left-center, and a view of the famous Angels A sign over the short right field porch. Every Angels home run and victory is saluted with fireworks.

In the stands it's a laid-back California scene. A gourmet restaurant behind home plate has tables in places that would be prime real estate at most other parks. There are usually plenty of seats available, especially early in the season. All of the views are unobstructed and the stadium is steeply raked, making all seats relatively close to the field.

The Angels were the unexpected winner of the 2002 World Series, defeating coastal rivals the San Francisco Giants.

Edison Field is located at 2000 East Gene Autry Way in Anaheim, about ten minutes from Disneyland. For information, call (714) 634–2000 or consult www.angels.mlb.com. For tickets by phone, call (888) 796–4256. Tickets range from about $7.00 to $26.00.

LOS ANGELES DODGERS

Dodger Stadium, 1000 Elysian Park Avenue, Los Angeles.

The Dodgers have played in Chavez Ravine for more than forty years. The stadium offers a handsome view of downtown Los Angeles to the south, and the

San Gabriel Mountains to the north and east. The field has real grass and a view of the sky; the team averages one rainout every two years.

The 56,000-seat stadium has parking for 16,000 automobiles on twenty-one terraced lots adjacent to the same elevations as the six different seating levels. Tickets range from about $6.00 to $43.00. (323) 224–1448. www.dodgers.mlb. com. Tickets by phone: (323) 224–1448.

COLLEGE BASEBALL

■ UCLA–UNIVERSITY OF CALIFORNIA, LOS ANGELES
For information on Bruins baseball games and tickets, call (310) 825–2101 or consult uclabruins.fansonly.com/sports/m-basebl.

■ USC–UNIVERSITY OF SOUTHERN CALIFORNIA
For information on USC Trojans baseball games, call the ticket office at (213) 740–4672 or consult usctrojans.fansonly.com/sports/m-basebl/usc-m-basebl-body.html.

PROFESSIONAL BASKETBALL

The Los Angeles Clippers and the Los Angeles Lakers alternate possession of the Staples Center in downtown for National Basketball Association games. They play each other about four times a year, as well.

The Staples Center is located in downtown, near the intersection of the I–10 (Santa Monica) and the I–110 (Harbor) Freeways, at the corner of Eleventh and Figueroa Streets, adjacent to the Los Angeles Convention Center.

For information, consult the individual teams or www.staplescenter.com.

■ LOS ANGELES CLIPPERS
The Los Angeles Clippers began in 1970 as the Buffalo Braves, one of three expansion franchises to join the National Basketball Association that year along with the Portland Trail Blazers and the Cleveland Cavaliers, as the league dealt with the challenge of the upstart American Basketball Association. The franchise later moved from Buffalo to San Diego and then to Los Angeles, changing its name from the Braves to the Clippers.

To be charitable, the Clippers have not been one of the leading lights of the league in its more than three decades of existence, finishing with a .500 or greater record only half a dozen times. Through 2002, they had not retired a single star player's uniform number. For information, call (213) 745–0400. www.nba.com/clippers. Tickets by TicketMaster, (213) 480–3232.

■ LOS ANGELES LAKERS
The other hoopsters at the Staples Center have a much more storied history. Born as the Minneapolis Lakers in 1948, they moved to lakeless Los Angeles in

1960. They won fourteen NBA titles through the 2002 season, and the uniform numbers of seven of their players are retired: Wilt Chamberlain, Elgin Baylor, Gail Goodrich, Magic Johnson, Kareem Abdul-Jabbar, James Worthy, and Jerry West. In 2002, the team was led by a brilliant odd couple, Kobe Bryant and Shaquille O'Neal. (310) 419–3100. www.nba.com/lakers. Tickets by Ticket Master, (213) 480–3232.

COLLEGE BASKETBALL

■ UCLA BASKETBALL
Pauley Pavilion, UCLA Campus, Westwood. (310) 825–2101. uclabruins.fans only.com/sports/m-baskbl.

■ USC BASKETBALL
Sports Arena, 3939 South Figueroa Street, Los Angeles. (213) 740–4672. usc trojans.fansonly.com/sports/m-baskbl/usc-m-baskbl-body.html.

COLLEGE FOOTBALL

■ ROSE BOWL FOOTBALL GAME
The big football game traditionally pits the best of the Pacific Coast Conference against the best of the Big Ten Conference on New Year's weekend. (The famed Rose Bowl Parade is held on New Year's Day.) Tickets are hard to come by and usually sell out well in advance. (626) 449–4100. www.tournamentofroses.com.

■ UCLA BRUINS
The Rose Bowl, 1001 Rose Bowl Drive, Pasadena. (626) 577–3100. uclabruins. fansonly.com/sports/m-footbl.

■ USC TROJANS
LA Coliseum, 3911 South Figueroa Street, Los Angeles. (213) 740–4672. usc trojans.fansonly.com/sports/m-footbl/usc-m-footbl-body.html.

HORSE RACING

■ HOLLYWOOD PARK
1050 South Prairie Avenue, Inglewood. Thoroughbred racing April to July and November to December; harness racing August to October. (310) 419–1500. www.hollywoodpark.com.

■ LOS ALAMITOS
4961 Katella Avenue, Los Alamitos. Harness and quarter-horse racing May to August. (714) 995–1234. www.losalamitos.com/laqhr.

■ SANTA ANITA

285 West Huntington Drive, Arcadia. Thoroughbred racing at one of the country's most famous tracks. Morning workouts open daily from 7:30 to 9:30 A.M. during racing season, which is December to April and October to November. (626) 574–7223. www.santaanita.com. General admission, $5.00; clubhouse, $8.50; Turf Club, $15.00.

PROFESSIONAL HOCKEY

■ ANAHEIM MIGHTY DUCKS

Arrowhead Pond of Anaheim, 2695 East Katella Avenue, Anaheim. NHL hockey. Not your basic hockey club, the team is owned by Disney; rumors of a sale have been common for several years. October to April. Tickets range from about $15 to $175. (714) 704–2701. www.mightyducks.com. Tickets through TicketMaster (714) 740–2000.

■ LOS ANGELES KINGS

Staples Center, Eleventh and Figueroa Streets. NHL hockey. Tickets range from about $21 to $350. (310) 419–3100. www.lakings.com.

ICE SKATING

■ CULVER ICE ARENA

4545 Sepulveda Boulevard, Culver City. (310) 398–5718. www.culverice arena.com.

■ PASADENA ICE SKATING CENTER

310 East Green Street, Pasadena. (626) 578–0801. www.skatepasadena.com.

ROLLER SKATING

■ MOONLIGHT ROLLERWAY SKATING RINK

5110 San Fernando Road, Glendale. (818) 241–3630.

SKIING

Los Angeles's local ski region lies mostly due east in and around **Big Bear City** and **Big Bear Lake** in the San Bernardino National Forest. The resorts are about a hundred miles from Los Angeles, about a two-hour drive on Interstate 10 and State Route 18.

■ BEAR MOUNTAIN

Big Bear Lake. Vertical drop 1,665 feet. Longest run, 2.5 miles. Nine chairlifts including two high-speed quads, plus three surface tows. Tickets can be reserved by telephone, over the Internet, and at various ski shops. (909) 585–2519. www.bearmtn.com. Lodging information: (909) 866–5877 or (909) 866–4601.

■ MOUNT BALDY

San Bernardino. The biggest vertical drop in southern California, at 2,100 feet. Located about 45 miles from Los Angeles. Four chairlifts. (909) 981–3344. www.mtbaldy.com.

■ MOUNTAIN HIGH

Wrightwood. First opened in 1937. Vertical drop 1,600 feet. Ten chairlifts and two tows. Tickets can be reserved in advance. (760) 972–9242. www.mthigh. com. Lodging: (619) 249–5477.

■ SKI SUNRISE

Wrightwood. Smaller and less crowded area with one chairlift, three Pomas, one rope tow, and limited facilities. Vertical drop 816 feet. (760) 249–6150 or consult www.skisunrise.com.

■ SNOW SUMMIT

Big Bear Lake area. Vertical drop 1,200 feet. Eleven chairlifts. Longest run, 1.25 miles. (909) 866–5766. www.snowsummit.com. Lodging: (909) 878–3000.

■ SNOW VALLEY

Big Bear Lake area. Eleven chairlifts. Longest run, 1.25 miles. Vertical drop 1,030 feet. (909) 867–2751. www.snow-valley.com. Lodging: (909) 878–3000.

■ MOUNT WATERMAN

La Canada (North of Pasadena). Vertical drop 1,001 feet. Small ski area. Three chairlifts. Longest run, .5 mile. (818) 790–2002.

PART IX

TOURING AROUND SOUTHERN CALIFORNIA

CHAPTER SEVENTEEN

DOWNTOWN LOS ANGELES

EL PUEBLO DE LOS ANGELES HISTORIC MONUMENT

El Pueblo was a group of mud huts established in 1781 by eleven families from Mexico. Today, a forty-four-acre park is the home of the city's first church, firehouse, theater, and other restored buildings from the original settlement of Los Angeles.

There's a visitors center in the 1887 Sepulveda House on Main Street. Other notable structures include the Garnier buildings used by Chinese immigrants at the turn of the twentieth century. Free guided walking tours are offered Wednesday through Saturday at 10:00 A.M., 11:00 A.M., and noon.

El Pueblo is located within the area of Main Street, Sunset Boulevard, Macy Street, Alameda Street, and Arcadia Street. For information, call (213) 628–1274 or consult www.ci.la.ca.us/ELP.

Nearby to El Pueblo is **Olvera Street,** one of the oldest commercial streets of Los Angeles. Street vendors and colorful shops line the street between Alameda and North Main streets. South of Olvera is **The Plaza,** once the center of the pueblo, and now the location of festivals and celebrations, including Cinco de Mayo.

Avila Adobe, at 10 Olvera Street, is the oldest remaining home in Los Angeles. It was built in 1818 by Francisco Avila, who was mayor of the pueblo at the time. The ravages of time and earthquakes have been repaired and the restored adobe is furnished with period artifacts. Free guided walking tours are offered Wednesday through Saturday at 10:00 A.M., 11:00 A.M., and noon. For information, call (213) 628–1274.

The **Old Plaza Firehouse** at 134 Paseo de la Plaza dates from 1884 as Los Angeles's first fire station. Restored as a museum of old firefighting equipment, the firehouse is open daily except Monday.

El Mercado at 3425 East First Street is a three-story indoor Mexican market, including a supermarket, restaurants, and stores.

El Pueblo de Los Angeles. *Photo by Jeff Hyman,* © *Corel Corporation*

Among the interesting restaurants along Olvera Street is **La Golondrina,** located within the Pelanconi House. The restaurant, whose name means "The Swallow," was Los Angeles's first brick edifice, dating back to 1850. Strolling mariachi musicians entertain guests.

CHINATOWN

Near El Pueblo and historic Union Station, Chinatown is bordered by Alpine, Spring, and Yale Streets and Bamboo Lane. Most of the shops and restaurants can be found on streets off Gin Ling Way, the "Street of the Golden Palace."

Chinese labor helped open California to the world and helped build Los Angeles. The Chinese did not, at first, share in the success of the Golden State. Laborers cut an early wagon road through the mountains near Newhall, worked on the mines of the Comstock in Nevada, and dug the difficult San Fernando tunnel that brought the Southern Pacific to Los Angeles in 1876. Most of the Chinese chose to—or were forced to—live in a small area located close to Olvera Street. Living conditions were marginal, and anti-Chinese prejudice included what has become known as the Chinese Massacre of 1871, when nineteen men and boys were killed.

The Chinese influence continued as Chinese immigrants became fishermen, cooks, and servants and established farms that provided most of the vegetables sold in Los Angeles.

CHINATOWN–EL PUEBLO–LITTLE TOKYO AREA

The old Chinatown was torn down in the 1930s to make way for the construction of Union Station. The new Chinatown, off North Broadway, opened in 1939 with businesses ready to serve the several thousand residents and with an eye on tourism. Shopping is a major pastime, and most stores are open in the evening. For authentic Chinese markets and restaurants, North Spring Street is worth a visit. There is also a Chinese cinema. About 10,000 people reside in Chinatown today.

Although small in comparison to Chinatown in San Francisco, the Los Angeles version is just as lively and colorful, especially in February. During the celebration of the Chinese New Year, traditional parades take to the streets and the sounds of music and firecrackers fill the air as dragons wind their way along.

The main entrance to Chinatown is through the ornamental **Gin Ling Way** pagoda gate at 900 North Broadway near College Street. Facing the gate is a statue of Dr. Sun Yat-sen, who led the overthrow of the Manchu dynasty in 1911 and is regarded as the founder of the Republic of China. As you walk through the area, look at the roofs and upper structures of many of the buildings for images of animals and fish, considered good luck talismans.

Guided walking tours of the district are offered by the Chinese Historical Society of Southern California; call (213) 621–3171 for more information. The Los Angeles Old Chinatown Merchants Association maintains a Web site with information about the area, at old china townla.com.

During the years, new waves of Asian immigrants have added to the mix. You'll find cuisine from China, Taiwan, Hong Kong, Vietnam, and more. Several tightly jammed shopping arcades transport you thousands of miles once you are through their gates. On Broadway you will find **Dynasty Center, Chinatown Plaza,** and **Saigon Plaza.**

Wing On Tong, at 701 North Spring Street, is a Chinese herb store that dates back nearly a century, little changed over time.

Farther down the street is the **Capitol Milling Company** at 1231 North Spring Street. Originally established in 1855 as the Eagle Mills, it was one of the earliest flour mills in California; it was also one of the original seven telephone subscribers to the Los Angeles Telephone Company in 1881. It continues as a commercial mill.

The gateway to Chinatown. *Photo by Jeff Hyman,* © *Corel Corporation*

Philippe the Original is one of those only-in-Los Angeles places, a deli-catessen established by a French cook in 1908, which moved to Chinatown in 1948. According to the official legend, chef Philippe Mathieu accidentally dropped a sandwich into the roasting pan filled with juice still hot from the oven; the customer, a policeman, ate the sandwich anyway, and brought back friends for more "French Dip" sandwiches. The restaurant, at 100 North Alameda Street, has a Web site at www.philippes.com.

Mandarin Plaza at 970 North Broadway includes several dozen restaurants and stores. Near the intersection of North Broadway and Bernard Street is Association Row, home of many family and fraternal associations set up by Chinese immigrants.

F. See On Company at 940 Chungking Court is a renowned gallery for the sale of Asian art.

Those with a literary bent may want to visit the Chinatown Branch of the **Los Angeles Public Library** at 536 West College Street. Its collections include materials on Chinese, Vietnamese, and Spanish cultures. For information, consult www.lapl.org/branches/63.html.

LITTLE TOKYO

Bordered by First, Alameda, Third, and Los Angeles Streets, Little Tokyo is the cultural and commercial center for Japanese-Americans of the Los Angeles region. This is the largest Japanese community outside Japan with a population of more than 100,000. Older enterprises can be found in the many small shops and restaurants; newer development includes several large shopping malls, including the spectacular Yaohan Plaza at Alameda and Third Streets. Yaohan includes a sprawling supermarket of Japanese foods and a branch of the Japanese toy store Hello Kitty.

At Weller Court at Weller and Second Streets is another grouping of interest-ing stores; the central mall includes a monument to Japanese-American astro-naut Ellison Onizuka, one of the victims of the *Challenger* disaster.

The **Japanese American Cultural and Community Center** at 244 San Pedro Street offers information on cultural events and festivals in Nisei Week in August, which celebrates American-born citizens of Japanese extraction. The center offers traditional Kabuki theater performances and the Doizaki Gallery of Art. For information, call (213) 628–2725 or consult www.jaccc.org.

The **Little Tokyo Business Association** offers guided tours during the week. For information and reservations, call (213) 628–2725.

The **Higashi Hongwangi Temple,** at 8505 East Third Street, is an authentic Buddhist temple with a spectacular golden altar.

The **Japanese Village Plaza,** on First and Second Streets between San Pedro and Central, includes Japanese food stores, Japanese and Korean restaurants, and other unusual outlets. For information, call (213) 620–8861.

The **Little Tokyo branch of the Los Angeles Public Library,** at 244 South

Alameda Street, includes a large collection of Japanese-language books and research materials. The library's Web site is www.lapl.org/branches/64.html.

LOS ANGELES FARMERS' MARKET

The Farmers' Market of Los Angeles is a bit of heaven for anyone who eats. Begun in the 1930s when farmers gathered in a field at what was then the edge of town, the market grew to include restaurants, food stands, art galleries, and shops. The stands sell items from all around the world. Market stands include cheese, poultry, meats, breads, ice cream, fruits, vegetables, and health food.

One after another are restaurants from Mexican to Chinese to Japanese to American. On one Sunday morning visit, I had some New Orleans gumbo and corn bread washed down with fresh limeade and topped off with a sinful slice of pie.

You'll also find some spectacular fruits and vegetable stands, although there are not as many as there used to be. Some interesting crafts and gift shops are located across the parking lot.

The Farmers' Market is located at 6333 West Third Street off Fairfax between downtown Los Angeles and Hollywood. Three free hours of parking are allowed at the lot. The market is open daily except for major holidays, from 9:00 A.M. to 6:30 P.M. Monday through Saturday, and from 10:00 A.M. to 5:00 P.M. on Sunday. During the summer, the market stays open half an hour later. For information, call (323) 933–9211, or consult www.farmersmarketla.com.

CITY HALL

As Sergeant Joe Friday used to say as he drove past this place each week on his *Dragnet* beat: "Just the facts, ma'am." A mixed message of a building, unlike almost any other City Hall we know, it has a pyramid at its top with an observation deck on the twenty-seventh floor, and a domed rotunda at the base.

The building, located at 200 North Spring Street, has been a star in motion pictures from the moment it was completed in 1928; at that time Lon Chaney starred there in *While the City Sleeps*. Perhaps its most famous setting was in *War of the Worlds* in 1953; an eight-inch model of the building was destroyed with explosives in one of the major scenes.

City Hall was police headquarters for ten seasons of *Dragnet*; it was transformed to the Daily Planet in the *Superman* television series. *Kojak* and *Cagney and Lacey* used the building as a stand-in for New York City. Other cameos include scenes in *The Rockford Files, Matlock, Hill Street Blues,* and *LA Law.*

A major restoration of the building began in 2001; in addition to preserving the building's significant architectural and artistic features, City Hall is being strengthened against the effects of earthquakes. During the project, the building is closed to visitors; tours are expected to resume sometime in 2003.

Los Angeles City Hall. *Photo by Jeff Hyman, © Corel Corporation*

KOREATOWN

Olympic Boulevard between Crenshaw Boulevard and Vermont Avenue. Another fascinating, far-flung outpost of an ancient Asian culture. Korean restaurants, grocery stores, and shops, as well as the Korean Cultural Center on Wilshire Boulevard at La Brea Avenue with a performance space, gallery, and library. For information on the center, call (323) 936–7141 or consult www. kccla.org.

WATTS TOWERS

A world-renowned example of primitive art and a landmark of the Watts area, Watts Towers were built by hand during a thirty-year period from the 1930s through the 1960s by Sabatino Rodia, an Italian tile setter. The towers are made up of steel rods decorated with pieces of tile, dishes, pieces of bottles, bedframes, and other objects, including thousands of seashells. The towers are located at 1765 East 107th Street in Watts. For information, call (213) 847–4646.

The **Watts Towers Art Center** at 1727 East 107th Street, Watts, offers displays of art, poetry readings, and special exhibits that explore and celebrate the area's African-American culture. It is open Tuesday through Saturday 10:00 A.M. to 4:00 P.M., and noon to 4:00 P.M. on Sunday. Admission: free. For information, call (213) 847–4646.

The skyline of downtown Los Angeles. *Photo by Jeff Hyman,* © *Corel Corporation*

LOS ANGELES CENTRAL LIBRARY

A Los Angeles landmark from the moment of its completion in 1926, the library was reborn and expanded in 1993 from the ashes of a disastrous fire seven years earlier. It is now the third largest library in the country. It sits beneath a somewhat fanciful colored-tile pyramid tower. The library, located at Fifth and Hope Streets, is open Monday to Thursday from 10:00 A.M. to 8:00 P.M.; Friday and Saturday from 10:00 A.M. to 6:00 P.M.; and Sunday from 1:00 P.M. to 5:00 P.M. Guided tours are available daily. For information, call (213) 612–3200 or consult www.lapl.org/central/clhp.html.

HISTORIC WALKING TOURS

The Los Angeles Conservancy offers one- and two-hour walking tours on Saturday of historic neighborhoods and commercial areas, including the theater district, Union Station, and Pershing Square. Different tours are offered each day; tickets cost $8.00. Tickets for the tour of Angelino Heights, the oldest suburb in Los Angeles, are $10.00. Advance reservations are required. For information and reservations, call (213) 623–2489 or consult www.laconservancy.org/tours.

BONNIE BRAE STREET

The 800 and 1000 blocks of South Bonnie Brae Street, near MacArthur Park, are beautifully preserved Victorian residences dating from the 1890s. They are regular locations for film shoots.

BROADWAY THEATER DISTRICT

Los Angeles's original theater district, cleverly named as Broadway, stretches from Third to Ninth Streets in downtown. The oldest of the legitimate theaters date to about 1910, and the first movie palaces opened in the 1920s.

Most of the movie houses have gone to seed, or at least to new roles as neighborhood homes to second- and third-rate films, but the exteriors and interiors remain interesting. Among the tired gems are the Art Deco Doremus Building at Ninth Street; the Cameo Theater at 528 Broadway, built in 1910 as a nickelodeon; and the Million Dollar Theater at 307 Broadway, built in 1918 by impresarios Sid and D. J. Grauman, of Chinese Theatre fame.

LOS ANGELES FLOWER MARKET

The wholesale market for florists and decorators, at 754 Wall Street, opens in the middle of the night for commercial clients. The public can enter after 9:00 A.M. on weekdays and Saturday. Get there early to browse and buy from the spectacular leftovers. For information, call (213) 622–1966.

CHAPTER EIGHTEEN

LOS ANGELES EAST TO BEVERLY HILLS, BURBANK, HOLLYWOOD, PASADENA, ANAHEIM, SAN BERNARDINO, RIVERSIDE, AND PALM SPRINGS

BEVERLY HILLS

From its very humble beginnings as a lima bean farm, Beverly Hills has grown to become a place where a different kind of bean is counted; the local sport is the barely disguised pursuit and display of wealth. How many other places do you know where the ZIP code (90210) can identify a television series, a line of clothing, and a way of life?

The small town (less than 6 square miles) lies within the City of Los Angeles but is an independent entity fiercely protected by its mostly upscale residents. Developed in 1906, the town was named after Beverly, Massachusetts; many of the early stars of Hollywood moved there, and the area became the center of attention in 1921 when Mary Pickford and Douglas Fairbanks built their famous mansion Pickfair in Beverly Hills.

Today many of the homes of the glitterati are hidden in the hills above the Hills, in the canyons above Sunset Boulevard, and behind massive hedges and imposing fences. You can, though, see the hangers-on of the lifestyles of the rich and famous: trendy and overpriced restaurants, overpriced and trendy clothing and jewelry stores, theatrical agents, production companies, stockbrokers, and more. The main street of all of this excess is Rodeo Drive, a short connector that runs between Wilshire Boulevard and Santa Monica Boulevard.

Other famous structures include the **Beverly Hills Hotel** at 9641 Sunset Boulevard, built in 1912. There is a pink Mission-style main building as well as twenty-one bungalows on twelve lush acres. Howard Hughes rented Number 3 for years at a time; many other legends of Hollywood have made the cottages their temporary homes. For information, call (310) 276–2251 or consult www.thebeverlyhillshotel.com.

BURBANK

Beautiful downtown Burbank, which is neither downtown nor especially beautiful, is not quite Hollywood, but it is nevertheless the vital heart of the modern television and movie industry. It was built around the sprawling Warner Bros. Studios, where stars including James Cagney, Humphrey Bogart, Lauren Bacall, and others made many of their most famous films.

Today, major operations include Warner Bros., the Disney Studios at 500 South Buena Vista Street, and the NBC production facilities at 3000 Alameda Avenue. *You can read about tours of the Warner Bros. Studio in Chapter 14.*

HOLLYWOOD

Hooray for Hollywood, a state of mind as much as a place.

The area was first developed in the 1880s; the wife of the developer named the area Hollywood after an all-but-forgotten place of the same name near Chicago. Hollywood, California, began as a quiet fruit-farming community; things began to change soon after an early silent picture was filmed on a ranch there in 1906. The landscape and weather were perfect for tableau films, including Westerns, and the infant moviemaking industry moved from its mostly East Coast origins to Hollywood.

The famed Hollywood sign that looms over much of the area, by the way, dates to 1923 when it was built to publicize a housing development named Hollywoodland. The "land" is gone, but the 50-foot-high, 450-foot-long advertisement sign remains.

By the 1940s nearly the entire American film industry was located in Hollywood. In the years that have followed, the rising price of real estate has resulted in relocation of large portions of the business a bit farther outside of Hollywood proper.

A&M Records. Located in the former Chaplin Movie Studios at 1416 North La Brea Avenue and operated since 1966 as one of the premier recording studios, A&M was founded by musicians Herb Alpert and Jerry Moss. Chaplin's footprints are immortalized in front of Stage 3.

Capitol Records Tower. An unusual circular office building, at 1750 Vine Street, it was likened by some to a stack of records when it was built in 1956; perhaps, in this modern day, it would be thought of as a pile of CDs. A rooftop light flashes "Hollywood" in Morse code.

Capitol Records has purchased land just north of its building and announced plans to build a museum to house memorabilia from recording artists such as

HOLLYWOOD

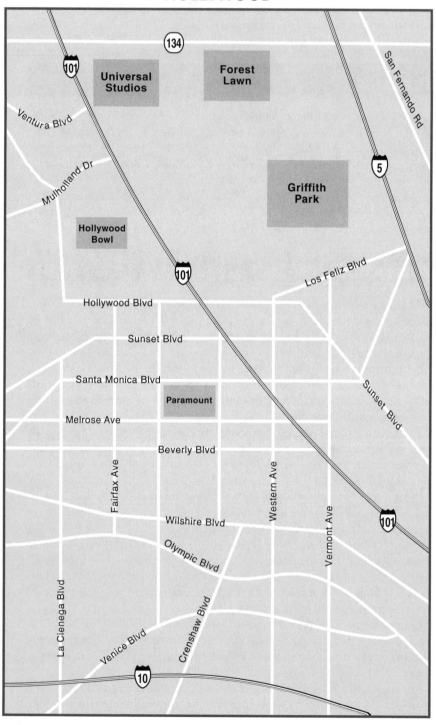

The emporium is located at 8200 Sunset Boulevard; just look for the 15-foot-high statue of Bullwinkle J. Moose holding Rocky the Flying Squirrel in his hand. For information, call (323) 656–6500 or consult www.rockyandbullwinkle.com/jwt/history_productions.html.

Mann's Chinese Theatre. During the years the theater has been as much of an attraction as the great films that have debuted and played there. It was designed as a fanciful version of a Chinese temple inside and out.

Sid Grauman built the theater in 1927, and his name is noted in many of the early handprints and signatures in the concrete outside. The theater is in the heart of Hollywood at 6925 Hollywood Boulevard. For film schedules, call (323) 464–6266 or consult mann.moviefone.com/services/graumanmain.adp.

Ozzie and Harriet House. A must-see for those of a certain age. This was the actual home of the Nelson family, and it was used as the model for the house occupied by the family in their TV series. The home, at 1822 Camino Palmero Drive, is now a private residence and not open to visitors.

GLENDALE

Just above Hollywood in the shadow of the San Gabriels, this old settlement is best known for its proximity to a very quiet neighborhood: the **Forest Lawn Memorial Park.** This 300-acre final resting place (they're positively ghoulish about their desire that it not be called a cemetery) resembles more a rolling green religious theme park. There are several famous church replicas, including the Wee Church o' the Heather and the Church of the Recessional. Displays include huge murals of Jesus and a mural of the signing of the Declaration of Independence accompanied by patriotic music. Residents of the necropolis and the nearby Forest Lawn Hills Memorial Park include Clark Gable and Carole Lombard, Stan Laurel, Buster Keaton, and Liberace.

Forest Lawn is free to the public, and visitors can view some of the spectacular artwork, including the *Paradise Doors,* made from a cast of Lorenzo Ghiberti's original Gothic masterpiece; *Bronco Buster,* an original bronze by Frederic Remington; a mosaic rendering of John Trumbull's *Signing of the Declaration of Independence;* a full-size re-creation of Michelangelo's *David;* and a large collection of coins mentioned in the Bible.

For information, call (800) 204–3131 or consult www.forestlawn.com.

CENTURY CITY

Century City is mostly famous for what it once was—the formal sprawling back lot of **20th Century–Fox** and, before that, the ranch of cowboy actor Tom Mix.

Just a small part of 20th Century–Fox remains, at 10201 Pico Boulevard. The studio is not open to the public, but you can drive by the formal gates to catch a glimpse of the huge New York set used in *Hello, Dolly!* and many other classic films.

The back lot was mostly sold off in 1961 and became an almost-instant city of office buildings, restaurants, shops, and condominiums mostly catering to the entertainment industry.

PASADENA

The end of the trail for numerous parties of settlers from Indiana in the 1880s, the city became a winter playground for the East Coast wealthy; many of their fabulous mansions can be still be seen along Orange Grove Avenue. The name Pasadena means "crown of the valley" in the language of the Chippewa Indians.

Today Pasadena has a population of more than 132,000 and includes some of the best museums in the West, including the **Norton Simon Museum of Art** and the **California Institute of Technology,** which includes the NASA Jet Propulsion Laboratory. Pasadena is most famous, of course, for the Rose Bowl football game and the Tournament of Roses Parade that precedes it each New Year's Day. For more information about Pasadena, consult www.ci.pasadena.ca.us.

ANGELES NATIONAL FOREST

On top of Old Baldy (known on the maps as Mount San Antonio), the view from 10,064 feet is unsurpassed. The huge wilderness area also includes lowland deserts and verdant meadows.

If you're not up to using the hundreds of miles of hiking trails, campsites, ski trails, and downhill slopes, you can take a spectacular 64-mile drive from one side of the forest to another along Route 2 from La Canada off Interstate 210 near Pasadena. The road threads its way among many of the larger peaks with views of Crystal Lake and Old Baldy; the road connects to Route 138 southbound to San Bernardino on the other side of the forest. For information on facilities, call (626) 574–5200 or consult www.r5.fs.fed.us/angeles.

ANAHEIM

German immigrants took "ana" from the nearby Santa Ana River and "heim," meaning home, and named their remote village in 1857. They also brought cuttings from the Rhine and made Anaheim California's first important winemaking region and, before long, the leading wine area of the country. A blight caused by a plant virus some thirty years later wiped out the grape crops, and growers switched to oranges.

Industry and the discovery of oil changed the economy again. The opening of Disneyland in 1955 changed the nature of the area once more, and now tourism is one of the leading industries. For information about Anaheim, consult www.anaheimoc.org.

For details about Disneyland and Knott's Berry Farm see Chapters 4 and 8.

ONTARIO

Graber Olive House. Free tours of one of California's leading olive processing companies, located at 315 East Fourth Street in Ontario. C. C. Graber established his olive farm and packaging facility in 1894. For information, call (909) 983–1761 or (800) 996–5483 or consult www.graberolives.com.

BARSTOW

Calico Ghost Town. Step back into California's mining past to a restored boomtown of the 1880s. The Calico Mountains included some of the richest silver finds of the West; for example, the Maggie Mine, which is part of today's ghost town. Most of the buildings in the park are real; there is also a museum with artifacts from the mining past.

The town was restored by Walter Knott, the founder of Knott's Berry Farm in Buena Park. Knott had worked in the mining camp near the end of its use. Today the ghost town is run by San Bernardino County as a park.

Special events include the Calico Hullabaloo, held over Palm Sunday weekend and featuring "horseshoe pitchin', stew cookin', and tobacco spittin'" competitions. Calico Days, held on the Columbus Day weekend, includes a Wild West parade, gunfights, games, and other events. The Heritage Festival over Thanksgiving weekend includes Old West and Indian art and sculpture.

Located on Ghost Town Road, off I–15, 10 miles northeast of Barstow, Calico is open daily from 9:00 A.M. to 5:00 P.M., except Christmas. Admission: adult, $6.00; child (6–15), $3.00. For information, call (760) 254–2122 or consult www. calicotown.com.

VICTORVILLE

Roy Rogers–Dale Evans Museum. Sure, there are old guns, saddles, boots, and lots of pictures from the fabled movie and television career of Roy and Dale. But you really want to see the stuffed carcass of Trigger, right?

The museum includes artifacts of Roy Rogers and his singing partner and wife Dale Evans through their long careers. On display are family photos, colorful costumes, parade saddles, memorabilia from movies and early television, and the couple's collection of firearms.

The museum, located at Seneca Road and Civic Drive in Victorville off the Roy Rogers Drive exit of I–5 is open daily from 9:00 A.M. to 5:00 P.M. Closed Easter, Thanksgiving, and Christmas. Admission: adult, $8.00; child (13–16), $7.00; child (6–12), $5.00; senior, $7.00. For information, call (760) 243–4547 or consult www.royrogers.com/museum.html.

SAN BERNARDINO

Big Bear Lake. A recreation area in the San Bernardino Mountains, about a hundred miles east of Los Angeles. Summer activities include swimming and boating (rentals available) in Meadow Park, hiking, and camping. In the winter, there are several downhill ski areas and numerous cross-country trails. Call the Big Bear Ranger Station at (909) 866–3437 for information. For information about resorts in the area, call (800) 424–4232 or consult www.bigbearinfo.com. To get to Big Bear Lake, take I–10 to San Bernardino, to State Route 18 into the mountains.

Drivers can explore the Holcomb Valley—location of some of the sites of the 1860–75 Gold Rush—on a three-hour tour north of the lake. Maps and descriptions are available at the Ranger Station.

From Memorial Day through the end of October, visitors can take a ninety-minute tour of Big Bear Lake aboard a trimaran that departs several times a day from Pine Knot Landing in Big Bear Lake. For information, call (909) 866–2628 or consult www.pineknotlanding.com.

RIVERSIDE

March Field Museum. From antique flying machines to the U-2 spy plane and the modern F-14, this museum at March Air Force Base, Van Buren Boulevard is open daily 10:00 A.M. to 4:00 P.M. Donations requested: adult, $5.00; child, $2.00. For information, call (909) 697–6602 or consultwww.pe.net/~marfldmu.

Orange Empire Railway Museum. A sprawling museum of old railroad, trolley, construction, and maintenance cars from in and around Southern California is in the landmark 1893 terminal in Perris. On the weekends several trains or trolleys (still decked out in their original colors and advertising placards) cruise about on the museum's tracks.

Located at 2201 South A Street in Perris, the collection is open daily from 9:00 A.M. to 5:00 P.M. Closed Thanksgiving and Christmas. Trains and trolleys operate weekends and holidays from 11:00 A.M. to 5:00 P.M. Admission: free to museum; all-day train pass adult, $8.00; child (5–11), $6.00.

For information, call (909) 657–2605 or consult www.oerm.mus.ca.us.

UCR California Museum of Photography. A collection of photographs and equipment from the dawn of art through modern day, at a museum operated by the University of California, Riverside. Open Tuesday to Sunday from 11:00 A.M. to 5:00 P.M. Admission: free. 3824 Main Street, Riverside. For information, call (909) 784–3686 or consult www.cmp.ucr.edu.

PALM SPRINGS

Palm Springs is a thriving, even booming, oasis in the desert, a fascinating mix of desert heat and desolation, lush greenery, splendid spas, and snow-capped mountaintops.

Palm Springs is at the western edge of the Coachella Valley, about 107 miles southeast of Los Angeles. The city itself is only 487 feet above sea level, but it is all but surrounded by mountains, including 10,831-foot Mount San Jacinto; the Palm Springs Aerial Tramway climbs the mountain to the 8,516-foot level, sometimes taking visitors from summer heat to winter cross-country skiing and hiking conditions at the top.

Palm Springs averages 354 days of sunshine and fewer than 5.5 inches of rain per year. The "high season" of Palm Springs runs from January to May; there is still plenty to do in the summer months, but the heat in the desert can be brutal. However, don't overlook the desert as the site of some spectacular and unusual vistas, wildlife, and vegetation.

Palm Springs Regional Airport is a mile from downtown. Los Angeles International Airport is two hours away by car.

There are more than 140 hotels in Palm Springs ranging from modest bungalow courts to European-style bed and breakfasts to full-service luxury resorts and spas. You can call the Palm Springs Visitor Information Center at (800) 347–7746 for details on hotels and to make reservations or consult www.palm-springs.org.

There are four gambling casinos in and around Palm Springs, each operated by an Indian tribe. You won't find the flash of Las Vegas here, but you will have the chance to lose your paycheck at blackjack, pai gow, poker, and other table games, and at slot machines and sports books.

The **Spa Hotel & Casino,** operated by the Agua Caliente Band of Cahuilla Indians, is located in Palm Springs at 140 North Indian Drive. For information, call (760) 323–5865 or consult www.sparesortcasino.com.

Casino Morongo, operated by the Morongo Band of Mission Indians, is about seventeen minutes west of Palm Springs off the Cabazon Apache Trail exit of I–10. For information, call (800) 252–4499 or consult www.casinomorongo.com.

Fantasy Springs Casino, operated by the Cabazon Band of Mission Indians, is located near Indio off I–10. For information, call (760) 342–5000 or consult www.cabazonindians.com/fantasysprings.html.

Trump 29 Casino, operated by the Twenty-Nine Palms Band of Mission Indians, is in Coachella off I–10. For information, call (760) 775–5566 or consult www.trump29casino.com.

Indian Canyons. Just minutes from downtown, Andreas, Murray, and Palm Canyons shelter North America's largest natural fan palm oases. There is also a trading post, hiking and horse trails, and picnic areas. The region is part of the domain of the Agua Caliente Band of Cahuilla Indians.

Palm Canyon, 15 miles long, is home to several thousand *Washingtonia filifera* palms that stand in striking contrast to the barren desert and rock formations. A trading post operated by the Cahuillas sells art and artifacts.

In 1876 the Agua Caliente Indians were deeded in trust some 32,000 acres to be used as their homeland; today, some 6,700 acres lie within the city limits of Palm Springs. What was once considered worthless desert today is among the most valuable real estate in the country.

Open daily from 8:00 A.M. to 5:00 P.M. in fall and winter, and until 6:00 P.M. in spring and summer. Admission: adult, $6.00; child (6–12), $2.00; senior (62 and older), $4.50. For information, call (760) 325–3400 or consult www.indian-canyons.com.

Desert Adventures. Guided tours to the natural and historic wonders of Palm Springs, Indian Canyons, Joshua Tree, and the Santa Rosa Mountains. Other offerings include off-road jeep safaris, agriculture tours, and earthquake fault tours.

I took a tour of Indian Canyons in one of the company's signature red jeeps; the canyons are just a few miles outside of Palm Springs but a world away. Among the stops was a lush desert oasis; alongside it was an ancient grinding rock used by families of Indians for generations. The streams are overflows of entrapment areas in mountains; these aquifers of ancient rainfall provide all the drinking water for the Palm Springs area. (Imported Colorado River water is used for irrigation purposes in the valley.)

Back out on the desert floor we were introduced to plants such as the Thorn Apple, a hallucinogenic member of the nightshade family; the poisonous Jimson Weed, also used in some religious and personal experimentation as Sacred Datura; and the Yrba Senta plant, used as a poultice and mouthwash and smelling very much like Juicy Fruit gum.

And then there were the Jumping Cholla (pronounced choy-ah), which are especially nasty plants whose heads seem to fly off when a human or animal passes nearby. The barbs swell up and pull themselves as much as half an inch into the body. Very patient gourmets cook the cholla flowers for as long as fifteen hours for an artichoke-like flavor.

The desert is also home to sheep, goats, deer, 30-inch-long chuckwalla lizards, scorpions, tarantulas, black widows, and recluse spiders.

Rates run from about $59 to $99 per person for scheduled tours. For information, call (760) 324–5337 or consult www.red-jeep.com.

Living Desert. A 1,200-acre desert interpretive center featuring exotic birds and animals, nature trails, botanical gardens, and a visitors center that has geological exhibits.

It's a stroll in the Coachella Valley desert, among coyotes, bighorn sheep, oryx, zebras, cheetahs, and meerkats. There are some interesting displays about the local ecology. Open 9:00 A.M. to 5:00 P.M. daily from September through mid-June; call for summer hours. Admission: adult, $8.50; child (3–12), $4.25; seniors (62+), $7.50. For information, call (760) 346–5694 or consult www.palmsprings.com/points/desert.html.

Palm Springs Desert Museum. Collection of classic western American and contemporary California art, as well as natural science exhibitions and a full schedule of performing arts in the 450-seat Annenberg Theater.

The unusual collection includes an active seismograph charting current earth movement in the area, several dinosaur skeletons, a collection of intricate Apache baskets, a set of paintings by Frederic Remington, portraits by actor William Holden, and sculptures by Western actor George Montgomery.

The museum is open daily except Sunday and Monday. Adult, $7.50; youth (6–17), $3.50; and senior (62 and older), $6.50. Free to the public on the first Friday of each month. For information call (760) 325–7186 or consult www.psmuseum.org.

Moorten Botanical Garden. Nature trails in a setting of two thousand varieties of giant cacti, trees, birds, succulents, and flowers. Located at 1701 South Palm Canyon Drive, the garden is open daily 9:30 A.M. to 4:00 P.M. Admission: adult, $3.00; child (5–15), 75 cents. For information, call (760) 327–6555.

Knott's Soak City Palm Springs. A twenty-one-acre water playground—formerly **Oasis Waterpark**—with eighteen waterslides and other attractions including body- and board-surfing, and an inner tube ride. Located at 1500 South Gene Autry Trail, the water park is open from mid-March through late October. Admission: adult, $21.95; child (3–11), $14.95; after 3:00 P.M., $12.95; child (under 40 inches), free. For information, call (760) 327–0499 or consult www. soakcityusa.com.

Adjacent to the waterpark is the **Uprising Rock Climbing Center** with three covered, micro-misted towers. For information, call (760) 320–6630 or consult www.uprising.com.

Wind Farm Tours. They're one of the great unnatural wonders of the world—thousands of whirling windmills in the valley just north of Palm Springs along Interstate 10. The operation claims the mantle as the world's most efficient power-producing wind farm. And they're open to the public for ninety-minute tours that go out onto the farm and into the machinery. Tours are offered daily at 9:00 and 11:00 A.M. and 1:00 and 3:00 P.M. Admission: adult, $23; student, $15; child (6–12), $10. For information, call (760) 251–1997 or consult www.wind milltours.com.

Palm Springs Air Museum. One of the world's largest collections of World War II aircraft, many of which are still in flying condition. The museum, in a sparkling new building and hangars, sits alongside one of the runways at the Palm Springs Regional Airport. On most weekends, one or another of the lumbering bombers or surprisingly fragile-looking fighters takes to the air.

The museum's collection includes a working B-17 Flying Fortress, and a P38 long-range fighter bomber named *Joltin' Josie*. You'll also find some unusual automobiles, including a three-headlamp 1948 Tucker and a 1930 Pierce Arrow. On the day of my visit, a B-25 bomber was offering tours to members and paying guests; its throaty engines echoed throughout the valley as it made low-altitude passes over the airport.

The museum, located at Palm Springs Regional Airport, 745 North Gene Autrey Trail, is open daily 10:00 A.M. to 5:00 P.M. Admission: adult, $8.00; child (6–12), $3.50; senior, (65+) and military personnel, $6.50. For information, call (760) 778–6262 or consult www.air-museum.org.

Palm Springs Aerial Tramway. A spectacular climb more than a mile up the side of Mount San Jacinto in an eighty-passenger tram. The view from the cool top of the tram extends across the San Jacinto Valley; on a clear day you can see as far as the Salton Sea, nearly 50 miles away, created in 1905 as the result of a flood on the Colorado River diversion channel. A trail from the top of the tram leads six miles to the peak of Mount San Jacinto. During the winter you can rent sleds and saucers for use on a snow hill.

The base station for the tram is at 2,463 feet, and the mountain station tops out at 8,516 feet, where the temperature averages forty degrees cooler than the base. The tram travels about 12,800 feet in total over the fourteen-minute ride. There's a gift shop, cafeteria, and cocktail lounge at the top, too. You can watch a video about the making of the tram, and you can plant yourself on a mule for a twenty-minute tour on a trail. From the top, you can see the San Andreas Fault as it snakes through the valley about 8 miles away. The Nordic Ski Center is open November 15 to April 15, snow conditions permitting.

The attraction, located on Tramway Road, Palm Springs, off Highway 111, is open weekdays from 10:00 A.M. to 9:15 P.M.; weekends from 8:00 A.M. The last car up is at 8:00 P.M., and the last car down is at 9:45 P.M. The tram usually closes for maintenance for about a week in August; call for details. Admission: adult, $20.80; child (3–12), $13.80; senior, $18.80. The tram also offers a Ride 'n Dine ticket at the end of the day that includes a meal for adult, $28.80; child, $18.80.

For information, call (760) 325–1391 or consult www.pstramway.com.

Palm Springs Follies. If you happen to find yourself in Palm Springs in winter or spring, put aside dreams of Broadway and Hollywood and head for the Follies, a somewhat modernized vaudeville show that has become a local favorite since it was revived in the Historic Plaza Theatre.

You'll find singers, tap dancers, comedians, magicians, trained dogs, and a flashy chorus line with an age restriction: dancers must be older than sixty.

The Follies usually run from early November through the end of May, with breaks around Christmas. Tickets range from about $35 to $70. For information, call (760) 327–0225 or consult www.palmspringsfollies.com.

Joshua Tree National Monument. Off Highway 62, at Twenty-Nine Palms and Joshua Tree (another gate can be found at Cottonwood Springs, 25 miles east of Indio off I–10).

The stark beauty of the Colorado Desert in the valleys and the high Mojave Desert is within an easy drive from Los Angeles or Orange County. The two deserts come together at the Joshua Tree National Monument, which draws its name from the many Joshua trees found there. (Joshua trees are actually giant desert lilies that can reach 40 feet or more.) They were given their names by Mormon emigrants who thought they resembled the biblical prophet Joshua with upraised arms.

You can take your car on an 18-mile exploration on Geology Road, which goes to many of the park's more interesting areas. Hiking trails reach to Twenty-Nine Palms Oasis and other destinations. For information, call (760) 367–5500 or consult www.joshua.tree.national-park.com.

CHAPTER NINETEEN

ALONG THE COAST TO LONG BEACH, THE *QUEEN MARY*, AND CATALINA ISLAND

LONG BEACH

The long beach was a strip of sand used as a trading area between Indians of the mainland and those who came across from Catalina Island in canoes.

Outsiders built up the area after the turn of the twentieth century when Henry Huntington's Pacific Railroad arrived. When oil was discovered at Signal Hill in 1921 the population nearly doubled to 100,000. Today's economy is built on shipping and tourism, including the ocean liner *Queen Mary*, which is moored in the harbor. Fort MacArthur in San Pedro is an important military installation. The Long Beach Grand Prix is held in the city each spring.

Long Beach features two restored parks that are worth an afternoon stroll. Both are open Wednesday through Sunday afternoon and are free. A beach within the harbor is a popular spot for swimming, water skiing, and other water sports.

For information about Long Beach, call (562) 436–3645 or (800) 452–7829 or consult www.golongbeach.org.

El Dorado Park Archery Range, site of the 1984 Olympic competition, is open to visitors and competitors. call(562) 570–1765 or consult www.ci.long-beach.ca.us/park/facilities.

Farmers' Market. Friday from 10:00 A.M. to 4:00 P.M. at Long Beach Promenade. Call (562) 436–4259 or consult www.harborareafarmersmarkets.org.

Rancho Los Alamitos. 6400 East Bixby Hill Road. A ranch house from the early nineteenth century with period furnishing and half a dozen agricultural buildings, including a working blacksmith's shop. Admission: free. Call (562) 431–3541 or consult www.ci.long-beach.ca.us/park/facilities.

Rancho Los Cerritos. 4600 Virginia Road. Includes a Spanish-style adobe dating from the mid-nineteenth century and surrounding gardens. Call (562) 570–1755 or consult www.ci.long-beach.ca.us/park/facilities.

Whale Watching Tours. January through March. Catalina Cruises, (800) 228–2546; Pier Point Landing Sport Fishing, (562) 983–9300; Spirit Cruises, (562) 495–5884. Dinner cruises available.

LONG BEACH AQUARIUM OF THE PACIFIC

Skin divers equipped with microphones serve as underwater tour guides at the Long Beach Aquarium. With one million gallons of Pacific Ocean water in twenty-one exhibition tanks and twenty-six smaller tanks, the aquarium's three permanent exhibits offer visitors a virtual journey along the Pacific Rim from temperate Southern California and Baja to the more frigid waters of the Bering Sea and Kuril Islands, and on to the spectacular paradise of a Micronesian barrier reef. The collection includes more than 550 different Pacific marine species.

Shaped like an ocean wave, the building is the anchor of the Queensway Bay project in downtown Long Beach, across the bay from the *Queen Mary*.

Highlights of the exhibit include close encounters with the seals and sea lions of Santa Catalina Island, the leopard sharks and barracuda of Predator Place, and the sea turtles and other creatures of Baja and the Sea of Cortez. The Northern Pacific exhibit includes sea otters; puffins and other diving birds; and giant spider crabs, octopuses, and sea stars. The largest tank is devoted to the Tropical Pacific, including the dazzling Palauan living coral lagoon and the barrier reef of Micronesia.

The Long Beach Aquarium of the Pacific is located at 200 South Shoreline Drive, Queensway Bay, off the Aquarium Way exit of I–710. Admission: adult, $16.95; child (3–11), $9.95; senior (60+), $13.95. Parking $6.00. Open daily 9:00 A.M. to 6:00 P.M. For information, call (562) 590–3100 or consult www. aquariumofpacific.org.

Long Beach Aquarium of the Pacific. *Photo courtesy Anaheim/Orange County Visitor & Convention Bureau*

▦ MUST-SEE THE *QUEEN MARY*

The *Queen Mary* is a most unusual floating museum, a sixty-two-year-old relic of the grand era of transatlantic ocean liners. Tours of the vessel take visitors from the keel to the upper decks with stops at the engine room, luxury staterooms, spectacular dining rooms, and the bridge.

The self-guided tour gives access to the many public rooms of the ship, as well as the engine room and the upper deck, including the bridge. The escorted Royal Historic tour adds visits to the first-class salon and dining room, a luxury stateroom, the boiler rooms, and more; it is worth the extra charge.

Moored alongside the liner is the retired Russian submarine *Scorpion,* also open for tours. Combination tickets include both vessels.

The *Queen Mary* is an easy twenty- to thirty-minute drive from Anaheim. You will see the big ship as you drive alongside the harbor across from the City of Long Beach.

Open daily 10:00 A.M. to 6:00 P.M.; from July 1 to Labor Day open until 9:00 P.M. Fireworks summer Saturday nights. For information, call (562) 435–3511 or consult www.queenmary.com.

At her height the *Queen Mary* was the queen of the Atlantic, a floating palace of elegance, grace, and power. At her creation, she was unlike anything ever seen on the sea, a combination of engineering, craftsmanship, and artistry.

The *Queen Mary* began life as the glamorous solution to a difficult problem facing Cunard, the leading steamship company of its time. Cunard had lost many of its best vessels during World War I and faced competition unlike anything it had seen before. The company decided to create two ships that would be bigger and faster than any ocean liner in existence, two ships that would do the work of three.

Designing the plans for the ships took two years, with revolutionary solutions in hull shape, propeller design, and powerplant. The four steam turbines each generated 40,000 horsepower, making the ship the fastest ever made.

If the *Queen Mary* were in service today, she would still be one of the fastest boats afloat, capable of a top speed of up to thirty-six knots, equivalent to about forty miles per hour. The speed came at some expense, though; at full cruising speed, the *Queen Mary* got 13 feet per gallon of fuel.

When completed the *Queen Mary* was a bit more than 1,019 feet in length, with the showcase Promenade Deck stretching 724 feet; there were twelve decks in all. The hull's draft was nearly 40 feet, and the ship weighed 81,237 gross tons with hull plates from 8 to 30 feet in length and up to 1.25 inches thick. The hull was held together with more than ten million rivets; there were more than 2,000 portholes.

The ship's rudder weighed 140 tons. There were two 18-foot-tall anchors at the bow, each weighing sixteen tons; the 900-foot anchor chain added forty-five tons, with each 2-foot-long link weighing 224 pounds. The *Queen Mary* could hold 1,957 passengers, plus 1,174 officers and crew.

Queen Mary Tickets

Prices were in effect in mid-2002 and are subject to change.

	ADULT	CHILD	SENIOR
GENERAL ADMISSION PASSPORT	$19	$15*	$17
Behind-the-Scenes Guided Tour (plus admission passport)	$8	$5*	$8
SCORPION SUBMARINE	$10	$9*	$9
FIRST CLASS PASSAGE	$23	$19**	$21
Queen Mary, Guided Tour, *Scorpion* Submarine			
Parking: $8			

*ages 3 to 11
**ages 4 to 11

Air conditioning was a new art at the time the ship was constructed, and only three rooms on the *Queen Mary* were cooled: the first-class dining room, the ballroom, and the ship's kennel.

Finally, in 1934, Cunard was ready to launch the greatest, most luxurious ocean liner ever built. Queen Mary herself pressed the launch button to release her floating namesake into the River Clyde. It took two more years to outfit her as a passenger vessel.

In May 1936 with her three massive, one-ton steam whistles blasting, the *Queen Mary* embarked on her maiden voyage to New York with nearly 2,000 passengers and a crew of almost 1,200 aboard. She received a spectacular greeting as she steamed up the Hudson River, including an airborne drop of thousands of white carnations.

In 1939 a round-trip first-class ticket sold for about $2,000, which was a lot of money back then; third-class passage was a pricey $500.

Dining aboard the *Queen Mary* was an event. All 800 first-class passengers could be served at once in the largest room ever built within a ship. The wine cellar on board contained more than 15,000 bottles, rivaling the finest restaurants in Europe.

The ship's engines were improved in 1938, allowing her to cross the Atlantic in just under four days, a world record, which she held for fourteen years.

By the summer of 1939 the *Queen Mary* was an unqualified success. In September of that same year her first career was abruptly halted when Great Britain was drawn into war with Germany. The *Queen Mary* was conscripted into the war effort for use as a troop carrier.

Camouflaged with gray paint and capable of evading warships and even out-maneuvering torpedoes, the *Queen Mary* became known as the Gray Ghost. Berths were stacked up to six high, with troops sleeping in shifts during the five-day crossing. Sleeping accommodations were set up in drawing rooms, in lounges, and even within drained swimming pools. Five double-barreled cannons were installed, and 20-mm guns lined the upper decks; four sets of antiaircraft rocket launchers were installed. The guns, though, were never fired in anger.

On one memorable voyage, some 16,000 troops and crew were shoehorned into every corner of the vessel. No ship before or since has carried so many. Special assignments included transporting British Prime Minister Winston Churchill three times to conferences. Churchill approved the D day invasion plans aboard the ship. During the course of the war, Adolf Hitler put a $250,000 bounty on the ship and offered Germany's highest military honor to the captain who could sink her.

By the end of her war service the *Queen Mary* had carried more than 800,000 troops, had traveled more than 600,000 miles, and had played a part in every major Allied campaign of World War II. She was also used to carry German and Italian prisoners of war to camps in North America.

At the end of the war the *Queen Mary* was fitted out as a floating hospital with surgical and intensive care units to bring home the wounded. She later carried many returning troops and their war brides.

Regular passenger service resumed on July 31, 1947. After completing 1,001 crossings of the Atlantic, the *Queen Mary* retired from regular passenger service on September 19, 1967; she made one "Last Great Cruise" from October 31 to December 9, 1967, pulling into port for the last time at Long Beach. The RMS Foundation, which took over operation of the *Queen Mary* in 1993, signed a new twenty-year lease in 1996, and the ship was added to the National Register of Historic Places, so the queen may have found a very long-term home.

The *Queen Mary* at dock. *Photo courtesy The* Queen Mary

Among the interesting stops on the guided tour is the first-class lounge, an extraordinary room paneled with rare woods collected from around the world—some are from species no longer available.

On the wall of the first-class dining room is a huge mural showing the North Atlantic from England to the United States. Two tracks, occupied by small glass ships, mark the progress of the *Queen Mary* and her sister ship the *Queen Elizabeth;* at the peak of Cunard's history, the two ships crossed the Atlantic weekly on opposite schedules, passing in mid-ocean.

■ A *TITANIC* COMPARISON

The *Queen Mary* was longer, wider, taller, and faster than the *Titanic.* And as her current owners point out with a straight face, the *Queen Mary* made 1,001 transatlantic crossings while the *Titanic* made, well, half a crossing.

Here are some of the statistics on the two ships:

	Queen Mary	*Titanic*
Length	1,019 feet	883 feet
Breadth	118 feet	93 feet
Height	181 feet	175 feet
Tonnage	81,237 gross tons	46,329 gross tons
Decks	12	8
Cruising speed	28.5 knots	21 knots

■ ART OF THE *QUEEN MARY*

Among the sometimes overlooked treasures of the *Queen Mary* are her works of art. Many of the original art pieces, including the huge murals and decorations of the principal public rooms, many smaller works of art, and decorative items are located throughout the ship in areas where the public does not usually visit.

In 1995 the ship opened a permanent exhibition of some of the art pieces in her own gallery on the *Queen Mary*'s Promenade Deck, immediately forward of the Queen's Salon.

Featured in the gallery are Dame Laura Knight's *The Mills Circus* from one of the first-class private dining rooms; S. Nicholson Babb's *Jupiter and Europa,* and Gilbert Bayes's *The Sea King's Daughter,* both bronze figure groups borrowed from the corner niches of the Queen's Salon. Kenneth Shoesmith's *Madonna of the Atlantic,* originally the altarpiece for the Roman Catholic Chapel, and Walter and Donald Gilbert's bronze doors, which originally adorned side entrances of the first-class restaurant, are also included.

■ RESTAURANTS AT THE *QUEEN MARY*

Sir Winston's. The *Queen Mary*'s most elegant restaurant offers a spectacular view of the coastline from the upper deck, with dinner served from 5:30 to 10:00 P.M. Specialties in the range of $18 to $36 include Swordfish Filet Nicoise and Beef Phylo Sir Winston's. For reservations, call (562) 499–1657.

Chelsea. A seafood eatery with a view of the sea. Specialties in the range of $14 to $24 include Lobster Pappardelle (rainbow pappardelle pasta with lobster tail and spinach in roasted bell pepper sauce) and Seafood Phylo. Open weekdays for lunch, and Wednesday through Sunday for dinner from 5:30 to 10:00 P.M. For reservations, call (562) 499–1685.

Promenade Cafe. Open for breakfast, lunch, and dinner, from 6:30 A.M. to 10:00 P.M. Specialties priced from about $8.00 to $20.00 include chicken linguine and blackened halibut. Salads and pasta dishes are also available.

Sunday Champagne Brunch in the Grand Salon. A buffet featuring food from around the globe with more than fifty entrees, including a special island for children. The Grand Salon is the former first-class dining room of the ship. Served from 10:00 A.M. until 3:00 P.M. Adult, $29; child (4–11), $9.95.

Observation Bar. Evening entertainment, cocktails, and dancing in the original first-class bar, an Art Deco masterpiece. Open nightly.

■ THE HOTEL *QUEEN MARY*

The Hotel *Queen Mary* today offers 365 first-class cabins for rent at rates as low as $109 per night for a standard inside cabin without a porthole to $500 per night for a royalty suite.

One of the rooms not available for rent but visited on the escorted tour is the Duke of Edinburgh Room, a luxury suite that was occupied by the Duke and Duchess of Windsor, Winston Churchill, and comic actors Laurel and Hardy, among others.

LONG BEACH CRUISE TERMINAL

Carnival Cruise Lines plans to open a cruise ship terminal alongside the *Queen Mary* in Long Beach in early 2003. The single berth will be large enough to accommodate vessels the size of one of the line's mammoth 102,000-ton "Destiny" class ships. The terminal is expected to serve as home port for the company's West Coast–based fleet. The project also includes a parking garage capable of accommodating more than 1,200 vehicles.

Guests arriving for a cruise will be able to check their bags and enter a waiting lounge on board the *Queen Mary* before boarding their ship. Debarkation for passengers returning to Long Beach after a voyage would take place within a portion of the **Dome at the *Queen Mary*.** Originally constructed in 1983 to house Howard Hughes's gigantic *Spruce Goose* seaplane, the dome is the world's largest clear-span dome. The structure closed in 1992 when the plane was sold to a museum in Oregon.

The facility has been used as a motion picture soundstage; it was home of the Batcave in *Batman Forever,* and was used in *Stargate, The Cable Guy,* and *The Haunting.*

NEWPORT BEACH

Orange County Museum of Art. 850 San Clemente Drive, Newport Harbor. Contemporary paintings, sculpture, and photography. Open 11:00 A.M. to 5:00 P.M., closed Monday, major holidays, and between major exhibitions. For information, call (949) 759–1122 or consult www.ocma.net.

Newport Harbor Cruise. 400 Main Street, Newport Harbor. Harbor cruises from the Balboa Pavilion. Open daily except Christmas. For information, call (714) 673–5245 or consult www.caladventures.com/PavQueen.htm.

Newport Harbor Showboat Cruises. 700 East Edgewater Avenue, Newport Harbor. Open daily except Christmas and Thanksgiving periods. For information, call (949) 673–0240.

BALBOA ISLAND

Balboa Island in Newport Harbor is an old-style amusement zone that includes the Balboa Pavilion, built in 1905 and restored to its former glory. Nearby is a Ferris wheel, bumper cars, arcade games, and fast-food stands.

A ferry costing 25 cents per pedestrian runs from the end of Palm Street on the Balboa Peninsula, twenty-four hours a day in the summer and all day for the rest of the year.

From Balboa Island you can take harbor cruises, including one on board a replica of a Mississippi River riverboat, or a more traditional boat. For information, call (949) 673–5245 (riverboat) or (949) 673–0240 (traditional boat). For information on the island, consult www.balboa-island.com.

CATALINA ISLAND

About 27 miles off the coast and a world away, Catalina Island was a pirate and smuggler's outpost after its discovery in 1542 by Juan Rodríguez Cabrillo. The original occupants of the island were Gabrieleno Indians, who were wiped out by various later arrivals including Russian seal hunters. The island was bought and sold by several wealthy Californians until it came into the hands of the Wrigley (as in chewing gum) family. William Wrigley, Jr., built the famous circular casino in 1929, and the modern era of the island as a tourist destination began.

Current residents of the island include a herd of free-running buffalo. The original animals were brought over to the island for the filming of a Hollywood movie, *The Vanishing American;* the beasts have flourished ever since.

You can travel to the island by ferry (about one to two hours) or by small plane (a twenty-minute hop). The 8-mile-wide, 21-mile-long island offers spectacular beaches. The principal settlement on the island is Avalon, which includes the famous casino; another port is located at Two Harbors. Nearly all of the island is owned by the Santa Catalina Island Conservancy and will be preserved as forever wild.

Cars may not be brought to the island, but bicycles and golf carts can be rented in Avalon. For information about Catalina Island, consult www.catalina.com.

ATTRACTIONS ON CATALINA ISLAND

Visitors come here to hike, ride horses, scuba dive, play golf, sportfish, or explore the Mediterranean charm of Avalon, which is home to numerous shops, hotels, restaurants, and cafes.

The **Avalon Casino,** constructed at a cost of $2 million at a time when a dollar was worth, well, a dollar, it houses a charming ballroom still used for big-band concerts; an art gallery; and the Catalina Island Museum, where fossils, Native American artifacts, and natural history exhibits are on display. The museum is open daily, from 10:30 A.M. to 4:00 P.M.

Beyond Avalon, Catalina's 42,000-acre interior is a designated nature preserve with unique plants and animals. Developed campsites, cabins, and primitive camping areas are available.

There are numerous services, including tours and taxi (by land and sea) on the island. An intriguing attraction are the *Starlight* and *Emerald* semi-submersible vessels. Not quite submarines, they are tour boats with a basement. Passengers sit in a cabin beneath the sea level with a panoramic view of the waters and marine life around Catalina Island. Admission: adult, about $30; senior, $27; and child, $15. Tickets are available at Discovery Tours outlets on the island.

BOAT SERVICE TO CATALINA

Catalina Express. San Pedro, Long Beach, and Dana Point to Avalon. San Pedro to Two Harbors. (800) 481–3470. www.catalinaexpress.com.

Catalina Passenger Service. Fast catamaran ferry service on the 500-passenger Catalina Flyer from Balboa Pavilion in Newport Beach, about a seventy-five-minute trip. (949) 673–5245. www.catalina.com/catalinainfo_outlink.htm.

AIRLINE SERVICE

Island Express Helicopter Service. Long Beach and San Pedro Ferry Terminals to Catalina. (310) 510–2525 or (800) 228–2566. www.islandexpress.com.

Island Hopper Catalina Airlines. San Diego to Avalon. (858) 279–4595.

HOTELS ON CATALINA

Hotels and standard accommodations on Catalina generally range from about $50 to $200 per night with more expensive luxury rooms and condos also available. Fans of the Old West might want to consider staying at the Zane Grey Pueblo Hotel, the 1926 "pueblo" home of author Zane Grey. Because Catalina is an island, it is generally very important that you have a reservation.

Write to the Catalina Chamber of Commerce, P.O. Box 217, Avalon, CA 90704, for a copy of the visitor's guide, or call the Visitors Information Bureau at (310) 510–1520 for accommodation information.

■ CAMPING ON CATALINA

For hiking and biking permits, call the Catalina Island Conservancy office in Avalon at (310) 510–2595. Reservations only by mail, fax, or Web. www.catalina. com.

You can also obtain information and reservations for camping through the Santa Catalina Company at (888) 510–7979 or by consulting www.scico.com.

Hermit Gulch Campground. Avalon. Nearby to Wrigley Memorial and Botanical Garden and hiking trails; about 1.5 miles up Avalon Canyon. (310) 510–8368.

Two Harbors Campground. Seaside camping. Tents and camping gear available for rent. Call (310) 510–2800 or (800) 322–3434 for reservations.

Little Harbor is southeast of Two Harbors, in a protected cove with a sandy beach 17 miles from Avalon, and 7 miles from Two Harbors; it is very popular with youth groups. Call (310) 510–2800 or (800) 322–3434.

Parsons Landing is a remote site on the northwest shore accessible by a 7-mile trail from Two Harbors or by boat. Call (310) 510–2800 or (800) 322–3434 for reservations and information.

Blackjack is in a grove of pine trees on 1,600-foot Blackjack Mountain in the center of the island, a 10-mile hike to Avalon or Two Harbors. Call (310) 510–2800 or (800) 322–3434 for reservations.

Ten undeveloped coves on the coastline, accessible by boat only, include **Frog Rock Cove, Willow Cove, Italian Gardens, Goat Harbor, Gibraltar Point Beach, Lava Wall Beach, Paradise Cove, Rippers Cove, Starlight Beach,** and **East Starlight Beach.** Call (310) 510–3577 for information. Reservations by mail or fax only.

MISSION SAN JUAN CAPISTRANO

The Mission at San Juan Capistrano is a place of quiet beauty, as old and redolent of history as any place in California. The mission was founded by Father Junipero Serra, a Spanish Franciscan priest, on November 1, 1776—four months after the Declaration of Independence of the original thirteen colonies on the other side of the still-wild American continent. It was the seventh in a chain of twenty-one California missions.

Constructed of adobe (mud and straw), many of the early missions have fallen apart; San Juan Capistrano and several others were restored around 1900. Today the Mission San Juan Capistrano's chapel is the oldest building in California still in use. Fund raising for a $20 million restoration project is now under way.

The native Americans who greeted Father Serra were the Acagchemem, a peaceful tribe; the Spanish renamed them the Juaneno. Some descendants of the Juaneno work at the mission today.

In 1821 the newly independent Mexican government took over California and forced the Spanish padres to leave; the mission was sold and the Indians evicted. After the Americans were victorious in the Mexican-American war in 1850, California came under dominion of the United States. In 1865 President Lincoln gave some of the California missions back to the church.

On the grounds of the mission is the remains of an old stone church, which was destroyed by an earthquake in 1812, an event that killed forty Indians who were in the church at the time. You'll be able to visit a number of rooms of the mission, restored as a museum. There's also a display about Native Americans, an archaeological field office, and even an homage to the swallows.

Today the place may be best known for the celebration of the miraculous return of thousands of swallows to the mission each March 19, on St. Joseph's Day. (Of course, some also come on March 18 and March 20, but there's no party for them.) The locals have a parade and other events on March 19; by the way, the sparrows traditionally pack their bags and fly south on October 23.

Those square-tailed cliff swallows traditionally come to southern California in March to nest; they return to their homes in Argentina, 6,000 miles away, in October. The oldest recordings of the migration of the swallows date to the late 1700s; however, there is evidence that the birds had been regular visitors well before then, nesting in the silt stone cliffs near the ocean.

To their credit the modern-day keepers of the mission do not make the claim that the swallows magically reappear on exactly March 19. A few "scouts" often arrive ahead of time. The arrival date of the main flock may vary from year to year because northward migration is affected by the weather's influence on available insect food as the birds travel. They move northward when the temperature warms up to about forty-eight degrees.

The mission is open daily from 8:30 A.M. to 5:00 P.M., except for Thanksgiving, Christmas, New Year's Day, and Good Friday afternoon. Admission: adult, $6.00; child (3–12), $4.00; and senior, $5.00. For information, call (949) 248–2049 or consult www.missionsjc.com.

CHAPTER TWENTY

Western Beach Communities from Santa Barbara to Malibu and Santa Monica

SANTA BARBARA

Located 92 miles north of Los Angeles, Santa Barbara is one of the oldest settlements in California. In 1542 explorer Juan Cabrillo entered the channel and claimed the region for Spain. He was greeted by the true discoverers of the area, the Chumash Indians, who lived in small villages along the Santa Barbara coast and the Channel Islands.

Sixty years later three Spanish frigates under the command of Sebastian Vizcaíno arrived in the channel after surviving a fierce ocean storm. A Carmelite friar on board one of the ships named the area after that day's saint, Barbara. It wasn't until 1782, though—after the birth of the United States on the other side of the continent—that Spain established a permanent presence in the area led by Father Junipero Serra, Captain Jose Ortega, and Governor Felipe de Neve.

The Spanish governed the area until 1822 when California became a territory of Mexico; in 1846 Santa Barbara was taken for the United States by Colonel John Fremont.

Santa Barbara was one of the leading film capitals of the world when the American Film Company opened its Flying A Studio around 1910 in what is now downtown. The studio made more than 1,200 silent pictures, mostly Westerns, over a ten-year period before moviemaking's center moved south to Los Angeles.

Santa Barbara Airport, 8 miles north of downtown, is served by America West, American Eagle, United Airlines, and United Express. For information on the airport, call (805) 967–7111 or consult www.flysba.com.

Arlington Theatre. Home to Santa Barbara's performing arts center, it was built in the 1930s as a grand motion picture palace. It includes a Spanish village in the lobby and a curved ceiling painted with stars. The facility is located at 1317 State Street. For information, call (805) 963–4408.

Botanic Garden. A public garden devoted to the display and study of California's native flora. Five miles of trails pass through re-creations of the deserts, the Sierra Nevadas, and the offshore islands. Open daily from 9:00 A.M. to 4:00 P.M., weekends from 9:00 A.M. to 5:00 P.M.; guided tours are offered at least once a day. The garden is located at 1212 Mission Canyon Road. Admission: adult, $5.00; senior (60+), students and teens (13–19), $3.00; and child (5–12), $1.00. For information, call (805) 563–2521 or consult www.santabarbarabotanic garden.org.

Carriage Museum. An unusual collection of horse-drawn carts and carriages used by pioneers and early settlers. The vehicles include stagecoaches, buggies, firefighting equipment, and an antique hearse. Some of the carriages take to the streets of Santa Barbara each August during the Old Spanish Days parade. Located at 129 Castilo Street, the museum is open daily from 9:00 A.M. to 3:00 P.M.; on Sunday, the exhibit is open from 1:00 P.M. to 4:00 P.M.; closed Saturday. Admission: free, but donations are accepted. For information, call (805) 962–2353 or consult www.sbceo.k12.ca.us/%7Ecrane/carriage/index.html.

El Paseo. Within the area of State, De la Guerra, and Anacapa Streets, a historic Spanish-style shopping arcade was built around a 1920s residence. The arcade includes specialty shops, art galleries, and restaurants. For information, call (805) 962–6050.

El Presidio de Santa Barbara State Historic Park. Founded in 1782, the Presidio includes part of the original Presidio Real, the last Spanish military outpost in California. Among the restored buildings are the Presidio Chapel, the Padre's and Commandant's Quarters, and El Cuartel, the guard's house. El Cuartel, built in 1788, is the oldest building in Santa Barbara and the second oldest in California. Located at 123 East Canon Perdido Street, the park is open daily from 10:30 A.M. to 4:30 P.M. Admission: free; suggested donation is $1.00. For information, call (805) 966–9719 or consult www.parks.ca.gov/default.asp? page_id=608.

Mission Santa Barbara. Established in 1786 by Spanish Franciscans, it was the tenth of the California missions. The buildings were severely damaged in earthquakes in 1812 and again in 1925 but have been rebuilt. The mission continues as a Roman Catholic parish church and is open to the public for self-guided tours that include a museum, gardens, and the chapel. Located at 2201 Laguna Street, the mission is open daily from 9:00 A.M. to 5:00 P.M. Admission: adult, $3.00; free to children younger than 12. For information, call (805) 682–4713 or consult www.sbmission.org.

Santa Barbara County Courthouse. A stunning Spanish-Moorish building completed in 1929, it is worth a visit for a peek at its ornate interior and to make a climb up the 80-foot clock tower for a panoramic view of the city. Guided tours are offered once a day on weekdays. The courthouse is located on Anacapa

Street, between Anapamu and Figueroa Streets; open weekdays 8:00 A.M. to 5:00 P.M. and weekends from 9:00 A.M. to 5:00 P.M. Admission: free.

Santa Barbara Historical Museum. A broad collection of regional history, including artifacts, books, maps, and photographs from the Spanish exploration, the Wild West, and the settlement of California. Nearby the museum are two nineteenth-century adobes, including the Casa de Covarrubias at 715 Santa Barbara Street, built in 1817. Located at 136 East de la Guerra Street, the museum is open Tuesday through Saturday from 10:00 A.M. to 5:00 P.M. and Sunday from noon to 5:00 P.M. Donations accepted. For information, call (805) 966–1601.

MALIBU

The Chumash Indians called this place by a word meaning "where the mountains meet the sea." Taken first by the Spanish, Malibu was then bought by a Frenchman named Leon Victor Prudhomme, who sold off the land at 10 cents per acre in 1857. Today, of course, the land is worth hundreds of thousands or even more per acre.

The view of the beach is blocked in many areas by private homes. Malibu Surfrider State Beach is reserved for wave riders, but it's worth a peek for any visitors. For information, consult www.malibu.org.

SANTA MONICA

Portuguese explorer Juan Rodríguez Cabrillo discovered the broad bay that today runs from about Malibu to Redondo Beach in 1542 as part of a journey that included the first European visits to the Santa Barbara Islands and San Diego.

First named "Bay of Smokes" because of the rising smoke from Indian campfires in the area, it was later renamed as Santa Monica in honor of the mother of fourth-century Saint Augustine.

The town became an important area in the 1870s with the arrival of a railroad line from Los Angeles; developers sold off small lots for beach cottages. With the growth of Hollywood, many movie stars built homes there. For information, consult www.santamonica.com.

The famous **Santa Monica Pier** (which includes the carousel used in the movie *The Sting*) is worth a visit, as are the many shopping and dining areas. For information, consult www.santamonicapier.org.

VENICE

Developer Abbott Kinney dreamed of a spectacular town in 1904 near the growing community of Santa Monica. It was to be an American re-creation of Venice.

He built a system of canals, spectacular beach pavilions, a huge amusement park, and other facilities, and the resort enjoyed a brief success before economic problems and competition from other communities brought it into decline.

In the 1950s Venice became one of the centers of the beatnik culture. Today a few of the original canals and some of the buildings remain, and it has become a fashionable area once again. It is well known for its large artists' colony, and the boardwalk is one of the world capitals of weirdness. For information, consult www.venicebeach.com.

MARINA DEL REY

A large man-made harbor usually jammed with thousands of pleasure boats. Tours of the harbor and rental boats are available. **Fisherman's Village** in Marina del Rey at 13755 Fiji Way is a replica of a New England town with shops and restaurants, open daily. For information, call (310) 823–5411 or consult www.marinadelrey.com.

REDONDO BEACH

Railroad magnate Henry Huntington added to his fortune by selling lots next to the new railroad system. California's first serious surfers discovered the beach about 1907, and their descendants still rise early to catch the best waves. Today the area has a spectacular marina at King Harbor.

Redondo Beach is a local center for whale, porpoise, and seal watching in King Harbor from December to April. California gray whales migrate south each year from the Arctic Circle to the warm-water lagoons of Baja California, Mexico.

Redondo Beach Pier is a favorite dining, shopping, and amusement spot and a popular sport fishing pier for visitors, located at the west end of Torrance Boulevard. For information, call (310) 374–2171 or (310) 374–3481 or consult www.redondo.com/pier.html.

Seaside Lagoon, at Harbor Drive and Portofino Way, has a heated saltwater pool, a beach, and volleyball courts. For information, call (310) 318–0681.

HEARST CASTLE SAN SIMEON

William Randolph Hearst built his ultimate monument on a hilltop in the Santa Lucia Mountains overlooking the Pacific Ocean. An army of craftsmen labored for nearly twenty-eight years on the castle and guest cottages with 165 rooms and 127 acres of gardens, pools, and terraces. Inside the buildings is a jaw-dropping collection of Spanish and Italian antiques. Hearst Castle, now a state historical monument, is in San Simeon, about midway between Los Angeles and San Francisco, a six-hour drive from either city.

There are four daytime tours, each lasting just under two hours; all include the spectacular Neptune outdoor and the Roman indoor pools. Tour 1 includes the Casa Grande main house and the Casa del Sol guest cottage. The upper floors of Casa Grande are included in Tour 2. Guests on Tour 3 visit the Casa del Monte guest cottage and the north wing of Casa Grande. Tour 4, offered April through October, includes the Hidden Terrace and the exterior gardens and grounds as well as the Casa del Mar, the largest and most elaborate of the guest cottages, overlooking the Pacific Ocean.

The evening tour, offered in the spring and fall, includes docents in period dress appearing as Hearst's guests and domestic staff and a tour of Casa Grande, Casa del Mar, and the pools and gardens by night.

Hearst Castle is open for tours daily except Thanksgiving, Christmas, and New Year's Day. Reservations are recommended for tours. In mid-2002 tours were priced at $10.00 for adults and $5.00 for children (6–12). The lengthier evening tour, offered from March to May, and September to December, was priced at $20.00 for adults and $10.00 for children. Call (800) 444–4445 to purchase tickets or consult www.hearstcastle.org.

CHAPTER TWENTY-ONE

ORANGE COUNTY ATTRACTIONS

MOVIELAND WAX MUSEUM

The perfect stars: handsome, well-dressed, and completely amenable to any pose, role, or setting. They won't sign autographs, though: they're made of wax.

Movieland is the home of more than 400 wax likenesses that have been seen by millions during the past three decades. The museum is exclusively dedicated to the entertainment industry and surrounds the wax figures with re-creations of famous movie sets.

Here are some of the things we saw on a visit:

Movieland Wax Museum. *Photo courtesy Anaheim/Orange County Visitor & Convention Bureau*

- Elizabeth Taylor as Queen of the Nile in *Cleopatra.* The wax figure was sculpted from a life mask of Taylor, and the gown is an exact copy from the movie.
- A scene from the remake of *Perry Mason,* with defense attorney Raymond Burr grilling O. J. Simpson on the witness stand.
- Abbott and Costello in baseball uniforms performing their famous "Who's on First?" routine.
- John Wayne in a scene from the film *Hondo,* with costar Lassie.
- A Chamber of Horrors including scenes from *The Exorcist, Psycho,* and *Friday the 13th.*

A full tour of the museum can take two hours. The museum, located at 7711 Beach

Boulevard in Buena Park, one block north of Knott's Berry Farm off the Santa Ana (I–5) and I–91 Freeways, is open every day of the year.

In 2002 adult tickets were $12.95; child (4–11) tickets were $6.95. Combination tickets are also available with Ripley's Believe It or Not! Museum, priced at $16.90 for adult and $9.75 for child tickets. For information, call (714) 522–1152 or consult www.movielandwaxmuseum.com.

RIPLEY'S BELIEVE IT OR NOT! MUSEUM

Here are some of the things we saw:

▪ A dead bird in a glass container that was killed by a golf ball in flight at the Coombe and Hill Golf Club in New York in 1920.

▪ A lifelike statue of the Lighthouse Man of Chungking, China, who once guided American military dignitaries through the streets by the light of a 7-inch candle inserted into a hole in the top of his head.

▪ Something to inspire every American homemaker: a large drawing made up entirely from lint, and a version of the Last Supper made from 280 slices of carefully toasted white bread

▪ A man who smoked through his eyes, and a talented chap who could inflate a balloon through his ear.

Robert L. Ripley was born in 1893 in Santa Rosa, California. He began his newspaper career at the age of sixteen. On December 19, 1918, while working as a sports cartoonist at the *New York Globe* and at a loss for an idea, Ripley gathered together a few sports oddities that happened to be on his desk, made them into a cartoon, and captioned them "Believe It or Not."

The museum is located at 7850 Beach Boulevard in Buena Park, just north of Knott's Berry Farm and across the street from its sister museum, the Movieland Wax Museum. Admission in 2002 was $8.95 for adult and $5.25 for child (4–11) tickets. Combination tickets are also available with Movieland. For information, call (714) 522–1152 or consult www.movielandwaxmuseum.com.

WILD BILL'S WILD WEST DINNER EXTRAVAGANZA

Ropin', ridin', and rowdy indoor entertainment in a cross between an Old Wild West review and the *Ed Sullivan Show*. On one of my visits the happy crowd was entertained by dancing girls, a handsome Wild Bill, a lariat-spinning lassie, a fascinating Native American dance troupe, an astounding Indian ring juggler and dancer, and an incongruous but very funny modern-day comedian. Several members of the audience are likely to be drafted to take part in a square dance and one man can expect to be enlisted by Miss Annie in removing her garter.

The two-hour show includes a fried chicken and barbecued rib dinner with salad, soup, beer and soft drinks, and good old American apple pie.

The 800-seat showroom is about a mile from the entrance to Knott's Berry Farm and a ten-minute drive from Disneyland. The theater is located at 7600

Medieval Times. *Photo courtesy Anaheim/Orange County Visitor & Convention Bureau*

Beach Boulevard in Buena Park. Admission: adult, about $39.95; and child (3–11), $25.95. For information, call (714) 522–6414 or (800) 883–1546.

MEDIEVAL TIMES

An eleventh-century medieval banquet, complete with jousting knights, fair damsels in distress, and horseback entertainment. A typical menu includes soup, whole roasted chicken, spare ribs, herb-basted potatoes, and beer or soft drinks. They didn't use silverware back then, so neither will guests today. There are more than 1,100 seats, often filled with raucous visitors.

The theater is located at 7662 Beach Boulevard in Buena Park, across from Movieland Wax Museum and up the road from Knott's Berry Farm. Performances nightly. Admission in 2002 was adult, $41.95; child (12 and younger), $28.95. Look for discounts in flyers and on-line. For information, call (714) 523–4740 or (800) 899–6600 in California or consult www.medievaltimes.com.

PART X
SAN DIEGO ATTRACTIONS

CHAPTER TWENTY-TWO

SAN DIEGO: SEAWORLD AND SAN DIEGO ZOO

THERE'S A LOT TO LIKE in San Diego: this sunny outpost near California's border with Mexico has more than a little bit of everything. There's beach and sand along the Pacific Ocean, the sprawling Anza-Borrego Desert to the east, and just a short drive outside of downtown is heavily wooded alpine country where the mountain peaks are often dusted with snow in winter.

In addition to its natural wonders, San Diego boasts of two world-class attractions: SeaWorld California and the San Diego Zoo.

SEAWORLD CALIFORNIA

SeaWorld likes to quote the African environmentalist Baba Dioum: "For in the end, we will conserve only what we love, we will love only what we understand, and we will understand only what we are taught."

SeaWorld California is a 166-acre marine life and entertainment park on San Diego's Mission Bay, 100 miles south of Anaheim and about a two-hour drive from the Disneyland area.

Opening and closing times vary by season. Hours are extended during holiday periods and summer nights from mid-June through Labor Day. Call (619) 226–3901 for current hours. www.seaworld.com.

From north or south, exit Interstate 5 at SeaWorld Drive. From the east, exit Interstate 8, to Interstate 5 north to SeaWorld Drive west.

■ AROUND SEAWORLD

The hallmark **Shamu Adventure,** narrated by TV personality and animal expert Jack Hanna, highlights spectacular natural behaviors of killer whales, starring Shamu, Baby Shamu, and Namu. An interactive Web page dedicated to the show is at www.shamu.com.

SeaWorld Tickets

Prices were in effect in mid-2002 and are subject to change. Admission includes all shows, exhibits, and attractions except SeaWorld's Skytower and Mission Bay Skyride.

	ADULT	CHILD (ages 3 to 11)	CHILD (younger than age 3)	SENIOR (55+)
ONE-DAY TICKET	$42.95	$32.95	Free	$39.95
TWO-DAY ADVENTURE TICKET Two consecutive days	$46.95	$36.95	Free	$46.95
SOUTHERN CALIFORNIA VALUE PASS One entry to both SeaWorld San Diego and Universal Studios Hollywood for up to fourteen consecutive days.	$79.00	$59.00	Free	$79.00

Parking: Cars $7.00, RVs $9.00

At **Shamu Close Up,** guests can interact with killer whales. Depending on special activities, visitors may be able to experiment with hand and sound signals for the whales and watch training and feeding activities. A 70-foot-long acrylic wall allows guests to view the whales from beneath the surface of the water.

Manatee Rescue is the only place in the country outside of Florida displaying the endangered West Indian manatee. Several rescued and rehabilitated animals live within the containment, which has a large glass viewing port.

Sea lions and river otters are among the creatures in *Fools with Tools* at the Sea Lion and Otter Stadium.

The **Cirque de la Mer** show is a strange journey to the mythical island of Amphibia where a variety of colorful Amphibians—a hybrid of sea creatures and humans—possess super abilities, which they display in whimsical acrobat-like moves. Actors move across the water in a strange craft they call a *zorb*.

One of the hottest attractions at the park is a very cool place: **Wild Arctic,** a trip to the top of the world. Visitors board *White Thunder,* a jet helicopter simulator that soars over the frozen landscape, offering breathtaking views of rocky glaciers and snowy ice floes; the craft barely escapes an avalanche by zooming into a narrow ice cave. We eventually land safely at Base Station Wild Arctic at the heart of the frozen North Pole.

We see the tools of the researchers who labor in the wreck of a 150-year-old exploration ship, the remnants of a failed expedition to find the Northwest Passage. Part of the hull, upside down in the ice, forms a pool in the ice floes where beluga whales swim and play.

In another area, majestic walruses can be observed moving their snouts along the floor of the pool, using their vibrissae (whiskers) to search for food, and

SeaWorld California San Diego. *Photo courtesy of SeaWorld*

hauling it out onto ice floes using their powerful tusks. Behind a wall of ice is a stunning view of polar bears swimming below the surface of the water.

At **Rocky Point Preserve,** visitors get a true appreciation of the beauty of bottle-nosed dolphins and Alaska sea otters in their natural environment in this two-part attraction. Alaska sea otters, survivors of the 1989 Prince William Sound oil spill, are displayed in the natural rocky habitat. The dolphin habitat also includes a sophisticated wave pool.

Shipwreck Rapids takes castaways on a wet and wild journey in nine-passenger tubes through raging rapids; roaring waterfalls; a near-collision with a ship's propeller; and a dark, forbidding tunnel through the interior of a mysterious ship's engine room.

Shark Encounter presents the world's largest display of these fascinating animals. A submerged viewing tube allows SeaWorld guests to enter the sharks' habitat, a 700,000-gallon tank.

At **Forbidden Reef,** California moray eels and bat rays are displayed in one of SeaWorld's most popular displays. Visitors can touch and feed the graceful rays and enjoy underwater viewing of hundreds of moray eels.

The majority of SeaWorld's nearly 400 penguins live in the twenty-five-degree indoor display of **Penguin Encounter.** Featured nearby are auklets, puffins, and murres, the penguin's Northern Hemisphere cousins. An outdoor area houses Magellanic penguins, a temperate-zone species.

The **California Tide Pool** re-creates one of the ocean's richest environments, an intertidal zone. Guests are invited to roll up their sleeves and touch starfish and view sea urchins, sea cucumbers, California moray eels, spiny lobsters, and a variety of fishes.

The **Marine Aquarium** displays hundreds of fish and marine invertebrates from oceans throughout the world. Marine species as exotic as the lionfish and chambered nautilus live in re-creations of their natural habitats. Fish from freshwater habitats in Africa, Asia, and the Amazon River Basin are at the Freshwater Aquarium. The archerfish, capable of downing insects perched on branches overhead using bullets of water, is among the species on exhibit.

Shamu's **Happy Harbor** is a two-acre dream world for children of all ages, but especially adventuresome youngsters. Happy Harbor is like any other playground, although much more so. There are more than twenty places to explore, crawl, slide, jump, bounce, climb, and get wet.

The **Skytower,** a 320-foot-tall structure offering a panoramic view of San Diego's Mission Bay, skyline, foothills, bays, beaches, and the Pacific Ocean in a fifty-seven-seat cabin. Enclosed gondola cars ascend to a height of 100 feet on a 0.5-mile, round-trip journey over Mission Bay at the Skyride.

SAN DIEGO ZOO

To call the San Diego Zoo a "zoo" is sort of like calling Disneyland an "amusement park."

The unique animal collection, set within a one-hundred-acre tropical garden, includes four thousand animals of eight hundred species from the standard favorites—lions, tigers, bears, elephants, giraffes, gorillas, and hippos—to the rare and exotic, including giant pandas from China, cuddly koalas from Australia, tree kangaroos from New Guinea, fierce Komodo dragons from Indonesia, and a collection of exotic Asian hornbills. There's also the Polar Bear Plunge, a refrigerated pool for bears and reindeer.

The best way to begin a visit is to take the forty-minute guided tour bus through miles of winding roads, down the canyons and up the mesas. Another option is the Kangaroo Bus Tour that follows the same bus route but allows visitors to hop on and off at nine stops. Finally, there is the Skyfari aerial tramway across the treetops over the Reptile House, Hippo Beach, Monkey Mesa, the Scripps Flight Aviary, and Gorilla Tropics.

The San Diego Zoo is located north of downtown in Balboa Park. Open daily from 9:00 A.M. to 4:00 P.M., until 9:00 P.M. in summer months. Deluxe admission with bus tour and Skyfari aerial tram: adult, $32; child, $19.75. Two-park ticket (zoo and wild animal park within five days): adult $46.80; child $31.40. (619) 234–3153. www.sandiegozoo.org.

SAN DIEGO WILD ANIMAL PARK

In Escondido, 32 miles northeast of San Diego, the San Diego Wild Animal Park is a sprawling wildlife preserve that allows visitors to view herds of exotic animals as they might have been seen in their native Asia and Africa. On a 1,800-

acre piece of land (about twenty times larger than its parent, the San Diego Zoo), more than 3,500 animals from 250 species roam.

The park includes the largest crash of rhinos in any zoo, as well as California condors, Przewalski's wild horses, lowland gorillas, Arabian oryx and addax from the Middle East, and herds of antelopes and gazelles.

The **Heart of Africa** is a walk through thirty acres of a re-created African wilderness with habitats from dense forests to grassy savannas and water holes. Guests walk near animals including okapis, cheetahs, rhinos, giant eland, colobus monkeys, wattled cranes, warthogs, hornbills, and flamingos.

The Wgasa Bush Line Railway is a 5-mile, fifty-minute excursion into the bush.

Also popular are **Photo Caravan Tours,** truck rides into the heart of the large-animal enclosures. Caravans range in price from about $95 to $115 per person, depending on the length of the tour. Reservations are required; call (760) 738–5049 or (800) 934–2267.

The San Diego Wild Animal Park is located at 15500 San Pasqual Valley Road in Escondido, and is open every day. Winter hours are 9:00 A.M. to 4:00 P.M.; in the summer, the park is open later in the day, depending on the hour of sunset. Admission prices in mid-2002, including Wgasa Bush Line Railway and all shows and exhibits: adult, $26.50; child (3–11), $19.50; child (2 and younger), free. Two-park ticket (San Diego Zoo and Wild Animal Park general admission to use within five days from day of purchase): adult, $46.80; child, $31.40. Parking is $6.00 per vehicle.

For information, call (760) 747–8702 or consult www.sandiegozoo.org/wap/visitor_info.html.

QUICK-FIND INDEX
TO ATTRACTIONS

ABOUT THE AUTHOR

———

Corey Sandler is a former newsman and editor for the Associated Press, Gannett Newspapers, Ziff-Davis Publishing, and IDG. He has written more than 160 books on travel, video games, and computers; his titles have been translated into French, Spanish, German, Italian, Portuguese, Polish, Bulgarian, Hebrew, and Chinese. When he's not traveling, he hides out with his wife and two children on Nantucket island, 30 miles off the coast of Massachusetts.

WORLD'S LARGEST
MOVIE STUDIO AND THEME PARK™

Save $4 Off
Park Admission
(Up to 4 people)

www.UniversalStudiosHollywood.com

Take $4 off admission per person when you present this coupon at the USH ticket booth. Good for up to 4 people. Offer valid through 12/31/03. This offer cannot be combined with any other offer or with per-capita sightseeing tours. Distribution of this coupon on Universal Studios Hollywood property is prohibited. Not valid for separately ticketed events or Universal Studios Florida. Spider-Man, the character: TM & ©2002 Marvel. Jurassic Park TM and ©2002 Universal Studios, Inc. and Amblin' Entertainment, Inc. The Mummy ©2002 Universal Studios, Inc. ©2002 Universal City Studios LLLP. All Rights Reserved. Econo Guide 02-ADV-607

0 02035 12791 2   0 02035 24042 0

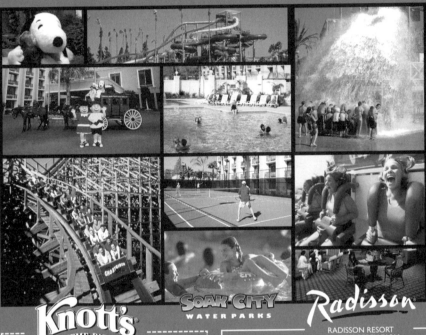

hotels.com rebate coupon

1. You must book and confirm online to be eligible for offer. No call-ins or faxes accepted.
2. The online coupon is only valid for reservations in Albany, NY, Albuquerque/Santa Fe, Alexandria, VA, Amsterdam, Anaheim, Annapolis, MD, Arlington, VA, Asheville, NC, Atlanta, Atlantic City, Austin, Texas, Baltimore, Barcelona, Spain, Berlin, Biloxi, Mississippi, Birmingham, AL, Boston, Branson, Missouri, Brussels, Belgium, Cancun, Caribbean, Cayman Islands, Charleston, SC, Charlotte, NC, Chicago, Cincinnati, Ohio, Cleveland, Colorado Springs, Columbia, SC, Columbus, Ohio, Dallas/Fort Worth, Daytona Beach, FL, Denver, Detroit, Flagstaff/Grand Canyon, Florence, Italy, Florida Keys, Frankfurt, Germany, Ft. Lauderdale/Palm Beach, Ft. Myers/Captiva, Gatlinburg/Pigeon Forge, TN, Greenville-Spartanburg, SC, Hartford, CT, Hawaiian Islands, Hilton Head, SC., Hong Kong, Houston, Indianapolis, Jacksonville/St. Augustine, FL, Kansas City, Knoxville, Tennessee, Las Vegas, Lisbon, Portugal, London, Los Angeles, Louisville Kentucky, Memphis, TN, Miami, Milan, Milwaukee, WI, Minneapolis, MN, Montreal, Myrtle Beach, SC, Nashville, Naples/Marco Island, FL, New Orleans, New York, Niagara Falls, Norfolk, VA, Omaha, Nebraska, Orlando, Palm Beach, Florida, Palm Springs, Panama City, FL, Paris, Philadelphia, Phoenix, Pittsburgh, Portland, Oregon, Puerto Rico, Raleigh-Durham, NC, Reno-Tahoe, Richmond, VA, Rochester, NY, Rome, Sacramento, CA, Salt Lake City, San Antonio, San Diego, San Francisco, Santa Fe, NM, Savannah, GA, Seattle, Silicon Valley/San Jose, Spacecoast, Florida, St. Louis, MO, St. Thomas USVI, St. Croix, USVI, Tallahassee, FL, Tampa, Toronto, Tucson, Vancouver/Victoria, Venice, Italy, Vienna, Austria, Washington D.C., Williamsburg, Virginia, and Yellowstone, Wyoming, booked and prepaid through hotels.com
3. Rebate Levels are as follows: 3 Nights - $20 Rebate, 5 Nights - $30 Rebate, 8 Nights - $50 Rebate, 10 Nights - $75 Rebate, 12 Nights - $100 Rebate.
4. Cut out this coupon, write in your name, hotel and dates of stay and mail after your completed stay.
5. After Check Out, please send this coupon to: **hotels.com – Rebate**
   807 S. Jackson Road, Suite B
   Pharr, TX 78577
6. Not valid with any other offer, including, but not limited to, frequent flyer miles.
7. For faster processing time, rebates will be credited back to your credit card within 3 weeks of receipt of this form.
8. One rebate per customer or household.
9. Coupon valid for reservations booked online between September 1, 2002 through September 30, 2003 for stays anytime.
10. "Booking" means a completed stay booked on one calendar day.
11. Offer may be revoked without notice at any time.
12. hotel.com's interpretation of the rules of this offer are final.

Book online or Call 1-800-2-HOTELS